John Lingard by James Lonsdale, 1834.

LINGARD REMEMBERED

Essays to mark the Sesquicentenary of
John Lingard's Death

edited by

Peter Phillips

CATHOLIC RECORD SOCIETY
LONDON
2004

ISBN 0 902832 21 2

Published 2004

Information about the Catholic Record Society
and its publications may be obtained from the Hon. Secretary,
c/o 114 Mount St., London, W1X 6AH

Printed by Newton Printing Ltd., London
www.newtonprinting.com

CONTENTS

		Page
	Acknowledgements	viii
	List of Figures	x
	List of Abbreviations	xi
	Editor's Introduction	1
1	Natural Philosophy at Douai, Crook Hall and Ushaw *Michael Sharratt*	9
2	Lingard's Anglo-Saxonism: A Post-Colonial Reading *J. A. Hilton*	23
3	Lingard v. Barrington, et al.: Ecclesiastical Politics in Durham, 1805–1829 *Leo Gooch*	35
4	John Lingard and the English Catholic Periodical Press 1809–1841 *Paul Richardson*	65
5	John Lingard: Historians and Contemporary Politics, 1780–1850 *Rosemary O'Day*	82
6	John Lingard and the Simancas Archives *Edwin Jones*	105
7	Every Picture tells a Catholic Story: Lingard's *History of England* illustrated and the 1850s Transition in Catholic Historiography *Rosemary Mitchell*	125
8	John Lingard and the Liturgy *Emma Riley*	143
9	The *New Version of the Four Gospels* *Peter Phillips*	157
10	Off Duty: Lingard's Letters to Women *John Trappes-Lomax*	170
	Appendix 1: Lingard's Published Works	184
	Appendix 2: Lingard's Letters and Papers	191
	Appendix 3: Portraits of Lingard	205
	Notes on Contributors	211
	Figures 1 to 14	
	Index	213

ACKNOWLEDGEMENTS

It seems appropriate to mark the 150th anniversary of the death of the priest and historian John Lingard (1771–1851). As these essays hope to reveal, his contribution to the life of the Church in the first half of the nineteenth century was far ranging. The editor of this volume is grateful for the enthusiasm and support his fellow contributors have brought to their task of exploring aspects of his work.

The editor thanks the Pro-Vice-Chancellor and Chair of Publications Board of Durham University for permission to publish as Chapter 2 Leo Gooch's article 'Lingard v. Barrington, et al.: Ecclesiastical Politics in Durham, 1805–1829', first published in *Durham University Journal*, January 1993, pp. 7–26.

Thanks are due to Cambridge University Press for permission to include a slightly revised version of Edwin Jones' article 'John Lingard and the Simancas Archives', first published in the *Historical Journal*, vol. 10, (1957), pp. 57–76, as Chapter 4.

The material in Chapter 5 is based on work previously published as part of Chapter 3 in Rosemary O'Day, *The Debate on the English Reformation* (Methuen, 1986).

Much of Chapter 8 has already appeared in Rosemary Mitchell, *Picturing the Past: English History in Text and Image 1830–1870* (Oxford University Press, 2000). The editor is grateful to Oxford University Press for permission to publish this chapter.

Acknowledgements are also due to the History Faculty Library, Oxford, and Mr. Michael Dudley, formerly of the Ashmolean Museum in Oxford, for permission to reproduce Figures 2–9.

Appendix 2 would not have been possible without the kindness and generosity of many people. The librarian at Ushaw, Dr. Alistair MacGregor, has always been ready to open the Lingard archives and the Revd. Dr. Michael Sharratt has been at hand to share his wide knowledge of this material. Close by in Durham, Dr. Jan Rhodes and Dr. Ian Doyle have offered valued advice, while Roger Norris kindly searched out letters in the Dean and Chapter Library. Canon Nicholas McArdle has shared the hospitality of Lingard's table at Hornby, where a large collection of memorabilia keeps Lingard's memory vividly alive. A delightful visit to Rome as the guest of the Rector and staff of the Venerable English College allowed the editor time to explore the extensive archives of the College, opened to him by the kindness of the student archivist, Nicholas Schofield. In Rome he was also made warmly welcome at the Scots College and was able to examine Lingard papers there. Antony and Elizabeth Leeming offered the hospitality of Skirsgill Park enabling him to read Lingard's correspondence with James Whiteside in the comfort of their library.

The support, interest and hard work of a host of archivists and others interested in Lingard has lightened the burden and added to its enjoyment: the Revd. Dr. John Sharp (Birmingham Archdiocesan Archives); John

Trappes-Lomax (Bury St. Edmunds); Peter Meadows (Cambridge University Library); the Revd. Dr. J.A. Harding (Clifton); Dom Philip Jebb OSB (Downside Abbey); Paul Richardson (Durham); Dr. Christine Johnson (Scottish Catholic Archives, Edinburgh); Mgr. George Bradley and Robert Finnigan (Leeds Diocesan Archives); Dr. Philip Cattermole (Leicester); Dr. Meg Whittle (Liverpool Archdiocesan Archives); the Revd. Thomas McCoog SJ, and Br. James Hodkinson SJ (Archives of the British Province of the Society of Jesus, Mount Street, London); Mrs. Margaret Osbourne (Northampton Diocesan Archives); the Revd. Denis Carlin (Scots College, Salamanca); the Revd. Martin Broadley (Salford); H.R. Tempest (Broughton Hall, Skipton); the Revd. Michael Clifton (Southwark Diocesan Archives); the late Revd. Francis Turner SJ (Stonyhurst College); Dr. Edwin Jones (Swansea); the Revd. Ian Dickie (Westminster Diocesan Archives); Emmeline Garnett (Wray). The editor would like to thank staff at the British Library, London; the Bodleian Library, Oxford; the Lancashire Record Office, Preston. He apologises to any who might inadvertently have been omitted from this list; their help is none the less valued.

No doubt, even with the painstaking work of such a valiant band, further letters of a letter-writer as indefatigable as Lingard remain to be searched out: the editor would appreciate a note of them.

x

LIST OF FIGURES

Frontispiece   John Lingard by James Lonsdale, 1834.

Figures 1 to 14 appear between pages 212 and 213.

Fig. 1   J. E. Doyle, 'The Barons at Edmondsbury swearing to obtain the Great Charter', J. Lingard, *The History of England* (1854–55), vol. 2, frontispiece.

Fig. 2   J.E. Doyle, 'Alfred presenting Gothrun for Baptism A.D. 878', Lingard, *History* (1854–55), vol. 1, facing p. 108.

Fig. 3   H. Dudley, 'The Burial of William I', Lingard, *History* (1854–55), vol. 1, facing p. 255.

Fig. 4   H. Dudley, 'The Arrival of Cardinal Wolsey at the Abbey of Leicester', Lingard, *History* (1854–55), vol. 4, facing p. 264.

Fig. 5   J.E. Doyle, 'Escape of Charles II after the Battle of Worcester', Lingard, *History* (1854–55), vol. 8, facing p. 156.

Fig. 6   J.E. Doyle, 'Death Warrant read to Mary, Queen of Scots', Lingard, *History* (1854–55), vol. 6, frontispiece.

Fig. 7   H. Dudley, 'Lord Stafford led to Execution', Lingard, *History* (1854–55), vol. 9, facing p. 248.

Fig. 8   H. Dudley, 'Last Interview between the Duke of Monmouth and his wife', Lingard, *History* (1854–55), vol. 10, facing p. 85.

Fig. 9   John Lingard by James Ramsay, c. 1819–1822.

Fig. 10   John Lingard, engraving by L. Stocks, after the miniature by Samuel Lover, 1837.

Fig. 11   John Lingard, lithograph by Thomas Skaife, 1849.

Fig. 12   St. Mary's Church, Hornby.

Fig. 13   The presbytery at Hornby.

Fig. 14   Inkstand, black inlaid with silver, formerly belonging to the poet Cowper, a gift to Lingard from Lady Throckmorton, and quill used by him.

LIST OF ABBREVIATIONS

AAW	Archives of the Archdiocese of Westminster.
ABSI	Archivum Britannicum Societatis Iesu.
BAA	Birmingham Archdiocesan Archives.
BL	British Library.
CUL	Cambridge University Library.
DNB	*Dictionary of National Biography*, founded by G. Smith, ed. L. Stephen and S. Lee, 63 vols. (Oxford, 1885–1900). Also reprinted, with some corrections, in 21 vols., 1908–1909.
Chinnici	Joseph P. Chinnici, *The English Catholic Enlightenment: John Lingard and the Cisalpine Movement, 1780–1850* (Shepherdstown, W.Va., 1980).
CRS	Publications of the Catholic Record Society.
Gillow	Joseph Gillow, *A Literary and Biographical Dictionary or Bibliographical Dictionary of the English Catholics*, 5 vols. (London, 1885).
Haile and Bonney	Martin Haile and Edward Bonney, *Life and Letters of John Lingard, 1771–1851* (London, 1911).
Lingard-Lomax Letters	John Trappes-Lomax (ed.), *The Letters of Dr John Lingard to Mrs Thomas Lomax Letters 1835–1851*, vol. 77 (Records Series), CRS (London, 2000).
Lingard Transcript	(See Appendix 2) Transcripts have been made of both the original Lingard letters held at Ushaw and copies of other Lingard letters not at Ushaw. Though scholars usually quote from the originals, the transcript numbers provide a very convenient finding system for Lingard's extensive correspondence in Ushaw's archives. Individual footnotes indicate cases in which Ushaw does not hold the original letter (e.g. Walker Transcripts, Farm Street Transcripts).
Milburn	David Milburn, *A History of Ushaw College: A Study of the Origin, Foundation and Development of an English Catholic Seminary, with an Epilogue, 1908–1962* (Durham, 1964).

SEC	St. Edmund's College Archives, now located at the Westminster Diocesan Archives.
RH	*Recusant History.*
UCA	Ushaw College Archives.
VEC	Archives of the Venerable English College, Rome.

Additional abbreviations used in particular chapters are listed at the ends of those chapters.

EDITOR'S INTRODUCTION

John Lingard walked for the last time in his garden on Easter Sunday 1851, examining the saplings he had planted out from acorns provided by his oak, itself once an acorn picked up by Lingard on the shores of Lake Trasimeno during a tour of Italy. The following day he took to his bed. His last years had been dogged by illness which brought considerable pain, and cataract which made reading in anything but the brightest light more and more difficult. These ailments were met with a characteristic lack of self-pity and a humour marked with what we might now consider an overly brash and Georgian delight in the vagaries of our internal systems. There were days when he became increasingly incoherent, failing to recognise even the closest of friends. Difficulty in breathing made it more convenient to spend those last days and nights propped up on the sofa in his library and there, amidst his books, he died just before midnight on July 17th 1851.

This volume of essays has been collected to mark this event and to look back over a fruitful life as Catholic priest and historian. While celebrating the considerable contribution Lingard made to the Catholic community in England, it is important also to acknowledge the part he played in the transformation of historical scholarship in the first half of the nineteenth century. By an assiduous attention to primary sources newly rediscovered in archives at home and abroad, and often overlooked by his contemporaries, he sought to challenge the Protestant interpretation of England's past. Lingard's is a political history, but offers one of the earliest in a series of revisionist accounts of England's past which has flowered in the historical scholarship of the late twentieth century.

Lingard had been missioner in the little Lancashire parish of Hornby, eight miles inland from Lancaster, for forty years and, to the end, he had reflected on Catholic life in this country with a gentle and probing irony. In the months before his final illness, he witnessed the restoration of the hierarchy, and his pupil Nicholas Wiseman, now a Cardinal and Archbishop of Westminster, with wry humour: 'I always thought it ridiculous myself because Westminster was a bishopric created by Henry VIII, and to make it an archbishopric for Catholics would be strange.'[1]

Westminster and its See is now a familiar part of Catholic, and not only Catholic, life in the country: a result, in some ways, of Lingard's contribution to the redefinition of what it means to be English and a Catholic. The whole course of Lingard's life marked a period of transition for the Catholic community and Lingard himself played a major part in this. He was born in Winchester on February 5th 1771 before the first Penal Laws

---

1. John Lingard to John Walker, October 20th 1847, UCA, Lingard Transcript 1256. The letter is written three years before the Restoration of the Hierarchy, when discussions for the names of the new Sees were in the air.

had been struck from the Statute Book, and during a summer break from
Douai had joined his father in signing the required oath of allegiance to
George III in 1791. He was a few years short of sixty before the process
was complete and he could write to congratulate Charles Butler on the part
he had played in bringing about Catholic Emancipation in 1829.

John Lingard entered the English College, Douai, as a schoolboy of
eleven, to escape for home in 1793 amidst the turmoil of the French
Revolution and War. He was a key figure in the gathering of the northern
exiles from Douai and in the difficult journey towards the setting up of a
new English seminary at Crook Hall and Ushaw. A visit to Rome in 1817
meant that he was at hand to play a part in the reopening of the English
College there after the ravages of the French occupation of the city. It was
at Crook that he was ordained deacon, but he travelled down to the Bar
Convent in York for ordination as priest in April 1795.

For most of his time at Crook and Ushaw Lingard is listed as Professor
of Philosophy, but he was also acting vice-president of the College and
bursar. He was caught up in a welter of matters. A major concern of the
staff at Crook was to preserve a continuity with what had gone before:
Crook and its sister college, St. Edmund's, Ware, in Hertfordshire, were
the inheritors of a proud tradition which reached back to the founding of
the English College at Douai in 1568. Michael Sharratt explores one
aspect of this in his study of Lingard's course in Natural Philosophy
offered to the small group of students preparing for ordination (Chapter 1).
The College at Douai had become something of a back-water in the late
seventeenth and eighteenth century but Sharratt's study of student dictates
from the period reveals how philosophy lecturers at Douai College
became increasingly at ease in their acceptance of Newtonianism.

Lingard's teaching differed little from that of Joseph Hodgson, his own
philosophy tutor at Douai, but he did include a reference to Uranus, the
planet newly discovered by Herschel in 1781, and shows himself familiar
with recent developments in other areas of science. While no innovator,
Lingard appears to have provided a workmanlike introduction to aspects
of contemporary science. Such a course of studies might be considered as
providing an excellent context for the formation of an historian.

It was at Crook that Lingard wrote his first book, *The Antiquities of the
Anglo-Saxon Church* (1806), as well as entering into a pamphlet controversy fired by the anti-Catholic propaganda of the 1807 election campaign
following the fall of the generally pro-Catholic Ministry of All the Talents.
These are issues explored by J.A. Hilton and Leo Gooch. Lingard's early
work reveals him at his most Cisalpine. While Lingard echoes the interests of contemporary scholars in their assessment of the Saxons, Hilton's
essay (Chapter 2) shows how Lingard's work brings to the fore a Gallican
emphasis on the legitimate authority of the state and a tolerant respect for
the individual conscience. Lingard took pains to show how Christianity
brings culture and civilisation together with its promise of salvation, and
was as keen, quietly and subtly, to undermine an aggressive approach to

the English Church on the part of Rome as he was to indicate England's long-standing links with the See of Peter.

These same concerns are revealed in Lingard's controversy with the staunchly anti-Catholic Bishop Barrington of Durham, who republished his 1806 visitation address to the clergy of his diocese during the parliamentary crisis which preceded the election campaign. Barrington's riposte to Lingard's conciliatory response was to reissue his *Charge* for a national readership. The bishop was supported by a host of *Replies*, *Answers*, *Letters* and *Defences* from various Anglican clergy and there was a controversy in the pages of the *Newcastle Courant*. Leo Gooch examines Lingard's response to these pamphlets and explores the aftermath of the controversy (Chapter 3). Curiously, as Gooch shows, it was Henry Phillpotts, one of Barrington's most vociferous supporters in the Durham controversy, whose correspondence with Wellington paved the way for the emancipation of Catholics in 1829.

With the sudden death of Ushaw's first President, Thomas Eyre, in 1810, Lingard became acting President of the College. The work was not to his taste and relations with Bishop Gibson became increasingly difficult. After seeing John Gillow comfortably settled in as Ushaw's second President, Lingard left in the early autumn of 1811 for the quiet mission of Hornby in the Lune valley. Here he remained for the rest of his long life. Lingard always preferred to work in the wings than to strut in the limelight. He found a home and good neighbours in Hornby and did his most important work here. Lingard built the Catholic Chapel at Hornby out of the profits of the early volumes of his *History*: 'Harry the Eighth's chapel', he joked, because his study of that king had paid the bills. He shared what he had earned generously. The quiet daily round of service to his flock and the life of scholarship he found congenial: for this he turned down bishoprics and academic appointments. He was a valued advisor to the bishops as well as to laity, a forthright controversialist, and a warm friend. If he had been prepared to give up Hornby for Rome in 1826, there is little doubt that Leo XII would have made him a Cardinal. Whether he became a Cardinal *in petto*, remains unknown; he certainly enjoyed sharing the tale in the more expansive mood of old age. Leo's predecessor, Pius VII, had conferred on him the triple degrees of Doctor of Divinity and of Civil and Canon Law in 1821 and gradually he achieved European acclaim, his *History of England* being published in French, German and Italian editions. He become an associate of the Royal Society of Literature and in 1839 was elected a corresponding member of the French Academy.

The first decades of the nineteenth century bear witness to a growing confidence in the Catholic community in Britain. Less compromising than the generation that had gone before, Catholics none the less wished to identify themselves with the mainstream of British life. As Paul Richardson shows, this period marks the emergence of a Catholic periodical press (Chapter 4). Some of the titles lasted only a few editions; some survived longer. Lingard's contribution to these is not inconsiderable:

here Lingard spells out his views on Catholic faith and practice, his preference for clarity and simplicity in devotion. Such journals represent a battle for the soul of English Catholicism. The doughty Bishop Milner and William Eusebius Andrews of the *Orthodox Journal* carried on a fierce campaign against what they considered a yielding to Protestant sentiments; by 1820 Rome was forced to intervene in this unseemly public debate, formally warning Milner to cease contributing to the periodical on pain of being deprived of his vicariate.

Cardinal Wiseman, though delighting to acknowledge that he had been a student of Lingard's at Ushaw, regarded him as a representative of the old school, cold and Gallican, and lacking the new found fervour of nineteenth century Ultramonatism. It was an opinion echoed in *The Tablet* obituary and by many scholars since. This was certainly true of his approach to liturgy: he preferred liturgy to be intelligible and attractive both to the Catholic community and to Protestant visitors, disliking repetitious litanies and the flowery metaphors of the new devotions being introduced from the Continent. He wanted his congregation to understand and follow the celebration of Mass. Emma Riley takes up this theme in her discussion of Lingard's *Manual of Prayers on Sundays and During the Mass* (1833) and compares Lingard's work to other examples of the genre (Chapter 8). There is little doubt that he would have approved the liturgical changes of Vatican II. He sought simplicity, disdaining both the medievalism of Pugin's Gothic Revival and the unwarranted pomp that often accompanied the opening of churches, the church being 'turned into an opera house' and 'the bishop performing as the first dancer in the ballet'.[2] It is to him we owe one of the most beloved of English Catholic hymns, his translation of the Ave Maris Stella, *Hail Queen of Heaven*, which has survived into our modern repertory of hymns, while many a Victorian contribution has been quietly laid to rest.

Lingard's *History of England* (1819–1830) and his later works of controversy reveal a marked development from the early Cisalpinism of *The Antiquities of the Anglo-Saxon Church*. The transition is demonstrated by his reply to Sir John Cox Hippisley's *Report on the Laws and Ordinances existing in Foreign States respecting the regulation of their Roman Catholic Subjects in Ecclesiastical Matters*. Hippisley, a bencher of the Inner Temple and M.P. for Sudbury from 1790 to 1796 and from 1802 until his retirement in 1819, had long been a supporter of the Catholic cause; living in Rome in 1779–1780 and again between 1792 and 1796, he was able to act as unofficial go-between for the British Government and Papal Court. Hippisley's *Report* represents the Cisalpinism of an earlier generation. Lingard's response testifies to a change of mood, something revealed even more clearly in correspondence with William Poynter, Vicar Apostolic for the London District, and in the five resolutions drafted by

---

2. John Lingard to John Walker, November 16th 1843, UCA, Lingard Transcript 1362.

Lingard. These, though initially signed by the Vicars Apostolic (but excluding Milner) and printed in 1817, were withdrawn at the last minute by Poynter, who sensed the hesitations of his fellow bishops. Lingard shows that control of the civil power over episcopal appointments and the promulgation of papal decrees was dependent on some sort of civil establishment of the Church. As this could in no way be applied to the Catholic Church in England, the Church must in turn be guaranteed freedom from civil interference.

Here we see Lingard's view maturing to a position which, though more subtle than Wiseman's was later to be, brings Lingard and his erstwhile pupil closer than perhaps either appreciated. This is something brought out in the editor's contribution to this volume which examines Lingard's translation of the four Gospels, made rather unusually from the Greek text rather than the Latin Vulgate familiar in Catholic circles, and published anonymously in 1836 (Chapter 9).

Lingard made clear in a long self-justificatory letter to John Kirk that he sought in his *History* to refute the accepted Protestant reading of the history of England. The early volumes were to set the scene, but the chief test of his work would be how he handled the Reformation. Lingard's motive for composing his *History* might lie in religious conviction, but he refused to allow apologetic intent to compromise his integrity as an historian:

> …I have no doubt that [my own account] is far the most correct history extant… Through the work I made it a rule to tell the truth, whether it be for or against us, to avoid all appearances of controversy, that I might not repel protestant readers, and yet furnish every necessary proof in our favour in the notes: so that if you compare my narrative to Hume's for example, you will find that with the aid of the notes it is a complete refutation of him, without appearing to be so. This I think is preferable – in my account of the reformation I must say much to shock protestant prejudices: and my only chance of being generally read by them (protestants) depends on my having the reputation of a temperate writer. The good to be done is by writing a book which protestants will read. Had it been like the Anglo-Saxon Church, it would have been read only by Catholics. This, however, I can say: that I have not conceded a single proof in our favour, nor omitted a single fact in useful observation through fear of giving offence to Mawman [Lingard's Protestant publisher], as Bp Milner asserts. Such a thing never entered my mind. Whatever I have said, or purposely omitted, has been through a motive of serving religion. Yet I heard long before the book was published from some of Dr. M's friends that I had sold my principles with my Ms….[3]

---

3. John Lingard to John Kirk, December 18th 1819, AAW, A 68, Lingard Transcript 197.

The volumes of his *History* dealing with the English Reformation did their job and were to provide ammunition for the virulent anti-Anglican polemic of William Cobbett's *The Protestant Reformation* (1824–1827): Cobbett's pages abandon Lingard's subtle undermining of the prevailing Protestant interpretation for a flagrant propagandising.

Rosemary O'Day explores the strengths of Lingard's approach to the Reformation by setting his historical researches firmly in the context provided by contemporary historians, both Catholic and Protestant (Chapter 5), while Rosemary Mitchell shows that the illustrators of the later editions of the work are able to bring to the fore Lingard's underlying polemical intent by a careful choice of subject (Chapter 7). The five editions of the *History* published during his lifetime allowed Lingard to include new collections of materials as they were brought to his notice, and gradually set out a more explicit statement of Catholic revisionism than he felt appropriate as the task was beginning.

Lingard's historical achievement is considerable. He is the first English historian to make serious use of rare printed material and manuscript sources in the Vatican and other Italian libraries. He early appreciated the significance of the detailed reports from the Venetian Ambassadors, asking Gradwell in 1818 to look out such material in the Barberini Library,[4] which Lingard himself had visited during a trip to Rome the year before: Leopold von Ranke was, of course, later to come to a similar appreciation of this outstanding collection. Lingard sought out French despatches, as well as material from the State Papers of Ferdinand and Isabella and of Philip II of Spain preserved almost inaccessibly in the Spanish castle of Simancas. The complexities of gaining access to these holdings through the good offices of English and Scots colleagues in nearby Valladolid are explored in the essay by Edwin Jones (Chapter 6). The pioneering use of such material enabled Lingard to move away from a tendency towards parochialism in English political history by placing it firmly in its European context.

Though he did not bear fools gladly, he approached others always with a delicate respect, numbering non-Catholics among friends and correspondents. As Appendix 2 reveals, Lingard was an indefatigable letter-writer and many of these letters have been preserved in archives and private collections. Rarely away from Hornby for long, Lingard relied on a variety of correspondents for the information he needed for his historical studies and parcels of books and manuscripts were regularly sent to his door, as well as notes of research done for him in the British Museum and other collections.

Lingard had a sound instinct for searching out archive material, but this was an instinct allied with remarkable good fortune. A noteworthy example of this is his publication of the Secret Treaty of Dover: writing to Lord

---

4. John Lingard to Robert Gradwell, June 3rd or 4th 1818, VEC, 66: 8, 6, Lingard Transcript 101.

Stourton for information which might enable him to present a more favourable picture of Charles II, Lingard intimated that he thought 'the Clifford family may be in possession of some documents respecting him' and asked Stourton to approach them in the hope that they might 'entrust material to the mail'. What came in the post turned out to be a batch of papers relating to Charles II's reign, and including the final protocol of the Secret Treaty ratified at Dover in 1670. Lingard published the Treaty in volume seven of his *History* (1829). It was something of a coup. The documents had been passed on by the king for safe keeping to the first Lord Clifford, one of the signatories to the Treaty, and knowledge of its existence was preserved only within the Clifford family circle. As Lingard comments of the Treaty: 'though much was afterwards said, little was certainly known'.[5] By publishing the document, Lingard offered proof that Charles II's alliance with Louis XIV was political rather than religious in motive, and he was able to discredit the view, popularised by Whig historians, that it formed the final piece in a Catholic conspiracy to undermine the Protestant cause.[6] It was no such thing.

Lingard's correspondence was not only a matter of historical enquires. In later years he corresponded sometimes more than twice weekly with his friend John Walker, missioner in Scarborough, and with others. These letters provide a delightfully unbuttoned commentary on Catholic life during the first half of the nineteenth century. It is interesting to compare his support for the convert Mary Sanders in her difficulties with her family with his letters to Hannah Joyce, a Liverpool Unitarian: there is no attempt to convert Miss Joyce, though there is a little gentle teasing of her as a heretic. He was remarkably at ease with women and, as John Trappes-Lomax shows (Chapter 10), Lingard's correspondence with both women ranges far and wide.

Friends also were swift to beat a path to his door; he was a good host, though he did not encourage visitors. Both Henry Brougham, who became Lord Chancellor in the Whig administration which saw the Reform Bill through Parliament, and the Tory, James Scarlett, Lord Chief Baron of the Exchequer, looked forward to the chance of sharing Lingard's table when they were travelling North. Lingard liked nothing more than a quiet evening with the Anglican priest across the road, who on his death bequeathed his pets into Lingard's care. Hornby has one of the few Anglican churches where there is a monument to the local Catholic priest and it attests his ecumenical sensitivity.

5. John Lingard, *History of England* (1819–1830), vol. 7, p. 510. For the Treaty itself see pp. 626–634.

6. Clifford Papers, BL, Additional Mss. 65138–65141. This material formerly preserved by the Clifford family at Ugbrooke, Devon, and now in the British Library, contains, in addition to the Treaty, autograph letters of Louis XIV and Charles II and other material relating to the Charles II's reign. The collection also contains letters from Lingard to William Stourton, Hugh Clifford and George Oliver, relating to Lingard's enquiries. See R. Hutton, 'The Making of the Secret Treaty of Dover', *Historical Journal*, 29 (1986), pp. 297–318.

A public controversialist, an historian who sought to include, rather than exclude, the Catholic in the pattern of our English history, an ironic observer of all types and conditions of people, Lingard was the most unclerical of clerics. As these essays hope to show, this unassuming priest contributed significantly to a sense of burgeoning confidence on the part of the English Catholic community in the early nineteenth century and laid the foundations for a renewal of historical studies reaching far into the future.

1

NATURAL PHILOSOPHY AT DOUAI,
CROOK HALL AND USHAW

Michael Sharratt

At both Crook Hall and Ushaw John Lingard is listed as Professor of Philosophy from 1794 until 1810. On the death of the President, Thomas Eyre, on May 7 1810 he became acting President and was listed as Professor of Theology for his final academic year in the College, 1810–1811. He himself had studied a full two-year course of philosophy at the English College, Douai (1789–91) and had commenced his study of theology in 1792 after one year of teaching the class of Grammar as a minor professor. But French hostility to English residents was beginning to make the future of the College more than doubtful. The College was occupied on February 18th 1793. Lingard was one of those who managed to escape three days later.[1] (The bibliography on pp. 21–22 below gives fuller details of works referred to in the footnotes.) A year and a half later he was helping to continue the work of the College in the north of England.

The novel venture of transplanting seminary formation to native soil might have led to a radical break with the Douai tradition, but the conscious aim both at Old Hall, Ware and Crook Hall in county Durham was to bring Douai back to life, as far as was possible, in its twin daughter colleges. Lingard was one of those who provided much needed continuity. In this essay I show where his teaching of what we would now call science fits into the Douai tradition.

The attachment of Crook and Ushaw to the traditions of Douai is evident in the daily timetable, in the spirituality of the College and in the course of studies and methods of teaching. The evidence for this traditionalism, though by no means as complete as one would wish, is most accessible in the case of studies and teaching methods.

In Ushaw's Big Library (and in the Lisbon Collection which came to Ushaw in 1974–75 from the English College, Lisbon) there are several dozen manuscript volumes of courses given at the English College, Douai. These are known as 'Douai Dictates', because dictation was, according to the College's Constitutions, the chief method of teaching.[2] Most of these dictates come from the eighteenth century, most are courses in theology and all are written in Latin; how much the Latin makes use of contractions to lessen the drudgery of writing seems to have depended on the skill of the student. Sometimes one can be quite sure of the accuracy of the manu-

---

1. The lists for Crook Hall and Ushaw are in the College Diary in the Ushaw College Archives; Lingard's progress at Douai can be traced by using the index in P. Harris, ed., *Douai College Documents*, CRS, vol. 63, (London, 1972); Lingard's is at p. 332.
2. *Constitutiones Collegii Pontificii Anglorum Duacensis*, (Duaci, 1690), p. 12 and p. 14.

script, since there are two virtually identical copies of the same course
taken down by different students; in such a case, it may be that some correction or rewriting outside of class was involved. In other cases, lacunae,
grammatical clumsiness or misunderstanding of the subject would suggest
that very little in the way of correction or supervision by the lecturer has
taken place. Some dictates are, in fact, what the lecturer himself used
when dictating.

One cannot assume that students always paid proper attention to writing their dictates. In 1781 Henry Rutter wrote to his uncle, Robert
Banister:

> I must, however, have some good divine to supply the place of our dic-
> tates, which to my sorrow I have not completed, for as my breast has
> been but weak these two years past I followed the custom of not writ-
> ing them.[3]

Still, where dictates have survived, they are a pretty reliable indication of
what was taught and how it was taught.

There is sometimes, moreover, another type of source which is both eas-
ier to use and more reliable than lengthy hand-written treatises. Daily and
weekly disputations were another important part of the teaching methods
prescribed the College's Constitutions. More solemn versions of these
took place annually. At the end of the academic year it was customary for
lecturers in both theology and philosophy to stage exhibitions of learning
in the form of disputations to which people outside the College were invited. These occasions were advertised publicly by means of broadsheet
posters. The poster consisted of a summary of the topics to be discussed,
with each topic reduced to a series of theses which the chosen student or
students undertook to defend in response to questions. Since the printed
poster itself was a form of publication, responsibility for its contents lay
with the presiding lecturer rather than with the student. Since the prestige
of the College was at stake, the publication had to be vetted for orthodoxy
by the Prefect of Studies, whose brief would extend to ensuring that the
Latin was both correct and reasonably stylish.[4] This was a point which
Lingard drew to the attention of Charles Newsham, the recently appointed President of Ushaw:

> You publish Latin Theses: for the credit of the House they ought in
> point of style to be excellent: for no one will attribute the faults, if faults
> there be, to the composer merely, but to the house in general: as it will
> be taken for granted that the composition was seen [by] several before
> it was sent to the press.[5]

The printed theses are known variously as 'theses', 'disputations', 'conclusions' or 'defensions'. Ushaw has a collection of such theses from
Douai College, some of which will be used in this essay.

3. L. Gooch, *The Revival of English Catholicism*, p. 18.
4. *Constitutiones Collegii Pontificii Anglorum Duacensis*, p. 28.
5. Lingard to Newsham, undated but probably the autumn of 1837, Lingard Transcript 521.

The tradition of dictating lectures continued throughout Lingard's career as a teacher, while annual disputations in Latin lasted at Ushaw for nearly all the nineteenth century. Although only one or two dictates have survived, Ushaw does have a collection of printed theses from Crook Hall and Ushaw, the later ones in the form of pamphlets or leaflets rather than posters. This collection includes courses taught by Lingard, so a comparison of what he was taught as a student with what he himself taught will provide hitherto unpublished evidence of the continuation of the Douai tradition in England. There is also a single copy of a dictate of a course given by Lingard in his final year as Professor of Philosophy.[6] This does not deal with science and in any case merits separate treatment so it will be referred to only incidentally in this essay.

The course of studies at both Douai and Ushaw kept more or less the same external pattern until the 1960s. The typical church student who entered as a boy of about eleven and was ordained as a young man of about twenty-four would start in Rudiments (sometimes called Figures) which usually lasted three years and then would ascend through the classes known as Grammar, Syntax, Poetry and Rhetoric. After completing these courses in the humanities he would proceed to study philosophy for two years and theology for four – at least a fourth year of theology was prescribed by the Constitutions (p. 13), though in each case one has to check whether a student did the full four years. (In the 1890s the Governing Bishops of Ushaw had to extend the theology course to four years from what had become a customary three years or less.)[7] An able student might be asked to prolong his time in the College by spending a year or more as a 'minor' professor; during that time he would be deputed to teach a class (or, sometimes, a subject) to the boys in the College. The use of minor professors was discontinued in the 1940s. Lingard's progress as a student was typical until he completed his philosophy; as we have already noticed, his entry into theology was postponed for his year of minor professorship and his first year of theology at Douai was cut short when he, with others, left Douai on February 21 1793.

Students in the first year of philosophy were known at Douai as 'Logici', those in the second year as 'Physici'. This terminology survived at Ushaw but sometimes 'Low Philosophy' and 'High Philosophy' were used, and eventually prevailed, alongside First and Second Philosophy. To understand what the names of the various classes referred to it is helpful to realise that one is dealing with sixteenth-century terminology applied to a syllabus which had ostensibly been finalised in detail in the Douai Constitutions of 1690 but in fact had continued to develop in response to changing needs throughout the eighteenth century. It is something of a curiosity that the method of dictation, which had been a necessity in the

6. See the bibliography for Lingard's dictate of 1809–10 on Logic, Metaphysics and Ethics.
7. Milburn, p. 306.

medieval universities, continued to be insisted on long after printed books were widely available. In the last days of Douai and the early days of Crook Hall no one was more insistent than Robert Banister on the advantages of dictation, which he seemed to think was a guarantee of maintaining the distinctive traditions of Douai College. But though he presented himself as an upholder of an unchanging tradition and has succeeded in being accepted ever since as a consistent conservative, I shall use recently discovered evidence to show that he was a significant contributor to an important change in Douai's teaching of that part of the philosophy course which we would now class as science.

When Douai College was founded in 1568 it was natural enough for the shape of the philosophy syllabus to be Aristotelian. That was the norm throughout Europe, even in leading educational institutions of the Reformation. By the time the College's Constitutions were published in a booklet in 1690, its provisions seem to hindsight far less appropriate. If Lingard had had to follow a course in natural philosophy which conformed to the Constitutions' requirement to follow the well-worn ways of the Aristotelian school, one would have had to say that he was the victim of an anachronism. In fact, things worked themselves out much more satisfactorily without, as far as is known, anyone expressly taking up the task of revising the syllabus in the light of increased knowledge. It was simply assumed that parts of the Constitutions were a dead letter.

I shall illustrate what one might call the natural process of curriculum development by examining what was taught in the second year of the course (under the title Physics or Natural Philosophy) in the sixty or so years from 1740. (I have described elsewhere the College's teaching of theology in the first half of the eighteenth century.)[8] But first a brief description of what was usually treated in the first year of the course under 'Logic' will serve to show that Lingard and his predecessors did not feel at all bound to give a course that was recognisably Aristotelian. I take as a typical example the theses in *philosophia universa* presided over in 1787 by the man who taught Lingard philosophy, Joseph Hodgson. Where it is possible to check, it is clear that Hodgson made no major changes in the course before starting to teach it to Lingard a couple of years later.

The subjects covered in the first year were logic itself, metaphysics and ethics. Logic covers what would later more usually be termed theory of knowledge or epistemology. A principal adversary is Descartes. Lockean empiricism is much more favoured than Cartesian methodical doubt: in fact, on the origin of ideas, Locke is the only one to be listened to. Metaphysics deals with immaterial things. It includes ontology, where natural theology finds its place (with Spinoza the chief adversary), and pneumatology, which covers rational psychology or philosophy of mind.

---

8. M. Sharratt, ' "Excellent Professors and an Exact Discipline": Aspects of Challoner's Douai', pp. 112–125. Still useful is B. Hoban's 'The Philosophical Tradition of Douay', *Ushaw Magazine*, Vol. 63 (December 1953), pp. 145–159.

Ethics overlaps with natural theology in so far as God is the *summum bonum*; here atheists, who anticipate post-modernism in explaining away religion as a device to exercise political control, are thoroughly impious and quite foolish into the bargain.

In all this it is not difficult to find important ideas which can be traced back to Aristotle, but they sit alongside things no Aristotelian could allow. Lingard himself, in his own lectures at Ushaw, was quite happy to disagree with Aristotle on the origin of ideas.[9] It would be easy to quote other sources to confirm, what has long been known, that in the second half of the eighteenth century lecturers in philosophy at Douai College sat loosely to the provisions in the Constitutions about Aristotelianism and that on occasion they explicitly distanced themselves from the Peripatetics, as they usually called Aristotle's followers.

Although one can find examples from the mid-eighteenth century of Catholic educational institutions stubbornly rehearsing chunks of Aristotelianism that had long been junked nearly everywhere, lecturers who did not feel tied to Aristotelian accounts of knowledge were hardly likely to cling to Aristotelian physics. Yet the rubric covering the second year of the course was 'Physics', so in effect the lecturers found themselves having to provide a course in Natural Philosophy and, given the obsoleteness of Aristotelian physics, having a pretty free hand to model it on whatever lay to hand.

But there was one very important constraint and to understand what it was a brief excursus into the history of science is necessary. It is still customary to refer to 'the Copernican Revolution' and to use the label 'scientific revolution' to indicate the major changes in astronomy and physics which transformed much of science in the sixteenth and seventeenth centuries. Although labels like these have their drawbacks, it is sometimes convenient and allowable to talk as though this scientific revolution started with the publication in 1543 of Copernicus's book *De Revolutionibus Orbium Coelestium* and was completed by Newton's *Principia Mathematica* in 1687. As is well known, Catholics who had the inclination and aptitude to benefit from the 'new philosophy' faced a problem over and above the inherent difficulty of the subjects treated by scientists. In 1616 the Congregation of the Index of Prohibited Books had ruled that no Catholic could hold that the earth is a planet. This ruling had been reinforced in 1633 by the condemnation of Galileo. Although technically that condemnation concerned only Galileo himself, it gave a message to all other Catholics, a message broadcast and reinforced in Catholic countries by instructions to nuncios and Catholic universities. The President of Douai, Matthew Kellison, was prompt in assuring the authorities that such unorthodox ideas would never be taught in his College.[10]

---

9. For instance, on p. 42 of his dictate on Logic.

10. I have dealt with this whole issue at length in *Galileo: Decisive Innovator*, especially at pages 107–131 and 153–180; for Kellison see pp. 178–180.

Galileo died in 1642. A hundred years later a scrupulous, or even an ordinarily conscientious, Catholic lecturer in Natural Philosophy could well be troubled by the fact that his Church would not allow him to accept a key component of contemporary science. Yet his plight could have been worse. There was nothing to stop him saying that he treated the orbital and rotational motions of the earth as *hypotheses*. That much, as everyone knew, had been allowed since the ruling of the Congregation of the Index in 1616 and made crystal clear by its 'corrections' of Copernicus's book published in 1620. It is sometimes said in defence of the Congregation that their intervention was both sagacious and prescient. Copernicus's heliocentrism had not been proved true, so it was only a hypothesis and, as we now know, no scientific conclusion is ever established beyond the possibility of revision, so the authorities of the Church, it is claimed, were the ones who got it right and have been unfairly traduced ever since. Such a defence of the Congregation is entirely misplaced: it rests on a complete misunderstanding of what the Congregation meant by 'hypothesis'. All it meant was this: for centuries it had been customary in astronomy to treat the devices used by working astronomers (devices such as eccentric circles and epicycles) as mere calculating devices employed to enable astronomers to make accurate predictions of planetary positions. Such devices made no claims about the true nature of the heavens or of the actual motions of heavenly bodies. If one wanted to know what the heavens are like then one went to the philosophers: such questions did not lie within the competence of astronomers.

So 'hypothesis' in the eyes of the Congregation – and of the Congregation of the Inquisition at the time of Galileo's condemnation – did not mean an unproven guess which might, with further supporting evidence, come to be accepted as true. Truth or falsity did not come into it: a mere calculating device is not the sort of thing that could be true or false, not even probably true or probably false. It can be neat or cumbersome, but that is a different matter.

Still, any Catholic lecturer was entitled to expound Copernican, Keplerian or Newtonian ideas, provided that he insisted that these were mere calculating devices and that the earth is in fact a unique body fixed motionless at the centre of the universe. He could even allow that all the planets went round the sun, as in the 'system' sketched by the great Danish astronomer, Tycho Brahe, towards the end of the sixteenth century, but again with the proviso that the sun itself went round the central and immobile earth.

With the passage of time, anything except a whole-hearted acceptance of the fact that the earth is a planet became less and less plausible. We can now trace how the philosophy lecturers at Douai College became quite comfortable in their acceptance of Newtonianism (though the discovery of further dictates or theses would fill out the picture).

Alban Butler, the author of the *Lives of the Saints*, is sometimes given credit for having taught Newtonianism at Douai. The evidence for this is a passage from his nephew Charles. But what Charles Butler says is carefully phrased: 'He adopted it, in part, into the course of philosophy which he dictated to the students.' The part he could not accept was that the earth is in fact a planet. What stopped him was, of course, the authority of scripture, as interpreted by the Church. I have described Butler's teaching of science at Douai in 1740–41. From the theses he published it is not clear whether Butler accepted Tycho Brahe's compromise or whether he was content to treat sun-centred ideas as mere calculating devices, but it is clear that he was not a heliocentrist. One might call him 'moderately progressive' in his treatment of physics and astronomy, but he could not ignore the official rulings on the subject of heliocentrism.[11]

Yet, as I showed in another article which drew on both a dictate and a disputation poster, by 1757–58 at the latest William Wilkinson seems quite comfortable in treating the earth as a planet. It is possible that he did so earlier since he began to teach philosophy in 1752–53. Evidence that the climate of opinion was changing can be found in the fact that the 1758 edition of the Index of Prohibited Books omitted the entry which condemned all books advocating Copernicanism. Thus, by 1757 when the new edition was being prepared, the Congregation had decided that acceptance of heliocentrism as the true system of the universe was compatible with a Catholic interpretation of scripture. The change was made unobtrusively, with none of the fanfare which followed Galileo's condemnation and, perhaps through an oversight, Galileo's own work remained on the list of condemned works. But it seems pretty certain that Wilkinson will have designed his course without any knowledge of an imminent change on the part of the authorities in Rome.[12]

Since writing those articles on Butler and Wilkinson I have discovered that one of Wilkinson's former pupils in philosophy was teaching Newtonianism as early as 1754–55. It is a matter for some surprise that the lecturer in question is Robert Banister. He began to teach philosophy in 1753, but his disputation poster of 1755 is the only evidence I have come across of what he taught. There are two copies of the poster and they owe their survival to the fact that they were used as wrappers for packets of sermons, with some consequent damage to one or two sentences. Thanks to expert restoration by the Palaeography Department of the University of Durham they now give an almost complete summary of what is an introductory course in Newtonian natural philosophy.

Here I can give only samples of Banister's course. He calls physics a genuine though imperfect science, presumably because it does not attain the Aristotelian goal of providing conclusive demonstrations. It used to be a rather abstruse treatise and did not enjoy the light of experiments. He gives Newton's laws of motion. On Newtonian attraction he actually gives a specific reference to the *Principia*. Copernicanism accounts very

---

11. See my 'Alban Butler: Newtonian in Part'.
12. For Wilkinson's dictate and disputation see my 'Copernicanism at Douai'.

happily for all the phenomena of the heavens and has nothing to fear from physics. His whole treatment is a competent introduction to the work of the man he calls 'the most sagacious Newton'.[13]

Respect for Newton's genius is even more marked in a disputation I have already mentioned, Joseph Hodgson's Universal Philosophy of 1787. Although the disputation covers the whole of philosophy, in other words, the complete two-year course, Hodgson's first love seems to have been natural philosophy. He goes out of his way to preface his theses with a rhetorical introduction extolling the value of philosophical studies. Two thirds of this preface concern natural philosophy. Hodgson warns against a rash and forbidden excessive ardour for philosophizing; he may have in mind the what were thought to be the excesses of a predecessor, Joseph Berington, who had to leave the College in 1772 because of his unacceptable philosophical views.[14] Or it may be the sort of remark he thought appropriate to the occasion. In any case, there is no problem: he simply exhorts the reader to investigate nature safely by taking Newton as guide and patron. After praising Newton's work on optics he concludes by saying that mortals rightly congratulate themselves on such a glory of the human race.

When Hodgson says in the astronomy section that he prefers the Copernican hypothesis to Ptolemy's or Tycho's and explains it in terms of Newtonian attraction and Kepler's laws of planetary motion he is not harking back to the days when heliocentrism could be held by Catholics only as a hypothesis or calculating device. His whole treatment of mathematical physics, including astronomy, takes the English genius Newton as a safe guide. One of Banister's complaints in a letter of 1794 about the teaching at Douai in the College's last years would apply, among others, to Hodgson:

Philosophy consisted of Locke's ideas and Newtonian attraction and a waste of time in the Experimental Room.[15]

We need not suppose that Banister thought his earlier espousal of Newtonianism had been a mistake. It is much more likely that he thought that science was being given disproportionate time, to the neglect of more metaphysical topics. Nor do we know whether in his earlier days he ever expressed any sympathy for Locke's ideas. It should also be noted that Banister had become unremitting in his criticism of the College. In a letter of May 17 1791 to James Haydock, a student at the College, he is particularly sweeping in his condemnation of the idleness of staff and students. Some years later Haydock's brother, George Leo wrote:

What informations – I was then at ye Col from 1785 29 Ap & found ye masters zealous enough. On play-days good Pedagogues would improve ye pupils as much.

13. Banister's disputation on *Philosophia Naturalis* is dated March 3 1755.
14. On Berington see Milburn, pp. 10–11.
15. R. Banister to H. Rutter, in L. Gooch, *The Revival of English Catholicism*, p. 213.

He adds:
> The Col broke up 5 days after I ran away 5 Aug 1793 some sent to Dourlens & all at last lost.[16]

So George Haydock did not endorse the complaints of the elderly Banister and I have not come across any evidence that Lingard was dissatisfied with how he was taught by Hodgson.

There is also a disputation on Rational Philosophy which was presided over by Hodgson and defended by Lingard in 1790. In this there is a hint of patriotism in the way Descartes' innate ideas are rejected, while 'our countryman Locke', who treated the mind as a *tabula rasa*, is taken as the man to follow. Again, I leave to another occasion a comparison of the teaching of Hodgson and Lingard on the subjects covered by this disputation (logic, metaphysics, natural theology and rational psychology). I note only that Hodgson is severe on the way the Peripatetics, with their agent and passive intellect and their impressed and expressed species, greatly darkened the topic of the origin of ideas. Their opinion is dismissed as obscure and false.

Lingard's teaching at Crook Hall and Ushaw is very much in the Douai tradition. He employed the traditional methods of dictation and disputation and he taught in Latin. He himself was considered something of a Latin stylist. Even in old age he was often called upon to provide the text for petitions or protests to the Congregation of Propaganda or to devise epitaphs for presidents and vicars apostolic. He considered it essential that some clergy should be able to draw up documents in a Latin style that would not strike Roman bureaucrats as incorrect or inept. But he became convinced that Latin defensions ought to be abolished, as is shown by a letter he wrote to John Walker on July 31 1845: 'Latin composition is not sufficiently studied to make them tolerable'.[17] Yet only a few years earlier, in a letter of April 25 1838 to the recently appointed President, Charles Newsham, his position had been more nuanced:

> Many years ago I used to think that it would be a great improvement to introduce *occasional* disputations in English into the theological schools, as it would prepare the young men for the explication of the Catholic doctrines to their congregations; and at the same time allow such as could not express themselves with facility in Latin, to distinguish themselves, partially at least, at the defensions.

> That the defensions should be entirely in English I am not prepared to assert. Is it so in other colleges? Is it so at the universities? Is not the speaking of Latin considered as a mark of classical education, or rather I should say, of a place of classical education? – I should not like to have it said that the classical studies are at so low an ebb at Ushaw that they are obliged to defend in English. Your rivals will say so.[18]

16. G.L. Haydock's comments are written on Banister's letter to James Haydock, UCA, Douai Papers, XVIII F 2 17 (6).
17. UCA, Lingard to Walker, Lingard Transcript 1064.
18. UCA, Lingard to Newsham, Lingard Transcript 527.

It was in natural philosophy that Latin seemed most inappropriate and the theses in that subject were printed in English as early 1830. Perhaps that is what Lingard had in mind when he wrote:

> I care not much for the Latin defensions. I think I had a hand in introducing the English. But I want the writing of Latin to be cultivated on account of the necessity of corresponding with Rome.[19]

Whatever may have been his later opinion, Lingard's own teaching was, as far as we know, all in Latin and the theses on the first year of the course were printed in Latin until the defensions were discontinued.

In one respect he was at a disadvantage compared with his predecessors. They had had the use of an extensive College library, not to mention other libraries in Douai. From a chance remark of Lingard's half a century later, we know how insignificant Crook Hall's library was when he presided over a disputation on Rational and Natural Philosophy in 1796, because even two years later all it amounted to was a collection of a hundred books in a mean room or closet. Even when the College moved to Ushaw in 1808 its library amounted to only about 4,000 volumes.[20]

The College Diary shows how many students there were in each class each year at Crook Hall and Ushaw. The data are for the start of the academic year, usually the traditional date used in the Douai Diaries, the feast of St. Remigius, October 1. It will be seen that there were never many pupils in a class and sometimes, because there were no students, the course was not taught. In Lingard's final year at Ushaw he taught Theology, while Richard Albot taught 'physica'; the College diary does not make clear who taught 'Logic' or Low Philosophy that year. I shall give the figures simply by year followed by the number of students for High Philosophy and the number for Low Philosophy:

> 1795: 3,2; 1796: 2,5; 1797: 2,4; 1798:3,0; 1799: 0,0; 1800: 0,4; 1801: 2,0; 1802: 0,2; 1803: 0,2; 1804: 2,3; 1805: 3,0; 1806: 4,0; 1807: 0,6; 1808: 4,0: 1809: 0,3; 1810: 3,7.

So in the sixteen years covered by this list, there was one without any philosophy course at all and another ten in which either High or Low Philosophy was omitted. In the courses that were taught there were very few students, but it is worth noting that even at Douai there were only six in the class when Lingard studied Low Philosophy and five when he went on to High Philosophy.

For Lingard's teaching on science I use the disputation of 1796 on Rational and Natural Philosophy. This covers both Low and High Philosophy, as is confirmed by the fact that the theses were defended on the first day by first-year students and by second-year students on the following day. In general, one may say that his approach is very similar to

---

19. UCA, Lingard to Walker, August 10 1842, Lingard Transcript 1033. For the English theses in natural philosophy see Milburn, pp. 141–42.

20. UCA, Lingard to Walker, December 23 1845, Lingard Transcript 1082; see my 'The Origin and Growth of the Ushaw· Library', p. 23.

what he was taught by Hodgson, so most of what follows will be concerned with variations of emphasis or new topics introduced by Lingard.

In comparing Lingard with Hodgson, I start with some epistemological considerations in their respective treatment of rational philosophy. In 1787 Hodgson said that Descartes' methodical doubt is to be eliminated from philosophy since it does not keep within proper bounds, whereas in the theses Lingard defended in 1790 it is dismissed as impossible. Lingard in 1796 is more nuanced: he would not disapprove of methodical doubt if kept within just limits, but he rejects it as absurd and useless if it is extended to things that are absolutely clear.

On the origin of ideas we have already seen Hodgson saying that Locke is the only one to listen to. Lingard does not name Locke. He is content to say that the opinion which attributes our ideas to sensation and reflection fits nature better and is more likely (*veri similior* – nearer the truth, we might say, in the later language of Karl Popper who actually makes verisimilitude a key concept). It is preferable to the occasionalism of Malebranche or Descartes' innate ideas. Lingard also agrees with Hodgson that the impressed and expressed species of the Peripatetics have long been abandoned by everyone.

In passing I note that in his theses on natural theology and ethics Lingard introduces names from the relatively recent past: Pierre Bayle (1647–1706) and Anthony Collins (1676–1729) and their opponents Samuel Clarke (1675–1729) and William King (1650–1729). A major adversary for both Hodgson and Lingard is Benedict Spinoza (1632–1677), but in his theses on ethics we find Lingard mentioning someone who was still very much alive, namely Jeremy Bentham (1748–1832). Given Lingard's own personal experience of the effects of the French Revolution, one might expect him to enliven his opposition to atheism and deism with references to what he had seen only a few years before. So far, however, I have not found anything of the kind: to that extent he could be considered detached, though in general he has no qualms about indulging the traditional rhetorical device of describing adversaries as absurd or mad.

Clearly Lingard is very much in the Douai tradition of the second half of the eighteenth century, a tradition which from the 1750s had moved away decisively from Aristotelianism. With this knowledge in mind, when one comes to his natural philosophy, one does not look for any startling departure from what he had been taught a few years before. Like Hodgson he has theses which summarise elementary arithmetic, geometry and algebra. One addition worth noting is that he adds a passage on conic sections and the properties of curves, so he must have included something under this heading in his teaching or at least in his coaching of the students who were to defend the theses.

There are instances where he seems to be paraphrasing theses he had defended as a student under Hodgson and he occasionally uses phrases which he almost certainly lifted from his teacher. This is not surprising, since he is defending very similar views and Hodgson's course was perfectly respectable. So there was no reason for Lingard to take a very different tack in his treatment of motion, hydrostatics or astronomy. But even if he is heavily influenced by Hodgson's teaching he has clearly taken the trouble to rewrite the theses in his own words and there is one instance where he adds something which one would rather expect an enthusiast like Hodgson to have included. This is the discovery of Uranus in 1781 by William Herschel. Herschel called this 'the Georgian star' in honour of George III. Lingard does not name it but lists seven planets: Mercury, Venus, Earth, Mars, Jupiter, Saturn and 'the one which after so many centuries Herschel was the first to see'.

A comparison with Lingard's *Theses Philosophicae* of 1807 shows that in his years of teaching at Crook Hall he made no major changes in his course of natural philosophy. Since the theses also cover what he taught in Low Philosophy I first note a few changes in presentation. Generally he lifts whole sections from the earlier disputation, with stylistic changes made necessary where he has omitted something. Most of the omissions are summaries of what adversaries held, though there is no reason to think that they were also omitted in the actual course he dictated. He still rejects the Peripatetic theory of impressed and expressed species, but he is noticeably more polite than he was on the earlier occasion:

> There is an old opinion, one time and again strengthened by the authority of most learned men, that ideas are a sort of images, representing external things, pictured either in the mind or in the brain (for there is no agreement on this): but we cannot assent to this, since we think it is the external things in themselves and without any representation which are perceived by the mind.[21]

His own opinion seems to remain Lockean, though again he makes no mention of Locke. I note, in passing, that in the second half of the nineteenth century Lingard's successors regularly mentioned Locke for the explicit purpose of rejecting his account of the origin of ideas, but the revival of neo-scholasticism was still a long way off when Lingard was teaching.

In the theses on Natural Philosophy there is little change to remark and some of the changes are merely consequences of arranging the theses under different headings. To show that light does not travel instantaneously Lingard mentions how this was first shown by Roemer's observations of the satellites of Jupiter and later confirmed by Bradley's observations of the aberration of starlight, both discoveries which had been made long before. In the theses on hydrostatics we learn that water is not, as the ancients thought, a simple body: it is 85% oxygen and 15% hydrogen, as

---

21. *Vetus est enim opinio, eaque doctissimorum hominum auctoritate saepius comprobata, ideas esse quasdam imagines, rerum externarum repraesentatrices, vel in mente, vel in cerebro (de hoc enim non convenit) depictas: cui tamen assentiri non possumus, cum nobis non rerum imagines, sed res ipsae in se et sine ullâ repraesentatione à mente percipi videntur.*

recent experiments have shown. This leads to something which seems new in the syllabus.

By what is presumably a slip or a misprint the heading *Ex Physica* is repeated. It may well be that something like *Ex Chimia* was intended, since there is a subheading *De Calorico*. *Calor*, we are told, is heat, whereas the cause of heat is 'caloric'. But the nature of caloric is disputed. Some take it be found in the internal agitation of the parts of a body, whereas Lingard favours the rival view which treats it as a very subtle and extremely elastic substance. To assess his grasp of the work of scientists such as Lavoisier is beyond my competence, so I merely note that here Lingard does seem to be introducing a new topic into the syllabus.

In general, Lingard is no great innovator in the syllabus. There is no good reason why he should have been. Like Hodgson, he gives a very serviceable summary of the subjects he has been teaching. Whether it was Wilkinson or Banister or some yet to be discovered predecessor of theirs who made the initial breakthrough to espousing contemporary science, it is clear that for both Hodgson and Lingard the scruples of Alban Butler were a thing of the past. In conclusion, it is a curiosity that is not often attended to that Douai, Crook and Ushaw all allotted a prominent place in the philosophy syllabus to the study of science, whereas in recent decades seminaries have been content to make the unreliable assumption that any seminarian studying philosophy and theology will already have an adequate acquaintance with contemporary science.[22]

BIBLIOGRAPHY

Banister, Robert, [Disputation poster, two copies] *Philosophia Naturalis* [theses on Physics and Astronomy], Duaci, apud Derbaix, March 3 1755. [Ushaw College Library: kept in protective folder with no pressmark.]

Butler, Alban, [Disputation poster] *Philosophia Naturalis* [theses on Physics and Astronomy], Douai, February 20 1741. [Ushaw College Library: kept in protective folder with no pressmark.]

Doyle, Peter, 'Seminary Education: A Conservative 18th Century View', *North West Catholic History*, Vol. 1, No. 1 (February 1969), pp. 26–38.

Gooch, Leo (editor), *The Revival of English Catholicism: The Banister Rutter Correspondence 1777–1807*, North West Catholic History Society, Wigan, 1995.

Hoban, Brendan, 'The Philosophical Tradition of Douay', *Ushaw Magazine*, Vol. 63 (December 1953), pp. 145–159.

Hodgson, Joseph, [Disputation poster] *Philosophia Universa* [theses on Logic, Metaphysics, Ethics, Mathematics, Physics, Astronomy and Optics], Duaci, apud Derbaix, June 25 1787. [Ushaw College Library: kept at XVIII D 5 8.]

——— [Disputation poster] *Philosophia Rationalis* [theses on Logic and Metaphysics], Duaci, apud Derbaix, June 15 1790. [Ushaw College Library: kept at XVIII D 2 12; these theses were defended by Lingard.]

22. On this see my 'Science in a Seminary'.

Lingard John, [Disputation poster] *Philosophia Rationalis et Naturalis* [theses on Logic, Metaphysics, Ethics, Mathematics, Physics and Astronomy], Crook Hall, June 22 and 23, n.y. [1796; Ushaw College Library: kept at XVIII D 5 8.]

—— [Disputation poster] *Theses Philosophicae ex Logica, Pneumatologia, et Ethica Depromptae,* June 20 1798. [Ushaw College Library: kept at XVIII D 5 8.]

—— [Disputation poster] *Theses Philosophicae* [theses on Logic, Metaphysics, Ethics and Natural Philosophy], Novo Castri, Typis Edvardi Walker, 1807. [Ushaw College Library: kept at XVIII D 5 8.]

—— [Dictate written by Henry Gradwell] *Logic* [98 pages, completed March 15 1810], *Metaphysics* [134 pages, completed May 14 1810], *Ethics* [54 pages, completed July 6 1810], Ushaw College Library.

Sharratt, Michael, 'Copernicanism at Douai', *Durham University Journal,* New Series, Vol. 36, No. 1 (December 1974), pp. 41–48.

—— 'Alban Butler, Newtonian in Part', *Downside Review,* Vol. 96, No. 323 (April 1978), pp. 103–111.

—— ' "Excellent Professors and an Exact Discipline": Aspects of Challoner's Douai', in *Challoner and His Church: A Catholic Bishop in Georgian England,* edited by Eamon Duffy, London, Darton, Longman & Todd, 1981, pp. 122–25.

—— 'The Origin and Growth of the Ushaw Library', *Northern Catholic History,* No. 24 (Autumn 1986), pp. 22–34.

—— *Galileo: Decisive Innovator,* Oxford, Blackwell, 1994; Cambridge University Press, 1996.

—— 'Science in a Seminary', in *The Place of the Scientist in the Life of the Church: Papers Presented at the Meeting of the Secretariat for Scientific Questions,* St. Albans, Pax Romana, 1998, pp. 81–87.

2

LINGARD'S ANGLO-SAXONISM:
A POST-COLONIAL READING

J.A. HILTON

John Lingard made his name as a scholar with his *Antiquities of the Anglo-Saxon Church* (first published in 1806 and reprinted in 1810, and revised for republication in 1845), and he returned to the subject as part of his massive *History of England* (first published between 1819 and 1830 and continually revised until 1849), which confirmed his reputation as a historian. He made a significant contribution to Anglo-Saxonism, defined as the study of the Anglo-Saxons. A critical reading of his Anglo-Saxonism, using the insights of post-colonial criticism, will help to reveal the implicit assumptions of Lingard's scholarship.[1]

Lingard's life spanned the emergence of English Catholics from persecution. He was born in 1771: the Catholic Relief Acts were passed in 1778 and 1791 and the Emancipation Act in 1829; the English Catholic hierarchy was restored in 1850; he died in 1851. Lingard's life also fell within an age of revolution which began with the American Revolution of 1776, progressed to the French Revolution of 1789, saw the Reform Act of 1832, and ended with the year of revolution in 1848. He also lived to see the abolition of the slave trade in 1808 and the abolition of slavery in the British colonies in 1834.

Lingard was one of the last students of the English college at Douai, and a founder of its successor at Crook Hall and Ushaw. Despite his love of the college, he declined the burden of teaching and academic administration, and became, from 1811 until his death in 1851, the priest of the quiet rural mission at Hornby in Lancashire, where he had leisure to devote himself to historical scholarship. His *History* with its pioneering use of primary sources was acknowledged as a masterpiece. He was awarded a triple papal doctorate in 1821, and was elected to the Académie Française in 1839, and his reputation continues to grow. He also became the acknowledged leader of the Cisalpine clergy who worked for Catholic Emancipation and the restoration of the English hierarchy.[2]

In his 'Preliminary Notice' to the *History* he 'disclaimed any pretension to that which has been called the philosophy of history', as 'writers of history know nothing more respecting motives than the little which their

---

1. I am grateful to Chetham's Library, Manchester (it was a privilege to study where Lingard studied), the John Rylands Library of the University of Manchester, the Talbot Library, Preston, the British Library, Mr. J. McDermott, and the Rev. P. Phillips.
2. M. Haile and E. Bonney, *Life and Letters of John Lingard* (London, 1911); J.P. Chinnici, *The English Catholic Enlightenment* (Shepherdstown, 1980); M. Mullett, 'John Lingard, Historian', *North-West Catholic History*, XII (1995), pp. 36–38; E. Jones, *John Lingard and the Pursuit of Historical Truth* (Brighton, 2001).

authorities have disclosed, or the facts necessarily suggest'.[3] It is just this disclaimer that alerts us to the possibility of an undisclosed, implicit, and, indeed, unconscious philosophical and political agenda, which is revealed by a post-colonial reading of Lingard's Anglo-Saxonism. Such a reading makes explicit not only some of the presuppositions of Lingard's scholarship but also casts light on the attitudes of the English Catholic community he represented.

Hostile critics of such a reading may fall back on Lingard's contempt for 'speculative and philosophical historians',[4] but a post-colonial approach to Lingard is only looking, as he did, at 'the little which' he 'disclosed'.[5] Post-colonial critical theory divides the study of a subject, Orientalism par excellence but also Anglo-Saxonism, into manifest and latent. Manifest Anglo-Saxonism is the changing academic discipline and increasing body of knowledge that constitutes Anglo-Saxon studies. Latent Anglo-Saxonism is the unconscious certainty about the subject, what might be called Anglo-Saxony, which regards pagan Anglo-Saxons as uniformly barbarous and violent, as the Other. It is significant that, although Lingard availed himself 'of the additional help offered by the present improved state of Anglo-Saxon literature'[6] in preparing the third edition of the *Antiquities*, he repeats virtually word for word what he wrote in the first edition about the character of the Anglo-Saxons. Post-colonial theory implies a colonial and pre-colonial past, which requires analysis, and draws attention not only to the writer's use of language but also to the identity it reveals.[7]

Lingard made a major contribution to the manifest Anglo-Saxonism of the early nineteenth century. Contemporary Anglo-Saxonists included Sharon Turner, whose *History of the Anglo-Saxons* appeared between 1799 and 1805, and Francis Palgrave, whose *History of the Anglo-Saxons* was published in 1831, as well as John Mitchell Kemble, whose *Saxons in England* appeared in 1849 towards the end of Lingard's life. These specialist works were set against the general histories of England, pre-eminently Hume's *History of England* ((1745–61), which Lingard was at pains to refute, as well as Gibbon's *Decline and Fall of the Roman Empire*, and novels, such as Scott's *Ivanhoe*, which appeared in 1819.[8]

3. *History of England*, vol. 1, p. xvii.

4. *History of England*, vol. 1, p. xviii.

5. *History of England*, vol. 1, p. xvii.

6. *History and Antiquities* (1849), vol. 1, p. vi.

7. P. Barry, *Beginning Theory* (Manchester, 1995), pp. 191–201; B. Ashcroft, G. Griffiths, and H. Tiffin, *Key Concepts in Post-Colonial Studies* (London, 1998); E. Said, *Orientalism* (New York, 1978); L. Stiebel, *Imagining Africa* (Westport, 2001); A.J. Frantzen and J.D. Niles (eds.), *Anglo-Saxonism and the Construction of Social Identity* (Gainesville, 1997); A.J. Frantzen, *Desire for Origins: New Language, Old English, and Teaching the Tradition* (New Brunswick, 1990).

8. John M. Kemble, *Saxons in England*, 2 vols. (London, 1849); P. Phillips, 'John Lingard and *The Anglo-Saxon Church*', *Recusant History*, vol. 23, no. 2, (1996), pp. 178–89; Haile and Bonney, p. 166; C.T. Berkhout and M.McC. Gatch (eds.), *Anglo-Saxon Scholarship: The First Three Centuries* (Boston, 1982).

Anglo-Saxonists, like Orientalists and Africanists, were concerned to map the territory of their subject, to name its places and spaces. Lingard's *Antiquities* includes a map of Anglo-Saxon England, naming its settlements and kingdoms. However, when it came to the original German homeland of the Anglo-Saxons, what Palgrave calls 'the real *Old England*',[9] they had only the vaguest of information. Lingard describes the origins of the Anglo-Saxons in the *Antiquities* thus:

> the Saxons, in the commencement of the second century, were a small and contemptible tribe on the neck of the Cimbrian Chersonesus: in the fourth, they had swelled to a populous and mighty nation, whose territories progressively reached the Elbe, the Weser, the Ems, and the Rhine.[10]

In the *History of England* he provides a little more detail:

> about the middle of the second century the Saxons, an obscure tribe of barbarians, occupied the district between the Elbe and the Eyder, on the neck of the Cimbrian Chersonesus: in the course of two hundred years the same appellation had been extended to all the nations from the extremity of the peninsula to the Weser, the Ems, and the Rhine ... the Angles were their neighbours on the north as far as the present town of Flemsburgh; and beyond the Angles dwelt the nation of the Jutes, with no other boundary than the ocean.[11]

Turner conveys the same information. The Anglo-Saxons came from 'the Cimbric peninsula, and its vicinity ... they were branches of the great Saxon confederation, which from the Elbe, extended itself to the Rhine'.[12] They were originally contained by 'a territory of the neck of the Cimbric Chersonesus, and three small islands',[13] and they occupied 'the western side of the Cimbric peninsula, between the Elbe and the Eyder'.[14] Palgrave adds another detail: 'the Jutes [and] the Angles dwelt in the peninsula of Jutland ... and in the adjoining Holstein, where there is still a district called *Anglen* ... The Saxons were more widely dispersed'.[15] They have little to add to Hume's popular account written in the previous century: the Saxons 'had diffused themselves from the northern parts of Germany and the Cimbrian Chersonesus, and had taken possession of all the sea coast from the mouth of the Rhine to Jutland'.[16] Gibbon summarised the prevailing knowledge thus: 'The successive colonies which issued in the period of a century from the mouths of the Elbe, the Weser, and the Rhine were principally composed of three valiant tribes or nations of Germany; the *Jutes,* the *old Saxons* and the *Angles*'.[17] Despite the best

9. Palgrave, p. 33.
10. *Antiquities*, vol. 1, pp. 7–8; *History and Antiquities*, vol. 1, p. 16.
11. *History of England,* vol. 1, pp. 70–71.
12. Turner, vol. 1, p. 88.
13. Turner, vol. 1, p. 111.
14. Turner, vol. 1, p. 117.
15. Palgrave, p. 33.
16. Hume, vol. 1, p. 16.
17. Gibbon, vol. 4, p. 102.

cartographic efforts of these scholars, the Anglo-Saxon homeland remained what Tolkien called 'the nameless North'.[18]

This empty space served as a blank screen on to which the Anglo-Saxonists could project their image of the Other, an exotic, homogeneous embodiment of vices. According to Lingard the original Anglo-Saxons were 'hordes of ferocious pirates',[19] whose 'favourite occupation was piracy',[20] 'the most barbarous of the nations', 'disgraced by ... brutality', who 'generally preferred the blood of their captives', governed by 'the ferocity of their passions', by 'Avarice and the lust of sensual enjoyment'.[21] They were 'barbarians', 'pillage by land, piracy by sea, were their only professions', and 'their whole time was alternately devoted to indolence and to rapine'.[22] Turner paints a similar picture of their 'ferocious qualities', 'their cruelty and destructiveness', and their 'love of plunder and cruelty'.[23] Palgrave concurs, calling them 'wild and ferocious'.[24] Similarly, Hume states that the Saxons were 'one of the most warlike tribes of this fierce people [the Germans], and had become the terror of the neighbouring nations',[25] and Gibbon describes them as 'warlike barbarians'.[26] Modern civilised scholars look back with horror at these ancient, barbarian pirates. 'I wants to make your flesh creep', as the Fat Boy says in Dickens's *Pickwick Papers*. Obviously Lingard and his contemporaries find the characteristics of the Anglo-Saxons in their sources. They are, perhaps, strongly influenced by the *locus classicus* for ancient Germany, Tacitus' *Germania,* in which the author compares and contrasts the civilised, vicious, and effeminate Romans with the barbarian, virtuous, and warlike Germans.[27] However, the Anglo-Saxonists find what they are seeking. Of course, the Anglo-Saxon conquest of Britain was led by barbarian warriors, but despite Lingard's reference to 'the meaner labour of women and slaves',[28] the Anglo-Saxons are seen as homogeneous – they, or at least, the free men – are all 'warriors', and they are all motivated by violent emotions, by the lust for pillage and blood. The racism of latent Anglo-Saxonism is quite explicit in Turner, who writes in a reference to the parallel discourses of Orientalism and Africanism:

the ferocity of the Saxon character would seem to suit better the dark and melancholy physiognomies of Asia and Africa, than the fair, pleas-

18. H. Carpenter, *The Inklings* (London, 1997), p. 29.
19. *Antiquities*, vol. 1, p. v.
20. *Antiquities*, vol. 1, p. 8.
21. *Antiquities*, vol. 1, p. 43; *History and Antiquities*, vol. 1, pp. 45–46.
22. *History of England*, vol. 1, pp. 70–71.
23. Turner, vol. 1, pp. 204–205.
24. Palgrave, p. 55.
25. Hume, vol. 1, p. 16.
26. Gibbon, vol. 4, p. 100.
27. H. Mattingley, (ed.), *Tacitus on Britain and Germany* (Harmondsworth, 1948), pp. 23–29, 101–40.
28. *History of England,* vol. 1, p. 71.

ing, and blue-eyed countenances by which our ancestors are described. But though nature had supplied them with the germs of those amiable qualities which have become the national character of their descendants, their direful customs, their acquired passions, and barbarous education perverted every good propensity.[29]

The Anglo-Saxons were heathens as well as barbarians. As Lingard explains 'to the worship of the true God succeeded the impure rites of Woden; and the ignorance and barbarism of the north of Germany were transplanted into the most flourishing provinces of Britain'.[30] He goes on to describe some of the features of Anglo-Saxon religion:

> their religion was accommodated to their manners. In their theology they acknowledged no sin but cowardice; and rewarded no virtue but courage. Their gods they appeased with the blood of human victims. Of a future life their notions were faint and wavering; and if the soul were fated to survive the body, to quaff ale out of the skulls of their enemies was to be the great reward of the virtuous; to lead a life of hunger and inactivity the endless punishment of the wicked.[31]

Lingard's Catholic view of the benighted heathen is supported by the atheist historians Hume and Gibbon. Hume writes that the Anglo-Saxons worshipped Woden, 'the god of war' as 'their supreme deity' and that 'if they obtained the favour of this divinity by their ardour ... they should be admitted after their death into his hall; and reposing on couches, should satiate themselves with ale from the skull of their enemies'.[32] Hume takes the opportunity to score a point against all religion: the heathen Anglo-Saxons 'admitted in general a system of doctrines, which they held as sacred, but which like all other superstitions, must carry the air of the wildest extravagance, if propounded to those who are not familiarised to it from their earliest infancy'.[33] Gibbon writes that the ancient Germans 'adored the great visible objects and agents of nature, the Sun and the Moon, the Fire and the Earth; together with those imaginary deities, who were supposed to preside over the most important occupations of human life', that they were exposed 'naked and unarmed to the blind terrors of superstition',[34] and goes on to assert that 'All agreed that a life spent in arms, and a glorious death in battle, were the best preparations for a happy futurity either in this or another world'.[35] The Catholic recoils with horror from 'the impure rites' of the Anglo-Saxons and the Enlightened *philosophes* smile pityingly at their 'superstition'. Turner finds something positive in Anglo-Saxon religion. He points out that they called the

---

29. Turner, vol. 1, pp. 206–207.
30. *Antiquities*, vol. 1 p. 11; *History and Antiquities*, vol. 1, pp. 18–19.
31. *Antiquities*, vol. 1, pp. 43–45; *History and Antiquities*, vol. 1, pp. 45–46.
32. Hume, vol. 1, p. 27.
33. Hume, vol. 1, p. 27.
34. Gibbon, vol. 1, p. 254.
35. Gibbon, vol. 1, p. 256.

supreme being 'GOD, which is literally THE GOOD'.[36] Similarly, Palgrave remarks that, while their religion was 'evidently a compound of the worship of the celestial bodies ... and of hero-worship',[37] and 'Of the conception of the essence of the Divine Being, the Anglo-Saxon language affords a singular testimony, for the name of *God* signifies Good. He was goodness itself and the author of goodness'.[38]

This appreciation of the positive aspects of Anglo-Saxon heathenism indicates that, paradoxically, Anglo-Saxony is seen as the repository of admirable physical characteristics and moral virtues. After all, from an English point of view, there would have to be some good in the Anglo-Saxons, for, as Gibbon writes, 'an Englishman may curiously trace the establishment of the barbarians from whom he derives his name, his laws, and perhaps his origin'.[39] Indeed, the study of the German origins of English characteristics and institutions amounted to a so-called Germanist school of history.[40] For Lingard the Saxons had 'swelled to a populous and mighty nation', they were 'intrepid' and possessed 'audacity'.[41] Turner described them as 'fearless, active, and successful', as well as 'fair, pleasing, and blue-eyed', and they had 'the germs of those amiable qualities which have become the national character of their descendants'.[42] For Palgrave the Saxons 'though wild and ferocious towards their enemies,... were less corrupted than the more polished Greeks and Romans. They were faithful, chaste, and honest – turning towards the light and seeking amendment'.[43] For Hume the ancient Germans 'carried to the highest pitch the virtues of valour and love of liberty'.[44] Again the ultimate authority is probably Tacitus, as Gibbon asserts: 'In their primitive state of simplicity and independence the Germans were studied by the discerning eye, and delineated by the masterly pencil, of Tacitus, the first of historians who applied the science of philosophy to the study of facts'.[45] Lingard remarks that 'of these [Anglo-Saxon institutions] the most important, and that which formed the groundwork of the rest, may be discovered among the Germans in the age of Tacitus'.[46]

Nevertheless, the Anglo-Saxon conquest of Roman Britain, the history of which deserves a post-colonial analysis, serves only to demonstrate their vicious qualities, their 'ferocity' and 'brutality'. The early stages of the Anglo-Saxon settlement were apparently accomplished by the exter-

---

36. Turner, vol. 1, p. 217.
37. Palgrave, pp. 51–52.
38. Palgrave, p. 55.
39. Gibbon, vol. 4, p. 100.
40. *Cambridge History of English and American Literature,* 18 vols. (Cambridge, 1907–21), chapter 11 (http://www.bartleby.com/224/0201.html).
41. *Antiquities,* vol. 1, pp. 7–8; *History and Antiquities,* vol. 1, p. 17.
42. Turner, vol. 1, pp. 206–207.
43. Palgrave, p. 55.
44. Hume, vol. 1, p. 15.
45. Gibbon, vol. 1, p. 237.
46. *History of England,* vol. 1, p. 377.

mination of the native inhabitants, the destruction of Roman civilisation, and the extirpation of Christianity. Lingard explains that:

> the natural ferocity of the Saxons had been sharpened by the stubborn resistance of the Britons. They spared neither the lives nor the habitations of their enemies; submission was seldom able to disarm their fury: and the churches, towns, and villages, all the works of art, and all the remains of Roman grandeur were devoured by the flames. But while they thus indulged their resentment they dried up the more obvious springs of civil and religious improvement. With the race of the ancient inhabitants disappeared the refinements of society and the knowledge of the gospel.[47]

Similarly, Hume points out that 'a total extermination of the Britons became the sole expedient for providing a settlement and subsistence to the new planters'.[48] Gibbon remarks that 'conquest has never appeared more dreadful and destructive than in the hands of the Saxons'. He points out that 'this strange alteration has persuaded historians, and even philosophers, that the provincials of Britain were totally exterminated; and that the vacant land was again peopled by the perpetual influx and rapid increase of the German colonies'.[49] Lingard and his contemporary Anglo-Saxonists were writing during the colonial era, during the rapid growth of the British Empire. He looks back at its Elizabethan origins and concluded that:

> the adventurers brought wealth and honour to their country. But among them there were many who, at a distance from home, and freed from the restraints of law, indulged in the most brutal excess; whose rapacity despised the rights of nations and the claims of humanity; and whom, while we admire their skill, and hardihood, and perseverance, our more sober judgement must pronounce no better than public robbers and assassins.[50]

The later stages of the Anglo-Saxon conquest were accompanied by the enslavement of the natives, and the development of a trade in Anglo-Saxon slaves, which Lingard compares with the African slave trade. The slave trade was abolished only in 1806, a couple of years after the first edition of the *Antiquities,* and British West Indian slavery was abolished only in 1833, three years after the completion of the first edition of the *History.*[51] Lingard writes in the *Antiquities*:

> the man, whose life they condescended to spare, was taught to consider perpetual slavery as a gratuitous favour … The savages of Africa may traffic with Europeans for the negroes they have seized by treachery, or captured in open war: but the more savage conquerors of the Britons

47. *Antiquities*, vol. 1, pp. 10–11; *History and Antiquities*, vol. 1, pp. 18–19.
48. Hume, vol. 1, p. 24.
49. Gibbon, vol. 4, p. 111.
50. *History of England,* vol. 4, pp. 479–80.
51. H. Thomas, *The Slave Trade* (London, 1997).

sold without scruple to the merchants of the continent, their country-
men, and even their own children.[52]

He makes the same point in the *History*:

> like the savages of Africa, they are said to have carried off, not only
> their own countrymen, but even their friends and relatives; and to have
> sold them as slaves in the ports of the continent. The men of Bristol
> were the last to abandon this nefarious traffic.[53]

His contemporaries would have recognised the role of Bristol in the
recently abolished slave trade. He also writes that 'The work of devastation was checked by views of personal interest ... and the labours of the
captives were found necessary for the cultivation of the soil'.[54] Gibbon
argues that 'after the sanguinary barbarians had secured their dominion
and gratified their revenge, it was their interest to preserve the peasants, as
well as the cattle of the unresisting country'.[55] Lingard also points out that
in Elizabethan times:

> the renowned John Hawkins first acquired celebrity by opening the
> trade in slaves. He made three voyages to the coast of Africa; bartered
> articles of trifling value for numerous lots of negroes; crossed the
> Atlantic to Hispaniola and the Spanish settlements in America; and in
> exchange for his captives returned with large quantities of hides, sugar,
> ginger, and pearls.[56]

Anglo-Saxon slaves in the market of Rome 'caught the eye' of the
future Pope Gregory the Great, who eventually sent Augustine to convert
the Anglo-Saxons.[57] This mission allowed Lingard to instil upon his
Protestant readers the unpalatable fact that from its origin the English
Church had been subject to Rome: 'the belief of the Anglo-Saxon church
respecting the supremacy of St Peter'.[58] Anglo-Saxon 'ferocity soon
yielded to the exertions of the missionaries, and the harsher features of
their origin were insensibly softened under the mild influence of the
gospel'.[59] Indeed, 'by religion they were reclaimed from savage life, and
raised to a degree of civilisation, which, at one period, excited the wonder
of the other nations of Europe'.[60] They went on to carry Christianity into
their original homelands in Germany, and beyond: 'The rays of the gospel
were reverberated from the shores of Britain to the banks of the Weser, the
Rhine, and the Danube'.[61] However, for Lingard their pagan vices clung

---

52. *Antiquities*, vol. 1, pp. 43–45; *History and Antiquities*, vol. 1, pp. 45–46.
53. *History of England*, vol. 1, p. 420.
54. *History of England*, vol. 1, p. 85.
55. Gibbon, vol. 4, p. 112.
56. *History of England*, vol. 4, p. 480.
57. *Antiquities*, vol. 1, pp. 11–19.
58. *Antiquities*, vol. 1, p. 339.
59. *Antiquities*, vol. 1, pp. 45–46; *History and Antiquities*, vol. 1, p. 45.
60. *Antiquities*, vol. 1, p. v.
61. *Antiquities*, vol. 2, p. 332.

to the Anglo-Saxons like the vestiges of Original Sin, and Catholic Christianity was the source of their virtues:

> but the impartial observer will acknowledge the impossibility of eradicating at once the fiercer passions of a whole nation; nor be surprised if he behold several of them relapse into their former manners, and on some occasions unite the actions of savages with the professions of christians. To judge of the advantage that the Saxons derived from their conversion, he will fix his eyes on their virtues. *They* were the offspring of the gospel; their vices were the relics of paganism.[62]

The role of the Anglo-Saxon kings in the conversion of their subjects and in settling disputes about the discipline of the English Church also allowed Lingard to imply that Anglo-Saxon Catholicism, whilst honouring the supremacy of the papacy, had a Gallican, Cisalpine view of the legitimate authority of the state and a tolerant respect for the individual conscience.[63] It was the Pope who sent Augustine and his fellow missionaries to convert England, but it was the King of Kent who became their first and most eminent convert, and whose example led to the voluntary conversion of his people:[64]

> from the natural ferocity of the Saxon character, there was reason to fear that the royal convert, in the fervour of proselytism, might employ the flames of persecution to accelerate the progress of christianity. But his teachers were activated by motives more congenial to the mild spirit of the gospel: and with a moderation which is not always the associate of zeal, sedulously inculcated that the worship of man to be grateful to the Deity, must be the spontaneous dictate of the heart; and that the obstinacy of the idolater was to be overcome, not by the sword of the magistrate, but by the labours of the missionary.[65]

Faced with the disputes about discipline between the Roman and Celtic missionaries, 'the merit of restoring concord was reserved for the zeal and authority of Oswio, King of Northumbria'.[66] The Cisalpines attempted to win relief from the penal laws by appealing to the principle of religious toleration, and were even prepared, in return, to admit some measure of influence by the English Protestant State over the English Catholic Church.

With the Anglo-Saxons safely gathered into the fold of Catholic Christianity and Roman civilisation, history repeated itself, and they fell victim to the Vikings, who replace them as the Other. The Vikings, Lingard explained, came from the same regions as the pagan Anglo-Saxons, and behaved in the same way:

---

62. *Antiquities*, vol. 1, pp. 48–49.
63. See P. Phillips, 'John Lingard and *The Anglo-Saxon Church*', *Recusant History,* vol. 23, no. 2, (1996), p. 185.
64. *History,* vol. 1, pp. 88–90.
65. *Antiquities*, vol. 1, p. 18; *History and Antiquities*, vol. 1, p. 25.
66. *Antiquities*, vol. 1, p. 57.

the peninsula of Jutland, the islands of the Baltic, and the shores of the Scandinavian continent were the birthplace of a race of men, who, like the Saxons of old, spent the best portion of their lives on the waves, despised the tranquil enjoyment of peace, and preferred the acquisitions of rapine to the laborious profits of industry.[67]

The Danes, according to Lingard,

sought no other occupation than war, and possessed no other wealth than what they had acquired by the sword ... No injury was necessary to provoke their enmity. The prospect of plunder directed their attack; and carnage and devastation were the certain consequences of their success. They could conceive no greater pleasure than to feast their eyes with the flames of the villages, which they had plundered, and their ears with the groans of the captives expiring under the anguish of torture.[68]

Similarly, Turner writes that the Vikings 'plundered every district they could approach',[69] Palgrave that 'the Danes became the incessant and inveterate foes of Britain and its inhabitants, visiting every part of the island with fire and sword',[70] Hume that the Danes 'kept the Anglo-Saxons in perpetual inquietude, committed the most barbarous ravages upon them, and at last reduced them to grievous servitude',[71] and Gibbon that 'every sea and land were invaded by the adventurous spirit of the Scandinavian pirates' who indulged in 'rapine and slaughter'.[72]

Finally, the Anglo-Saxons were conquered by the Normans, who, according to Lingard, 'proud of their superior civilization, treated the natives as barbarians'.[73] Hume draws the parallel between the Anglo-Saxon and Norman conquests: 'except the former conquest of England by the Saxons themselves, who were induced, by peculiar circumstances, to proceed even to the extermination of the natives, it would be difficult to find in all history a revolution more destructive, or attended with a more complete subjection of the antient inhabitants'.[74] The colonisers were now the colonised. This situation provides the background for Scott's *Ivanhoe*:

A circumstance which greatly tended to enhance the tyranny of the nobility and the sufferings of the inferior classes, arose from the consequences of the Conquest by Duke William of Normandy. Four generations had not sufficed to blend the hostile blood of the Normans and Anglo-Saxons, or to unite, by common language and mutual interests, two hostile races, one of which still felt the elation of triumph, while the other groaned under all the consequences of defeat.[75]

67. *History of England*, vol. 1, p. 169.
68. *Antiquities*, vol. 2, p. 219; *History and Antiquities*, vol. 2, p. 219.
69. Turner, vol. 1, p. 449.
70. Palgrave, p. 105.
71. Hume, vol. 1, p. 56.
72. Gibbon, vol. 5, p. 609.
73. *History of England*, vol. 1, p. 431.
74. Hume, vol. 1, pp. 226–27.
75. Walter Scott, *Ivanhoe* (Wordsworth Classics edition, Ware, 1995), p. 4.

First developed in the seventeenth century, the concept of the Norman Yoke had been developed by Whigs and Radicals in the eighteenth century, and continued to have political resonance into the nineteenth. It has been defined by the historian, Christopher Hill as follows:

> Before 1066 the Anglo-Saxon inhabitants of this country lived as free and equal citizens, governing themselves through representative institutions. The Norman Conquest deprived them of this liberty, and established the tyranny of an alien King and landlords. But the people did not forget the rights they had lost. Concessions (Magna Carta, for instance) were from time to time extorted from their rulers, and always the tradition of lost Anglo-Saxon freedom was a stimulus to ever more insistent demands upon the successors of the Norman usurpers.[76]

It is one of the themes underlying *Ivanhoe*, in which Scott shapes the idea into a proverb:

> Norman saw on English oak,
> On English neck a Norman yoke;
> Norman spoon in English dish,
> And England ruled as Normans wish;
> Blithe world to England never will be more,
> Till England's rid of all the four."[77]

Protestants and Puritans used the concept to denounce the papacy, episcopacy, and the clergy. It was used again as an argument against Catholic Emancipation, a cause in which Lingard was active.[78] Lingard, therefore, made a careful appraisal of the effects of the Norman Conquest, and concluded that 'the natives submitted to the yoke in sullen despair',[79] and that 'England presented the singular spectacle of a native population with a foreign sovereign, a foreign hierarchy, and a foreign nobility',[80] but he argued that these new rulers took over the institutions of the Anglo-Saxons, and that apparent innovations, such as feudalism, were based upon Anglo-Saxon precedents.[81] He also made a strong case for acknowledging the close links between the Anglo-Saxon Church in Britain and the See of Rome.

The identities of Lingard and the English Catholics he represented are reflected in his Anglo-Saxonism. As an Englishman he identifies with his Anglo-Saxon ancestors and with contemporary Englishmen. As a Roman Catholic he regards the pagan and barbarian Anglo-Saxons as the Other, but he is able to identify with the Christian Anglo-Saxons. His account of

---

76. C. Hill, *Puritanism and Revolution* (London, 1958), p.57.

77. *Ivanhoe*, p. 223.

78. Hill, pp. 50–122; C.A. Simmons, *Reversing the Conquest: History and Myth in Nineteenth-Century British Literature* (New Brunswick, 1990); G. Miller, *The Policy of the Roman Catholic Question discussed in a Letter to the Right Honourable W.C. Plunket* (London, 1826); Haile and Bonney, pp. 204–56.

79. *History of England*, vol. 1, pp. 466–67.

80. *History of England*, vol. 1, p. 468.

81. *History of England*, vol. 1, pp. 648–92.

the barbarian Anglo-Saxons as colonial conquerors, who exterminate and enslave, implies criticism of the contemporary British Empire. His description of the English Catholic Church before the Protestant Reformation and the effects of that Reformation, amounts to an account of English Catholicism's pre-colonial and colonial past from the post-colonial viewpoint of toleration. Marginalised as a Catholic and living in the margins of England in rural Lancashire, he asserts, by writing English history, his identity as an Englishman.

ABBREVIATIONS

Antiquities	John Lingard, *The Antiquities of the Anglo-Saxon Church,* 2 vols. (Newcastle, 1806).
Gibbon	Edward Gibbon, *The Decline and Fall of the Roman Empire,* 6 vols. (Everyman's Library edition, London, 1993).
History and Antiquities	John Lingard, *The History and Antiquities of the Anglo-Saxon Church,* 2 vols. (London, 1845).
History of England	John Lingard, *The History of England,* 10 vols. (5th edition, London, 1849).
Hume	David Hume, *The History of England,* 6 vols. (Liberty Classics edition, Indianapolis, 1983).
Turner	Sharon Turner, *The History of the Anglo-Saxons,* 3 vols. (London, 1828).
Palgrave	Francis Palgrave, *History of the Anglo-Saxons* (London, 1841).

3

LINGARD V. BARRINGTON, ET AL.: ECCLESIASTICAL POLITICS IN DURHAM, 1805–29

Leo Gooch

In his Charge to the diocesan clergy of Durham in 1831, Bishop William van Mildert expressed deep regret at the passage of Catholic Emancipation, but he instructed them to put it out of their minds:

> Far better is it, for the peace of the community, and for its future welfare, that such things should be left to the historian hereafter to dilate upon, with a cooler judgement and a more impartial spirit than can be expected from contemporary observers.[1]

That was sound advice, for the Catholic Question had been argued vehemently and unceasingly for more than forty years throughout the diocese by the clergy as well as by leading members of the pro- and anti-emancipation groups who had their bases in the north.

The See of Durham was occupied between 1791 and 1826 by Shute Barrington who had kept alive, almost singlehandedly, the spirit of No-Popery since the imprisonment (and conversion to Jewry) of Lord George Gordon in 1788. Barrington placed a number of anti-Catholic divines in the more lucrative livings of the diocese and continually exhorted them to write and preach against the abominations of Rome, and they did so. Barrington's protégés can be counted among the more distinguished anti-Catholic campaigners in the land and the most vociferous and persistent of them was the Rev. Henry Phillpotts, whose sixty-year career in political and theological controversy began in Durham in 1805 over the Catholic Question.[2]

At the same time, the diocese of Durham was home-base for some of the most determined secular pro-Catholics in the country, chief among them Charles Grey, later Lord Howick and finally Earl Grey, Member of Parliament for Northumberland, leader of the Whig party, and champion of Catholic Emancipation, parliamentary reform and the abolition of slavery. In County Durham, Grey's son-in-law John ('Radical Jack') George Lambton, afterwards Earl of Durham, was equally committed to Catholic relief and other liberal causes. He helped to found the *Durham Chronicle* in 1820 as a counterblast to the *Durham County Advertiser* (published until 1814 as the *Newcastle Advertiser*) which was the mouthpiece of the Tory and Anglican establishment in the north-east. Many of the principal landed magnates of the region were Whiggish on the Catholic Question, as were many of the lesser gentry, though the Tories had powerful advo-

---

1. C. Ives, *Sermons on Several Occasions and Charges by William van Mildert, DD*, etc. (1838), p. 542.
2. J.C.D. Clarke, *English Society* (1985), p. 354.

cates such as the Duke of Northumberland. John Lingard, the Catholic priest later to be celebrated for his *History of England*, was a professor at the newly-established seminary at Crook Hall and Ushaw until 1810, and he was the principal Catholic clerical voice in the debate.

The proximity of strongly pro- and anti-Catholic national figures in the region, then, was bound to give a keen edge to any local discussion of Catholic Emancipation, particularly during election campaigns; the topic came up, more or less routinely, at all electoral contests in the region during the period. So as to accommodate the various objections, ecclesiastical and civil, within a single argument, it was usual to conflate the individual aspects of the anti-emancipation debate into the one politico-theological concept of Popery, which could be used by all indiscriminately. It is appropriate, then, to begin with a brief summary of this highly convenient, and potent, idea.

Anti-Catholicism comprised two main elements. Firstly, to a greater or lesser extent, Protestants held that Catholic beliefs and practices were idolatrous, blasphemous and sacrilegious. Secondly, religious conformity was required by English law. Since the crown claimed spiritual as well as temporal authority, it was treasonable to adhere to a religion which owed spiritual allegiance to any other authority such as the Pope (who was himself, in any case, a temporal ruler). Dissent from the religion of the state was equivalent to opposition to the state; religious deviance was regarded as politically subversive and hence a matter of national security.

There were other elements in the anti-Catholic case arising out of the main propositions. From 1688 to 1788 the Catholic exiled House of Stuart maintained a claim to the English throne. It did not help that the Jacobite court in exile was on papal territory after 1715. In 1817, Grey argued that John Locke's objections to relieving the Catholics had rested on their attachment to the Stuarts; and now that that objection could no longer be advanced, there was no justification for their political exclusion. The extinction of the Stuarts made little difference to the substantive Protestant argument about the nature of Catholic loyalty, however, for the Pope remained as an alternative and supposedly more dangerous focus of Catholic allegiance. Catholics were held to support the Pope's deposing power by which he could relieve them of their civil allegiance. Catholics were also held to believe that it was sinful to keep faith with heretics, and that they could entertain mental reservations on any oath tendered to them which conflicted with Catholic tenets; they could not, therefore, be entrusted with English citizenship. This line was developed by the Bishop of Durham in a debate in the House of Lords in 1805. It was sufficient, he said, to show charity and kindness to people holding a different faith, but that did not mean they should be given political power. England had received and protected French émigré priests with all the warm charity of Christians, and the liberality of Englishmen, undeterred by the lack of 'security against the introduction of spies and enemies'. He would treat the Irish with similar kindness, and improve their social and economic condition, but without granting them political power: 'Let us keep inviolate the barriers of our religious and political constitution'.[3]

John Wesley believed that 'No government not Roman Catholic ought to tolerate men of the Roman Catholic persuasion'. In the nineteenth century, Wesleyan Methodism was politically, ecclesiastically, and socially conservative, a position necessarily opposed to Catholic Emancipation. Wesleyan opposition to the Catholic claims was part of a wider fear of radicalism, popular discontent and infidelity. The development of a highly authoritarian central bureaucracy among the Wesleyans alienated many in the Methodist movement and, in 1810, a group of working-class radicals, calling themselves Primitive Methodists, broke away to recover their more revivalist origins. The Primitive Methodists were no less opposed to Catholic Emancipation than the Wesleyans, because of the perceived illiberalism of Popery. Nonetheless, official Methodism did not wish to become involved in a question 'so decidedly political', and the leadership made attempts 'to discourage anti-Catholic sentiment from becoming anti-Catholic political activity'. For the majority of Methodists out in the country, however, the issue was primarily a religious one, and they disregarded the advice from London and vigorously opposed Catholic Emancipation in their own localities.[4]

Similarly, within the Dissenting bodies the leadership and the rank and file went their own ways. The Dissenters were chiefly concerned with the repeal of the Test Act, and the Committee of the Three Denominations expressed support for the Catholics in what was seen as an analogous case to their own. No such equivalence was acknowledged in the country, however, and individual Dissenters campaigned alongside Methodists against Catholic Emancipation. Consistency was also lacking among the Radicals with no religious affiliation. Officially, Catholic Emancipation was a simple question of religious toleration and equality. After Emancipation, however, it became clear that the support of the Radicals had not been based on any principle of religious toleration, but was merely an adjunct to their main aim of political reform. From 1832 Radicals were seen to be

3. T.C. Hansard, *Parliamentary Debates* (1803–29), First Series, vol. 36, col. 667 [hereafter *PD* (I) with vol. and col.]. U. Henriques, *Religious Toleration in England 1787–1833* (1961), p. 26; *PD* (I), 4, pp. 708–11. Bishop W. Gibson was told in 1790 that the government was very willing to relieve the Catholics if it could secure their allegiance: 'The difficulty is not about ye Stuarts, but ye interference of papal authority' (Leeds Diocesan Archives [hereafter LDA], Gibson Papers, Pilling to Gibson, Nov. 26th 1790).

4. J. Todd, *John Wesley and the Catholic Church* (1958), p. 100. Wesley does not seem to have come across many Catholics. He did meet one 'cursing, swearing, drunken papist' in Newcastle in 1743 who insisted that Wesley read Challoner's *The Grounds of the Old Religion* (cf. *Journal*, vol. 3, p. 75). He believed that Catholics could be regarded as sincere though deluded Christians. When his nephew became a Catholic, Wesley remarked, 'better a Catholic than a pagan'. (Todd, pp. 29–30, 86–87); D. Hempton, *Methodism and Politics in British Society, 1750–1850* (1984), Ch. 5; J.H. Hexter, 'The Protestant Revival and the Catholic Question in England, 1778–1829', *Journal of Modern History*, 8, (1936), p. 300.

as anti-Catholic as most other Englishmen by conflating Catholicism with reactionary politics and illiberal Popery.[5]

Roman Catholicism, then, aroused a powerful dual antagonism – religious bigotry and xenophobia; those disinclined to religious persecution could join the crusade to keep out the foreigner, and vice versa. Anti-Catholicism served as a national-cum-religious identity; Papists were not just non-Protestant but un-English. Idolaters, blasphemers and those owing any kind of loyalty to a foreign power could not be tolerated. It would, therefore, be a constitutional outrage to admit to English citizenship Roman Catholics who were idolatrous subjects of a foreign prince. Places of trust and authority under the crown could not be given to Papists, but were to be reserved for fully-fledged British citizens.

The Catholic laity fully appreciated the deep-rooted fears of the Protestants, and they were prepared to go to considerable lengths to remove the stigma of Popery. They would accept the appellation 'Protesting Catholic Dissenters' and they would concede a crown veto on episcopal appointments. They sought the restoration of the English hierarchy so that their bishops would have ordinary episcopal jurisdiction over day-to-day matters which Vicars Apostolic had to refer to Rome. In 1814, for example, a number of laymen called for a relaxation of the laws of abstinence for the various vigils, Ember and Rogation days which, 'because of the constant and daily intercourse between persons of different religions' in Great Britain, made them so difficult to observe. The abolition of these rules, in their submission, would reduce the differentiation of Catholics in their daily socio-economic environment, and they would also enhance the congruity with their fellow-citizens the Catholics wished to emphasise. But it was a question which could only be decided in Rome.[6]

The laity would also agree to an *exequatur*, the censorship of all correspondence between English ecclesiastics and the Roman Curia. So far as the English Vicars Apostolic were concerned, an *exequatur* would have little effect since communications with the Holy See were irregular and largely confined to abstruse questions of canon law. In 1773 Propaganda told Bishop Petre to send an account of his vicariate, it was so long since they had heard from him. Propaganda complained in 1821 that they would have to publish its *Status Missionum* from reports sent in seven years before. In any case, that from the Northern District was missing and should be sent immediately. Bishop Poynter urged Bishop Smith to respond quickly and to include details of 'the Durham controversy, Mr. Lingard's history and other works' to mollify the Curia. On another occasion Bishop Hay felt it necessary to advise Bishop Gibson to show a little

5. Hexter, *art. cit.*, pp. 304–6; Hempton, *op. cit.*, p. 141; P. Cadogan, *Early Radical Newcastle* (Newcastle, 1975), p. 37.

6. L. Gooch, 'The Durham Catholics and Industrial Development 1560–1850' (York, M.A., 1984), p. 34.

more deference to Rome. In 1839 the Pope asserted that he had to learn what he could about the state of the Church in England from the newspapers.[7]

The proofs of loyalty to the British Constitution and detachment from Rome proposed by some representatives of the English laity illustrate the anxiety of many Catholics to allay Protestant fears, as well as their passionate desire for political emancipation, almost to the exclusion of other factors, even the danger of schism. More generally, the Catholics entertained the hope that their evident peaceable behaviour would lead to their emancipation. Grey told the House of Lords in 1810 that there were in Northumberland, Catholics 'of ancient and respectable families, who, as friends and neighbours, as parents of families, and in all the relations of society, conducted themselves with the greatest propriety, and this he believed to be the general character of that body'.[8]

The English Catholics lived in a state of some ambiguity in the late eighteenth century. The anti-Catholic laws remained on the statute book although they were not strictly enforced. Catholics were able to worship in their own houses and in unobtrusive public chapels without interference, and they maintained friendly contacts with their neighbours. Those social relationships tended to mitigate hard-line anti-Popery. Earl Grey again told the House of Lords that 'he enjoyed the honour of an acquaintance' with many Catholics in Northumberland and that in the

exemplary discharge of the duties of life they could not be excelled, and if religion was to be appreciated by the conduct of those who professed it, he must at least say that the religion which produced such fruits could not be a bad one.[9]

Another pro-Catholic argument advanced in parliament was that the English Catholics were 'as a body of men, however respectable, small in number and forming only an exception to the general mass of the population'. The converse was advanced in relation to Ireland where, it was pointed out, three-quarters or more of the Irish were Roman Catholics. Indeed, by far the most important advantage held by the Catholics was the risk posed to national security in Ireland. The Irish had to be kept loyal in a time of war, and they were, therefore, in a powerful bargaining position. After 1798 the Catholic Question became an Irish political question; and throughout the campaign for emancipation the English Catholics and pro-Catholic Protestants took care to remind parliament of the danger represented by an aggrieved Ireland.[10]

---

7. Propaganda to Gibson April 6th 1821, LDA, Gibson Papers, IV; Propaganda to Petre, August 11th 1773, UCA, Ushaw Collection of Manuscripts [hereafter UCM] vol. 3, 189; B. Ward, *The Sequel to Catholic Emancipation*, vol. 1, pp. 125–150; Northumberland Record Office, Roman Catholic Diocese Archives [hereafter NRO RCD] 4/89. Hay to Gibson, Oct. 4th 1794.

8. M. Roberts, *The Whig Party 1807–12* (1965), p. 39; E. Norman, *The English Catholic Church in the Nineteenth Century* (1984), p. 45; *PD* (I), 15, p. 504.

9. PD (I), 17, p. 430.

10. PD (I), 4, p. 654.

Finally, the French Revolution benefited the British Catholics in two ways. Firstly, the severity of French anti-Catholic persecution served to mitigate English intolerance, and the Relief Act of 1791 was passed without substantial opposition. Ideologically, the Act was justified under a principle of toleration which could countenance different kinds of non-Anglican worship, but exclude non-Anglicans from political power. In any case, an oath of loyalty was required under the Act. Secondly, patriotic feelings against France allowed the British to welcome over five thousand exiled French priests, and to accept the repatriation of English Catholic schools and religious communities from the continent. The presence of large numbers of Catholics in various parts of England transcended, at least superficially, the mistrust of Papists.[11]

All these factors, the extinction of the Stuarts, the willingness of lay Catholics to demonstrate their detachment from Rome, their small number and social integration, the Irish problem and the effects of the French Revolution, went towards creating a climate favourable to Catholic Emancipation, and were exploited by the English Catholics throughout the campaign. They certainly did not cringe in the face of intolerance or meekly accept their political disabilities. On the contrary, they became energetic and confident campaigners. Tracts, letters, speeches and petitions poured forth, most of which were couched in persuasive and responsible terms, intended to soften, if not eradicate Protestant suspicions of Roman Catholicism. The primary aim of the Catholics was to convince their fellow-countrymen that the Constitution would not be imperilled by Catholic Emancipation but strengthened, for the English Catholics were law-abiding not seditious, Catholic not Papist, tolerant not fanatic. These arguments and counter-arguments all appeared in the campaign but probably the most extensive and detailed examination of the question occurred in a lengthy controversy between Shute Barrington, Bishop of Durham, and the Rev. John Lingard, which began at the general election of 1807. This dispute was joined by a number of the Durham clergy and it affected the outcome of several parliamentary elections. The pamphlets thrown up by the controversy became standard texts and were studied throughout the kingdom; they were republished regularly in the quarter-century before the matter was finally resolved.[12]

In 1807, the Ministry of All the Talents proposed a bill relieving Catholics in the Army and the Royal Navy. King George III forced its withdrawal and demanded a promise that the ministers would never raise the Catholic Question again. Unable to accept such a constraint, the ministry resigned in March and brought about a general election. The Tories

---

11. Clarke, *op. cit.*, pp. 350–353.
12. The vigour of the Catholics in the political arena is well brought out by R.W. Linker in 'English Catholics in the Eighteenth Century: An Interpretation', *Church History*, 35 (1966), pp. 288f. and 'The English Catholics and Emancipation: The Politics of Persuasion', *Journal of Ecclesiastical History*, vol. 27. no. 2 (1976), pp. 151f.

under Spencer Perceval made it a 'No-Popery' election by going to the country on one issue: 'Support the King and the British Constitution'.

During the parliamentary crisis, Barrington published his diocesan visitation address of 1806 as a pamphlet: *A Charge Delivered to the Clergy of the Diocese of Durham*. Lingard was somewhat disturbed by the offensive tone and inaccuracy of this work and he published, anonymously, a response to it entitled *Remarks on A Charge....* The tone of Lingard's pamphlet was conciliatory; the line he took was that he was responding to the bishop more in sorrow than in anger that Roman Catholicism had been so wrongly represented. Certainly he neither sought nor expected the attention his *Remarks* attracted, nor did he appreciate the long-term consequences on his own life its publication would entail. Indeed, it might have been forgotten entirely had not the bishop followed up with what Lingard regarded as sharp practice.[13]

No sooner had Lingard's *Remarks* appeared than the bishop reissued his *Charge* for a national readership during the election campaign in May 1807, but under a new title: *The Grounds on which the Church of England Separated from the Church of Rome*. Lingard immediately reissued his *Remarks* but with a new and less conciliatory preface, in which he accused the bishop of having taken advantage of 'the ferment of a general election' to whip up the anti-Catholic prejudices of the electorate: 'From one extremity of his diocese to the other he preached a holy crusade against the opinions, I had almost said the persons of Catholics'. Barrington had now extended 'the benefits of his Charge to the whole nation... After such provocation', Lingard said, 'we certainly may be allowed to speak in our own defence', and that was precisely what he intended to do.[14]

Lingard was thirty-five years of age at this time and he had been a priest for ten years; he was Vice-President of the seminary at Crook Hall. Lingard had spent much of his life in an academic environment, the first fruits of which was the publication in 1806 of his *Antiquities of the Anglo-Saxon Church*. It is unnecessary to comment on this work save to note his historical method, for it was also the approach he adopted in his polemical writings. Lingard believed that if the misunderstandings which the English Protestants had of the Roman Catholic faith were corrected, not only would the penal laws be repealed, but the way would be clear for Christian unity. This was a fond hope, but it was nonetheless the sense in

---

13. The precise chronology of this dispute in its early stages is difficult to establish; the sequence given here is based on internal evidence. Barrington's *Charge* was delivered in the cathedral at Durham in the summer of 1806 but it was not published until Feb./Mar. 1807. It went into three editions but Lingard issued his *Remarks* after the first. This must have been in April, for Lingard notes that 'within two months' of publication, Elijah Index and A. Clergyman responded. The former dates his contribution to June 5th 1807. Barrington issued his *Grounds* in May 1807 and Lingard reissued his *Remarks* with a new preface. He reviewed the *Protestant's Reply* in June, and Elijah Index replied in July. Subsequent interventions came after the election (parliament met on June 22nd).

14. Preface to the second edition of *Remarks*.

which Lingard has to be read. He knew, moreover, that his only chance of reaching the audience he desired lay in a sober and unimpassioned exposition of the facts. He wished to be a man of reason rather than a bigot, and to use irony and humour to make his case rather than sarcasm and ridicule. Lingard might perhaps be regarded as the Catholic Sydney Smith, but he was never to attempt the satirical heights achieved by Smith, whose wit so effectively exposed the confusions and inconsistencies of the anti-Catholic argument. Smith's *Peter Plymley's Letters* of 1807–8 were written as a direct result of the fall of the Talents; the *Letters*, which went into eleven editions within a year, were much enjoyed by his northern friends, the Greys of Howick, the Lambtons of Lambton Castle and the Howards of Castle Howard, but not by Bishop Barrington.[15]

Barrington was twice Lingard's age. He was the son of a peer, his brothers included an admiral, a general, a judge and a Chancellor of the Exchequer; he married the daughter of a duke and he became Chaplain in Ordinary to Kings George II and III. Barrington has been described as 'a fine example of the harmless and even meritorious clergyman who owed great preferment to family interest'. It has also been said that he 'perhaps owed his religiosity to having been one of the few men of his age to have survived a lithotomy'. Barrington had been made a bishop in 1769, that is, two years before Lingard's birth. He was firstly Bishop of Llandaff, then of Salisbury (1782) and he was translated to Durham in 1791.[16]

Bishop Barrington spoke in a parliamentary debate on only ten occasions in an episcopate of fifty-seven years, and all those utterances were in fervent support of the establishment. He was a staunch opponent of Catholic Emancipation, in accordance with the Tory doctrine of the indivisibility of Church and State. He preached to the House of Lords in 1799 on the need to preserve the English Protestant establishment from Popery on the grounds that the French Revolution could be traced to the corruptions of the Church of Rome – a similar fate would befall England if Catholics were granted political emancipation. He said much the same thing in his *Charges* to the clergy of Durham in 1797, 1801 and again in 1806. The topic was clearly something of a fixed idea for which he had become notorious. In 1802 the Rev. Joseph Berington wrote to Hannah More asking her to drop the use of the 'insulting words' Papist, Popery

---

15. Bishop Milner condemned the *Antiquities* for its reticence and good manners (Haile and Bonney, p. 97). He suspected Lingard of heresy. Unaccountably, the *British Critic*, vol. 32, p. 422, held the impression over a year later that the author of the *Remarks* was Milner. Perhaps this was because Milner published a second edition of his *Case of Conscience Solved*, to which he added, 'Observations on a publication by the Rev. T.L. Mesurier entitled "A Sequel to the Serious Examination into the Catholic Claims"' (1807) (cf. F.C. Husenbeth, *The Life of the Rt. Rev. John Milner* (1862), p. 40). G. M. Trevelyan. *Lord Grey of the Reform Bill* (1920), p. 170.

16. *DNB.* Some of Barrington's anti-Catholic 'tracts became standard treatises in the religious world', *VCH*, County Durham, vol. 2, p. 68; F.K. Brown, *Fathers of the Victorians* (1961), pp. 31–32; R. Solway, *Prelates and People; Ecclesiastical Social Thought in England 1783–1852* (1969), p. 72, note 3; W. Fordyce, *The History & Antiquities of the County Palatine of Durham* (2 vols., 1857), vol. 1, pp. 86f.

and Romanist which, he said, were 'fit only for the Bishop of Durham'. Now, in 1807, much to Lingard's disgust, Barrington presented his latest *Charge* to the general public for purely political purposes.[17]

In the *Charge* the bishop inveighed against Rome and Geneva; Romanist excesses, he said, had complicated the plain message of the gospel by 'ostentatious pageantry'. On the other hand, the English Dissenters who, 'in reforming the reformed', had over-simplified the Christian liturgy and had 'deprived religious worship of many interesting auxiliaries without adding any thing to its spirit and its truth'. The clergy of Durham were therefore urged to be vigilant in the defence of authentic, that is, Anglican Christianity. In particular, the 'zeal of the Romanist especially should operate as a strong caution against indifference to the corruptions of their church'. The French Revolution had driven 'numerous societies of the Romanish Church' to settle in England, 'this land of charity and freedom'. Furthermore,

> The education which the English Catholics used to seek in foreign countries, they now have it in their power to obtain at home in ample seminaries of their own communion. Various other civil privileges and indulgences have within these few years been granted them by the Legislature.[18]

The danger from this apparent encouragement was clear.

Barrington went on to outline the reasons for the Anglican separation from Roman obedience. The material was familiar, and consisted of all those beliefs and practices with which the reformers had been concerned. He held that statues were idolatrous for they led to image-worship; prayers addressed to the Blessed Virgin and the Saints, as well as penances and indulgences, detracted from the honour due to Christ. The Doctrine of the Real Presence was unfounded, and the denial of the communion cup to the laity was 'not only an unjust deprivation of their rights' but 'a daring mutilation of that holy sacrament'. The Roman Church's great stress on external ritual tended to lessen the spirituality of religious duties. The use of Latin in the liturgy was inconsistent with the purpose of public devotion, and it also removed Scripture from the reach of the 'common enquirer'. All these injurious beliefs and usages, the bishop said, should make the English zealous to maintain their 'national Church, which has cost so much learning, and so many lives to establish'. Barrington's real concern, then, was with the undisturbed Anglican supremacy, which was not actually threatened, by the Catholics, at any rate, as Lingard was to observe, albeit somewhat equivocally:

> The Protestant is the established church. This should satisfy her ambition. In the present temper of mankind, while she remains in possession of wealth and honour, she may deem herself secure.[19]

17. G.G. Armstrong, 'The Life and Influence of Shute Barrington, Bishop of Durham, 1791–1826' (Durham, King's College, M.Litt., 1936), p. 616.
18. *Charge*, p. 4.
19. *Ibid.*, p. 9; *Remarks*, preface.

Clearly, Lingard could not have expected to convince Barrington of his mistaken evaluation of the Catholic faith, but he could hope to appeal to the better selves of those less prejudiced than the bishop that the theological arguments in the *Charge* were false or distorted. He opened his *Remarks* by insisting on the worthiness of his adversary. He pointed out that the arguments in the *Charge* were the most plausible and satisfactory that could be adduced by the most able and zealous prelate in the Church of England. Delivered as they had been in the most solemn circumstances in Durham Cathedral, each assertion would have been carefully weighed so that no unguarded word would have fallen from the learned preacher's mouth. 'With eagerness', Lingard opened the book, as he 'anticipated the moderation, the liberality, the benevolence of an aged Prelate, who was unwilling to sink into the grave without leaving to posterity a lasting monument of his piety and pastoral solicitude'. But, as we were by now bound to expect, Lingard was 'most grievously disappointed' with the bishop's angry polemic, which was calculated to assist 'the diffusion of religious prejudice, and to misrepresent the creed of a most numerous class of his Majesty's subjects'. The bishop was, in fact, 'combating a phantom of (his) own creation'; the *Charge* was more like the 'fabrications of some obscure controversist' determined to exalt his own insignificance, than the publication of the respectable occupant of the see 'first in opulence in the United Kingdom':

> That this expedient should have been frequently adopted by the herd of minor and hungry writers is not surprising. It has often proved the most certain road to reputation, and, what they probably valued more than reputation, to wealth and preferment. But the Bishop of Durham is placed far above such paltry temptations.[20]

Lingard proceeded to examine each of Barrington's assertions in turn. The essential point he wished to make was that the bishop had wilfully misunderstood Catholic belief and was, in any case, inconsistent, for there was a large number of similarities between Anglican and Roman practice. Lingard suggested, moreover, that Barrington was not perhaps aware how easily his reasoning could be turned against himself. Indeed, that feature of the *Charge* gave Lingard the opportunity to write his *Remarks* as 'an exact parody' of the bishop's logic. He did this in a number of genial observations. On the matter of the Latin liturgy, Lingard observed that the English Church was a modern Church and so its liturgical language was modern; the Church of Rome was an ancient Church and it, therefore, preserved its ancient liturgy. He also reminded the bishop that in 1560 the English parliament had prevented the use of the Irish vernacular in the reformed liturgy. On the invocation of the saints and on indulgences, Lingard pointed out that both were practices of the Church of England and gave examples. About statues, he merely noted that 'six new statues of

20. *Remarks*, pp. 1–2.

very large dimensions have been lately made by order of the Dean and Chapter of Durham, and are now standing on the eastern transept of the cathedral'. On the supposed failure of Catholics to disseminate scriptural knowledge, Lingard reminded the bishop that the attention of the nation had lately been turned to the subject by 'Mr. Whitbread's plan for the instruction of the poor: and the result has been a general conviction that the ignorance, superstition and immorality of the lower orders are an evil of the most alarming magnitude'. Lingard suggested that had the English clergy 'made the diffusion of religious knowledge the great object of their labours and solicitude', such evils would not have arisen. Lingard was aware that Barrington, Sir Thomas Bernard, and William Wilberforce had founded the Society for Bettering the Conditions of the Poor in 1796.[21]

On the Catholic doctrine of the Real Presence of the Body and Blood of Christ in the Eucharist, Lingard contented himself with the observation that it was something of a paradox for the bishop to approach the altar to receive that which he believed did not really exist. Insofar as the reception of the Sacrament under both kinds was concerned, Lingard simply said that this was 'a mere matter of discipline, which may vary according to times and circumstances'. In any case, if the Sacrament consisted merely of bread and wine, as the bishop believed, how then could Christ be dishonoured in the taking of communion under one kind? As to the French Revolution being the culmination of the degeneracy of the Church of Rome, Lingard said that 'far from thinking, with the Bishop of Durham, that catholicity was favourable to their projects', the revolutionaries actually treated it as their natural and most formidable enemy'. That was, after all, why thousands of French priests had sought refuge in England, and why the expatriate English Catholics had returned to their native shores to open the schools which so worried the bishop. Lingard sought to allay Barrington's anxiety, particularly about Ushaw College, just outside the city of Durham, which was then almost ready for occupation:

> The toleration which has been granted us by a gracious Sovereign and an enlightened ministry, has encouraged us to open schools in England. The country will not lose by it. A domestic education will strengthen our attachment to our native land, and will retain at home the sums which formerly were of necessity expended abroad. The present ruler of France has made us the most tempting offers to resume our former plan of education in that country. His offers have been refused by our Prelates. The Bishop of Durham will, I trust, applaud their patriotism, and wish success to their endeavours.[22]

But he did not.

21. *Ibid.*, verse on p. 71, p. 78, note; pp. 81, 90, note y. See also *A General Vindication*, p. 30, note o; G. Best, *Temporal Pillars* (1964), p. 141; J. Milner, *The End of Religious Controversy* (1818), p. 290.

22. *Remarks*, pp. 6, 79, 83, 95.

On the other hand, Charles Butler, a Catholic and Barrington's almoner, remarked favourably on the bishop's charity. Bishop Barrington had been generous to a community of Poor Clares who lived in St. Helen's Auckland Hall for ten years. Barrington was their close neighbour at Auckland Castle and he gave the nuns annual alms. This reflected the bishop's approach which he had outlined in his *Charge*, 'Charity is certainly not incompatible with the most active zeal against erroneous and defective institutions'. He did not, however, contribute to Crook Hall or subscribe to the building costs of Ushaw College. He did, nonetheless, employ Ignatius Bonomi, a Catholic architect of Italian parentage, to work on Auckland Castle in 1817.[23]

Bonomi designed five Catholic churches in the North East (six, including a rejected design for St. Mary's, Hexham). However, he obtained four times as many Anglican commissions in the diocese of Durham. Moreover, Dean John Banks Jenkinson appointed him Consultant Architect of Durham Cathedral in 1827. Evidently, Bonomi's Catholicism, like Butler's, was no bar to Protestant patronage. Bonomi was not, however, strongly attached to his religion and he lapsed from it in 1840. He became a Freemason, and in 1837 he married Charlotte Fielding, the daughter of a local Protestant clergyman. Three years later he was listed as a church-warden of St. Mary-le-Bow in Durham. Bonomi received no further commissions from Catholics except from the Charltons who were his personal friends and for whom he built St. Oswald's church in Bellingham and renovated Hesleyside. Bonomi was on close terms with the cathedral clergy, especially Dr. William Gilly, an advocate of the Waldensian Church in Italy, in which Bonomi and his wife became interested as a consequence. In 1852 Charlotte Bonomi published an anti-Catholic novel, *Edith Grey, or Ten Years Ago*, to caution young girls against rubbing brasses for the Camden Society or poring over drawings of Gothic architecture in *The Ecclesiologist*, since such interests led only to Rome. During the course of the novel, Edith visited Piedmont to take encouragement from the persecuted Waldensians. Ignatius thought an Italian edition of the novel might buoy up the Italian Protestants; more practically, he built two churches for them.[24]

Lingard hardly used the political arguments for Catholic Emancipation in his dispute with Barrington; clearly, he was more concerned, as a priest, to debate points of theology. Only occasionally did he refer explicitly to the bishop's avowed purpose of denying some five million British subjects the common rights of citizenship on what were irrelevant (and, in any case, fraudulent) grounds:

> Some readers of the Bible, perhaps, may wonder what religious doctrines can have to do with petitions for political privileges... If I believe

23.   Armstrong, thesis cited, p. 660; W. Fordyce, *op. cit.*, vol. 1,p. 89; C. Butler, *Reminiscences* (Collected Works Vol. 1, 1824), pp. 126–129. See also Vol. 10, p. 94, note.
24.   J. Crosby, *Ignatius Bonomi of Durham, Architect* (1987), *passim*.

Christ to be really present in the Eucharist and you believe him to be present by faith only, what is there in my opinion that should incapacitate me, or in yours that should qualify you for civil employment.

Religion was beside the point; together with 'Jews, deists and atheists', Catholics 'might aspire to places of trust, emolument and rank, and obtain the privileges for which our fathers fought and which are the birthright of every Englishman'.[25]

In this brief departure from the strictly theological, Lingard highlighted the alleged relationship between the religious belief and civil allegiance of Catholics, but he concentrated on the former, leaving the latter to others to deal with. He did, however, join a correspondence which appeared in the *Newcastle Courant* in May 1807, during the election campaign, initiated by 'A Liege Subject' who contended that there was a Catholic doctrine of Papal infallibility which superseded all national political obligations. He wrote *An Address to the Electors of Northumberland* in which he described the Catholics as 'half-subjects' and as 'a class of British subjects who acknowledge a foreign power superior to the power of the state under which they live'. Catholics, he said, would do well to remember that 'they are only tolerated, and not sue for privileges which they are constitutionally incapable of holding'. The editor printed the *Declaration of the Irish Catholics* of 1792 alongside that letter, to show that the idea that Catholics had divided loyalties had been specifically repudiated. The Liege Subject objected to the reprint of the *Declaration* and quoted a Catholic catechism of 1688 which he said proved his point. Again the editor struck a balance by adding a note to the effect that he had examined all Catholic catechisms in use and could find no such doctrine of infallibility in any of them. He also reprinted in full the *Address of Several of His Majesty's Roman Catholic Subjects to their Protestant Fellow-Subjects*, which had been issued ten days previously (and had been signed by all the prominent North-Country Catholics), and which also denied the charge of disloyalty.

It was the reference to the catechism, however, that prompted 'J.L.' (Lingard) to write to the *Courant* to point out that the catechism had, in fact, been written by John Williams, a Protestant clergyman, in a deliberate attempt to mislead the English people; J.L. suggested that the Liege Subject should look at the catechism's title page where its provenance was admitted. The significant remark made by Lingard in his contribution was that Catholics 'would not be obliged to conform to any dispensation from their allegiance and would defend the country, even against the Pope himself, in case he should invade the nation'. Latimer remarks that this 'caused some sensation', as well it might, for though Lingard had only said precisely what most lay Catholics would have said, not many priests would have put it in such blunt terms.[26]

---

25. *Remarks*, p. 77; J. Lingard, *Remarks on a Late Pamphlet Entitled 'The Grounds...'* (1809), p. 4.

26. 'Liege Subject' was the Rev. Henry Cotes. Two Catholic gentlemen appealed for peace and fairness in the *Courant*: George Gibson, under the pseudonym 'A Friend to Peace and

The purpose of Barrington's *Charge and Grounds* was to influence the outcome of the general election of 1807 by raising, as Lingard put it, the 'war-whoop of no popery'. In the event, the election showed that support for the Catholics was not a popular vote-catching issue, although Lingard evidently thought Barrington's campaign had failed. On 20th May, at the height of the campaign, Lingard wrote,

We are in a great ferment here about the elections. Notwithstanding all the influence of the Bp of Durham and the chapter, the old members have been returned for the city. Every attempt is making to throw out one of the old members for the county, but I think it will be in vain. At Newcastle the old members are also returned. In Northumberland I expect that Lord Percy will turn out Col. Beaumont Lord Howick will come in. Is it not surprising that all the members in the North (two counties) with the exception of one should vote for the catholics; and of all these I think only one is in danger of losing his seat.[27]

Lingard was not well informed. Although Durham City, Morpeth and Newcastle all returned an unopposed Tory/Whig combination of members, the two counties went to a poll and the Catholic Question was an important issue on the hustings.

At a Durham County meeting on 1st June, a loyal address declaring approval of Tory policy on the Catholic Question was proposed. The tenth Earl of Strathmore (Bowes) said that the Catholics he knew had always behaved with the 'most gentlemanly conduct' and that they ranked high in loyalty; nonetheless, he opposed the policy of the Talents. He was seconded by Matthew Russell of Brancepeth Castle. The ultra-Tory Richard Wharton (unopposed candidate for Durham City) also spoke against any concessions and, as Lingard suggested, the Durham clergy and college may be reasonably suspected of being influential if not the instigators of the address. The policy of the Talents was defended by Dr. J.R. Fenwick who proposed a counter-address. This was seconded by Ralph Milbanke (a Whig candidate) and supported by Sir H.T. Liddell, the retiring county member, and R.J. Lambton, already elected for the city. The Tory address was, however, 'carried by a very great majority'. In the election, Cuthbert Ellison, the second Whig candidate, was defeated by Sir H.V. Tempest, a staunch Tory.

Union', and Thomas Selby as 'A Loyal Freeholder'; all are identified in *Orthodox Journal*, vol. 3, no. 99, July 26th 1834, p. 62. The Rev. T. Gillow, Catholic chaplain at Callaly Castle, published a short treatise, *Catholic Principles of Allegiance Asserted in 1807* in which he explained that the Pope's supremacy was confined to spiritual matters and that English Catholics would never suffer any foreign power whatsoever to divide their affections or estrange their allegiance. The book does not appear to have been noticed.

27. Lingard to Orrell, May 20th 1807, UCA, Lingard Transcript 25. For all this section see *Proceedings of the Durham County Meeting on Monday June 1st 1807*, etc. (n.d., published by G. Walker, Durham); Fordyce, *op. cit.*, vol. 1, pp. 152, 348–349; C. Daykin, 'The Parliamentary Representation of Durham 1675–1832' (Durham University, M. Litt., 1961), p. 308; W. Garnet, *A Collection of Papers, Speeches, etc., Relating to the Northumberland Election of 1807* (Newcastle 1807), *passim*.

The election in Northumberland produced the most significant result. The Duke of Northumberland decided to run his son, Lord Percy, in tandem with the sitting Tory, Colonel Beaumont, against Lord Howick, Foreign Secretary, Leader of the House of Commons and leader of the Whig Party, who was the great champion of Catholic Emancipation. Indeed, it was Howick who had introduced the measure which had brought about the general election. Howick could not afford to fight an election against the wealthy duke (polling would take place at Alnwick, under the castle walls, so to speak) and so he withdrew on the eve of the poll; Howick had been the member for twenty-one years. In his election address Howick had argued for freedom of conscience and he had singled out the Catholics Mr. Selby of Biddleston and Mr. Haggerston of Ellingham as ornaments of society. Percy did not refer to the matter; Beaumont would not be heard by the mob.

Howick had been humiliated in his home constituency over a fundamental Whig policy. He was accommodated in other seats before his elevation to the House of Lords as Earl Grey in November that year, where he was to continue the fight, and eventually succeed, but his defeat in 1807 on the Catholic Question was particularly disappointing, and he never forgave the duke. He could not have held the Bishop of Durham in any high regard either, for that matter. Of the two electoral contests in the North East in 1807, the anti-Catholics gained a seat in each.

The controversy between Lingard and Barrington was joined by a number of (mostly anonymous or pseudonymous) Anglican clergymen who published *Replies*, *Answers*, *Letters* and *Defences* in support of their diocesan, although most came out after the election. Lingard said that many members of the established clergy had condemned the acrimony of the bishop's pamphlet and had lamented that it was ever made public; but, scarcely two months after the first publication of the *Remarks*, 'two reverend apologists emptied the vials of their vengeance on the head of the writer'. The first was Henry Cotes, Vicar of Bedlington, under the pseudonym of Elijah Index, with *A Protestant's Reply* of 5th June 1807. Lingard immediately brought out a *Review*, and Cotes responded with a *Reply to the Reviewer* on 15th July. Meanwhile there appeared *A Letter to the Author of Remarks...* by 'A Clergyman of the diocese of Durham', who was Henry Phillpotts, newly-appointed Chaplain to Bishop Barrington and Rector of Stainton le Street, a benefice he held with that of Bishop Middleham. Phillpotts justified Barrington's concern for the safety of his people's religion in his reference to the new college at Ushaw; the bishop could not be expected to suffer 'such an institution to be established within his sight, without calling on his clergy to provide, with vigilance tempered by charity, against the efforts of their zealous and active rivals'. Under his own name, the Rev. George Faber, Vicar of Stockton upon Tees, published *An Answer*, and in a similarly open manner, the Rev. Thomas Le Mesurier, Rector of Newton Longville, in Buckinghamshire, issued *A Reply*. (The latter gave the Bampton Lectures at Oxford in 1807 on an anti-Catholic theme and in the same year he published an examination of the Catholic case in answer to Dr. Milner.)

These tracts elaborated, at inordinate length, the arguments raised and answered in Barrington's *Charge* and Lingard's *Remarks* on it. They tended to concentrate on the relationship between the French Revolution and Popery, and on the doctrine of the Real Presence, the two subjects on which the bishop had himself dwelt at length. No one responded to the other, admittedly minor, points on which the Anglicans were more vulnerable, nor did anyone betray the slightest sense of humour. Furthermore, as Lingard had already lamented, no one had taken the trouble to check that the beliefs attacked were in fact held by Catholics. This was a continual theme in Lingard's contributions to the debate and accounts for the quite marked change of tone evident from the second edition of his *Remarks* and the subsequent tracts in response to the minor clergy. The exasperated Lingard complained:

I have often considered it as an extraordinary phenomenon in the history of the human mind that in England the Catholics are not allowed the faculty of understanding their own belief... Objections which have been a thousand times refuted, are confidently brought forward as demonstrations of our folly and impiety; and the misrepresentations of prejudice are eagerly received with the veneration due to simple unvarnished truth.

Again, after reading one such tract, he described the author as a 'positive lying scoundrel', but that was in a private letter. In public he was more civil, though more belligerent than he had been initially, and less soothing than he had originally intended.[28]

Lingard composed *A Vindication* in response to the bishop's renamed pamphlet and the contributions of Cotes and Phillpotts. He took the opportunity to dispose of George Stephenson, Vicar of Kelloe and Curate of Bishopwearmouth, who had 'composed, preached and published twenty sermons for the charitable purpose of exposing the abominations of the church of Rome', which, Lingard considered, contained nothing but the rakings of 'filth out of the common sewer'. Lingard questioned why so much effort had been necessary since the parishioners of Bishopwearmouth and Kelloe would hardly have needed to be warned 'against seduction to a religion so absurd as that which (Stephenson had) delineated'. The sermons would, however, no doubt have pleased Bishop Barrington, to whom they were dedicated.[29]

A *Second Letter* was issued by Phillpotts at the beginning of 1808, and Lingard responded immediately. Later that year he dealt with all his cor-

---

28. All these pamphlets were published in Newcastle and they are all referred to in Haile and Bonney, pp. 383f; see also p. 122; J. Lingard, *A Vindication of The 'Remarks'...* (1807), p. 4.

29. *Ibid.* p. 32, note. G. Stephenson refers to 'the more opulent Roman Catholic families with which this northern country abounds', *Sermons* (1808), p. 20.

respondents in *A General Vindication*, comprising his *Vindication* of the previous year and separate replies to Phillpotts, Le Mesurier and Faber. There was little new in the work, but Lingard was at pains to insist that Catholics were good and sincere Christians. He challenged Phillpotts to compare the morals and piety of Catholics with those of his own parishioners, and then to say whether the Catholics were inferior to their neighbours: 'If he cannot, let him cease to affirm that the rites of the Catholic Church are injurious to piety'. In a similar way he challenged the conventional view of the Catholic priest:

A Romish priest is no longer an unknown character in this island. There was a time when Protestant liberality was allowed to paint him in the most hideous colours: and I have known many an orthodox churchman stare at a Catholic clergyman as if he were an ourang outang or an infernal being in a human shape.[30]

Lingard hoped that such days had passed away.

To close his *General Vindication*, Lingard thought it appropriate to include 'Observations on some fashionable interpretations of the Apocalypse'. In his earlier reply to Faber he had suggested that 'Prophecy not controversy (was) Mr Faber's peculiar department'. This was a reference to Faber's pre-millennialism, that is, to his numerous attempts to assimilate contemporary events to the prophecies about the Second Coming and the advent of the millennium in the Book of Daniel (chapters 7 and 8) and the Apocalypse (chapters 10 to 18). Unlike post-millennialists, who believed in a progressive and peaceful transition to the millennium (one thousand years of felicity), Faber held that the biblical texts foretold the violent overthrow of the existing order, by which he meant Popery, Mohammedanism and Infidelity in the person of Bonaparte. Since this was to be achieved by a 'prevailing maritime power of faithful worshippers', Faber took a particular interest in the naval battles of the war. He greeted the British victory at Trafalgar in 1805 with considerable relief because he saw in it confirmation of the prophecies, and proof that God was on England's side. For Faber, Daniel O'Connell and his campaign for Catholic Emancipation was to Britain what Napoleon was to France; just as the British success in arms would destroy Bonaparte, so O'Connell would be vanquished and the remnants of Popery in Britain eliminated. Bishop Barrington attacked Faber's millennialist views, although he did not go so far as Lingard, who recommended that Faber consult Dr. Thomas Trotter's recently published treatise, *A View of the Nervous Temperament*.[31]

The Rev. N.J. Hollingsworth now entered the field with five letters on justification, and Barrington returned to the attack in June 1809 with *The Grounds on which the Church of England Separated from the Church*

---

30. Lingard, *A General Vindication of The 'Remarks'*...(1808) pp. 26–40.
31. *Ibid.*, p. 51. The apocalyptic prophets of doom had their heyday in the first half of the nineteenth century and were reinforced in their beliefs by the appearance of brilliant comets (in

Reconsidered... The sub-title of this tract was 'A view of the Romish Doctrine of the Eucharist'. At some length Barrington sought to show that Christ's words in instituting the Eucharist were to be taken figuratively not literally. At equal length, Lingard argued in his *Remarks* on the pamphlet that Christ's words were to be taken literally not figuratively. He slipped in a teasing remark that the bishop's new tract had been made necessary because of the errors of Elijah Index ('of facetious memory') who was too dismissive of the Eucharist, and of Phillpotts whose theological exposition had been ambiguous.[32]

It is evident that there was no lack of stamina – staying power was essential if you were to have the last word – and Lingard was certainly prepared to go on. Indeed, he appears to have relished the prospect, for in an appendix to his *Remarks* on Barrington's pamphlet of 1809, he asked Hollingsworth to be content with a short answer because Lingard had to 'be allowed to attend the Bishop... it would be indecorous in me to leave the diocesan for the parochial minister'. Barrington's next contribution was his *Charge* of 1810 which considered Christian unity. He first alluded to Lingard's accusation that he was deliberately fomenting trouble. He said he spoke against giving countenance to the unscriptural errors of Popery as a duty, 'not with a view to excite animosities against the Papists, or to provoke their antipathies against us'. The Catholic claims, he said, were not enough considered from a religious point of view, although he himself continued to conflate the religious and the political, as when he said, 'the connection of their Church with a foreign jurisdiction is inconsistent both with those civil and ecclesiastical rights, which the King is sworn to maintain and for the support of which the Protestant succession was established by law'.[33] The main point of the *Charge* was that 'Catholic union' could not be achieved unless Rome abandoned all its sacrilegious and idolatrous beliefs and practices. This time Lingard did not respond: possibly Lingard felt constrained from replying to the *Charge*, and hence argue for unity, because as Vice-President of Ushaw College, he could not be seen to entertain such advanced opinions.[34]

There were, in any case, more immediate problems engaging Lingard's attention around this time. The new college at Ushaw was hardly finished when the staff and students moved into it in 1808. An outbreak of typhus laid low some fifty residents and eventually carried off five students. Then, in May 1810, the President, Thomas Eyre, died and Lingard acted in his place for thirteen months. By his own admission he was neither an administrator nor a disciplinarian, and that year was for him

1811 and 1843; Halley's comet appeared in 1835). W.H. Oliver, *Prophets and Millennialists* (1978) esp., pp. 20–22, 61–62; *New Annual Register* (1806), p. 291.

32. The Rev. N.J. Hollingsworth, *A Defence of the Doctrine and Worship of the Church of England in Five Letters* (1809); *Lingard's Remarks ...* (1809).

33. *Ibid.*, pp. 35–47; Shute Barrington, *Grounds of Union between the Churches of England and Rome* (1810), p. 436.

34. Haile and Bonney, pp. 108.

a time of anxiety and misery. Bishop Smith and Mr Gillow employed every inducement to prevail on me to stay with the latter. Though it hurt me to refuse, I did so because I was convinced that my health, my comfort, and even more than that was at stake. I resolved never more if possible to involve myself in a situation to which I was so ill adapted.

Bishop William Gibson, the Vicar Apostolic of the Northern District, had proved extremely difficult to deal with; he was autocratic, would accept no advice and he was regarded as unsound in financial matters. These pressures, then, prevented Lingard taking notice of every anti-Catholic pamphlet that appeared. Those same pressures led him to resign when John Gillow was appointed President of the college in 1811, and Lingard left Ushaw to become incumbent at Hornby, a small country mission near Lancaster, having 'a house well furnished, with a garden and croft and a good salary'.[35]

Barrington brought out another pamphlet in 1812 with the rousing title of *Vigilance, A Counterblast to Past Concessions and a Preventive of Future Prodigality Recommended*, with a 'Preface in reply to Mr Lingard's Preface', that is, to the *Remarks* of 1809. Lingard made no reply to that either, because he was engaged on a more important project: *Documents to ascertain the Sentiments of British Catholics in Former Ages Respecting the Power of the Popes*. At the same time he was composing a review of other episcopal anti-Catholic publications issued around that time. *The Protestant Catechism*, on the origin of Popery and on the grounds of the Catholic claims, had appeared from the Bishop of St. David's, Thomas Burgess, who was a protégé of Barrington, and who still held clerical appointments in Durham. Burgess had been Examining Chaplain to Barrington at Salisbury, where he also held a prebend. He moved with Barrington to Durham in the same capacities, and he was shortly presented to the 'sweet and delightful' living of Winston (£557). He was made Bishop of St. David's in 1803, but he continued to hold the sixth stall in Durham (£1,812). He published over a hundred works, many of an anti-Catholic character.[36]

The Bishops of Gloucester and Lincoln issued *Charges* to their clergy urging resistance to Catholic Emancipation, and Lord Kenyon published *Observations on the Catholic Question*. It was said that the review which Lingard published in response to these pamphlets was so temperate and well argued that that it probably exercised greater influence at the time

---

35. *Ibid.*, p. 111; Bishop Douglas had considered recalling Lingard from the Northern District in 1797 (cf. LDA, Gibson Papers, Douglas to Gibson June 14th 1797). Lingard would have preferred to stay in Durham and would have accepted the mission at Stella (offered to him by the sixty-year old William Hull), but Gibson would not sanction that (cf. Milburn, p. 117): Liverpool Archdiocesan Archives, Banister/Rutter Correspondence: Banister, Jan. 31st 1796.

36. Haile and Bonney, pp. 311, note, 384, items 14–16; for Burgess see *DNB*; W. Maynard, 'The Ecclesiastical Administration of the Archdeaconry of Durham 1774–1856' (Durham, Ph.D., 1973), p. 11. Figures in parentheses hereafter are the salaries/stipends of the parishes as given in the first edition of the Clergy List (1841).

than any other pamphlet written by a Catholic in favour of Emancipation. In 1813 it was resolved unanimously that the thanks of the Board of Catholics of Great Britain be given to Lingard 'for his zealous and successful defence of the Catholic Church in his many literary productions, and more particularly in his late able work entitled *A Review of Certain Anti-Catholic Publications*'. In 1815 Lingard dealt with Doctor Herbert Marsh's *A Comparative View of the Churches of England and Rome* (1814), and two years later he published his *Observations on the Laws and Ordinances which exist in Foreign States Relative to the Religious Concerns of their Roman Catholic Subjects*. It was clear by then, however that little could be added to the arguments; positions had been stated and reiterated, and nothing new could be said. At about this time the Protestant publisher of his tracts, Edward Walker of Newcastle, said to Lingard, 'After all, what is the use of these pamphlets? Few Protestants read them. If you wish to make an impression, write books that Protestants will read'. From this point Lingard concentrated on the research for his projected *History of England*, the first volume of which appeared in 1819.[37]

Lingard's primary aim in entering this controversy with the clergy of Durham was to refute the false beliefs attributed to Roman Catholics. He was particularly anxious to correct such errors because the civil rights of Catholics were being denied on fabricated (let alone irrelevant) grounds. He became increasingly angry with those who deliberately perpetuated misleading notions of Catholic dogma and it was partly their refusal to say accurately what Roman Catholic belief was that led him to accuse his Anglican opponents of entertaining hopes of preferment to 'rich and easy livings' in which 'to repose in the lap of wealth and indolence'. He also observed that it was truly edifying to see the alacrity with which the diocesan clergy had espoused their bishop's *Charge*; whereas Barrington had accused them of indifference, he would now have to applaud the zeal and promptitude of their exertions. At the outset, Lingard had scoffed at the herd of 'minor and hungry' writers looking for preferment; at the end, Lingard addressed Hollingsworth:

> If the real object of the parochial minister be to praise the Bishop of Durham, he acts wisely. The pious liberality of our Catholic forefathers has enabled that prelate to provide amply for the wants and conveniences of his advocates.

Since Lingard repeatedly hinted that clerical ambition lay at the root of the current round of anti-Catholicism, it is appropriate to enquire whether the careers of the clergy of Durham were noticeably advanced by their participation in anti-Catholic controversy.[38]

---

37. April 26th 1813 UCA, Lingard Transcript 43; Haile and Bonney, pp. 109, 384: Bishop Poynter suggested to Bishop Smith that Lingard be kept ready to respond to any further anti-Catholic publications (Apr. 4th 1821, LDA, Smith Papers).

38. *Vindication*, p. 5; *General Vindication*, pp. 23, 51; *Remarks* (1809), p. 45.

John Lingard declined all promotion; he refused the presidency of Oscott, a professorship at Maynooth, the rectorship of the Venerable English College in Rome, and the coadjutorships of the Western and Northern Districts. There was some speculation that Pope Leo XII made Lingard a cardinal *in petto* in 1826, but, in the nature of the case, there is no evidence to support the conjecture. Lingard may have declined it if it had been offered because he wished to stay in England, but he might, of course, have obtained permission to do that in any case, as Newman was to do later. At any rate, Lingard remained as missioner at Hornby for the remainder of his life, devoting himself to the mission, to his friends and to historical research.[39]

One of Barrington's first appointments in Durham was that of William Paley. Paley had already received substantial preferments in the dioceses of Carlisle, London and Lincoln for his theological work, and, in 1795, he was 'surprised by a letter from the Bishop of Durham Doctor Barrington, with whom he had not the smallest acquaintance', with the offer of the rectory of Bishopwearmouth (£2,899), which he accepted. In his Moral Philosophy of 1793 Paley had come out against revolutionary principles and he had defended the English establishment of Church and State. He had also argued for the toleration of all religions except where religious views were combined with political attitudes hostile to the constitution such as, he said, Popery. Paley therefore expressed the orthodox Anglican position, but that was as far as he would go. He was less sound in holding the view that if Papists and Protestants were permitted to live together in peace, the former would become 'more enlightened and reformed; they would by little and little incorporate into their creed many of the tenets of Protestantism as well as imbibe a portion of its spirit and moderation'. If Barrington expected a more forthright opposition to Catholic Emancipation from this renowned scholar, whom he had presented to the second richest living in his diocese, he was to be disappointed. Although he did dedicate his Natural Theology to Barrington, in his last years Paley, with Sydney Smith, was perhaps the best exponent of undogmatic Anglicanism. At any rate, Paley was not presented to a canonry in Durham although there were six vacancies which he might have filled.[40]

Stephenson, Paley's curate at Bishopwearmouth, who had published his anti-Catholic sermons in 1807 was presented by Barrington to the vicarage of Kelloe (£197) in 1809 and, in plurality, to Redmarshall (£365) in 1814. He became the first incumbent of the newly-created parish of St. Thomas, Sunderland (£200) in 1827, and he died there in 1845 aged eighty-five, the

39. Haile and Bonney, *passim*. The Rev. T. Gillow, who published a book in 1807 (see note 26 above) was offered a bishopric as Vicar Apostolic of the West Indies, but he declined, and went instead to the new mission at North Shields (cf. J. Stark, *St. Cuthbert's Church, North Shields* (North Shields, 1902), pp. 68f.)

40. Fordyce, *op. cit.*, vol. 2, p. 432, note; Mackenzie & Ross, *op. cit.*, vol. 1, p. 288; M. Clarke, *Paley* (1974), p. 84; Brown, *op. cit.*, *passim*.

senior clergyman in the diocese. That was not exceptional preferment, and Hollingsworth's reward was not much greater. He ended his days Vicar of Haltwhistle (£593) (and he was known as 'the Pope of Haltwhistle' by the *Tyne Mercury*), Perpetual Curate of Hartlepool, Minister of Tavistock Chapel, London, and Chaplain to the Dowager Viscountess Barrington. Cotes was Chaplain to the Duke of Portland (Prime Minister 1807–9) before the controversy opened, and he died in 1835, aged seventy-six, still Vicar of Bedlington (£454).[41]

Although George Stanley Faber gained preferment, it was not substantial, and his most senior clerical appointment was not in his parent diocese of Durham. Faber was made Vicar of Stockton (£245) in 1805; he resigned that living in 1808 for the rectorship of Redmarshall (£341). Shortly afterwards, the adjoining benefice of Great Stainton (£279) became vacant and Faber was offered it in plurality. He refused it, saying that one parish was enough for him to look after. When this was retailed to Robert Surtees of Mainsforth late one evening, he immediately called for his horse, declaring that he wished 'to take a look at a clergyman who has refused two livings'. Barrington collated Faber to the living of Long Newton (£604) in 1811, where he remained for twenty-one years. In 1829 Faber published *Letters on Catholic Emancipation* and in the following year Bishop Burgess promoted him to a prebendal stall in Salisbury Cathedral. In the spring of 1832 Faber was appointed Master of Sherburn Hospital in Durham (£1,164), and he died there in 1854. This was a respectable, though not very grand ecclesiastical career, and it seems that Faber's contribution to the debate on Catholic Emancipation in general, and in the controversy with Lingard in particular, did not arise out of self-seeking ambition but was the fervent expression of his millennialist beliefs (which were not, by any means, shared with his diocesan). Faber was to be disappointed late in his life over his nephew Frederick Faber, Rector of Elton, who was received into the Roman Catholic Church in 1845, taking seven of his parishioners with him. These were significant though not spectacular preferments for anti-Catholicism, but some others involved in the controversy did considerably better.[42]

Thomas le Mesurier, already Rector of Newton Longville and Domestic Chaplain to Lord Sidmouth, was presented additionally to the substantial living of Haughton le Skerne (£1,500) in Durham by Barrington in 1812, which he held to his death in 1822. Thomas Burgess, already Bishop of St. David's, received the surely unwarranted promotion (and increase of £500 in his stipend) from the sixth to the second stall in Durham Cathedral in 1820. That promotion was facilitated by the resignation of the previous holder of the second stall who had been appointed to the richest living in the diocese and was none other than Henry Phillpotts.[43]

41. Fordyce. *op. cit.*, vol. 2, p. 231, note; Haile and Bonney, p. 102.

42. *DNB*; Fordyce, *op. cit.*, vol 1., pp. 408–409; E.I. Watkin, *Roman Catholicism in England from the Reformation to 1950*, (1957), p. 179.

43. *VCH*, County Durham, vol. 2, p. 163; *DNB*.

It has to be said at once that Henry Phillpotts was a bellicose, ultra-High Church clergyman and active Tory. Greville thought Phillpotts was cast in the mould of Pope Sixtus. He was ordained in 1804, at the age of twenty-six, and presented to the crown living of Stainton le Street (£360) in December 1805 by Lord Chancellor Eldon, whose niece, Deborah Surtees, he had married. In 1806 he was made a chaplain to Bishop Barrington, a post he held for twenty years, and in June that year he was presented to the crown living of Bishop Middleham (£152), which he held for two years *in commendam*. Phillpotts lived in Middleham Castle and acquired the reputation of being a zealous though not always popular magistrate. Thereafter, as Lingard suggested, Phillpotts' 'labours were honoured with Barrington's approbation'. In 1808 he was collated by the bishop to the large and important parish of Gateshead (£1,300); in 1809 he was promoted to the ninth stall in Durham Cathedral (£2,065) and in the following year he was presented to the parish of St. Margaret, Durham (£330) by the Dean and Chapter, and he resigned Bishop Middleham. He was advanced to the second canonry (£2,313) in 1815, which he held for five years.

Phillpotts published, anonymously, a *Letter to Earl Grey* in 1819, the main point of which was that Roman Catholic disabilities should not be removed without adequate securities. He criticised Grey for suggesting that there was little difference between the doctrines of the Roman and Anglican churches (Grey was following Lingard, and Phillpotts Barrington). In 1820 Phillpotts was collated by Barrington to Stanhope in Weardale (£4,843), one of the richest livings in England. Barrington insisted that Phillpotts reside in the parish and so he resigned his stall at Durham. Three years later, the Prime Minister, Lord Liverpool, offered Phillpotts the bishopric of Clogher, worth £14,000 a year, but Phillpotts declined saying that he had pledged not to accept a bishopric during Barrington's lifetime. Phillpotts was, as Lingard acknowledged, 'an accurate and able controversialist', and it is quite certain that he would have risen in the church on his own abilities; he was, however, fortunate in his marriage and in his diosesan.[44] For Catholic and Protestant alike, then, it seems that participation in controversy did no harm to a clerical career; indeed, it probably enhanced the chances of promotion.

The *Edinburgh Review* while deprecating his work, nevertheless acknowledged that Henry Phillpotts had 'justly acquired the credit of being about the ablest of those who espouse[d]' the anti-Catholic cause. The unusual role he played in the late 1820s has, however, gone largely unremarked in spite of its importance and the means of its execution. His

44. L. Strachey & R. Fulford (Eds.), *The Greville Memoirs*, (1938), vol. 4, p. 84; *DNB*. Two biographies of Phillpotts are available: R.N. Shutte, *The Life, Times and Writings of the Rt. Rev. Dr. Henry Phillpotts, Lord Bishop of Exeter* (1863); G.C.B. Davies, *Henry Phillpotts, Bishop of Exeter 1778–1869* (1954); Lingard, *Remarks* (1809), p. 35; In addition to the individual stipend of each stall, prebendaries received £1,500 each from the income of the Dean and chapter of Durham; Schutte, *op. cit.*, p. 29; Haile & Bonney, pp. 103, 209.

elevation to the bishopric of Exeter has attracted most attention, not only for the scandal surrounding his bargaining over the appointment, but also because it is generally regarded as a reward for an overnight conversion to Catholic Emancipation. The reality is a little more complicated, and has to be seen over a longer timescale and in the exceptional circumstances in which Phillpotts found himself.[45]

Robert Southey's *The Book of the Church*, issued in 1824, was a defence of the Anglican establishment and an attack on pagans, papists and puritans. This inclusive assault came out in the midst of a sustained attempt to achieve Catholic Emancipation which appeared to be making considerable headway. Southey's book gained widespread approval in Tory circles (Bishop Barrington, for one, thanked him for it), and it raised yet another No-Popery furore. Appalled at the effect of the book on the cause of emancipation, Charles Butler responded with *The Book of the Roman Catholic Church* in 1825. Butler's intention was to show that since Roman Catholics held a great deal in common with Anglicans, Southey's remarks were not only out of place but they perpetuated falsehoods that were used to deprive Catholics of their civil rights, which was the same line of argument used by Lingard over twenty years before. This exchange led to a full-scale controversy with, inevitably, contributions from the clergy of Durham. George Townsend published *Accusations of History against the Church of Rome*, for which he was rewarded with promotion to the tenth prebendal stall at Durham (worth £2,900 a year).[46] Phillpotts published *Letters to Charles Butler Esq., on the Theological Parts of his Book,* etc. (1825), which he dedicated to Bishop Barrington.[47] George Faber brought out *The Difficulties of Romanism* in the following year. All these works repudiated Butler's attempt to reconcile Catholics and Anglicans, and the main lines of the argument have been discussed elsewhere.[48]

Phillpotts continued his anti-Catholic crusade into 1826 with *A Supplemental Letter to Charles Butler,* etc. Then, in 1827 there appeared his *Letter to Canning* in which Papal supremacy figured large, and he insisted that no concessions could be made unless Catholics accepted genuine securities to protect the Protestant establishment. He even formulated a new oath for the purpose. This letter went into several editions and it was widely welcomed by the ultra-Tories. Lord Kenyon was so impressed that he gave Phillpotts a series of letters that had passed between George III and Kenyon's father, the then Lord Chief Justice, relat-

---

45. *Edinburgh Review*, March 27th 1827, pp. 5, 19–22 (cf. Davies, *op. cit.*, p. 66).

46. *DNB*. Townsend went to Rome in 1850 to convert the Pope and he published an account of his visit: *Journal of a Tour in Italy* (1851). (See also R.A. Knox, 'The man who tried to convert the Pope', *Literary Distractions* (1958), pp. 114f.).

47. Butler was impressed with Phillpotts' book; he obtained an introduction to him and they remained on good terms (Davies, *op. cit.*, pp. 51–52).

48. Davies, *op. cit.*, pp. 43f; S. Gilley, 'Nationality and Liberty, Protestant and Catholic: Robert Southey's *Book of the Church*', *Studies in Church History*, 18 (1982), p. 409.

ing to the King's understanding of his responsibilities under the Coronation Oath, by which he had always refused to permit further relief to be granted to the Catholics. Phillpotts published that correspondence in May 1827 but, according to many, the letters showed that the oath was not the obstacle the King had thought it to be.[49]

Important as his pamphlets were, however, it was not directly through them that Phillpotts came to exercise the greatest influence on the Catholic Question, but through a fortunate personal encounter. The Duke of Wellington visited the North-East in September 1827 and met the Rector of Stanhope at Wynyard Park, the Durham home of the Marquess of Londonderry. Phillpotts gave the Duke copies of his pamphlets, and they discussed Catholic Emancipation. It may have been that the Duke acquainted Phillpotts with his private opinion that he would be prepared to reach a settlement with the Catholics, for the sake of peace in Ireland, on the basis of a Concordat with the Holy See which would give the British crown a veto on episcopal appointments. Wellington had come round to that view some two years before but he had kept quiet about it for fear of antagonising his ultra-Tory friends. At any rate, the Duke suggested that Phillpotts might usefully direct his thoughts 'to the question of communication with Rome'. That conversation would have had little significance had not the death of Canning later that year, and the resignation of his successor Goderich, unexpectedly brought Wellington to office as Prime Minister. His opinion on the Catholic Question was no longer academic.[50]

The Prime Minister sent for Phillpotts on 30th January 1828 and confided to him that concessions to the Catholics were under consideration, and he invited the canon to take discreet soundings as to how such a measure would be received by an unnamed individual. Phillpotts reported that his conversations had shown that the commonly held view was that if concessions had to be made, they should be accompanied by securities. With that, they opened a secret correspondence on the subject, which continued until the following February, when it was announced in the King's Speech that the government was to sponsor a settlement of the Catholic Question. Phillpotts frequently sought assurance from the Duke that his letters and memoranda were required, and he offered more than once to discontinue the correspondence. Wellington, however, proved receptive to Phillpotts' contributions, and he verbally encouraged him to do more research. It was not until February 1829 that Phillpotts told the Archbishop of Canterbury and his own diocesan of the correspondence.[51]

Phillpotts began by forwarding a background paper showing that the Catholics could accept securities without doing violence to their consciences; the corollary was that the King could then accept emancipation

49. Davies, *op. cit.*, pp. 64–65.
50. Duke of Wellington (Ed.), *Despatches, Correspondence and Memoranda of Arthur, Duke of Wellington* (8 vols., 1867–80), vol. 4, p. 317. [Henceforth *WND*].
51. *WND* vol. 4, p. 229; vol. 5, p. 486.

without doing violence to his. That view was also expressed in a new pamphlet, *A Letter to an English Layman*, issued by Phillpotts to rebut criticism of the George III – Lord Kenyon correspondence. It is at this point that we should notice Phillpotts changing tack. Hitherto he had maintained that further Catholic relief could not be granted, firstly because no test could be devised that would satisfy all parties. Secondly, the Coronation Oath bound the King 'for ever to reject every specious pretence of political expediency which may be urged to divert him from his purpose' of refusing emancipation. It now seemed to Phillpotts, however, that there was room for compromise after all, and that a mutually acceptable form of words could be found to overcome the King's scruples.[52]

This, by no means imperceptible, change of mind was due entirely to Phillpotts' knowledge of the line being pursued by the Prime Minister. Phillpotts was made Dean of Chester in March 1828, and he was in a difficult situation; he had a direct and confidential line to the premier on a matter about which his long-held and uncompromising views were well known, but he knew that the Duke was determined to grant Catholic Emancipation for the sake of peace in Ireland. Dean Phillpotts therefore had to recommend a policy to achieve the Duke's political aim without betraying his own, the preservation of the Anglican establishment. Like so many before him, Phillpotts insisted that if emancipation was inevitable then securities were the only worthwhile safeguards. His *Letter to an English Layman* prepared the public for his impending *volte-face*.

All through 1828 and the early months of 1829 Phillpotts sent Wellington a stream of memoranda on the various aspects of securities, and a related subject close to his ecclesiastical heart, the 'presumption' of Catholic clerics in taking episcopal and rectorial titles, and the need for 'some enactment which shall meet this most flagrant abuse'. The point here was that the Pope was exercising jurisdiction within the kingdom. In January 1829 Phillpotts forwarded a paper which included an oath drafted by an unnamed Catholic gentleman, but Phillpotts' ultimate solution to the vexed problem of securities was that there would be no need for the crown to insist on a formal veto if a political agent was placed in Rome, for he would be able to exert unobtrusive influence on the cardinals who were 'not inaccessible to presents adroitly bestowed'. His other major recommendation was to remedy the abuse of the forty-shilling freeholder's franchise in Ireland, by which life-tenants were treated as freeholders. This would remove large numbers of insolent Irish Catholics from the electoral registers at a stroke.[53]

Wellington was ready to declare his hand by the summer of 1828. Already convinced that emancipation was essential if Ireland was to be kept at peace, Wellington's next step had been to inform himself thorough-

52. *WND* vol. 4, pp. 254–255; Davies, *op. cit.*, pp. 65–67.
53. *WND* vol. 4, pp. 317, 324–329, 500–504; vol. 5, pp. 39, 48–49, 67, 71, 129, 386f., 444–449, 486.

ly on all aspects of the problem, privately and through the medium of an *advocatus diaboli*, an ultra-Tory churchman. With those necessary preliminaries completed, he turned to the tactical problem of achieving his aim. He told the King on August 1st that emancipation was in his mind. The King proved unreceptive and it was not until January 1829 that he (and Peel) would accept the measure, but only on the grounds urged upon them by Wellington – to avoid an Irish insurrection. It was also clear, by this time, that all bills relieving the Catholics were and would be passed by the House of Commons, and even in the House of Lords opinion was beginning to change.

There were four important northern peers in the upper house in addition to the Bishop of Durham: the Marquess of Londonderry, the Marquess of Cleveland, the Duke of Northumberland and Earl Grey. The latter's longstanding commitment to the Catholic cause has already been treated. William Henry Vane, Marquess of Cleveland was of a similar outlook. He had six parliamentary boroughs in his pocket and he was regarded by the *Dublin Morning Post* as one of the most zealous and useful friends of the Catholics: 'He makes it a positive condition with those to whom he gives his influence that they should vote for Catholic Emancipation'. His kinsman William Powlett was a member for County Durham.[54]

Lord Charles Stewart succeeded as third Marquess of Londonderry at the death of his half-brother Lord Castlereagh, the Foreign Secretary, in 1822. His sister was married to General Sir Henry Hardinge, M.P. for Durham City since 1820. Londonderry was an ultra-Tory who came round to the view that peace in Ireland was worth a few Catholic M.P.s. Provided emancipation became government policy, he said that 'his exertions would never be wanting in support of the Catholics'. Lord Ravensworth (Liddell) took a similar line; the other Durham peer, Lord Auckland (Eden) was unconditionally pro-Catholic.[55]

54. Vane (1766–1842) was the son of Henry Vane, second Earl of Darlington. As Viscount Barnard he had sat in the Commons for Winchilsea (1790–2) and County Durham (1812–4). He was created Marquess of Cleveland in 1827 and Duke of Cleveland in 1833. He abandoned the Whigs in 1830 over parliamentary reform (*DNB*). Seat: Raby Castle (DCA Nov. 11th 1826, quoting a Dublin newspaper.) His six boroughs were two each at Ilchester, Camelford and Winchilsea. He accommodated Howick at Winchilsea in 1826 (GEC, vol. 3, p. 284, note (b); Daykin p. 391). Powlett changed his name from Vane; he was afterwards third Duke of Cleveland (GEC, vol. 3, p. 285, note (d)).

55. Castlereagh had been pro-Catholic. Londonderry was not given office by Wellington, while Hardinge was given the War Office; relations between the two kinsmen cooled. The latter declined to stand for the City of Durham seat in 1830 and it was taken by the Marchioness's ultra-Tory nephew Arthur Hill Trevor, whom O'Connell described as 'the meek and modest representative of the clergy of Durham'. Londonderry's daughter Alexandrina became a Catholic. *PD* vol. 19, col. 1198; Edith, Marchioness of Londonderry, *The Life and Times of Frances Anne, Marchioness of Londonderry and her husband Charles, Third Marquess of Londonderry* (1958), pp. 141, 159, 169; M. Hyde, *The Londonderrys* (1979), p. xv; DCA Jun. 4th and 26th 1828. The other northern peers were Lords Morpeth and Howick in the Commons: both were pro-Catholic. *PD* (II), vol. 19, cols. 1294, 1330; vol. 20, col. 878.

Hugh Percy, third Duke of Northumberland, was also an ultra-Tory. He, it will be remembered, had defeated Grey in the No-Popery election of 1807 as a young man of twenty-two, and he had spent five years in the Commons until his elevation to the Lords in 1817 at the death of his father. Northumberland withheld his proxy from the opponents of the Catholic Relief Bill of 1825, but he would agree with emancipation only as a government measure, and he refused to join the Brunswick Club in 1828. Wellington offered him the Lord Lieutenancy of Ireland in January 1829 because Northumberland was 'the most moderate of men: and most particularly so upon the Roman Catholic question'. He told Wellington he could see no objection to the removal of all points of spiritual doctrine and discipline from the oaths. The government should impose a 'simple but strong' oath of allegiance as the qualification for all civil offices, except some of the higher offices of state which should remain closed to the Catholics; no other securities would be necessary. This clear and robust common sense satisfied the Prime Minister, and the appointment was confirmed. Northumberland allowed his proxy to be cast in favour of the Bill for Catholic Emancipation.[56]

Of the north-eastern members of the House of Lords, then, only the Bishop of Durham was anti-Catholic. Bishop Barrington died in 1826, and he was succeeded by the very junior Bishop of Llandaff, William van Mildert. He was an ultra-High Church bishop of whom it was said, 'orthodoxy oozed out of his pores', and that he 'stood as firmly as any churchman against the nineteenth century'. He made an effective speech against the Catholic Relief Bill in 1825 in which he said that Catholics were excluded from political life not for their religious errors, but because they were Papists, and he advanced the same view in 1829. He was another who used the age-old cliché that some of his good friends were Catholics but he would nonetheless vote against their emancipation. His views were simple enough, he said. 'Only keep the Papists out of Parliament, and I care little what else is done for them'.[57]

The voting record of the north-eastern peers and commoners between 1800 and 1829 on the Catholic Question was overwhelmingly pro-Catholic; only the Bishop of Durham, Matthew Bell, Richard Wharton and Sir H.V. Tempest consistently voted against. The Duke of

---

56. His grandfather, Sir Hugh Smithson of Stanwick (in the North Riding), was a Catholic until he succeeded as third baronet in 1733, aged 19. He married Elizabeth Seymour (daughter of the seventh Duke of Somerset), heiress to the Percy estates, in 1740. He was created Earl of Northumberland in 1750 and the dukedom (of the third creation) was revived for him in 1766 when he was appointed Lord Lieutenant of Ireland (*DNB*); *WND* vol. 5, pp. 453f.; A.S. Turberville, *The House of Lords in the Age of Reform, 1784–1837* (1958), p. 223.

57. O. Chadwick, *The Victorian Church* (2 vols., 1966), vol. 1, pp. 11–13; Solway, *op. cit.*, pp. 41, 90; G.F.A. Best, 'The Protestant Constitution and its Supporters, 1800–29', *Transactions of the Royal Historical Society* (5), 8, (1958), p. 113; C. Ives, *Sermons on Several Occasions and Charges by William van Mildert, DD, etc.* (1838), p. 99; *PD* (II), vol. 19, col. 1174.

Northumberland and Lord Ravensworth voted against until it became a government measure. In 1829, the Bishops of Chester (Sumner) and St. David's (Burgess!), both prebendaries of Durham, voted for Catholic Emancipation. The *Durham County Advertiser* smouldered with rage against the Act, the *Durham Chronicle* exulted.[58]

Catholic Emancipation was enacted with hardly a backward look at the interminable debates on securities of the previous twenty years. The only security contained in the Act was the disfranchisement of the forty-shilling Irish freeholders; there were no substantive ecclesiastical restrictions. The conclusion that the best security of all was emancipation without strings, reached by the Whigs long before, was at last, and more painfully, accepted by the Tories. Peace in Ireland was not only worth a Mass, it was worth an unfettered bench of bishops. Wellington, moreover, had not just achieved a surprise parliamentary majority for his Bill, he had avoided the public unrest that had followed upon the much more modest first Catholic Relief Act. This was partly due to a general acceptance of emancipation as a disagreeable but necessary measure; but it was also because the Bill had been introduced by the victor of Waterloo. It was sufficient for ordinary people that their military hero was prepared to emancipate the Catholics, for if he could not be trusted who could? He would see to it that the Catholics did not over-reach themselves. Wellington was no party ideologue but a disinterested and objective national leader; it is doubtful if any politician, Whig or Tory, could have carried Catholic Emancipation with so little adverse reaction from among the common people.[59]

Phillpotts was not in the least dismayed by Catholic Emancipation. He had already moved from outright hostility to an acceptance of mutually agreed verbal securities. Now, without demur, he accepted a bill with no effective ecclesiastical securities at all. He was raised to the episcopate as Bishop of Exeter the following year, and the conjunction of Catholic Emancipation with his elevation was not taken as coincidental. Phillpotts' promotion was inevitable at some point, however; it will be recalled that Lord Liverpool had offered him a bishopric long before. On the other hand, it seems clear that his relationship with Wellington engendered a pragmatism that modified his long-held and fervent anti-Catholicism. At any rate, Phillpotts became known in Oxford as the 'great rat'.[60]

---

58. W. Russell, Tory, who succeeded Lambton in the Commons on the latter's elevation to the Lords, declared himself in favour of Catholic Emancipation, but he was absent from the House during its enactment. DCA Feb. 16th 1828; Daykin, thesis cited, pp. 395–407.

59. Turberville, *op. cit.*, p. 227; Clarke, *op. cit.*, p. 359 (for Wellington's lack of ideology).

60. Clarke, *op. cit.*, pp. 394–399, note; Shutte, *op. cit.*, pp. 282f.; Fordyce, *op. cit.*, vol. 1, p. 651; vol. 2, p. 42. Phillpotts wished to retain the Stanhope rectorship to augment his episcopal salary of £5,000. In Oct. 1830, Cuthbert Rippon of Stanhope Castle, a violent anti-churchman, objected and raised a local petition to the King. Mr. Beaumont, M.P., outlined the matter in parliament on Nov. 10th, by which time the bishop had resolved the matter by appointing William Darnell to Stanhope. Darnell resigned his stall at Durham (£1,198) and it was given to Phillpotts. At the same time the Bishop of Exeter's salary was increased to £8,400 and Phillpotts felt able to manage on that.

James Losh, a Unitarian barrister of Newcastle, noted in his diary for May 1829 that 'the country is tranquil, and Catholic Emancipation is, I have no doubt, gradually producing the happiest effects'. Two years later the Earl of Durham said that events had proved emancipation to be essentially beneficial; parliament had been opened to 'as loyal, as honest, and as respectable men as are to be found in the country'.[61] His approbation no doubt stemmed partly from the fact that most of the northern Catholics were liberal in their politics and were keen to enter public life – in the Whig interest, of course. That would not have commended them to Bishop van Mildert but, as the tone of his 1831 *Charge* indicated, he was obliged to admit, if grudgingly, that his worst fears about Catholic Emancipation had not been realised, and that the clergy of Durham had best come to terms with it.

61. E. Hughes (Ed.), 'Diaries & Correspondence of James Losh', (*Surtees Society*, vols. 171–174, (1956/9)), May 1829; *The Speeches of the Rt. Hon. The Earl of Durham* (1836), note 62.

4

JOHN LINGARD AND THE ENGLISH
CATHOLIC PERIODICAL PRESS, 1809–1841

PAUL RICHARDSON

In November 1809, the Catholic publishing firm of Keating, Brown and Keating issued its prospectus for a quarterly work to be named the *Catholicon*.[1] The publication was promoted as a collection of literary reviews and essays which, it was hoped, would succeed both as a reflection and, more powerfully, as an example of Catholic unity, serving to promote the cause of emancipation. However, the *Catholicon* failed to appear. This satisfied one leading lay member of the Catholic Board, Charles Butler, who had confided in John Lingard his fear that the project emanated from the 'Milner School'.[2] The possible link with John Milner, the Ultramontane Vicar Apostolic of the Midland District, alarmed Butler who was concerned that the ecclesiastical hierarchy would use the *Catholicon* against the Board. Butler accordingly urged John Lingard to establish a reciprocal organ, to be conducted by the historian on a 'liberal plan' and without prelatic restraint.[3] But this plea was rejected by Lingard who, preoccupied with administrative and teaching duties at Ushaw College, had neither the time nor the inclination to make the required commitment.

More than two years passed before the idea of an English Catholic periodical was revived, albeit without any input from Lingard who, during the interim, had moved from Durham to Hornby in Lancashire. In June 1812, a monthly publication entitled the *Catholic Magazine* was founded by a Belgian émigré, Baldwin Janson, with the assistance of Bishop Milner. It circulated for six months until, in January 1813, it was taken over by Charles Butler. Renaming it the *Catholic Magazine and Review*, Butler renewed the work as a Cisalpine vehicle, completely liberated from episcopal stricture. Under his aegis, the journal tried to engender a Catholic-Protestant *rapprochement* in its pursuit of the 'great cause of Catholic Emancipation and the unlimited exercise of universal Theo-Political Rights'.[4] But the *Catholic Magazine and Review* suddenly ended in May

---

1. Cf. *Laity's Directory*, (London, 1810), pp. 33–36; Haile and Bonney, pp. 125–126. More detailed discussion of the publications and individuals referred to in this essay will soon be found in my Durham University Ph.D. Thesis, 'Conflict and Controversy: A Study of the English Catholic Periodical Press, *c.* 1660–1844'.
2. Charles Butler to John Lingard, November 23rd 1809, Charles Butler Letterbook, BL, Add. Ms. 25127.
3. *Ibid*. Cf. Butler to Lingard, December 22nd 1809: 'In respect to the [concept of a] review, I like the idea so well ... I should have no doubt that with the active exertions of yourself ... such a publication might be established ... I hope you will not entirely let the subject drop', CUL, Add. Ms. 9418.
4. Quotation from 'Prefatory Advertisement', *Catholic Magazine and Review*, vol. 1, January 1813.

1813 in the wake of the rejection by Parliament of a Relief Bill which Butler himself had engineered.

The demise of the *Catholic Magazine and Review* did not, however, signal the end of a Catholic periodical press in England. On 16th June, William Eusebius Andrews, a journalist and printer originally from Norwich, published in London his prospectus for the *Orthodox Journal*. The title, which first circulated later that same month, was founded as a battering-ram against Butler and the Board for promoting a Relief Bill which, incorporating clauses that granted to the Crown powers of veto and *exequatur* over the Catholic episcopate, was regarded by Andrews as a venal attempt to oppress the priesthood. Such sentiments earned Andrews encomiums from 'many of the first divines of our Church'.[5] Most vociferous in his approval was John Milner. He saluted the editor for having produced a work of 'undeniable ability, orthodoxy and independency' and promised to contribute to it regularly.[6] With this firm offer of support, an alliance was born which, in the seven years that followed, established the periodical as an organ of combat against Cisalpinism.

Unlike other prominent liberal Catholics who publicly responded to the attacks frequently levelled at them by Andrews and Milner, Lingard consciously avoided the 'miserable squabbles' that were a staple feature of the *Orthodox Journal*.[7] This remained so even when, in June 1819, Milner produced for Andrews a biting assessment of Lingard's *History of England*, the first three volumes of which, taking the narrative to 1509, had recently been published.[8] As Lingard later explained, one of his work's central aims was to promote Catholicism in a temperate way that would entice rather than repel Protestants.[9] In his critique of the *History of England*, Milner betrayed an ignorance of this objective and complained that the author had not dissipated Protestant calumnies but had rather flattered the enemies of Catholicism. He supported this assertion by pointing to Lingard's reluctance to use the titles of canonised saints and, in particular, to his treatment of Thomas Becket whose ardent piety, the bishop argued, had been pejoratively labelled 'enthusiasm'. Thus was initiated a controversy that, lasting seven months and occupying over fifty pages, allowed Milner's supporters and opponents to debate the validity of his denouncing Lingard as an un-Catholic disparager of authority.

Three individuals, writing as 'No Unbeliever', 'Minimus' and 'T', stepped forward to bolster Milner's prosecution.[10] The letters that attract-

---

5. *OJ*, vol. 1, October 1813, p. 205.

6. *OJ*, vol. 1, August 1813, p. 93.

7. Lingard to Butler, August 25th 1820, CUL, Add. Ms. 9418.

8. *OJ*, vol. 7, June 1819, pp. 228–231. Having read 'Milner's observations on my history', Lingard decided that he would 'not notice them' (Lingard to Butler, September 6th 1819, CUL, Add. Ms. 9418).

9. Lingard to Kirk, December 18th 1819, AAW/PP, A68.

10. *OJ*, vol. 7, September 1819, pp. 353–357 ('No Unbeliever'); October 1819, p. 376 ('Minimus') and pp. 393–396 ('No Unbeliever'); December 1819, pp. 468–469 ('T').

ed most attention, however, were those of 'Candidus' who argued in riposte that the *History of England* was a masterly work of 'uncommon merit' which did not deserve the bishop's 'unworthy and frivolous' comments.[11] Since the appearance of the first missive from 'Candidus' there has been much speculation about his identity. Initial reports ascribed the epistles to the two Cisalpine authors, John Fletcher and John Kirk. Independent rumours also circulated which implied that both John Lee, secretary to William Poynter, the Vicar Apostolic of the London District, and Thomas White, the Winchester-based missioner, were responsible. However, all these contemporary theories were unequivocally refuted.[12] Most recently, Joseph P. Chinnici has said that Lingard himself was 'Candidus', although external evidence indicates that he did not read Milner's critique until after the first letter in his defence appeared.[13]

My own opinion is that 'Candidus' was Thomas Michael McDonnell, a twenty-seven year old priest and controversialist of some repute who, at this time, was serving as chaplain to the Earl of Arundel and Surrey at Worksop Manor in Nottinghamshire. His profile fits exactly the little information we have about 'Candidus'. A Cisalpine and advocate of independent thought, McDonnell was also an admirer of Lingard. But, working in the Midland District, it was imperative that he 'remain unknown' to Milner lest the bishop exact revenge.[14] It was thus under a strict injunction to secrecy that 'Candidus' early disclosed this information to Lingard who, impressed by the 'sufficient castigation' meted out to Milner by 'Candidus', had initially vowed not to enter the contest.[15]

By September, however, Lingard was irked that Milner had not been silenced and decided to inform him through Andrews that he was preparing to attack his writings.[16] Accordingly, the following month, Lingard had the editor publish an article, written under the alias of 'Amicus Justitiae', in which he powerfully revealed the bishop to be an unreliable critic who had misrepresented the text under analysis.[17] As one commen-

11. The letters of 'Candidus' can be found in *OJ,* vol. 7, July 1819, pp. 266–269; September 1819, pp. 349–353; *OJ,* vol. 8, January 1820, pp. 22–27; February 1820, pp. 85–86. Quotations from *OJ*, vol. 7, July 1819, pp. 268–269.

12. For the popularly-espoused theories regarding the identity of 'Candidus', cf. Kirk to William Poynter, August 9th 1819, AAW/PP, A68; John Lee to Kirk, May 15th 1820; Milner to Charles Plowden, November 5th 1819, ABSI, Milner Letters; Frederick Charles Husenbeth, *The Life of the Right Rev. John Milner D.D.*, (Dublin, 1862), p. 396; Bernard Ward, *The Eve of Catholic Emancipation,* 3 vols. (London, 1911), vol. 2, p. 282. Haile and Bonney, p. 169, also gave witness that a copy of *OJ* belonging to the Durham-based Salvin family contained a note which ascribed the authorship to their chaplain, James Wheeler. However, no other documentary evidence has been found to support this theory.

13. Cf. Chinnici, pp. 119ff.; Lingard to Kirk, July 15th 1819, AAW/PP, A68; Lingard to Butler, September 6th 1819, CUL, Add. Ms. 9418.

14. Cf. *OJ*, vol. 7, July 1819, p. 268; September 1819, p. 351. Quotation from Lee to Kirk, May 15th 1820, AAW/PP, A68.

15. Lee to Kirk, May 15th 1820, AAW/PP, A68; Lingard to Butler, 6 September 1819, CUL, Add. Ms. 9418. Cf. above, note 8.

16. Lingard to Butler, March 5th 1823, CUL, Add. Ms. 9418.

17. *OJ*, vol. 7, October 1819, pp. 379–380. Cf. Lingard to Kirk, November 7th 1819; Poynter to Kirk, November 13th 1819, AAW/PP, A68.

tator remarked, the comments of 'Amicus Justitiae' were so direct that Milner could not possibly have ignored them.[18] Indeed, so humiliated was the bishop by Lingard's rigorous arguments that, in November, he tried to end the controversy by posing as 'Judex', a supposedly neutral arbitrator who summarised the contending viewpoints for the public to determine which was the more persuasive.[19]

In quick response, Lingard remarked that 'Judex' was suspiciously supportive of Milner.[20] McDonnell likewise complained that 'Judex' had given undue weight to the prosecution's case and he implored Andrews to intervene with a 'steady and unbiased hand'.[21] Having previously commended the editor for his impartiality, McDonnell expected Andrews to be objective but his trust was misplaced for, after deriding 'Candidus' as puerile and insolent, the publisher awarded Milner the victory.[22] In light of this decision, McDonnell resigned from the controversy in February 1820, expressing disgust at Andrews' 'low arts of misrepresentation and sophistry' and, despite a long association with the *Orthodox Journal*, suddenly became an 'angry disapprover of the publication'.[23]

Not content to let the discussion end at this point, Lingard presented Andrews with another two letters, written respectively under the pseudonyms of 'Justitiae Amicus' and 'Philorthodoxus', for the April issue of the *Orthodox Journal*.[24] As Lingard stated in the first missive, his purpose in writing was to expose Milner's errors and shake the misguided confidence placed in him by so many people. This plan was executed in the second letter which, focussing on the bishop's published history of Winchester, illustrated that he had written similar things to those for which Lingard had been condemned.[25] Both contributions, however, were rejected outright by Andrews who, in returning the essays, commented that they were the 'most worthless and self-refutable' that had ever been submitted to him since the 'commencement of his literary labours'.[26]

18. Richard Thompson to Kirk, February 12th 1820, AAW/PP, A68.

19. *OJ*, vol. 7, November 1819, pp. 423–428.

20. *OJ*, vol. 8, January 1820, pp. 21–22. Cf. Lingard to Kirk, December 18th 1819, AAW/PP, A68.

21. *OJ*, 8, January 1820, p. 23.

22. *OJ*, 7, September 1819, p. 353; *OJ*, 8, January 1820, pp. 27–34.

23. Quotations from *OJ*, 8, February 1820, p. 86 and *Truthteller*, 10, February 2nd 1828. McDonnell's reaction greatly confused Andrews who, unaware that the priest was the person he had slandered as a 'defeated and galled partisan', could not thereafter explain the sudden *volte-face* of his former devotee.

24. 'Justitiae Amicus', March 1820, AAW/PP, A68; 'Philorthodoxus', March 1820.

25. Quotation from Lingard to Butler, September 7th 1822, CUL, Add. Ms. 9418. Cf. John Milner, *The History, Civil and Ecclesiastical, and Survey of the Antiquities of Winchester*, 2 vols. (Winchester, 1798–1801).

26. William Eusebius Andrews to Mr. Last, March 16th 1820, AAW/PP, A68. Cf. Andrews to Lee, March 16th 1820, AAW/PP, A68; William Morris to Lee, March 16th 1820; Lee to Kirk, May 5th and 15th 1820; Lee to Lingard, March 1820, ABSI, Lingard Correspondence; Lingard to Butler, September 7th 1822, CUL, Add. Ms. 9418.

Although on this occasion Milner and Andrews stealthily subverted the representatives of liberalism, the final victory was not theirs because, shortly afterwards, the *Orthodox Journal* was denounced by Pius VII as a 'receptacle of factious insolence'. Furthermore, the Pope commanded the Prefect of Propaganda, Cardinal Fontana, to order Milner to 'reform and to tell him that otherwise his spiritual faculties will be withdrawn'.[27] Fontana did not prevaricate and, in a letter of 29th April, instructed Milner, on pain of removal from his vicariate, to take 'no further part henceforward, directly or indirectly, in the said journal, not to patronise or promote it in any way whatsoever, nor to furnish it with materials or arguments, and far less with any contribution'.[28] Milner's appeal against this decree was unsuccessful and the bishop had to inform Andrews that he could no longer help him with his literary efforts.[29] The loss of such a vital mainstay dealt a mortal blow to the periodical and, in December 1820, the original series of the *Orthodox Journal* ended.

Aware that his long-established work had been rendered unviable, Andrews had already founded a weekly replacement, the *Catholic Advocate of Civil and Religious Liberty*. Lamenting that Andrews' journalistic career had not been cut short, a group of priests belonging to the Midland District proposed, in June 1821, that a 'respectable Catholic monthly publication' should be started.[30] In commencing this work, they specifically enlisted the services of Lingard, who welcomed the idea of a new Catholic review, to write to Charles Brannan, a former pupil at Douai College, and ask him to undertake the management of the projected magazine. Lingard also attempted to solicit brethren clergy in the Northern District to donate literary and financial assistance to the periodical. Unfortunately, despite these efforts, the plans progressed no further because Brannan, then earning a comfortable living in London as a private tutor, was not interested.[31]

Following this brief period of activity, Lingard played no recognisable role in the development of English Catholic journalism until, in October 1830, John Kirk sought his opinion on another plan to establish in Birmingham a monthly publication. Like the majority of other individuals consulted, Lingard confirmed that he would support the projected *Catholic Magazine and Review*.[32] It is not difficult to understand why

---

27. Robert Gradwell to Richard Thompson, May 1st 1820, UCA, President's Archive, R29; Cf. Thompson to Lingard, June 1820, CUL, Add. Ms. 9418.

28. Cited Bernard Ward, *The Eve of Catholic Emancipation*, vol. 2, pp. 187–188.

29. Cf. Milner to Charles Plowden, January 30th 1821, ABSI, Milner Letters; Milner to Rev F. Scott, September 2th 1823, 175b.

30. Kirk to Poynter, June 12th 1821, AAW/PP, A68.

31. Cf. Lee to Kirk, June 27th 1821; Butler to Kirk, July 25th 1821; Kirk to Butler, July 27th 1821, AAW/PP, A68; Lingard to Kirk, June 1821, UCA, Lingard Transcript 207; Lingard to Butler, 1 April 1822, CUL, Add. Ms. 9418.

32. Kirk to Frederick Charles Husenbeth, October 14th 1830, Northampton Diocesan Archives.

Lingard was attracted to the prospectus that Kirk sent him, which outlined that the publication would, besides conveying domestic and foreign intelligence, carry articles generally concerned with literary and historical subjects. Consistent with this 'liberal and enlarged plan', the pages of the *Catholic Magazine* were also to be made available for readers to debate, with moderation and forbearance, a whole range of topics.[33] In essence, the new work was distinctly Cisalpine or, as Joseph P. Chinnici has styled it, an 'organ of enlightened opinion'.[34]

The *Catholic Magazine* first appeared in February 1831. It was edited by a syndicate of five clergymen belonging to the Midland District: John Kirk, Edward Peach, Francis Martyn, John Gascoyne and, in an executive role, Thomas Michael McDonnell.[35] During the initial stage of its development, McDonnell and his brethren editors established a concern which realised a healthy profit of 'between £15 and £20 monthly'.[36] One reason for this success was the considerable calibre of literary material that the editorial committee received from the 'best writers of the Catholic body'.[37] The leading contributor was Robert Gradwell, Coadjutor to James Bramston in the London District since June 1828, who conveyed regular domestic and foreign intelligence.[38] The pages of the *Catholic Magazine* also played host to Nicholas Wiseman, Gradwell's successor as Rector of the English College at Rome. Having greeted the establishment of the journal with 'ineffable delight', he quickly furnished two articles on the Chair of St. Peter and Catholic missions in North America.[39]

The vital connection with the Holy See that Wiseman gave the periodical was consolidated by Henry Weedall, the President of Oscott College. Recuperating from illness in Rome, where he had lived since the previous autumn, Weedall became foreign correspondent to the *Catholic Magazine*. The earliest dispatches that he forwarded to Birmingham dealt exclusively with the enthronement, in February, of Pope Gregory XVI and the subsequent upsurge of political insurrection across the Papal States.[40] By

33. The prospectus was reprinted in *CMR*, vol. 1, February 1831, pp. 1–4. Quotation from p. 3.

34. Chinnici, p. 144.

35. Cf. William Foley to Husenbeth, November 17th 1830, Diocesan Archives of East Anglia; *CMR*, vol. 1, February 1831, p. 5; Husenbeth, 'Memoirs', vol. 2, p. 330.

36. Kirk to Wiseman, July 7th 1831, UCA/WP, 172.

37. Husenbeth, 'Memoirs', vol. 2, p. 331.

38. Cf. Robert Gradwell to Kirk, March 8th and 21st 1831, ABSI, Kirk Papers, SM/7; Kirk to Gradwell, June 17th 1831 and March 17th 1832, AAW/BP, A72.

39. Quotation from Nicholas Wiseman to Husenbeth, January 22nd 1831, UCA/WP, 776. Cf. Kirk to Wiseman, April 30th 1831, UCA/WP, 169; Wiseman to Husenbeth, May 18th 1831, UCA/WP, 778; Kirk to Wiseman, July 7th 1831, UCA/WP, 172; Daniel Rock to Wiseman, March 19th 1832, UCA/WP, 182; *CMR*, vol. 1, May 1831, pp. 193–207; August 1831, pp. 402–415; Richard J. Schiefen, *Nicholas Wiseman and the Transformation of English Catholicism* (Shepherdstown, W.Va., 1984), p. 38.

40. Cf. Henry Weedall to Kirk, February 12th 1831, BAA, B53; Weedall to Wiseman, March 2th 1832, UCA/WP, 780; *CMR*, vol. 1, March 1831, pp. 127–128; April 1831, pp.

April, however, the revolution had been suppressed and Weedall travelled to Naples where he witnessed the liquefaction of the blood of St. Januarius. In a lengthy letter to the editorial committee, Weedall recorded his observations and, dismissing any scientific solution, argued that divine intervention alone had caused the previously congealed substance to liquefy.[41] Little did he know that this epistle, when printed in the *Catholic Magazine*, would ignite a ferocious argument over miracles between Cisalpines and Ultramontanes.

The opening blows were traded in September and October. Employing the pseudonym 'HY', Lingard produced a paper, his first for the periodical, in which he argued that, before a miracle could be confirmed, it must be demonstrated that the known laws of nature had not been functioning.[42] He then provided a rational explanation for the liquefaction, arguing that the solid matter had melted naturally when transferred from the cool treasury to the warm sanctuary. Of course, he accepted, this could be proven only by ascertaining, with a thermometer, the atmospheric conditions in which the substance altered: 'If it always happens at the same or nearly the same temperature', he wrote, 'the mystery will be solved; if at very different degrees of heat, the solution, which is here attempted, must be abandoned'.[43] This empirical approach, however, was contested by Frederick Charles Husenbeth and John Abbot, two Norfolk-based priests who had reputedly inherited Milner's zeal. They agreed that Weedall had indeed observed a miraculous event.[44] Ignoring a request from McDonnell for restraint, Husenbeth led the attack by denouncing the 'vapid effusions' of the 'irreverent' Lingard who, he declaimed, belonged with the incredulous Middletons, Addisons and Eustaces of a bygone age.[45] This view was seconded by Abbot. Writing as 'Philalethes', he asserted the ascendancy of belief, bolstered by authority, over positivistic conjecture and mockingly implored Lingard not to 'send Fahrenheit on a sleeveless errand'.[46]

The harsh tone adopted by Husenbeth and Abbot attracted support for Lingard from Robert Tate, a priest serving the mission at Hazlewood in Yorkshire. Objecting in the November issue of the *Catholic Magazine* to

---

176–182; May 1831, pp. 250–254; June 1831, pp. 309–310; Frederick Charles Husenbeth, *The Life of the Right Reverend Monsignor Weedall, D.D.* (London, 1860), p. 168; *Oscotian*, 6, 1887, p. 104.

41. *CMR*, vol. 1, July 1831, pp. 345–351. Cf. Wiseman to Husenbeth, May 18th 1831, UCA/WP, 778; Frederick Charles Husenbeth, *The Life of the Right Reverend Monsignor Weedall, D.D.*, pp. 169–170; Chinnici, pp. 137–139.

42. *CMR*, vol. 1, September 1831, pp. 484–487. Cf. Lingard to Robert Tate, December 7th 1831, UCA, Lingard Transcript 623; Lingard to Rock, January 11th 1832, UCA, Lingard Transcript 368; Haile and Bonney, p. 244.

43. *CMR*, vol. 1, September 1831, p. 487.

44. Cf. Lingard to Kirk, November 29th 1831, BAA, B76; Lingard to Tate, December 7th and 14th 1831, UCA, Lingard Transcripts 623 and 624; Lingard to Rock, January 11th 1832, UCA, Lingard Transcript 368.

45. *CMR*, vol. 1, October 1831, pp. 548–550. Quotations from pp. 548–549.

46. *Ibid.*, pp. 550–552. Quotation from p. 552.

the East Anglians' 'abusive' letters, Tate advanced, under the *nom de plume* 'RSY', that future discussion should be temperate rather than declamatory.[47] Unfortunately, this advice went unheeded and, refusing to retract his original missive, Husenbeth decried Tate's offering as 'savage'.[48] Abbot also reacted negatively, rejecting as 'nugatory' the renewed call made by Lingard's ally for experimental evidence to determine the cause of the liquefaction.[49] In response to such blatant obduracy, another correspondent, identified only as 'Y', entered the fray in January 1832 to condemn the 'futile zeal' of Abbot and lambaste the 'dictatorial insolence' of Husenbeth.[50]

By this stage, the general Catholic public had grown weary of the squabble and related its disgruntlement to the editorial committee.[51] One of the many who believed that the discussion had outlived its purpose was Lingard. In an effort to end it, he produced an article constructed as a dialogue between 'Antonio' and 'Ippolito', two Italians of 'learning and experience'.[52] Ruminating on the controversy, 'Antonio' queried why Catholics could not discuss issues with decorum and, not waiting for his companion to reply, blamed the 'guardians of orthodoxy' who considered 'every deviation from one of their favourite, though ill-founded and contracted notions' to be heretical.[53] Under the guise of 'Ippolito', Lingard urged such individuals to eschew that 'turbulent kind of zeal which burnt so fiercely in the heart of Dr M[ilner]' and embrace instead the 'zeal of charity'.[54] This sentiment was echoed by Henry Weedall, writing for the *Catholic Magazine* shortly after his return to England, who condemned the 'puerile' behaviour of participants on both sides.[55] Nevertheless, on the subject of miracles, the gulf separating the two men remained unbridged. Lingard still espoused that, without scientific evidence, the liquefaction could not be classified as miraculous, while Weedall maintained a diametrically opposed view. Stalemate thus reached, the controversy finally ended in March, much to the delight of Lingard who was relieved that he would 'hear no more about it'.[56]

Immediately after the hubbub over the blood of St. Januarius had subsided, John Gascoyne and Francis Martyn both resigned as editors. This

47. *Ibid.*, November 1831, pp. 625–628. Cf. Lingard to Tate, December 7th 1831, UCA, Lingard Transcript 623; Lingard to Rock, January 11th 1832, UCA, Lingard Transcript 368,
48. *CMR*, vol. 1, December 1831, pp. 690–692.
49. *Ibid.*, pp. 689–690.
50. *Ibid.*, January 1832, pp. 766–771. Quotations from pp. 766–767.
51. Cf. *ibid.*, February 2nd 1832, pp. 31–32; Rock to Wiseman, March 19th 1832, UCA/WP, 182.
52. *CMR*, vol. 2, February 1832, pp. 35–44. Quotation from p. 36. Cf. Lingard to Tate, December 7th 1831, UCA, Lingard Transcript 623.
53. *CMR*, vol. 2, February 1832, p. 37.
54. Cf. *ibid.*, pp. 38–39. Quotations from Lingard to Kirk, November 29th 1831, BAA, B76.
55. *CMR*, vol. 2, March 1832, pp. 73–99. Quotation from p. 74. Cf. Frederick Charles Husenbeth, *The Life of the Right Reverend Monsignor Weedall, D.D.*, p. 170.
56. Lingard to Kirk, May 1832, BAA, B91.

development was welcomed by John Kirk who, believing that the original large number of managers had hindered the publication, was optimistic that it would 'now be better conducted'.[57] Since the foundation of the *Catholic Magazine*, uncertainty had existed over which individual was responsible for correcting the press and, consequently, numerous errata had gone undetected. With the sudden change in the administration, the three remaining editors decided at once to rectify the problem and Edward Peach undertook the task of eradicating any typographical mistakes.[58] Nevertheless, in May, Lingard reported to Kirk that, despite such an effort, the technical quality of the publication remained far from perfect.[59]

Of far greater concern to the historian, however, was the hostile attitude that the *Catholic Magazine* shortly afterwards displayed towards those English Catholic parliamentarians who had lately supported a 'tyrannical enactment' which endowed each parson of the Irish Church with a portion of land belonging to local tithe-payers. In the July issue, McDonnell attacked Edward Petre, the Catholic MP for Ilchester, and promised to expose other individuals in the next number.[60] But this threat was not realised because Lingard warned the editors that, if they continued to use the *Catholic Magazine* against men of influence, vital subscriptions would be lost.[61] Heeding this advice, the editorial committee thereafter attempted to suppress contentious material, preference being given to benign papers from, among other notable authors, Lingard himself.[62]

However, controversy returned to the *Catholic Magazine* in January 1833 when a paper from Lingard on the perceived frailties of the Litany of Loreto was printed. Prompted by John Fletcher's decision to revise *The Catholic's Prayer Book*, the historian employed the magazine to 'feel the public mind' on the possible exclusion of the litany from the updated text.[63] Writing under the guise of 'Proselytos', a recent convert from the Protestant faith, Lingard delineated why this prayer to the Blessed Virgin troubled him. His essential problem was with the 'incomprehensible' appellations that were applied to the subject who was enigmatically described as 'the morning star, the gate of heaven, the ark of the covenant,

57. Kirk to Gradwell, March 17th 1832, AAW/BP, A72. Cf. *CMR*, vol. 2, May 1832, p. 307.

58. Cf. Kirk to Gradwell, March 17th 1832, AAW/BP, A72; Kirk to Husenbeth, 8 August 1832, Northampton Diocesan Archives; Husenbeth, 'Memoirs', 2, p. 16.

59. Lingard to Kirk, May 1832, BAA, B91.

60. Quotation from *CMR*, vol. 2, July 1832, p. 389. Cf. *ibid.*, May 1832, p. 243; Owen Chadwick, *The Victorian Church*, 2 vols. (London, 1966), vol. 2, p. 23.

61. Cf. *CMR*, vol. 2, August 1832, pp. 453–456, especially pp. 453–454; Lingard to Kirk, July 1832, BAA, B104.

62. Cf. *CMR*, vol. 2, August 1832, pp. 419–424; September 1832, pp. 557–558; Lingard to Kirk, July 1832, BAA, B104.

63. Quotation from Lingard to Tate, April/May 1833, UCA, Lingard Transcript 625. Cf. *CMR*, vol. 3, January 1833, pp. 17–22; Joseph Gillow, *A Literary and Biographical History, or Bibliographical Dictionary of the English Catholics*, 5 vols. (London, 1885–1903), vol 2, p. 300; Chinnici, p. 139; Emma J. Riley, 'Lingard as Liturgist' in J.A. Hilton (ed.), *A Catholic of the Enlightenment: Essays on Lingard's Work and Times* (Wigan, 1999), pp. 33–48.

the house of God, the tower of David and the tower of ivory'. While such language may have suited the period in which the litany was composed, Lingard argued, it now offended the 'more correct taste of the present age'.[64] Therefore, he concluded, the anachronistic invocation 'ought to be excluded from the public service'.[65]

This plea for liturgical reform roused vigorous opposition from two conservative subscribers to the *Catholic Magazine*. The first, writing as 'Lauretanus', was Joseph Curr, chaplain at Callaly Castle in Northumberland, and the second, signing his letter 'Pastor', was Frederick Charles Husenbeth.[66] Both men found the possible abolition of the Litany of Loreto reprehensible and, endeavouring to preserve it, unequivocally rejected any effort to 'reform and censure what past ages have approved and cherished'.[67] Such a defiant attitude towards the 'frivolity and degeneracy of the present generation' earned Curr and Husenbeth the support of William Eusebius Andrews.[68] Lingard, however, was less welcoming and, responding as 'Proselytos', berated these 'monopolizers of orthodoxy'.[69] Reiterating that it would be better to end the public practice of reciting the litany, a non-essential form of devotion, the historian claimed that it confirmed the prejudices of English Protestants and made them suspicious of Catholicism. Lingard then announced his retirement from the discussion, explaining to Robert Tate that it were more prudent to 'withdraw than to thrust my head into a hornet's nest'. In the same letter, Lingard also revealed a new dispirited attitude towards the periodical, stating a wish to see it 'discontinued'.[70]

Lingard's sudden resignation from the debate was lamented by John Walker, a Scarborough-based priest, who wrote to the *Catholic Magazine* as 'Augustinus'. In his letter, Walker complained that 'Proselytos' had been treated disgracefully by Curr and Husenbeth. He also blamed McDonnell for having allowed such 'disreputable' correspondents into the miscellany and warned him that, if they were granted further access, its demise would be assured.[71] This alarm was quickly responded to by the members of the Oscott Conference who, meeting on 8 May, urged the editors to purge the periodical of controversy.[72] However, McDonnell resisted such a call and, in June, a majority of Oscott priests dissolved the com-

64. *CMR*, vol. 3, January 1833, p. 19. The litany had originally been approved for use in 1587 by Pope Sixtus V.

65. *Ibid.*, p. 20. Cf. *Lingard-Lomax Letters*, p. 32.

66. *CMR*, vol. 3, March 1833, pp. 202–208 (Curr) and pp. 209–213 (Husenbeth). For the identification of both men as the authors, cf. Husenbeth to Kirk, February 3rd 1833, BAA, B133; Husenbeth to John Walker, December 6th 1864, UCA, Walker Papers, File 12: 48.

67. *CMR*, vol. 3, March 1833, p. 213.

68. *Penny Orthodox Journal*, vol. 1, March 9th 1833, pp. 212–213. Quotation from p. 212.

69. *CMR*, vol. 3, April 1833, pp. 302–309. Quotation from p. 303.

70. Lingard to Tate, April/May 1833, UCA, Lingard Transcript 625.

71. *CMR*, vol. 3, May 1833, pp. 384–389. For the identification of Walker as 'Augustinus', cf. Husenbeth to Walker, December 6th 1864, UCA, Walker Papers, File 12: 48.

72. *CMR*, vol. 3, June 1833, pp. 485–486.

mittee which had overseen the *Catholic Magazine*. At the same time, Edward Peach retired from the editorship in protest at the disputatious nature of the publication.[73]

During the weeks that followed, McDonnell himself made several attempts to resign his office but, on each occasion, was persuaded to remain in charge by members of the readership.[74] Emboldened by this repeated vote of confidence, he published in the August edition of the magazine a personal vindication, stating therein that his prime concern in employing the work as a controversial organ was to broker peace between opposing parties.[75] As a gesture of defiance to his detractors, McDonnell then reopened the debate over the Litany of Loreto by incorporating, from Husenbeth, a paper that dismissed the 'arrogant interference' of John Walker.[76] This was accompanied by another letter, written by 'Hieronymus', which goaded Lingard to re-enter the fray.[77] Unable to ignore this direct challenge, the historian retorted in September that he had retired previously from a reluctance to reason with men who 'substitute abuse for argument'.[78]

In the subsequent issue of the *Catholic Magazine*, a final response to Husenbeth and 'Hieronymus' was presented by Walker whose contribution concluded the argument between the main protagonists.[79] However, the ending of the debate did not appease Nicholas Wiseman who, in December, resolved to sever his links with the periodical for its allowing the Litany of Loreto to be denounced as 'unintelligible nonsense'.[80] The editors, he commented to a friend, were guilty of encouraging a discussion which countenanced principles displeasing to the Holy See. Therefore, Wiseman concluded, it was no longer appropriate that he, a Consultor of the Index, should prolong his association with Kirk and McDonnell.[81] Nevertheless, he deliberated informing the editors of his decision until he was quite satisfied that the *Catholic Magazine* had not shed its 'sadly reforming spirit'.[82] Wiseman's opinion was only confirmed after he read the edition for February 1834 which contained two more contentious articles by Lingard. The first paper, signed 'Sacerdos', called on the Vicars Apostolic to adapt the language incorporated in Richard Challoner's *The Garden of the Soul* so that it was rendered intelligible to the ordinary read-

73. *Ibid.*, September 4th 1833, p. xxvii.
74. *Ibid.*, August 1833, p. 2; September 1833, p. xxvii.
75. Cf. *ibid.*, August 1833, pp. 1–17.
76. *Ibid.*, pp. 36–40. Quotation from p. 37.
77. *Ibid.*, pp. 40–45.
78. *Ibid.*, September 1833, pp. 111–113. Quotation from p. 112.
79. *Ibid.*, October 1833, pp. 151–155.
80. Wiseman to William Tandy, December 2nd 1833, UCA/WP, 787.
81. Cf. *ibid.*; Chinnici, pp. 141–142; Richard J. Schiefen, *Nicholas Wiseman and the Transformation of English Catholicism*, p. 39.
82. Quotation from Wiseman to Tandy, March 15th 1834, UCA/WP, 790. Cf. Wiseman to Tandy, 14 April 1834, UCA/WP, 792; *CMR*, vol. 5, April 1834, p. xliv.

er. The second essay, signed 'Catechistes', proposed a thorough revision of the catechism so that it was made 'short and simple'.[83]

While the action taken by Wiseman was regretted by Kirk and McDonnell, it was not unexpected.[84] For some months prior to the receipt of this particular notice, it had become evident that numerous subscribers were renouncing the *Catholic Magazine*.[85] The precise details of this slump were disclosed in April with the release of the yearly accounts which revealed that, of the 750 copies printed each month, on average a meagre 500 were distributed throughout the United Kingdom and Ireland.[86] The main problem was that the editors had no strategy to entice back readers who had abandoned the magazine. Nicholas Wiseman said that he would recommence his contributions should the periodical ever be re-established as a non-controversial vehicle of 'Catholic feeling in its noblest form'.[87] However, with McDonnell exercising ultimate editorial power, there was little chance that it would ever be so modified. In fact, following the emergence of 'Sacerdos' and 'Catechistes', the *Catholic Magazine* remained as contentious as ever, as a battleground on which liberals and conservatives fought to control the way that Catholicism was taught and practised in England.

The heated discussions on devotional forms and the catechism that occupied the pages of the publication throughout 1834 were largely sustained by Lingard who, under his own name, also wrote a series of papers on the subject of Protestant ordinations.[88] Such regular exposure in the *Catholic Magazine* inevitably rendered Lingard open to abuse from less liberal-minded subscribers. One particularly hostile critic was Mariano Gil de Tejada, a Spanish curate working at Hammersmith. In a rambling letter, de Tejada accused Lingard of attempting to 'trample upon the old holiness' of the Catholic Church and urged him not to submit any more 'heterodox' correspondences to Kirk and McDonnell.[89] Whether or not de Tejada's words had any real impact remains unknown, but shortly afterwards Lingard told Robert Tate that, because the periodical no longer did Cisalpines any 'honour', he wished it were 'extinct'.[90] Thereafter, the historian wrote just one more piece for the work, a brief final letter on the topic of Protestant ordinations. When published in May 1835, this concluded Lingard's controversial association with the *Catholic Magazine*.[91]

---

83. *Ibid.*, February 1834, pp. 85–87 and pp. 89–90. For the identification of Lingard as the author of both pieces, cf. Haile and Bonney, pp. 387–388; Chinnici, p. 214.
84. Cf. Kirk to Wiseman, April 9th 1834, UCA/WP, 203.
85. Cf. *CMR*, vol. 5, January 1834, pp. 1–8.
86. *CMR*, vol. 5, May 1834, p. lxxix.
87. Wiseman to Tandy, April 14th 1834, UCA/WP, 792.
88. Cf. *CMR*, vol. 5, March 1834, pp. 142–146; April 1834, pp. 203–206 and pp. 232–234; July 1834, pp. 457–461; August 1834, pp. 499–503 and 508–513; September 1834, pp. 591–595; November 1834, pp. 704–719; December 1834, pp. 774–782; Lingard to Tate, June 22nd 1835, UCA, Lingard Transcript 627; Chinnici, pp. 142–144.
89. Mariano Gil de Tejada to Lingard, November 1834, BAA, B542.
90. Lingard to Tate, November 1834, UCA, Lingard Transcript 630.
91. Cf. *CMR*, vol. 6, May 1835, p. 221.

On 13 May, John Kirk followed Lingard's example and, deciding that he no longer wished to be associated with such a disputatious journal, tendered his resignation as editor and proprietor.[92] But McDonnell still continued to promote controversy between Catholics, a tactic that prompted John Abbot, during the late summer months, to campaign for his removal and, if this did not happen, the demise of the *Catholic Magazine*.[93] Such demands caused McDonnell, making one final effort to save the publication, to renew it as the *Catholicon* in January 1836.[94] However, this cosmetic gesture failed to prevent a mass exodus from the readership three months later.[95] The effect of this protest was so severe that, in early July, McDonnell admitted defeat and ended the continuous existence of the *Catholic Magazine* or *Catholicon*.[96]

Shortly before McDonnell's editorial career was effectively concluded, another major development in English Catholic journalism occurred. While visiting London towards the end of 1835, Nicholas Wiseman had been approached by Michael Joseph Quin, an Irish-born lawyer and writer, to assist in establishing a Catholic quarterly publication. Wiseman proved eager to help and, with additional backing from Daniel O'Connell, the three men began planning a non-controversial periodical entitled the *Dublin Review*.[97] One of the first people to whom they applied for a literary contribution was Lingard who, while happy to see founded a work as 'may do honour to our body', nevertheless rejected the request made for him to write an article. As Lingard carefully pointed out to Wiseman, his refusal to co-operate arose not from 'disinclination', but rather from 'inability' due to other commitments. However, the historian did promise that, as soon as the publication appeared, he would subscribe to it with a bookseller close to Hornby.[98]

The first issue of the *Dublin Review*, edited by Quin, was published in May 1836. Following the appearance of the second edition at the end of July, Wiseman felt confident that its future was assured and returned to Rome. Unfortunately, such optimism was premature because, in October, Quin abdicated the editorship, claiming that he had secured a more lucrative position working for the Spanish colonial service.[99] In tendering his resignation, Quin gave Henry Ridgard Bagshawe, a barrister and trusted

92. *CMR*, vol. 6, June 1835, p. clxxxii.

93. Cf. *CMR*, vol. 6, September 1835, pp. 453–454; October 1835, pp. 478–481.

94. *Catholicon*, January 1836, p. 19. Cf. Husenbeth, 'Memoirs', 2, p. 332.

95. *Catholicon*, June 1836, pp. cxix–cxx.

96. *Catholicon*, July 1836, p. clxxxi. Cf. Husenbeth, 'Memoirs', 2, pp. 331–332.

97. Cf. Nicholas Wiseman, *Essays on Various Subjects*, 3 vols. (London, 1853), vol. 1, pp. vi–viii; Josef L. Altholz, 'Early Proprietorship of the *Dublin Review*', *Victorian Periodicals Review*, 23, Summer 1990, pp. 54–56; Richard J. Schiefen, *Nicholas Wiseman and the Transformation of English Catholicism*, pp. 68–71.

98. Lingard to Wiseman, February 29th 1836, AAW, Stanfield Papers, 20/2/4.

99. Cf. Henry Ridgard Bagshawe to Wiseman, October 25th 1836, AAW, St. Edmund's College Papers, 7/4; Printed Circular, November 8th 1836, UCA/WP, 261; Bagshawe to Wiseman, 28 November 1836, UCA/WP, 263.

associate of Wiseman, all the materials that had been contributed for the third number. Bagshawe consequently employed the temporary editorial services of Mark Aloysius Tierney, an eminent historian and chaplain to the Duke of Norfolk, who ensured that the *Dublin Review* appeared, albeit belatedly, in late December.

Having secured the immediate future of the periodical, Bagshawe instigated Quin's removal from the proprietorship early the following year. At the same time, he reformed the management structure of the publication, implementing measures that permitted him to oversee its production alongside an advisory committee led by Wiseman as principal censor.[100] One final change that Bagshawe instigated was to set the *Dublin Review* on a sound financial footing by establishing a public fund to which Lingard subscribed £3. However, as the historian informed John Walker, this small donation did not demonstrate any close attachment to the periodical. On the contrary, Lingard clarified, he had been unable to refuse a request for financial assistance from Philip Henry Howard, the Catholic M.P. for Carlisle, who had kindly 'franked hundreds of letters' for him at Westminster.[101]

For the next two years, Lingard's only involvement with the *Dublin Review* was as a critical reader who complained in particular that the articles were too long and uninteresting.[102] Unwilling to be associated directly with the work, Lingard rejected repeated efforts made by Bagshawe to persuade him to contribute an essay.[103] Likewise, in April 1839, he refused an urgent request from Charles Dolman, the publisher of the periodical, to review Mark Aloysius Tierney's recently-printed first volume of a new edition of Charles Dodd's *Church History of England*. As Lingard explained, he was otherwise occupied and, in any case, did not like the 'profession of a puffer'.[104] However, Dolman persisted and sent Lingard a copy of the book together with a letter which stated that, unless the historian produced something quickly, the *Dublin Review* would not appear in May as scheduled.[105] Placed under such pressure, Lingard relented but,

100. Cf. Maurice O'Connell (ed.), *The Corespondence of Daniel O'Connell*, 8 vols., (Dublin, 1972–1980), vol. 5, p. 403; Bagshawe to Wiseman, December 31st 1836, January 28th and March 6th 1837, AAW, St. Edmund's College Papers, 7/4; Printed Circular, April 24th 1837, AAW/DRP.

101. Lingard to Walker, March/April 1837, UCA, Lingard Transcript 899. Cf. AAW/DRP, Printed Circular, 24 April 1837.

102. Lingard to Philip Henry Howard, February 1838, AAW/DRP. However, the second edition of Lingard's *Letter to the Lord Chancellor, on the 'Declaration' made and subscribed by Her Majesty, on her throne in the House of Lords, previously to the delivery of her most gracious Speech, to both Houses of Parliament, on Monday the 20th of November, 1837* was reprinted in its entirety in *DR*, vol. 4, January 1838, pp. 265–267.

103. Lingard to Walker, 1838, UCA, Lingard Transcript 919.

104. Lingard to Walker, July 6th 1839, UCA, Lingard Transcript 926. Cf. Charles Dolman to Mark Aloysius Tierney, March 27th and 29th and April 4th 1839, CUL, Add. 9419, Tierney Papers; Lingard to Tierney, April 2nd 1839, ABSI, Lingard Correspondence; Haile and Bonney, pp. 273–277.

105. Tierney to Lingard, 12 April 1839, CUL, Add. Ms. 9418; Lingard to Walker, May 4th and July 6th 1839, UCA, Lingard Transcripts 925 and 926.

as he told Tierney, 'I shall set to the work in bad spirits and almost with a presentiment that I shall not get through it'.[106]

Despite his evident reluctance to furnish an article, Lingard began the task immediately by asking Tierney to point out a passage from the *Church History* which would best illustrate how he had fulfilled the 'important office of editor'.[107] Tierney quickly suggested that the historian incorporate a controversial note in which he had argued that Thomas Becket, in protecting the traditional immunity of the clergy from civil prosecution, had been wrong to oppose Henry II.[108] Lingard agreed that this was a 'proper specimen for insertion' and featured it in the draft which Bagshawe received in early May.[109] However, Bagshawe objected to the provocative comments about Becket and, claiming that they would displease Wiseman, asked Lingard to 'withdraw the passage and substitute some other for it'.[110] In response, Lingard communicated his unwillingness to be guided by 'one who is a thousand miles distant' but, not wishing to cause trouble, gave his permission for the contentious section to be expunged.[111] This decision pleased Bagshawe who, after replacing the note on Becket with another on John Wycliffe, the fourteenth-century theologian, duly sent the paper to press.[112] Nonetheless, Lingard remained unhappy and told Tierney that he would 'never more write' for the *Dublin Review*.[113]

This promise might have been kept had Wiseman not personally asked Lingard, later that year, to write an historical refutation of the 'Puseyite doctrine that at the Reformation the Church of England reformed herself'.[114] Unimpressed by the Anglo-Catholic movement at Oxford, and keen to write on a period with which he was acquainted, Lingard accepted the challenge and completed the paper in April 1840. It appeared in the *Dublin Review* the following month and was received so positively that Bagshawe urged the historian to contribute more material.[115] Lingard

---

106. Lingard to Tierney, April 16th 1839, ABSI, Lingard Correspondence. Cf. Dolman to Tierney, April 26th 1839, CUL, Add. 9419, Tierney Papers.

107. Lingard to Tierney, April 21th 1839, UCA, Lingard Transcript 813.

108. Cf. Tierney to Lingard, April 24th 1839, CUL, Add. Ms. 9418; Mark Aloysius Tierney, *Dodd's Church History of England*, 5 vols. (London, 1839–1843), vol. 1, pp. 98–99.

109. Lingard to Bagshawe, May 14th 1839, UCA, Lingard Transcript 414. Cf. Lingard to Tierney, May 1839, UCA, Lingard Transcript 814; Tierney to Lingard, May 4th 1839, CUL, Add. Ms. 9418; Dolman to Tierney, May 10th 1839, CUL, Add. Ms. 9419.

110. Bagshawe to Lingard, May 13th 1839, CUL, Add. Ms. 9418.

111. Lingard to Tierney, May 14th 1839, UCA, Lingard Transcript 415. Cf. Lingard to Bagshawe, May 14th 1839, UCA, Lingard Transcript 414; Lingard to Tierney, June 17th 1839, UCA, Lingard Transcript 816; Lingard to Walker, July 6th 1839, UCA, Lingard Transcript 926.

112. Tierney to Lingard, May 31th 1839, CUL, Add. Ms. 9418. For the published article, cf. *DR*, vol. 6, May 1839, pp. 395–415.

113. Lingard to Tierney, May 14th 1839, UCA, Lingard Transcript 415. Cf. Bagshawe to Lingard, May 29th 1839, CUL, Add. Ms. 9418.

114. Lingard to Tierney, April 9th 1840, UCA, Lingard Transcript 820.

115. Lingard to Walker, May 1840, UCA, Lingard Transcript 937. Cf. Lingard to Walker, May 4th 1839, UCA, Lingard Transcript 925; Dolman to Bagshawe, March 10th and April 8th

replied that he was not against the idea of writing occasionally for the periodical, on condition that he was not 'bound either to time or subject', and asked Bagshawe to allow him a 'vacation for a few weeks' to consider the next article.[116]   In fact, one year passed before Lingard provided the *Dublin Review* with his next essay, another powerful piece which corrected the current idea circulated by the Tractarians that the English Church had been independent of Rome until the thirteenth century.[117]

The two articles that Lingard produced in 1840 and 1841 were later credited by Mark Aloysius Tierney for having done much in their 'unostentatious way to crush the pretensions and dissipate the sophistry' of the Oxford Movement.[118]   Both papers were also significant in that together they represented Lingard's final literary contribution to the English Catholic periodical press. Efforts were made in the autumn of 1841 by Bagshawe, Dolman and Tierney to persuade the historian to review the published second, third and fourth volumes of the *Church History of England*.[119]   However, Lingard rejected these applications principally because his failing eyesight would have prevented him from completing the work 'in such manner as to be of service' to Tierney and the *Dublin Review*.[120]   In any case, Lingard explained, he was 'desirous of quiet' and therefore chose this time to draw a conclusive line under an important and eventful, albeit occasional, career in Catholic journalism.[121]

ABBREVIATIONS

AAW/BP   Archives of the Archdiocese of Westminster, Bramston Papers.

AAW/DRP   Archives of the Archdiocese of Westminster, Dublin Review Papers.

AAW/PP   Archives of the Archdiocese of Westminster, Poynter Papers.

CMR   *Catholic   Magazine   and   Review*   (February 1831–December 1835).

1840, AAW/DRP; Tierney to Lingard, 13 April 1840, CUL, Add. Ms. 9418; *DR*, vol. 8, May 1840, pp. 334–373.

116. Lingard to Bagshawe, July 1840, AAW/DRP.

117. Cf. Lingard to Bagshawe, July 1841, AAW/DRP; Lingard to Tierney, 28 October 1841, UCA, Lingard Transcript 825; *DR*, vol. 11, August 1841, pp. 167–196.

118. Mark Aloysius Tierney, *A Memoir of Rev John Lingard D.D.* (London, 1854), p. 9. Cf. George Bowyer to [unknown], 1841, CUL, Add. Ms. 9418; Lingard to Mary Frances Lomax, October 16th 1841, *Lingard-Lomax Letters*, pp. 117–119.

119. Cf. Dolman to Bagshawe, September 25th 1841, AAW/DRP; Tierney to Lingard, October 25th 1841, CUL, Add. Ms. 9418.

120. Lingard to Tierney, October 28th 1841, UCA, Lingard Transcript 825.

121. Lingard to Bagshawe, October 6th 1841, AAW/DRP.

DR   *Dublin Review.*

Husenbeth,   Birmingham Archdiocesan Archives, SC/C21,
  'Memoirs'   Frederick Charles Husenbeth, 'Memoirs of Parkers:
                       that is Persons Educated at Sedgley Park, or
                       Connected with it by residence in that
                       Establishment, From its First Foundation, in 1763' 2
                       ms. vols. (1867–1868).

OJ   *Orthodox Journal* (June 1813–December 1820).

UCA/WP   Ushaw College Archives, Wiseman Papers.

5

JOHN LINGARD: HISTORIANS AND CONTEMPORARY POLITICS, 1780–1850

ROSEMARY O'DAY

This essay aims to set John Lingard's historical work within the context of contemporary discourse about the place of Catholicism in British life. Lingard's work was important not only because of what it said about the role of Catholics in the events surrounding the English Reformation but because of what it provoked among nineteenth-century Protestants. His careful marshalling of documentary evidence in the character assassination of Thomas Cranmer and Anne Boleyn and in the questioning of Henry VIII's motivations forced Protestant historians to review the origins of reformation. Moreover, he made assumptions about changing historical context and values that marked an advance in historical scholarship. In order to assess his importance as an historian, however, it is imperative that his contribution to the broader debates of the age is charted.

In the early nineteenth century, the history of the Reformation was written against the background of the debate about Roman Catholic emancipation that culminated in the passing of the Emancipation Act in 1829. Catholics constituted a tiny minority within England and Scotland – there were perhaps 60,000 in England and half that number in Scotland in 1780. This minority was led by a number of ancient and prominent Catholic peers. According to Cobbett, in October 1821 'to be sure the Roman Catholic religion may, in England, be considered as a gentleman's religion, it being the most ancient in the country'. At the beginning of the eighteenth century, severe penal laws had restricted the lives of these Catholics, but by the reign of George III the application of these laws was much more lenient. From 1771 onwards a number of relief acts were passed to modify the penal legislation. By the Relief Act of 1778, Catholics could henceforward acquire land by inheritance or purchase and open schools without fear of life imprisonment. Freedom of worship was granted by the Relief Act of 1791. In 1793 these concessions were extended to Scottish Catholics. These were tremendous steps forward, but Catholics still suffered from considerable religious and civil disabilities. In Scotland they could not open schools. Neither Scottish nor English Catholics could celebrate marriages or funerals in public. Catholics did not have the vote and they could not hold any rank in the army or navy. A Catholic could not sit in either House of Parliament. Whereas he could now become a barrister he could not proceed to become a High Court Judge. He could not attend either university, where the Test Acts were still in force. Living with such restrictions must have been irksome to Catholics, but even more offensive must have been the general animosity towards them of the population at large – they were regarded as a disloyal and alien minority in their native land. England and Scotland were Protestant countries, imbued with Protestant values and cultural forms even where active participation in religion was negligible. British Catholics had to accommodate themselves to a generally hostile environment. Civil and religious emancipation would ease this process, but only a change of heart in the British populace – aided by Catholic efforts at effective public relations – could truly integrate the Catholic community into British society. The Catholics who sought emancipation, therefore, were also concerned to display historical Catholicism in a more favourable light to the Protestant neighbours in order to improve the general attitude towards Catholicism.

Nineteenth-century historians had a multiplicity of traditions of Reformation history upon which to draw. The Roman Catholic tradition was represented both by the polemics of Catholic writers such as Reginald Pole, Nicholas Sanders, Nicholas Harpsfield, William Allen and Robert Parsons, and also by the much quieter, more conciliatory tradition of late Elizabethan writers such as William Watson (1601) and the Appellant priests. The non-Catholic tradition was yet more varied. Peter Heylyn and Thomas Fuller, with their clear memories of the Puritan revolution, and Jeremy Collier, affected by the non-juring schism, wrote of the beauty of holiness, of the apostolic succession, of the independence of the English church in convocation, and of the ancient church. John Foxe was representative of a virulently anti-Catholic and providential Protestant history – a tradition continued if modified by Gilbert Burnet and John Strype in the late seventeenth and early eighteenth centuries. The *Chronicle* of Edward Hall and the *Annals* of William Camden took a more nationalistic, political perspective. The providential and national traditions merged in the Whig histories of the late seventeenth, eighteenth and early nineteenth centuries, typified by those of Burnet and Rapin de Throyas.

Standing apart from the various Catholic and Protestant traditions stood the work of David Hume, *The History of England from the invasion of Julius Caesar to the abdication of King James II 1688*. Yes, Hume did have an animus against Roman Catholics, but this was coupled with an objection to all religious establishments. For him the word 'religion' spelt 'fanaticism and superstition'. And he challenged the Whig view that the Reformation had been accompanied by an extension of political liberty: he agreed that social progress had accompanied religious change, but saw the Tudor monarchies as despotic and tyrannical, and thoroughly contemptuous of the Constitution. He claimed that the people of England had acquiesced in their subjugation through 'the submissive, not to say slavish, disposition of his parliaments'.[1]

The party among us who have distinguished themselves by their adhering to liberty and popular government, have long indulged their preju-

---

1. D. Hume, *The History of England from the invasion of Julius Caesar to the abdication of King James II*, 1688 (Boston, 1868 edition), vol. 3, pp. 456, 308–309.

dice against the succeeding race of princes, by bestowing unbounded panegyrics on the virtue and wisdom of Elizabeth. They have been so extremely ignorant of the transactions of this reign, as to extol her for a quality which, of all others, she was the least possessed of; a tender regard for the constitution, and a concern for the liberties of her people.[2] All these various traditions were important resources for nineteenth-century British historians. But – a word of caution. Religion was a powerful influence upon nineteenth-century historical writing. Indeed, such writing was often undertaken in the context of contemporary religious controversy and, specifically, the cause of Catholic Emancipation. But, while religion united the Roman Catholic controversialists in this fight, politics often divided them, so that Catholics had varied interpretations of the past and wanted different things for the future. The division within Catholicism is best explained in terms of the division between the liberal Catholics who had been affected by the Enlightenment and who wanted a more tolerant Roman Catholicism, and the conservative Catholics who asserted the infallibility of the Pope and the divine authority of the bishops. The liberals, led by Charles Butler, a liberal layman, and Joseph Berington, a Staffordshire priest, had Catholic emancipation as their goal. In 1782 they formed the first Catholic Committee to this end, and in 1781 the second Catholic Committee. In 1792 they founded the Cisalpine Club and became known as the Cisalpinists. The tactic of this branch of Catholicism – to portray Catholics as loyal Britons with no superior allegiance overseas. In his *Appeal to the Catholics of England* (c. 1792), Berington persisted, 'I am no Papist, neither is my religion Popery.' But the Transalpinists, headed by John Milner, Bishop of Castabala and Vicar Apostolic of the Midland District, and Charles Plowden, defended papal infallibility and asserted clerical authority over the laity. In their eyes Cisalpinism appeared merely as a despicable Catholic form of Protestantism. So, while both the Cisalpinists and Transalpinists wanted Catholic Emancipation, they disliked one another cordially and fought with very different weapons.[3]

The Catholic protagonists, of whatever complexion, drew upon a historical armoury for their weapons. In his *Reminiscences*, Charles Butler, Secretary to the Catholic Committee, cheerfully admitted that he had never missed an opportunity to use history to prove his polemical points.[4] Similarly, John Milner's *The History, Civil and Ecclesiastical, and Survey of the Antiquities of Winchester* (1798–1801) was, in the words of the *Monthly Review* in April 1800, 'a deliberate design and laboured effort to

---

2. D. Hume, *op. cit*, vol. 3, p. 344.

3. For a more detailed account of the Catholic use of history see J. Drabble, 'The Historians of the English Reformation, 1780–1850' (Unpublished Ph.D., University of New York, 1975), and for a study of the position of the Catholics in early nineteenth-century England see B. Ward, *The Eve of Catholic Emancipation*, 3 vols. (London, 1911–12).

4. C. Butler, *Historical Memoirs of the English, Irish and Scottish Catholics since the Reformation* (London, 1819), vol. 1, p. 234.

vindicate the avowed patrons of this obnoxious system [Roman Catholicism] from deserved reproach, and to degrade the most distinguished advocates of that Reformation from popery, to which our country is principally indebted for the civil and religious liberty by which it has been blessed'. A writer in the *Quarterly Review* in May 1810 urged:

The History of Winchester is not be to be regarded as a mere topographical work... It is a vehicle for 'Truth severe in faery fiction drest'... The subject which Dr Milner has chosen, the period on which he enlarges with the great alacrity, the nimbleness with which he is ever stepping out of his way to disparage some distinguished character of the Protestant Church, or... to rescue some infamy, some champion of his own; these and many other appearances on the face of the work, lead to a suspicion that... narrative is but the vehicle for conveying his own principles and doctrines.

The contemporary politico-religious concerns of the nineteenth-century Catholic polemicists were served by history and shaped their interpretation of the historical past. The works of Joseph Berington provide an interesting case in point. In 1793 Berington published *The Memoirs of Gregorio Panzani*, with an introduction and historical supplement. His book contained a feature common to almost all early nineteenth-century Catholic writing: its emphasis upon the reign of Elizabeth, almost to the exclusion of the events of the early official Reformation. In Berington's case, the reason for this lay in his belief that Elizabeth had no particular religious settlement in mind when she ascended the throne in 1558, notwithstanding her parentage.[5] Rather, the activities of the Pope (Paul IV) and his agents had served to convince Elizabeth that a Protestant settlement was essential: 'Paul IV soon took to fix her resolution; and to him, perhaps... may be imputed the defection of England from the communion of Rome'.[6] Berington derived this opinion from Peter Heylyn's assessment in the *Ecclesia Restaurata* of 1660. Heylyn claimed that Paul IV had offered a direct insult to Elizabeth via her emissary, charging 'that the kingdom of England was held in fee of the apostolic see; that she could not succeed, being illegitimate'.[7] Berington concluded from this that 'the admission of such a monstrous prerogative could not consist with the safety and independence of her throne. If in high and indignant resentment she then made her choice... I may be sorry, but I cannot be surprised'.[8] The departure of England from the Roman communion was to be explained by the Pope's haughty action. Joseph Berington portrayed Elizabeth as rejecting the papacy in order to preserve her temporal sovereignty. The papacy had, in his opinion, laid claim to powers which were not acknowledged by the Catholic Church. For the power of the papacy had always

---

5. J. Berington, *Memoirs of Gregorio Panzani* (London, 1793), p. 4.
6. *Ibid.*, p. 5.
7. J.C. Robertson (ed.) Peter Heylin, *Ecclesia Restaurata* (Cambridge, 1849), vol. 2, p. 268.
8. J. Berington, *op. cit.*, p. 4.

been undefined and restrained by councils and bishops. In a series of works then, Berington attacked the 'prerogative which arrogant ambition had usurped, and which, for a long time, the weakness or ignorance of mankind durst not infringe'.

In adopting this line Berington was making a strong historical case for the tightening of restrictions upon the powers of the contemporary papacy. In 1790 the Pope had annoyed many of the Catholic laity by seeking to appoint to two vacant sees over the heads of the Catholic Committee. Democracy within the Catholic Church and national control were crucial contemporary issues. Berington was toeing the line of his patron, Sir John Throckmorton, who had in 1792 described His Holiness as a 'foreign prelate' who, by appointing English Bishops himself, had usurped the ancient privileges of the clergy. Throckmorton had in that same year argued that English Catholics might take the Oath of Supremacy because Queen Elizabeth had taken only the temporal power of the Pope and had been loath to assume spiritual power. Rubbing salt into the wounds of the Transalpinists, Berington supported his patron's argument by citing the work of Charles Plowden's brother, Francis, on the nature of the royal supremacy.

Praise was reserved by Berington for those loyal Catholics who had 'in silent resignations bowed their heads conscious that to submit to the laws... was their Christian duty' and blame showered upon those who, consumed with missionary zeal, had travelled to Catholic seminaries abroad and imbibed the traitorous tenets taught therein. Berington pointed out that persecution of English Catholics had not been severe until the 1570s and that it would not have grown severe 'if we had founded no foreign seminaries, we had provided no foreign laws'. Unfortunately for Catholics in England, the new priests courted and achieved persecution and martyrdom. All this, Berington urged, was proven by the fact that the old priests were not persecuted nor even the new in so far as they condemned papal tyranny.[9]

In making this case, Berington made Robert Parsons the arch-villain of the piece:

> a man with the sound of whose name are associated intrigue, device, stratagem, and all the crooked policy of the Machiavellian school... whose whole life was a series of machinations against the sovereignty of his country, the succession of its crown, and the interests of the secular clergy of his own faith. Devoted to the most extravagant pretensions of the Roman Court... pensioned by the Spanish monarch... his work has helped to perpetuate dissensions, and to make us, to this day, a divided people.[10]

This perspective, which so suited Berington's and Throckmorton's present purpose, was not original but was derived directly from the writings of the

9. *Ibid.*, pp. 15, 16, 24, 29.
10. *Ibid.*, pp. 25–28.

Elizabethan Appellant priests. In 1598 thirty priests had appealed to Rome against the appointment of George Blackwell by the Pope as arch-priest, coupling this with a denunciation of the seditious Jesuits. Of the Appellant writings, William Watson's *Important Considerations of a Vindication of Queen Elizabeth from the charge of unjust severity towards her Roman Catholic subjects*... is perhaps the best known to posterity and was certainly the most useful to Berington's case. Watson's charge that the Jesuits were guilty of high treason and the Appellant priests' signature of a declaration of allegiance, denouncing the bull deposing Elizabeth and affirming their loyalty to the Crown, were invaluable weapons in his arsenal.

This interpretation of royal policy – that of a queen anxious to create a church which would tolerate if not embrace Catholic subjects, provided that they were loyal – naturally did not find favour with the Transalpinist Catholic writers. Far from laying the blame for the persecution of Elizabethan recusants at the door of the Catholics, these writers returned it to the porticos of Elizabeth's palace: '...the penal laws were the cause of the seminaries, not the seminaries of the penal laws', stormed John Milner in the *Ecclesiastical Democracy*. Milner agreed that these laws were not rigorously enforced until after the founding of Douai in 1568, the Northern Rebellion and the Bull of Deposition, but Charles Plowden insisted that Elizabeth had never pursued a line of moderation towards her Catholic subjects. She had, he said, acted not only against Cardinal William Allen and Robert Parsons, but also against the adherents of the old religion. Plowden, moreover, vigorously defended Robert Parsons against the charges of treason. He alleged that Parson's letters were evidence of his charitable and peaceful spirit and that the education of seminary priests did not concern itself with politics.[11]

> I, who have searched for the guilt of the first seminarists through volumes of MS records and letters written, have not yet discovered a trace, a symptom of any plot or contrivance to dethrone or to destroy Elizabeth, in which the founders of the seminaries, or any of their friends or dependents had the smallest concern.[12]

His conclusion was that, as there existed no evidence of treacherous activity, Parsons and his co-religionists died for their speculative beliefs and not because of Elizabeth's well-founded fear for her kingdom at their hands.

The question of Catholic loyalty to the English Crown was indeed a pressing issue. The first Catholic Relief Act had been passed in 1778. This imposed an oath of allegiance upon Catholics. Transalpinists such as Milner and Plowden objected strongly. By the 1790s the issue of loyalty was again uppermost. Within England, the Catholics were finally admit-

---

11. C. Plowden, *Remarks on a book entitled Memoirs of Gregorio Panzani* (Liege, 1794), pp. 76, 84–86, 147–148.
12. *Ibid.*, pp. 147–148.

ted into the legal profession, and English Roman Catholic churches and schools were freed from penal disabilities. But there was widespread fear of Jacobins and in Ireland there was political unrest. The latter resulted in rebellion in 1798. The English government proposed a veto on Irish episcopal appointments for political reasons. Such suggestions were rejected both before the Act of Union (1801) and after (1808), but were still under discussion in 1813. In 1813 a Bill for the Relief of English Catholics, which contained a clause for a royal veto and a clause allowing commissioners to examine papal bulls on non-spiritual matters, was entered. This was defeated, at least partly due to the determined opposition of John Milner. Future Catholic Relief Bills (1813, 1819, 1821) all contained guarantees of Catholic loyalty.

Pressing though the issue of loyalty was, the English Catholics trod circumspectly when it came to dealing with the question in their histories. In his *History of Winchester*, Milner expressed sympathy for English Catholics who had acknowledged the Pope's spiritual supremacy without 'ascribing to him one atom of temporal authority' and who had never had any charge of treason proved against them.[13] Milner was understandably wary of treating the question of the papal claim to a right to depose heretical princes. In 1800 he considered the issue in *Letters to a Prebendary*. Here he alleged that this right was a speculative doctrine rather than an article of the faith and, moreover, one that had never gone unchallenged by Roman Catholics. In so far as the Pope did have such a right, it pertained to him as first bishop, and therefore arbiter, of Christendom rather than as a temporal prince. And Elizabethan Catholics had never accepted the bull deposing Elizabeth: 'The fact is, only one person in their whole number, John Felton, a lay gentleman, who affixed it to the door of the bishop of London's house, is known to have approved of it, for which he died, condemned by the whole Catholic body no less than by the Protestant'.[14] Berington, as had been noted, berated the papacy and the Jesuit priests of England for maintaining the papal right to depose the queen. He drew a picture of a Catholic community divided between the loyal and quiescent Marian priests and the disloyal missionaries. Charles Butler was more equivocal. In his *Historical Memoirs of English Catholics* he maintained that both Elizabeth and the Pope had acted imprudently, but he nevertheless felt that the Pope was more to be criticised than the Crown. The deposing bull of Pius V was, according to Butler, 'ever to be condemned and ever to be lamented'.[15] When it came to assigning guilt among the missionary priests, Butler's discovery of a British Museum manuscript which dealt with the responses of missionary priests to six questions on the deposing power of the papacy forced him into a moderate position. Campion and two others were found guilty and exe-

---

13. Milner, *History*, pp. 385–386.
14. Milner, *Letters*, Letter VI.
15. C. Butler, *op. cit.*, vol. 1, pp. 347–348.

cuted; three were explicitly exonerated; many were evasive. Butler noted that the pardon of those priests who answered the questions to the satisfaction of the examiners indicated that a specific disclaimer of papal claims to deposing power would have ensured better treatment for English Catholics. At the same time, he had to acknowledge that, while a few missionary priests were disloyal, the great majority of English Catholics were loyal to the Crown. However, when it came to the crunch, Catholics were killed, not because they acknowledged the deposing power of the papacy, but because Elizabeth had made treasonable the denial of her spiritual supremacy.[16]

John Lingard completely exonerated the missionary priests of charges of disloyalty. He argued that Elizabeth should not have executed men whose answers were merely evasive – instead she should have offered liberty of conscience in exchange for abjuration of the temporal pretensions of the papacy. Lingard went on to minimise the extent to which the Catholics had encouraged plotting against Elizabeth and to criticise the quality of the evidence against English Catholic rebels at the trials of the Duke of Norfolk, Throckmorton and Babington.[17]

If loyalty was a crucial contemporary issue projected back on to a historical screen, then intolerance was no less so. The entire Protestant tradition rested on the belief that Catholics had persecuted adherents of the new religion both cruelly and needlessly. The impact of Foxe's *Acts and Monuments* had been profound and lasting. Roman Catholics in the nineteenth century, as before, recoiled at such charges, but the matter had a new urgency at a time when these same Roman Catholics were seeking practical toleration and emancipation from the penal laws under a Protestant government. Once again, Catholic writers unashamedly sought to vindicate sixteenth-century Catholicism in order to improve their contemporary lot. In *Letters to a Prebendary*, John Milner put it like this:

> If it be proved that Catholics are bound by their principles to persecute and extirpate persons of a different religion from themselves, it is absurd in them to look up to a Protestant legislature for any extension of their civic privileges... But if this charge can be refuted, there does not remain a pretext for the continuance of these penal laws, which still exist against them.[18]

For this reason, he accorded the Marian burnings a good deal of attention – they had been used by Protestant writers to justify the spirit of resentment and counter-persecution of Catholics.

'First, then, it is to be observed, that, if Mary was a persecutor, it was not in virtue of any tenet of her religion that she became so', urged Milner in *The History of Winchester*.[19] Rather her persecutions were a defensive

---

16. *Ibid.*, vol. 1, pp. 212, 343–344, 347–348, 426; vol. 2, p. 46.
17. Lingard, *History*, vol. 8, pp. 113–114.
18. Milner, *Letters*, p. 111.
19. Milner, *History*, p. 355.

response to Protestant acts of militancy – Wyatt's rebellion; seditious printed propaganda; attempts on her life; prayers for her death. He conceded that there were a few intolerant Catholics who urged Mary to persecute, but alleged that their number was more than balanced by Protestant fanatics and was, moreover, unrepresentative of the majority of Catholics. Cleverly, Milner looked to earlier Protestant histories to indicate Mary's tolerance. He used Heylyn, Dodd, Phillips and Collier most skilfully. Other writers adopted a similar line – sometimes marshalling the evidence to better effect than Milner. John Lingard, for example, provided detailed evidence of Mary's tolerant attitude to Lady Jane Grey and Elizabeth after Wyatt's Rebellion, of Elizabeth's implication in Wyatt's Rebellion, and of Protestant provocation. Interestingly, he challenged the documentary foundation for Bishop Burnet's picture of Gardiner as a persecutor: 'This charge is not supported by any authentic document: it is weakened by the general tenor of the chancellor's conduct', and of Bonner as initiator of persecution.[20]

Both Lingard and Milner demonstrated at times an awareness that attitudes and values had changed since the sixteenth century. Lingard maintained, for instance, that, if Mary had been intolerant, then this was to a great extent because she was a product of her own times and of her own education. He stressed the discrepancy between her age and the more tolerant nineteenth century:

> After every allowance it will be found that, in the space of four years, almost two hundred persons perished in the flames for religious opinion;[21] a number at the contemplation of which the mind is struck with horror, and learns to bless the legislation of a more tolerant age, in which dissent from established forms, though in some countries still punished with civil disabilities, is nowhere liable to the penalties.[22]

Milner also sought to stress that intolerance had been a feature of sixteenth-century culture, not specific to Catholicism and, indeed, perhaps even more characteristic of Protestantism. Milner, Charles Butler and Lingard all expended a good deal of energy constructing a Catholic martyrology from a variety of sources and an analysis of penal legislation against the Catholics.

Once historians appreciated that historical context was all-important, it became, of course, much more difficult to project contemporary controversies back into the past. Catholicism in Mary's reign had been shaped by sixteenth-century events, habits of mind and education. Nineteenth-century Catholicism could, in reality, justify its claims to full integration into British society by an appeal to nineteenth-century conditions and attitudes. But neither Lingard nor any other Catholic historian faced up to this implication and took the next step. Blithely they sought to vindicate

20. Lingard, *History*, vol. 7, pp. 154, 158.
21. In fact, three hundred died.
22. Lingard, *History,* vol. 7, pp. 168–169.

contemporary Catholicism by an analysis of Catholic and Protestant behaviour under Mary despite their acknowledgement that this behaviour had been moulded by now extinct forces.

It was thought necessary to divert Protestant attention from the persecuting activities of Gardiner, Bonner and Pole under Mary I by vilification of Thomas Cranmer. Looking back upon writings of the period by Catholics and Protestants, Dean Hook explained:

> By party writers, on one side an attempt is made to represent Cranmer as a persecutor, and on the other, to explain away his share in the religious persecution under the reigns of Henry and Edward, and to make him appear as tolerant as... so far as the rack and the stake are concerned... men are compelled to be in the nineteenth century.[23]

This vilification took an extreme form in the works of Milner and Butler, but it was Lingard's *History* which prompted the Protestants to answer in the form of a veritable flood of lives of and defences of Cranmer in the 1820s and 1830s. In these writings much turned upon whether or not Cranmer had opposed the deaths of John Frith, John Lambert and Joan Boucher. The writers concerned became involved in a detailed examination of the evidence in order to establish the truth of their cases. For example, there was much debate about the true meaning of the *Reformatio Legum Ecclesiasticarum* – the reformed code of the canon law begun under Henry VIII and continued under his son – which Cranmer had helped to prepare. Lingard argued that the code was an instrument designed specifically with mass murder of Catholics in mind. In so doing he reviewed previous interpretations of the code, denying Burnet's assertion that Title Three (which dealt with the punishment of heretics) abolished capital punishment for heresy and following Jeremy Collier, who had in his *Ecclesiastical History* maintained that thenceforth heretics were handed over to the secular power for punishment by the death penalty. Lingard argued that the word 'punishment' in the *Reformatio* meant nothing less than 'privation of life'.

> Fortunately for the professors of the ancient faith, Edward died before this code had obtained the sanction of the legislature: by the accession of Mary the power of the sword passed from the hand of one religious party to those of the other; and within a short time Cranmer and his associates perished in the flames which they had prepared to kindle for the destruction of their opponents.[24]

Unsurprisingly, this sparked a Protestant outcry, particularly in the pages of Henry John Todd's *A Vindication of the Most Reverend Thomas Cranmer, Lord Archbishop of Canterbury and therewith of the Reformation of England against some of the allegations which have recently been made by the Reverend Dr Lingard, the Rev. Dr Milner and Charles Butler Esq.* (London, 1826). Todd argued that the British

23. W.F. Hook, *Lives of the Archbishops of Canterbury* (London, 1860–76), vol. 7, p. 62.
24. Lingard, *History*, vol. 7, pp. 153–154.

Museum manuscript of the code indicated, in a clarifying note, that no terror was intended by Cranmer, 'either that he may be driven into banishment for life, or thrust into the perpetual darkness of a prison... or punished at the discretion of the magistrate, in any other way which may seem to be most expedient towards his conversion'.[25]   But Lingard, using Strype, was able to show that the British Museum manuscript represented a draft and not the finished version of the code at all. In the final resort, Lingard, Milner and Butler were unable to make a watertight case against Cranmer, however, because of the inscrutability of the language used in the *Reformatio* and elsewhere. Careful textual criticism, appeals to past historians and the evidence of the persecutions themselves could yield just so much and no more. Ultimately, interpretation still had to be called into play.[26]

Already, by their efforts to vindicate the past behaviour of Catholics in Britain and thereby to make Catholic emancipation more acceptable to the British public and, especially, her ruling class, the Catholic historians had challenged the traditional Protestant interpretation of the Reformation in several important respects. Catholicism, they urged, had never been a disloyal, seditious and 'foreign' force in Britain. The persecuting spirit had never been a characteristic peculiar to Catholicism.   Catholics, like Protestants, had been products of their own age and had shared sixteenth-century attitudes to toleration of contrary beliefs. But they, unlike the Protestants, did not rejoice in the task of persecution.

It would be possible, on these grounds alone, to make a strong case that these Catholic historians had brought about a major revision of traditional interpretations of the Reformation, but their chief challenge to orthodox views of the Reformation lay elsewhere. Prior to this, Protestant historians had portrayed the English Reformation as a spiritual reformation – a cleansing operation, a purging of the corruption of the body of medieval Catholicism, a return to primitive purity. Even historians interested in the church as an institution, and even those concentrating upon the political and national ramifications of the process, nevertheless shared this overall view. Now Catholic writers of reputation forced a reassessment and a response from Protestant writers.

This is not to say, of course, that earlier writers had not acknowledged Henry VIII's baser motives. Catholic polemicists of the sixteenth century had not hesitated to expose that monarch's weakness: 'He gave up the Catholic faith for no other reason in the world than that which came from his lust and wickedness'. Protestant historians such as Gilbert Burnet were undeceived by Henry's claims to godliness, but preferred to marvel at the mysterious ways through which the Almighty worked and to draw attention to the sanctity of the reformers who carried out his work:

---

25. H.J. Todd, *Vindication of the Most Reverend Thomas Cranmer...* (London, 1826), p. 333.
26. Lingard, *History*.

He attacked popery in its strongholds in the monasteries, and thus he opened the way to all that came after, even down to our days. So, that while we see the folly and weakness of man in all his personal failings, which were many and very enormous, we at the same time see both the justice, the wisdom and the goodness of God, in making him, who has once the pride and glory of popery, become its scourge and destruction; and in directing his pride and passion so to bring about, under the dread of his unrelenting temper, a change that a milder reign could not have compassed without great convulsions in rescuing us by this means from idolatry and superstition; from the vain and pompous show in which the worship of God was dressed up, so as to vie with heathenism itself, into a simplicity of believing, and a purity of worship, conforming to the nature and attributes of God, and the doctrine and example of the Son of God.[27]

Nevertheless, the Catholic writers of the early nineteenth century forced Protestants to face up to the charge that the Reformation had not been a spiritual cleansing at all, but a division of the spoils of the wealthy but pristine Catholic church by money-grubbing monarchs, courtiers and climbers. Not only Henry came under attack, but also accepted Protestant martyrs and heroes. And the Catholic historians, moreover, backed up their charges with a reliance upon original documentation which their Protestant counterparts found more uncomfortable and more difficult to compass than mere polemic.

The Catholic attack upon the godliness of the Protestant Reformation was many-pronged. Broadly speaking, it combined a defence of Catholic sanctity with an assault upon Protestant spirituality. The balance struck between these two lines of attack in the writings of Catholic authors varied: those who wanted reconciliation with the Protestants (the Cisalpinists) tended to spend far less time vilifying the Protestants than did the hard-nosed Catholic Transalpinists.

Here it is sufficient to look in detail at the attacks made on the sixteenth-century Protestants in three areas – the dissolution of the monasteries; the Protestantism of Anne Boleyn; the character of Archbishop Cranmer – and the responses which these elicited among Protestants.

Most of the Catholic histories played down the corruption of the monastic ideal in England and emphasised the base motives for the Henrician dissolution. For Milner and Butler it was possible to sum up the motivation for the dissolution in one word – avarice. The results of the closure of the monastic houses had been felt in society as a whole immediately: charitable and educational provision had been irreparably damaged. The effects of the abolition of religious orders were, moreover, long-lasting. John Milner also decried the cultural effects of the plunder of England's monasteries and cathedrals. In his article on Gothic Architecture in *The*

27. N. Pocock (ed.), *Gilbert Burnet, History of the Reformation of the Church of England* (Oxford, 1865), vol. 3, p. 303.

Cyclopaedia (1800 edition) he lauded Gothic as an achievement both sub-
lime and beautiful, and regarded its defacement by the Protestants as barbarous and soulless in the extreme. To such writers the monastic ideal, in
its medieval flowering, characterised a Christian system in which the great
and powerful and wealthy cared for the poor and weak and needy in such
a way that God was praised. Alone among them stood Joseph Berington,
who seriously doubted the value of the monastic institutions as they stood
in the early sixteenth century.[28]

Milner's account left the reader in no doubt about his interpretation of
Henry VIII's motivation in suppressing the monasteries or his view of the
value of the religious houses in English society. Henry VIII was a hyp-
ocrite among hypocrites – even a Protestant historian such as Jeremy
Collier confessed that 'The suppression of the monasteries was thought
the easiest way of furnishing the exchequer' – but Milner exposed the
king's attempts to conceal this motivation:

> Nevertheless, to give colour to these proceedings, a visitation of all the
> convents, that were marked out for destruction, was set on foot, by they
> king's active vice-gerent, Thomas Cromwell, under pretence of reform-
> ing, by his ecclesiastical authority, the abuses that had crept into them.
> But the Commissioners... made use of such arts and violence, as did not
> fail of answering the intention of their employers, by furnishing a pre-
> text, grounded on the feigned motive of religion, for an act of parlia-
> ment, by which all monasteries, whose revenues did not amount to the
> sum of 200 l., were to be dissolved.[29]

Henry's deceit might have been bearable had the charges levelled against
the religious orders been true. But they were not. Milner looked at Stow's
chronicles for evidence that the religious houses had been popular and that
their closure was 'not generally acceptable to the people':

> These complaints of course became much louder at the suppression of
> the greater abbeys. These, as they had it more in their power, so they
> were generally more beneficial to the public. By their doles and alms
> they entirely provided for the poor, insomuch that no poor-laws existed
> until soon after their dissolution. The monks let their farms at easy
> rents, and made allowances for unfavourable seasons, so that abundance
> and population increased around them. They received into their houses
> and entertained strangers of all conditions, according to their rank,
> gratis. They provided hospitals for the indigent sick, and seminaries for
> poor children. Their management churches were the schools of the arts,
> both liberal and mechanical, and their scriptoria and libraries were the
> only asylum of the sciences and of classical literature.[30]

Yet the whole infrastructure of social welfare in Tudor England was swept
away simply 'to gratify the passions of one sensual king and to raise the
families of a few wicked courtiers'.

28. Milner, *History*, pp. 102–30; Milner, *Letters*, pp. 39–65; J. Berington, from *Gentleman's
Magazine*, vol. 69 (1799), p. 654.
29. Milner, *History*, p. 329.
30. Milner, *History*, p. 333.

This attack upon the traditional view of the monasteries and their position in English society before the Reformation is interesting to us chiefly because of the response it drew forth from non-Catholic contemporaries involved in nineteenth-century politics. It opened the floodgates for a Tory-radical critique of English society in the early nineteenth century, and particularly of the provision for the poor and needy within England.

The most significant work in this new tradition was undoubtedly William Cobbett's *A History of the Protestant Reformation in England and Ireland* (1824–7) which had as its subtitle the words 'showing how that event has impoverished the main body of the people in those countries'. Cobbett appears to have become interested in the subject as a result both of reading Lingard and of observing the plight of his many Catholic constituents in Preston, but he also related the matter to the contemporary debate over poor relief. At the same time his *Political Register* was actively espousing the cause of Catholic Emancipation in Ireland.

Cobbett's *Protestant Reformation* can scarcely be regarded as a work of history at all: it is a work of literary invective, of caricature, of political polemic. But it is extremely important because it is a prime example of the ease with which an interpretation of historical events can be popularised and seep almost unnoticed into national consciousness. Cobbett's book produced a new and powerful *social* interpretation of the Reformation which has had a profound influence upon both nineteenth- and twentieth-century perceptions of socio-economic developments.

For, to Cobbett, the Reformation signalled the introduction of oppression into English society. Prior to the dissolution of the monasteries, the religious had cared for the poor, sick and needy. As far as Cobbett was concerned, the punchline of Milner's account had been, 'insomuch that no poor laws existed until soon after their dissolution'. For the caring community had provided for the poor and there had been no need for oppressive legislation. After the Reformation all that had changed. Poverty and need were born. The rich rode roughshod over the rabble. Cobbett's *History of the Protestant Reformation* replaced the view of the Reformation as a blow fought for human freedom and intellectual honesty with a new and harsher indictment:

> The Reformation, as it is called, was engendered in beastly lust, brought forth in hypocrisy and perfidy, and cherished and fed by plunder, devastation, and by rivers of English and Irish blood, and that, as to its more remote consequences, they are, some of them, now before us in that misery, that beggary, that nakedness, that hunger, that everlasting wrangling and spite, which now stare us in the face and stun our ears at every turn, and which the 'Reformation' has given us in exchange for the ease and happiness and harmony and Christian charity enjoyed so abundantly, and for so many ages, by our Catholic forefathers.[31]

---

31. W. Cobbett, *A History of the Protestant Reformation in England and Ireland* (London, 1824–7), p. 4.

The Reformation had destroyed the natural unity of the English and Irish peoples, and had set them at one another's throats. It had provided a justification, by devious and deplorable means, for the hatred of and oppression of Catholics within the community. Worse still, it had impoverished the people: 'It was not a reformation but a devastation of England, which was, at the time when this event took place, the happiest country, perhaps that the world had ever seen, and, it is my chief business to show that this devastation impoverished and degraded the main body of the people'.[32]

In telling the story of the English Reformation, Cobbett was declaredly and unashamedly didactic for, to his mind, 'the great use of history is to teach us how law, usages and institutions arose, what were their effects on the people, how they promoted public happiness or otherwise; and these things are precisely what the greater part of historians, as they call themselves, seem to think of no consequence'. So he set out to show the ways in which the monasteries had benefited the community and 'especially how they operated on behalf of the labouring and poorer classes of the people', and to demonstrate the grievous consequences of their destruction. In particular, he attacked the system of tithe payments to the clergy and the married priesthood: 'In short, do we not know that a married priesthood and pauperism and poor rates all came upon this country at one and the same moment?'.[33]

To serve his didactic and partisan purpose Cobbett employed every trick in the book. Catherine of Aragon he portrayed almost as a saint, certainly as a paragon. Thomas Cranmer 'a name which deserves to be held in everlasting execration' and the justice of God was upheld only by 'our knowledge of the fact that the cold-blooded, most perfidious, most impious, most blasphemous caitiff expired, at last, amidst those flames which he himself had been the chief cause of kindling'. The *Acts and Monuments* was described as 'lying Fox's lying book of Protestant Martyrs!', Good Queen Bess became none other than a 'gross, libidinous, nasty shameless old woman'. The standard techniques of popular journalism – rhetorical questions, colourful language and heaped adjectival abuse – aided Cobbett's presentation: sarcasm and pillory abetted it. Speaking of the divorce from Aragon the Paragon, Cobbett wrote:

> Having provided himself with so famous a judge in ecclesiastical matters, the king lost, of course, no time in bringing his hard case before him, and demanding justice at his hands! Hard case indeed; to be compelled to live with a wife of forty-three when he could have, for next to nothing and only for asking, a young one of eighteen or twenty! A really hard case; and he sought relief, now that he had got such an upright and impartial judge, with all imaginable dispatch.[34]

32. *Ibid.*, p. 19.
33. *Ibid.*, pp. 19, 26–27, 123–124.
34. *Ibid.*, pp. 32, 188.

If we must not look to Cobbett for a work of historical accuracy, of scholarship and caution, we must none the less look to him for the popularisation of an interpretation of the Reformation which has had a profound effect upon the Reformation debate down to and including the present day – that the Reformation devastated social provision in the interests of a rapacious monarch and a hungry aristocracy.

As we can see, he also picked up on two of the other hallmarks of the Catholic school of writers in the early century – the role of Anne Boleyn and the character of Thomas Cranmer. The treatment of Cranmer by early nineteenth-century historians was in fact but a much-intensified version of their treatment of other Protestant heroes and martyrs. Milner, for example, associated Latimer, Hooper and Ridley with every imaginable vice. Ridley and Hooper were charged with pillaging the church; Hooper was accused of violating his vows as a Cistercian by leaving the order and marrying a former nun; Latimer and Ridley were both alleged to have dissembled their own Protestant views under Henry VIII and to have persecuted Protestants. Even Charles Butler, who wanted reconciliation with the Protestants, was tempted to describe Latimer as a mere temporiser. But by far the most potent attack on a Reformation leader was John Lingard's attack on Cranmer.

In examining the impact of Lingard's treatment, it is as well to be aware of the prevailing attitude to Cranmer's role in the English Reformation prior to Lingard's intervention. Although there had been criticisms of Cranmer from both Protestants and Catholics in the sixteenth and early seventeenth centuries, Cranmer had been eulogised by mainstream Protestant writers since the Civil War. Gilbert Burnet dubbed him 'a man raised by God for great services, and well fitted for them' and went on to set the record straight:

> He was naturally of a mild and gentler temper... and yet his gentleness did not lead him into such a weakness of spirit, as to consent to everything that was uppermost... He was a man of great candour; he never dissembled his opinion, nor disowned a friend. He laid out all his wealth on the poor and pious uses... His last fall was the only blemish on his life; but he expiated it with such a sincere repentance and a patient martyrdom.[35]

And Strype was the Archbishop's most ardent admirer:

> The name of this most reverend prelate deserves to stand upon eternal record; having been the first Protestant Archbishop of this kingdom, and the greatest instrument, under God, of the happy Reformation of this Church of England. He was a very rare person, and one that deserves to be reckoned among the brightest lights that ever shone in this English Church.[36]

---

35. N. Pocock (ed.), *op.cit.*, vol. 2, pp. 537–538.
36. J. Strype, *Memorials of the most reverend father in God, Thomas Cranmer* (London, 1693), vol. 2, pp. 1, 658.

What Lingard and Milner attempted to do was to strip Cranmer of the aura of spirituality with which he had been endowed by Burnet and Strype. Earlier we noted how he was vilified as a persecutor. Lingard and Milner went much further than this. Milner charged that, throughout his life, Cranmer 'exhibited such a continued scene of libertinism, perjury, hypocrisy, barbarity... profligacy, ingratitude, and rebellion, as is, perhaps, not to be matched in history'. The scandals regarding Cranmer's two marriages and the smuggling of his second wife into England in a chest; the tales of Cranmer's hypocrisy and the stories of his obsequious behaviour towards Henry VIII were all wheeled out as proof of the Archbishop's base nature.[37] Lingard, whose account was much more influential than Milner's because it was less partisan in tone, indicated that Cranmer was given position in order to secure a divorce for Henry and that he duly kept his part of the bargain. H.J. Todd contradicted this view of Cranmer as sycophantic time-server, but Lingard insisted that Cranmer was but a mere lap-dog of Anne Boleyn, intent only on doing her bidding. Lingard similarly countered Protestant arguments that Cranmer remained loyal to his friends, especially Anne Boleyn and Thomas Cromwell, at great personal risk and that he opposed the Six Articles of persecution. Lingard's case was all the stronger because he used original documentary sources to prove his points. Cranmer's sycophancy and extreme personal ambition were emphasised.[38]

Although as we shall see, Protestant writers sprang to the Archbishop's defence, the Roman Catholic critique had a pronounced effect upon the verdict of later nineteenth-century Protestants. For instance, both Canon Dixon and Dean Hook had absorbed the view that Cranmer had used the divorce as a route to preferment. It was now more difficult, given the evidence that Lingard adduced, to cast Cranmer as a plaster saint – if he was such then he certainly had feet of clay![39]

The defence of Cranmer immediately drawn forth by Lingard's *History* – H.J. Todd's *Vindication of the Most Reverend Thomas Cranmer* (1826) – was very largely a restatement of Burnet. Todd insisted that Cranmer had been extremely reluctant to accept the see of Canterbury, despite Lingard's suspicion of Burnet's account. Todd felt that Cranmer's own account of the affair should be accepted at its face value. Similarly, Todd followed Burnet in maintaining that Cranmer had publicly protested against the oath to the papacy, whereas Lingard alleged that the protest was only made in private. Todd, like Lingard, produced manuscript sources to defend his interpretation of Cranmer's activities, but his work did not further the debate.[40]

37. J. Drabble, 'The Historians of the English Reformation, 1780–1850' (Unpublished Ph.D., University of New York, 1975).

38. Lingard, *History*, vol. 6, pp. 153, 77–80.

39. W.F. Hook, *op.cit.*, vol. 4, pp. 467–468.

40. H.J. Todd, *Vindication of the Most Reverend Thomas Cranmer* (London, 1826), pp. 50–53.

There can be little doubt that Cranmer's stature as a saintly reformer was imperilled by Lingard's work and that Todd and other Protestant writers were hard put to it to defend his reputation.

If they found it difficult to protect Cranmer's Reformation standing, then they found it impossible to defend that of Anne Boleyn, a lady whose reputation was already besmirched. The issue of the Aragon divorce had long made historians uneasy. Catholics had tended to blame Cardinal Wolsey. Gilbert Burnet and David Hume saw that the issue was much more complicated than that: there had been problems in Henry's marriage to Catherine from the start; these problems intensified as time went on, especially as Catherine failed to produce a living heir male; Wolsey came to see Catherine as standing in the way of his vaulting ambition; and then Anne Boleyn captivated the king and monopolised him. Lingard, however, saw things in much simpler terms: 'The lust of Henry generated the independence of the English Church.' He revived the suggestion that Henry had had Anne's sister Mary as his previous mistress and he discovered the documentation to prove it. He alleged that Anne had been in England as early as 1522 and had been an early cause of Henry's dissatisfaction with Catherine of Aragon and not just the later catalyst of events – again he produced documentary evidence which supported this view. Lingard's character-assassination of Anne Boleyn was thorough. He maintained, like Cardinal Pole, that Anne 'artfully kept her lover in suspence, but tempered her resistance with so many blandishments, that his hopes, though repeatedly disappointed were never totally extinguished'. But her virginity was as tactical as that of her famed daughter, Elizabeth, much later. It served to make Henry scrupulous about his marriage with the wife of his late brother. It whetted his appetite and made him dream of marriage. Both Burnet and Hume had asserted that Anne maintained her chastity until her marriage to Henry in November 1532, ten months before Elizabeth's birth. Lingard shocked the public by alleging that Anne became Henry's mistress in 1529, months before the meeting of the Reformation Parliament. He even produced a letter, written by Cranmer, which suggested that the marriage did not take place until 25 January 1533, when Anne was already pregnant by Henry. And from the Vatican Archives he unearthed a dated letter from 1527 which contained the words: *'Ayant este plus qu' une anne attaynte du dart d'amours, non estant assure defaliere, trouver place en votre coeur et affection'*.[41]

Lingard's account elicited a response from an anonymous author in the *Quarterly Review* which attacked the nature of Lingard's interpretation:

Dr Lingard details the whole progress of the amour (between Henry and Anne) during five years, with the precision and accuracy of one of Marivaux' novels. His authorities for all this are a few dateless letters, and a furious invective by Henry's enemy, Cardinal Pole. The finished

---

41. J. Drabble, *op. cit.*

coquette, who, coldly and with ambitious calculation, for two years, refused a less price than a crown for her affection, who by consummate artifice, wrought the amorous monarch to divorce his wife and wed herself, is stated, nevertheless, to have lived as Henry's concubine during three years. Now, in the absence of all authentic evidence, would it not have been more natural, evidently more charitable, to attribute her long resistance to her virtuous principles, perhaps to her previous attachment to Percy? her weakness to the seductions of Henry's ardent attachment, and to her confidence in his promises. All that is proved against her is, that she was married on the 25th of January... and that Elizabeth was born the 13th of September.[42]

Such criticisms drew from Lingard a spirited reply in the form of his *Vindication of Certain Passages in the fourth and fifth volumes of the History of England.* One by one, he refuted the reviewer's arguments. There was, he said, a good deal of evidence that contemporaries regarded Anne as the king's mistress. Cardinal Wolsey had called Anne 'the nightcrowe, that cries ever in the king's ear against me'; the French ambassador, Du Bellay, a man in both Henry's and Anne's confidence, looked on Anne as Henry's mistress; papal briefs stated the same. And the circumstantial evidence was surely devastating:

We have the evidence of the facts. We find the king attempting to seduce a young and beautiful female. To overcome her objections, he promises her marriage, as soon as he can obtain a divorce from his wife. The cause is brought into court: but the delay of the judges irritates his impatience. He expels his wife; and sends for the object of his affection from the house of her father; he allots her appartments contiguous to his own, he orders his courtiers to pay to her all the respect due to the Queen; he suffers her to interfere in matters of state, and to claim a share in the distribution of favours. Thus they live for three years under the same roof. We find them taking their meals together; if the King ride out, we are sure to discover her by his side; if he hunt, he places her in a convenient station to partake of the sport; if he change his residence, she accompanies him; and, when he crosses the sea to meet the French king at Calais, he cannot leave her behind him. Let the reader couple all this with the amorous temperament of Henry, with his impetuous disposition, with his indelicate allusions and anticipations in his correspondence with her, and he will not want evidence to teach him in what relation they live together, nor feel any surprise, if her child was born within little more than seven months after the clandestine celebration of their marriage.[43]

Then Lingard proceeded to rebut the claim that Pole's testimony regarding Henry's relationship with Mary Boleyn was by its very nature suspect.

---

42. Anonymous review, *Quarterly Review*, vol. 56, p.13.

43. J. Lingard, *Vindication of Certain Passages in the fourth and fifth volumes of the History of England*, (London, 1827).

In fact, he urged, Pole assumed in his advice to Henry that the king's relationship with Mary was a known and undisputed fact. He assumed it when he sought to persuade Henry that he was divorcing Catherine not because of conscience but because of passion. The issue of consanguinity was not important, Pole argued, because Henry stood in the same relationship with Anne (the sister of his erstwhile mistress, Mary) as with Catherine (who had been his brother Arthur's wife).

Finally, he replied to the reviewer's charge that he had been unjust to Anne. Lingard claimed impartiality: he had recounted the rumours that Anne had been immoral and had taken servants as lovers, but he had refused to draw conclusions.[44]

It was indeed extraordinarily difficult to overturn Lingard's measured case against Anne Boleyn: contemporaries were quick to see that his work effectively besmirched the origins of the English Reformation. Sharon Turner's *Henry VIII* was by far the most ambitious Protestant attempt of the time to retrieve the situation. He tried to do this by diverting attention away from the embarrassment of Anne herself. He devoted an entire chapter to Cardinal Wolsey's part in instigating the royal divorce. Using Edward Hall and Polydore Vergil, he sought to demonstrate that the doubts about the legitimacy of the Aragon match originated not with Henry but with Wolsey, 'that Wolsey was the chief agent in the inception of the divorce; and that it was begun, and at first pursued, independent of Anne Boleyn'. To Turner, Anne was nothing more than 'an accidental and a temporary appendage' to a cause already under way and from which the king could not draw back. In an attempt to reassert the spiritual nature of the English Reformation, Turner emphasised the steady growth of Protestant ideas which were 'producing, every day, new stems and new fruit' and which formed a vital background to the passion and the politics at court.[45] But Turner was forced to deal with Anne's own tragic history. And there is no doubt that she was a severe embarrassment. As Lingard pointed out in the first edition of his *History*, even her daughter had made no attempt to clear her name, preferring rather to forget that there ever had been such a person as Anne Boleyn – as far as Elizabeth I was concerned, she was her father's and not her mother's daughter. She preferred to forget that she was a chip off the old block, when that block was located on Tower Green.

The main problem which Turner faced was that if he succeeded in clearing Anne's name of the charges made against her, he inevitably made Henry VIII the guilty party. He compromised. He withheld a verdict, claiming that the surviving evidence was immensely ambiguous, but he cast Anne in a favourable light. He was able to do this by consulting the

---

44. *Ibid.*, pp. 102–103.
45. S. Turner, *The History of the reign of Henry the Eighth comprising the political history of the commencement of the English Reformation* (London, 1828), vol. 2, pp. 179–180, 199–200.

commission for investigation into her behaviour and concluding that the commission and its findings suggested a fabricated accusation, and by maintaining that Anne herself acted throughout as someone would who believed that her indisputable innocence would save her. But Turner was worried by the nature of Mark Smeaton's confession and was unable to use evidence which later came to light to the effect that none of the five who were executed (Lord Rochford, Breton, Norris, Smeaton and Weston) declared their innocence or guilt at the execution. Turner's defence of Anne was not successful because he substituted mere assertion for documentary proof: his defence of the spiritual origins of the English Reformation suffered from the same defect.

Conclusion

In the late eighteenth and early nineteenth centuries the debate about the nature of the English Reformation became part of the language of politics. The controversy concerning Catholic emancipation preoccupied contemporaries. Features of the conflict between Catholic and reformer in the sixteenth century which illuminated this current debate were selected for attention. Were the Catholics traitors? Were the Catholics brutal persecutors of the adherents of the new religion? If so, were they any worse than the Protestants in this respect? Was persecution, in fact, a product of sixteenth-century society and culture rather than a necessary attribute of either Catholicism or Protestantism *per se*? Was the English Reformation really the act of spiritual cleansing which Protestant historians had proclaimed it? Had it not been an act motivated by lust, passion and greed? Had it not destroyed a pristine Catholic church, and a successful and caring social system, in the interests of a lustful monarch and his money-grubbing, capitalistic courtiers? All these questions were asked because they were seen to have a real bearing upon the current question – should the Catholics be accepted as full citizens or should they not? Nevertheless, the attempt to answer these questions had a profound effect upon the nature of the contemporary and future historical debate about the origins and nature of the Reformation in England.

How did it do this? The Catholic historians aired arguments about the nature of sixteenth-century Catholicism and Protestantism which had, in fact, appeared in many previous Catholic defences, but for the first time these arguments were widely read by non-Catholics and were actually countenanced by them. This owed much to the moderate approach of Butler and Berington, and yet more to the measured, scholarly work of Lingard. These writers were not polemicists, slinging mud at their enemies, but historians expressing balanced points of view supported by evidence. When the evidence was uncertain – as, for example, respecting the guilt of Anne Boleyn – they would say so. The relative detachment of such writers from the events of which they spoke – despite their involvement in current controversy – made readers sit up and take notice. Lingard's work had an air of objectivity about it which appealed.

In addition, the controversy about the nature of Catholicism and early Protestantism raised a very important issue – that of historical specificity. If it could be proved that Catholics persecuted Protestants in the sixteenth century and vice versa, then why was this so? Was it because Catholicism was for all time and of itself a persecuting creed or was it because conditions in the sixteenth century – political, cultural, social, historical – made active intolerance the order of the day? This was a very pertinent question *and one which still absorbs historians today*: how far are particular features of the past part of the general human condition and how far are they contingent upon specific contemporary conditions? Reflection on this theme became part and parcel of the Reformation debate in the early nineteenth century. Reformation historians began to delve deeper for explanations: they were not content to chronicle events or to provide an entirely one-sided perspective upon them.

Wait a minute, you may well cry. What about Cobbett? He is scarcely an example of balanced historical argument! He is the polemicist writ larger than life! What shall we do with him? Ironically enough, Cobbett derived his view of the English Reformation and its impact upon society from a reading of Lingard's *History* – a measured and careful account. But Cobbett was no historian: he used the work of Milner and Lingard and others to produce a caricature of the English Reformation. This caricature has had a profound impact upon later interpretations of the Reformation because it presents the official Reformation as the brainchild of a lustful monarch and his capitalist courtiers, and as the originator in England of the oppression of the poor by the rich. It is an overdrawn picture, but in it we find the beginnings of the multitudinous social and economic interpretations of the Reformation characteristic of the late nineteenth and twentieth centuries.

In what other respects did these early nineteenth-century treatments of the Reformation help to shape the nature of the historical debate? Certainly Lingard and others focused future attention on the official nature of the Reformation at the expense of the spiritual. Even ardent Protestants were converted to the view that the English Reformation was a political act first and foremost, and that the sanctity of Protestant heroes such as Thomas Cranmer and Anne Boleyn was not beyond doubt. If some attention was given to the spirituality of the Catholic church which was destroyed (by Milner, for example), the spirituality of the Protestant Reformation was merely attacked and demolished. Even Protestant historians such as Turner were able to give relatively little attention to the spread of the new faith which buttressed the official Reformation. Working with official state and church papers, and deprived of local materials, they were condemned to refute attacks on the spirituality of the Protestant Reformation with reiterations of Foxe and other histories and defences of the heroes of the Reformation based upon these. A corrective was not provided until the mid-twentieth century. For the time being, attention was concentrated upon the political leaders of the Reformation, be they lay or clerical. Henry VIII, Thomas Wolsey, Thomas Cranmer, Anne Boleyn – biographers abounded to explain and justify their Reformation roles.

Early nineteenth-century writings on the Reformation also drew attention away from the internal affairs of the Reformation church. Institutional history played little part in the debate: the focus was essentially political. This diversion from the path established by Strype in the early eighteenth century was, however, but temporary. The Church of England's family squabble of the mid-nineteenth century – when Anglo-Catholic and Protestant brethren fell out – revived this earlier interest in the nature of the Church of England both in terms of its institutional expression and also in terms of its creed and worship.

Catholics and Protestants alike openly used the historical past to support their contemporary political arguments. A study of the content and impact of the historical writings produced during the course of the debate about Catholic Emancipation should, however, alert us to the fact that historical arguments produced to support contemporary political causes should not be casually dismissed – they may well have a profound effect upon historical debate, upon the issues selected for treatment and the interpretations proffered.

John Lingard's careful and measured work played a pivotal role in shaping the popular view of the English Reformation in the nineteenth and early twentieth centuries. This was partly because his *History of England* was widely read and was prominent on library shelves. It was also because he was instrumental in determining the focus of contemporary historical debate on the major figures of that reformation and on the evidence of their motivations and actions. It was ironic that probably one of the most lasting legacies of his work was William Cobbett's caricature of the English Reformation – something that Lingard himself would have decried.

ABBREVIATIONS

Milner, *History*   J. Milner, *The History, civil and ecclesiastical, and survey of the antiquities of Winchester* (Winchester, 1798–1801).

Milner, *Letters*   J. Milner, *Letters to a Prebendary* (Baltimore edition, 1800).

Lingard, *History*   J. Lingard, *A History of England* (Philadelphia, 1827 edition).

6

JOHN LINGARD AND THE SIMANCAS ARCHIVES

Edwin Jones

John Lingard was the first English historian to attempt to look at the history of England in the sixteenth century from an international point of view. He was unconvinced by the story of the Reformation in England as found in the works of previous historians such as Burnet and Hume, and believed that new light needed to be thrown on the subject. One way if doing this was to look at English history from the outside, so to speak, and Lingard held to be a duty of the historian 'to contrast foreign with native authorities, to hold the balance between them with an equal hand, and, forgetting that he is an Englishman, to judge impartially as a citizen of the world'.[1] In pursuit of his ideal Lingard can be said to have given a new dimension to the source materials for English history. As parish priest in the small village of Hornby, near Lancaster, Lingard had few opportunities for travel. But he made good use of his various friends and former pupils at Douai and Ushaw colleges who were settled now in various parts of Europe. It was with the help of these friends that Lingard made contacts with and gained valuable information from archives in France, Italy and Spain. We shall concern ourselves here only with the story of Lingard's contacts with the great Spanish State Archives at Simancas.

The small and unimportant village of Simancas in Old Castile has been dominated in all senses through the centuries by the great Castle which overshadows it. Within the cold, damp, and cheerless precincts of this Castle, the opponents of the Spanish government met their fate in the sixteenth century. For here the marshal of Navarre was imprisoned and committed suicide in 1523, Acuna, bishop of Zamara, was tortured and executed after a bold and exciting dash for liberty in 1526, and the unfortunate Montigny was secretly strangled in 1570.[2] This ancient stronghold was the place chosen by Philip II in 1566 as a repository for the great mass of state letters and documents which had been accumulating at the royal court throughout the sixteenth century. The cautious and suspicious nature of the Spanish monarch is reflected in the strict regulations, formulated by Philip, which governed entry to these archives and which remained substantially unchanged until 1844. Nobody was allowed access to the originals; a special note, signed by the king's own hand, was necessary in order to obtain a copy of any document; this permission was given very

---

1. John Lingard, *History of England* (4th ed., 1837), Preface, p. vi.
2. R.B. Merriman, *The Rise of the Spanish Empire* (1925), vol. 3, p. 99, note 2; (1934), vol. 4, p. 284. See also R. Trevor Davies, *The Golden Century of Spain 1501–1621* (1937), pp. 49–50.

rarely, and never to foreigners; no fire was allowed in the archives, even in the heart of winter – and this is one of the colder places in Spain.[3]

The official opening of the Simancas Archives began in 1844. The Spanish National Archives had been established in an age when Spain dominated Europe; they were opened at a time when the imperial magnificence associated with the reign of Philip II had long departed, when Spain was governed by a regent and a provisional government which had to come to terms with the liberal movement. In 1566 Belgium had been a satellite of the great Spanish Empire. In 1844 the Belgians were playing an important role in the new archival work which had commenced about 1830,[4] the year in which they had gained their independence of Holland by revolution. It was M. Gachard, a representative of the Belgian government, who made the first great breach in the barriers of the richest – with regard to sixteenth-century documents[5] – and most jealously guarded archives in Europe. In his report to the Minister of the Interior, Gachard commended the contemporary Spanish government which, 'jaloux de seconder les progrès de la civilisation et des lettres, et le mouvement des esprits vers les études sérieuses', had allowed him entry to Simancas, 'un sanctuaire où n'avait jamais pénétré aucun étranger'. He added, however, that it was not without 'de nombreuses démarches' that the Belgian legation at Madrid had succeeded in persuading, first the regent, then the provisional government, to open the Archives.[6] M. Tiran, representing the French government, was also admitted to Simancas as a 'literary reader' at this time.[7]

About seventy years before Gachard gained entry to these Archives, William Robertson had been the first from the British Isles to be interested in the documents at Simancas. He had wanted materials for the activities of the Spaniards in the New World for his *History of America* (1777). His interest, however, was to no avail, and he had referred wistfully to the 'treasures' at Simancas:

> But the prospect of it, only, is all that I enjoyed. Spain, with an excess of caution, has uniformly thrown a veil over her transactions in

---

3. For these details, see L.P. Gachard (ed.), *Correspondance de Philippe II sur Les Affaires des Pays-Bas: D'Après les Originaux Conservés dans Les Archives Royales de Simancas*, 5 vols. (Brussels, 1848–79), vol. 1 (1848), 'Notice Historique et Descriptive', pp. 43–48. Gachard adds that 'De tous les historiens et chronistes espagnols, Geronimo de Zurita, qui écrivit, sous les règnes de Charles-Quint et de Philippe II, en qualité de chroniste d'Aragon, l'histoire de ce royaume… paraît avoir été le seul qui ait eu accès aux archives de Simancas' (*op. cit.*, p. 50, note 1).

4. H. Butterfield, *Man on His Past* (Cambridge, 1955), p. 79.

5. 'I have no doubt that from about 1480 to the end of the first quarter of the seventeenth century the Archives of Simancas surpass all the other archives I am acquainted with' (G.A. Bergenroth's letter to *The Athenaeum*, no. 1721, Oct. 20th 1860, p. 518). He added, however, that the Roman archives which he had not seen 'may be richer'.

6. 'Rapport à M. Le Comte de Theux, Ministre de l'Intérieur', Gachard, *op. cit.*, p. ix.

7. G. A. Bergenroth (ed.), *Calendar of… State Papers… at Simancas* (1862), vol. 1, Introduction, p. vii.

America. From strangers they are concealed with peculiar solicitude. Even to her own subjects the Archivo of Simancas is not opened without a particular order from the crown; and after obtaining that, papers cannot be copied, without paying fees of office so exorbitant... It is to be hoped that the Spaniards will at last discover this system of concealment to be no less impolitic than illiberal.[8]

So distant, in all senses, were the materials at Simancas from English historiography, that Robertson deserves mention for thinking in this direction, though he was not concerned with materials for English history.

It was not until 1862 that the first volume of the now familiar *Calendar of State Papers from Spanish sources relating to English affairs* appeared – the work of a German scholar, G.A. Bergenroth, employed by the Master of the Rolls. We can do no better in placing Lingard's connexion with Simancas in its proper perspective than to look first of all at the circumstances attendant upon the venture of Bergenroth about forty years after the events which we shall be relating.

Bergenroth wrote to his mother and sister in 1860, on the eve of his proposed visit to Simancas, that 'these Archives have been hardly at all used by historians, only by Spaniards, Frenchmen, and Belgians, not at all by Germans and Englishmen'.[9] In September of that year, he wrote that 'I am duly installed as the only literary reader in the Archives of Simancas'.[10] He said in a letter of the following month that he was searching 'for historical documents concerning the history of England during the reigns of our kings and queens of the house of Tudor' and that 'I am the first who has come to this remote village in the interests of English history'. He was certain of this because he had studied a list, belonging to the chief librarian, of those who had been there, and this was supported 'not only by the unanimous testimony of all the officers of the Archives, but also by a most detailed journal, into which every reader is obliged to enter his name, as well as each document which he receives for his perusal'.[11] He suggested that any previous English writer who had referred to these documents must have got his information from the Spanish and Belgian collections which were published after 1840.[12] In this, as we shall see later, Bergenroth was mistaken.

The difficulties and obstacles put in the way of Bergenroth after he had begun his work at Simancas are eloquent of the suspicion with which the Spanish authorities still regarded the entry of foreigners into their archives

8. W. Robertson, *The History of America* (1777), Preface, pp. ix–x.

9. Bergenroth to his mother and sister, July 11th 1860 (quoted in W.C. Cartwright, *Gustave Bergenroth. A Memorial Sketch* (Edinburgh, 1870), p. 51.

10. Bergenroth's letter of Sept. 20th 1860 in 'Foreign Correspondence' of *The Athenaeum*, no. 1721 (Oct. 20th 1860), p. 517.

11. Bergenroth's letter of October 1860 in 'Foreign Correspondence' of *The Athenaeum*, no. 1723 (Nov. 3rd 1860), p. 593.

12. Gachard, 5 vols., *op. cit..* Also M.F. Navarrete and others (ed.), *Coleccion de Documentos Inéditos para la historia de España*, 112 vols. (Madrid, 1842–95).

in 1860. In 1861 the 'Archivero' at Simancas 'went one step further in his
obstructions to my labours' and ordered the suppression of all parts of the
transcripts which did not seem 'calculated for publication'.[13] Bergenroth
immediately stopped work and went to Madrid where, with the help
chiefly of Mr. Edwardes, the English *chargé d'affaires*, and of the Prussian
embassy and the French ambassador, he was able finally to get the Spanish
authorities to agree to his requests.[14] But still there were difficulties, and
in 1863 Bergenroth was complaining:

> The greatest obstacle in my way came, however, from another source.
> The Archivero retains again all dispatches in cipher, of which no deci-
> pherings are to be found. He pretends that he has received orders from
> the Director General, in Madrid, to that effect. The Director General,
> on the other hand, denies to have given such orders, and calls the
> Archivero an 'ass' and a 'liar'. The fact, I think, is that here as well as
> in Madrid, there is a great amount of double-dealing.[15]

Having noticed the events connected with the 'official' opening of the
Simancas archives to English historiography in the years after 1860, we
may now turn to Lingard's attempts in this direction some forty years earlier. Bergenroth was not in fact the first to go to Simancas in the interests
of English history. For Lingard was using information which had been
sought after and gained in these archives in the interests of English history as early as 1820.

The great Spanish monarchy was the pivotal point of European politics
and diplomacy in the sixteenth century. The correspondence of the various Spanish envoys with Ferdinand and Isabella, Charles V and Philip II,
contains the keys to many problems not only of Spanish history but of that
of Germany, France, Italy and England. It was impossible to understand
certain aspects of English history without knowing the Spanish side of the
story, and Lingard seems to have been the first English historian to have
understood this. English Protestant historians had been satisfied with the
official version of sixteenth-century events based, in the first place, on the
Henrician statutes, and then on the '"Standard Works", accepted and
received as Canonical Books',[16] such as Foxe's *Book of Martyrs* and
Burnet's *History of the Reformation*, or on the less popular *Ecclesiastical
History* of the Non-Juror, Jeremy Collier. They had no real interest in
changing the story as it had come down to them and so they were psycho-
logically ill-adapted for the work of widening the basis of English source
material. Lingard, on the other hand, being a Catholic, was interested in
qualifying the old story and perhaps changing it at strategic points.

13. Bergenroth to master of the Rolls, Madrid, Apr. 30th 1861, quoted in W.C. Cartwright,
op. cit., p. 97.

14. *Ibid.*

15. Bergenroth to master of the Rolls, Simancas, June 14th 1863, quoted in W.C. Cartwright,
op. cit., p. 122.

16. Sir Francis Palgrave, *History of Normandy and England* (1851), Preface, p. xlvi.

Consequently he was anxious to find new evidence and new source materials. He wrote to a friend in 1821, 'I trust that by collating so many original letters and papers, I shall be able to make a history of Elizabeth etc., something different from those we now have'.[17] This interest, together with his talents as an historian and his international viewpoint, explains Lingard's importance as a pioneer in the work of extending English source materials.[18]

Amongst the papers and correspondence of Lingard to be found at Ushaw, near Durham, the first reference to the Simancas archives occurs in the summer of 1819 when Lingard was busy collecting materials for his volume on the reign of Henry VIII which appeared in 1820. On this occasion Lingard wrote to a friend that 'I am also promised several valuable documents from the archives of Simancas in Spain'.[19] We can take up the tale now in Lingard's Spanish correspondence.

Alexander Cameron, rector of the Scots College in Valladolid, a city about eight miles east of Simancas, proved to be a most valuable contact. He was in touch with Thomas Sherburne, former student and member of staff of the English College, Valladolid. Sherburne was to return to the English College as rector in 1822, but in 1820 he was missioner at Kirkham, in the Fylde, not too far from Lingard. Sherburne received a letter from Cameron who desired him to forward certain information to Lingard. Cameron mentioned the 'queries' of Lingard and answered them with information derived from Zurita[20] and Mariana,[21] 'the best informed of the Spanish historians'. He went on to say in the letter which Sherburne forwarded to Lingard, that the negotiations between the English and Spanish Courts up to the time of the death of Henry VII still existed at Simancas. No copies of these papers were given, however, without 'an express order from the Minister of State'. Cameron reported that even the Scottish historian William Robertson's attempt to gain entry to the Simancas in preparing his masterpiece, *The History of Charles V*, published in 1769, had met with rebuff. It was possible that something could be done through the medium of the British ambassador, Sir Henry Wellesley; but 'they are particularly delicate on such subjects in this country'. Some of Cameron's friends who were 'well informed in the history of those times' had promised to give him some information, and if this

---

17. Lingard to Kirk, March 26th 1822, UCA, Lingard Transcript 209.
18. Cf. 'Yours is the only history I can rely upon – The herd of historians follow in the same track – & the error of the first is copied throughout', Sir Cuthbert Sharp to Lingard, May 6th 1837, UCA, Lingard Transcript 1549. Sharp was the author of *Memorials of the Rebellion of 1569*, which was published in 1840.
19. Lingard to Kirk, July 15th 1819, AAW, Lingard Transcript 228.
20. Gerónimo de Zurita (1512–1580), who was patiently zealous 'in the search and use of manuscripts' and a founder of 'critical historical scholarship in Spain' (Merriman, *op. cit.*, vol. 4, pp. 482–483).
21. Juan de Mariana (1532–1624), who had 'modern views of contemporary affairs' (Merriman, *op. cit.*, vol. 4, p. 483).

threw any new light on the subject with which Lingard was concerned, it would be sent to him immediately.[22]

In another letter, fifteen days later, Cameron described the way in which certain facts had filtered through to him from the original materials in the Simancas Archives. Cameron had translated Lingard's letter, seeking information, into Spanish. Then 'I wrote to – you know the place and presented it to N.' – obviously Cameron wanted to hide the fact that he was writing to Simancas and also the name of the official there with whom he had some contact, in case this letter got into the wrong hands. The friendly official had later shown Cameron 'an Index of papers of those times', and 'sometime thereafter he remitted a few observations under cover to a friend of his here in town, with a strict charge that he should read them to me, but not allow me to inspect them', but he 'neither would nor could say anything more on the subject without an express order from Court'. So Cameron had to be content with 'hearing the paper read in a cursory manner, and pick up what I could'. He was annoyed at being 'so scurvily used', and wrote that

A mighty importance is given in this country to the papers lodged in Simancas. It is pretended that without admission to them, it is impossible to write any thing like a true history of the continent of Europe for the last three centuries, and that what has been hitherto published is a mere fable. What truth there may be in this, or whether it is merely a Spanish puff, is more than I can say. If Mr Lingard thinks it worth his while to take a trip to Spain, and spend a few months at Simancas, con las licencias necessarias [sic], all that I can do is to give him any little assistance in my power, and that I will do with pleasure.[23]

Cameron then proceeded to write out for Lingard the facts that he had learnt from the Simancas paper which had been read to him.

One of the subjects which formed the first episode of this Spanish correspondence in the Lingard letters of 1820 was the background to the marriage of Henry and Catherine of Aragon. There was a gap in the knowledge of English historians concerning the delay of this marriage until 1509. Moreover, the young Henry, in 1505, had 'protested' against the pre-contract made for his marriage with Catherine. Was this delay and protest due to any real doubts about the validity of the marriage, as English historians said?[24] The key to this problem would lie obviously in the correspondence between Henry VII and Ferdinand at this period which was at Simancas. Lingard wrote to his friends in Spain and the first letter in reply gave information derived from the works of the Spanish historians,

---

22. Cameron to Sherburne, May 5th 1820, Lingard Transcipt 1456a [not included in transcriptions], (re-addressed to Lingard by Sherburne).

23. Cameron to Sherburne, Valladolid, May 29th 1820, UCA, Lingard Transcript 1456.

24. Cf. P.F. Tytler, *Life of Henry VIII* (edition of 1851), p. 20 – this work had been first published in 1837; also J.A. Froude, *History of England* (1870), vol. 1, p. 227.

Mariana and Zurita who 'have no doubt... consulted the original documents from what I [Cameron] myself have seen'. Cameron continued:

That is what the Spanish historians say from which it appears that... the two Henries, father and son, considered themselves to act in the business of the marriage just as they pleased; which would not have been the case had they conceived the Pope's dispensation to be null, and which can only be explained by their believing, or affecting to believe, that the contract of marriage was not obligatory, no doubt because it was made during the Prince's minority, and because he had ordered a public protestation against it before he completed his fortinth [sic] year. If the dispensation was null, the contract was of course invalid; why then protest against it? or why protest at a particular age? When he might well at any age. I shall proceed to copy my Spanish vouchers and shall begin with Mariana...[25]

So far this information was conveyed only on the authority of the Spanish historians. But Lingard was anxious always to base his statements on original documents, and to check secondary sources in the light of these documents. Cameron wrote to the official at Simancas: 'I begged to call his attention in a particular manner to the cause of the protestation made by Prince Henry and to any steps that might have been taken by Ferdinand of Aragon to recall his daughter Catherine to Spain after the death of Arthur'. The official arranged for certain materials to be read out to Cameron who sent the information gained from them to Lingard. Cameron's notes gave a detailed account of the financial negotiations which preceded the marriage of Henry and Catherine in 1509 – complete with dates, sums of money involved, methods of payment and the various 'tactical' excuses used by both sides. On the subject of the 'protestation', Cameron wrote:

A correspondence was carried on between Ferdinand and Henry till the death of the latter; the correspondence turns principally on the payment of Catherine's portion. Henry complained that the payments were not made at the stipulated times; Ferdinand in reply offered different excuses... Henry the seventh in a letter... 1507, tells him that he could get a far better match for his son than Catherine, twice as much money, but that he preferred her on account of her beauty and her virtue, and that he was resolved to stand to his engagements (guardar los pactos) an evident proof that he had no doubt of the validity of Pope Julius' dispensation... The Protestation was evidently a political device intended to work on Ferdinand's fears. Henry pretended that he was at full liberty to conclude the marriage or not, just as he pleased.... Ferdinand was obliged to acceede [sic] to all his demands. This is the sum of what I have been able to find.[26]

25. Cameron to Sherburne, Valladolid, May 5th 1820, UCA, Lingard Transcript 1456a (re-addressed by Sherburne and forwarded to Lingard).

26. Cameron to Sherburne, Valladolid, May 29th 1820, UCA, Lingard Transcript 1456 (forwarded to Lingard).

It seemed evident from the Spanish papers that the delay in the marriage of Henry and Catherine, including the episode of Henry's protestation, was part of a prolonged piece of wrangling between Henry VII and Ferdinand, designed to gain a tactical advantage for the cleverer party[27] – an interpretation which was perfectly consistent with the shrewd character of Henry and the diplomatic ability of the Spanish king. In 1489, when the marriage of Catherine and Arthur had been arranged, Ferdinand of Spain had held the diplomatic advantage and made good use of it. When Arthur died in 1502 the European scene had changed and Ferdinand was now the suppliant. Henry liked his new position and tried to avail himself of it during the period 1502–9. Whether there was a real or merely a feigned possibility of Henry VII's abandoning the idea of the Spanish marriage for his son in 1505, the essential fact remains that, as Lingard saw, the protestation of 1505 was a political manoeuvre on the part of Henry VII and not a personal expression of conscience by the future Henry VIII.[28]

The development of historiography in England on particular points such as the protest of 1505 depended, in the first place, on a complete reorientation of the Englishman's general viewpoint on the history of his own nation. Thinking within the ideological framework of the Protestant-Whig interpretation of history, English historians saw far too many problems of sixteenth-century history in terms of an insular type of religious controversy. Nineteenth-century writers, like their predecessors for more than two hundred years, had forgotten that England was part of a greater whole, and that its history could not be explained properly in isolation. So the episode of 1505 became inevitably connected with the later Divorce question and was used mistakenly as a convenient piece of propaganda in the great historiographical debate on that subject. Only when we have understood all this does Lingard's work gain its true significance, for his introduction of foreign source materials acted as a disturbing breath of fresh air on the musty atmosphere of English historiography of the Reformation.

In November 1820 Lingard wrote to a friend of 'the new information which I have supplied & which he [another correspondent] will not find in any other English writer respecting the delay of Catherine's marriage...'[29] The information from Simancas had infused new meaning into these

---

27. Lingard, *History of England* (6th ed., 1883 reprint), vol. 4, pp. 328–329 and note 2.

28. Cf. the account of this episode in Merriman, *op. cit.* (1918), vol. 2, pp. 142, 276, 318, 321–2; and in G.R. Elton, *England Under The Tudors* (1955), pp. 39–41. A modern scholar has noticed that 'as from Lingard it became increasingly clear that scholarship endorsed many of the contentions on the Catholic side of the agelong argument whether or not certain crucial events had occurred: for example (1) the Catholic contention that the marriage between Catherine of Aragon and Prince Arthur had not been consummated, and that the lawfulness of Henry VIII's marriage had been generally endorsed' (B.H.G. Wormald, 'The Historiography of the English Reformation', in *Historical Studies*, 1 (1958), p. 56).

29. Lingard to Kirk, Nov 25th 1820, UCA, Walker Transcripts, Lingard Transcript 200.

events of English history and this is reflected in Lingard's treatment of the subject. He added in a footnote to his text, that

The English historians seem entirely ignorant of the causes which for so many years delayed the marriage of Henry and Catherine. For the preceding narrative I have had recourse to the Spanish historians Zurita and Mariana, and have compared their statements with the records at Simancas, which have been copied for me by a friend in Spain.[30]

The next episode in this Spanish correspondence occurred in the early months of 1823. By now Sherburne had returned to Valladolid and was acting as the 'middle man' between Cameron and Lingard. Sherburne had given some of Lingard's requests for information on certain topics to Cameron, but Cameron had been prevented from going to Simancas 'for several reasons, and it is not one of the least that I am unable to mount horseback or go up a stair in consequence of a dreadful fall'. This had made it necessary for him 'to make use of second hands' in the research and as a result he was afraid that 'all that I have to say will afford you but very little satisfaction'. Obviously Cameron had been going to Simancas previously. He mentioned certain 'originals..., which I have seen with my own eyes', by which he may have been referring to extracts taken from the originals by an official at the archives, for he continued:

Before I proceed to answer a few of your queries regarding Philip, let me observe that what has been written concerning him and Charles the fifth ought to be considered rather romances than *histories* as appears from the original documents in the Archives of Simancas, to which unfortunately no one is allowed access without special royal order. I understand that extracts have been taken from the principal papers, by a gentleman now employed in the archives, and that application is to be made for leave to print them. The whole of the correspondence with the Duke of Feria, while ambassador at London, is in Philip's own hand writing.[31]

There follows as much information as Cameron had been able to procure in answer to Lingard's queries and the remark: 'When I assert a fact without citing my authority, you may easily guess the source whence I derived it. I have requested Mr Sherburne to search his Archives [at the English College] to see if he can find what you want...'.

Sherburne transmitted this information to Lingard and added a comment of his own at the end, remarking that 'Had my leisure been equal to that of Mr. Cameron you [*sic*] inquiries should have been attended to with equal diligence', but 'my hands have been quite full, and mostly of dirty materials'. Sherburne then said that he was going to give a part of his time

---

30. Lingard, *op. cit.*, vol. 4, p. 335, note 2. Writing to his publisher in 1820, Lingard had to explain the spelling and meaning of the word 'Simancas' – so unfamiliar were these Archives to Englishmen (Lingard to Mawman, ? 1820, UCA, Lingard Transcript 457).

31. Cameron to Lingard, Valladolid, Jan 10th 1823, UCA, Lingard Transcript 1457 (through the medium of Sherburne who forwarded it to Lingard).

each day to the work of examining the correspondence of Cardinal Allen and Robert Persons[32] and others which was to be found in the archives of the English College at Valladolid; for there were 'immense loads of letters' and anything which appeared to be 'worth your notice' would be sent to Lingard.

The next letter in this Spanish correspondence heralded an important development in the story, for now Sherburne himself began to do some searching at Simancas, and he seemed determined to improve upon Cameron's efforts. In February of 1823 Sherburne, still acting as the 'middle man', wrote to Lingard. The first part of the letter is a transcript of Cameron's notes, together with Cameron's concluding comment, that

All this results from ocular inspection of the original documents, and not from hearsay. The Gentleman in whose custody they are, declined entering into further details because any communication of the kind is strictly prohibited, and for the same reason he cannot give a copy of the extracts he has made; intending to send them to the press if permitted by the government.[33]

Having transcribed Cameron's information, Sherburne continued:

So far as my friend Mr. Cameron. After reading his paper & transcribing it I thought it fitting to give him a scolding for not saying more... To make up for the deficiency I will take a ride westward tomorrow & see if something cannot be extorted. I know how delicate a matter it is and shall not be astonished if I return as I went...

There is now a break in the letter, corresponding to Sherburne's 'ride westward' to Simancas. He resumed writing on the following day:

Returned. I... have read a great part of the extracts made from the original documents & comprising the period from the beginning to the end of Philip's reign. There are several very curious things, of the ambassadors to Philip & of this monarch to his ambassadors.

Sherburne then proceeded to give information derived from two letters of Guerau de Spes, Philip's ambassador in London 1568–1571, and added that 'these two letters, among a thousand others have been before me this morning'. Another letter, in Philip's own handwriting from the Spanish king to his ambassador in London, revealed that Philip did not know of Pope Pius V's intention to excommunicate Queen Elizabeth in 1570 until this ambassador had informed him of it. It was revealed also that Philip considered the excommunication of Elizabeth 'as of very doubtful policy, & only to be justified by his [Pius V's] ardent zeal'. Philip showed himself to have been 'particularly slow in entering into any promises of assistance to the English malcontents'; the Duke of Alva showed the same attitude and most 'vehemently opposed every project of invasion that was proposed to Philip'.

---

32. Leaders of the 'Spanish Party' among the English Catholics of Elizabeth's reign. Persons was the founder of the English missionary college at Valladolid in 1589.
33. Sherburn to Lingard, Feb 19th 1823, UCA, Lingard Transcript 1550.

Facts such as these from the Simancas documents threw quite a new light on Philip II in English historical writing. English national feeling had been invoked against the twin 'threats' of Spanish dominance and 'popery' in the sixteenth century, and this had left its stamp on English historiography. English Protestants and nineteenth-century English 'liberals' gladly accepted the 'Black Legend' – depicting Philip as a 'monster of iniquity' – which had been created by William the Silent's *Apologia*.[34] This hostile presentation of Philip can be traced in Robert Watson's *History of the Reign of Philip II* (1777), and through influential works of the nineteenth century such as those of J.A. Froude, J.L. Motley and W.H. Prescott.[35] Lingard's contemporary Sharon Turner described Philip as 'the vindictive arm of the Papacy',[36] himself subject to the terrors of the Inquisition while he planned the Catholic invasion of Protestant England. Philip was indeed 'the relentless enemy of every patriotic Englishman'.[37]

But factors of political and national interest influenced Philip's actions just as they guided Elizabeth's. He was certainly not a servile instrument in the hands of the Papacy with which his relations 'might well have been those of a completely non-religious statesman'; the friendly part of these relations depended on the subserviency of the popes. Indeed 'few rulers – except, perhaps, Henry VIII of England – have ever maintained so consistently an anti-papal policy over a long period of years'.[38]

We have been told that Ranke was the first historian to produce this new view of Philip II after his researches into the reports of foreign ambassadors, which he found in various archives.[39] The modern portrayal of the Spanish king had emerged already, however, in the work of Lingard whose treatment of Philip, based partly on the materials from Simancas, anticipated the findings of modern scholarship and provided the first balanced account of Philip and his relations with England.

From Lingard we learn that Philip, a man of fortitude, was naturally slow and cautious. He had not supported the Marian persecutions in England and his confessor had preached strongly against them.[40] On the subject of the papal excommunication of Elizabeth, Lingard notes that:

It has been supposed that this bull was solicited by Philip; but, in a letter to his ambassador in England (June 30), he says that he never heard

---

34. R. Trevor Davies, *The Golden Century of Spain 1501–1621*, p. 118.

35. Froude, *History of England* (1856–70); Motley, *Rise of the Dutch Republic* (1855); Prescott, *History of the Reign of Philip II* (Boston, 1855–1888). Cf. Merriman, *op. cit.*, vol. 4, pp. 73–74. For the part played by nationalism in English historical writing in Lingard's day, see T.P. Peardon, *The Transition in English Historical Writing 1760–1830* (New York, 1933), ch. 6.

36. Sharon Turner, *The History of the Reigns of Edward the Sixth, Mary and Elizabeth* (2nd ed., 1829), vol. 4, p. 141, note 1.

37. A. Dimock, 'The Conspiracy of Dr Lopez', *English Historical Review*, 9 (1894), p. 471.

38. R. Trevor Davies, *op. cit.*, pp. 131–2.

39. R. Trevor Davies, *op. cit.*, p. 119.

40. See Lingard, *History* (6th ed., 1883), vol. 6, pp. 497, 513; vol. 5, p. 469.

of its existence before it had been announced to him by that minister, and attributes it to the zeal rather than the prudence of the pontiff.[41] This footnote is not included in Lingard's first edition of the volume on Elizabeth which appeared in 1823, though we know from the Spanish correspondence, cited above, that he had the information at this time. It is included in the fourth edition of 1838 and has a reference to the collection of reports on documents published in Spain in 1832 – the *Memorias de la real academia de la historia*.[42] Lingard had to be very careful in providing his evidence for any new treatment of a subject, and he was well aware of this. It may be that this new interpretation of Philip II's attitude in 1570 was so different from the usual version that Lingard did not want to introduce it until he could make a definite reference to a published source in support of it.

Indeed the rebellion in the Netherlands was caused by the 'arbitrary notions' of Philip by which he managed to antagonise every section of the community and the Spanish Inquisition was certainly an 'odious Institution'.[43] Yet Lingard was also the first English historian to disprove the old legend that Philip had arranged a meeting with the French monarch at Bayonne to plan the Massacre of St. Bartholomew and the total extirpation of Protestants in Europe.[44]

Again in his treatment of the Spanish Armada, Lingard breaks through the nationalist framework of English historiography to produce a more balanced interpretation. Elizabeth had provoked Philip into sending the Armada. She had offered him injuries 'almost annually', intercepted his treasure ships, helped his rebels, hired foreign soldiers to fight against Spanish armies, and had 'suffered her mariners to plunder and massacre his defenceless subjects on the high seas and in his American dominions'. Philip waited and hesitated. By 1583 the political situation in Portugal, France and the Netherlands was favourable enough for him to begin making plans against England; but still he was slow and cautious. Finally Elizabeth's sending of an English army to the Netherlands in 1585 was 'equivalent to a declaration of war' and the execution of Mary Queen of Scots hastened it. Philip was forced into action, exchanging his usual caution and procrastination for sudden temerity.[45]

Yet with regard to the immediate preparations for the Armada, we are told that 'of all men, the Spanish king should have been the last to acknowledge in the pontiff the right of disposing of the crowns of princes'. For he had declared war without hesitation against Pope Paul IV on a pre-

41. Lingard, *History* (4th ed., 1838), vol. 8, p. 56, note +. Cf. first edition (1823), vol. 5, p. 299, note 82.

42. See below, p. 121.

43. Lingard, *History*, (6th ed., 1883 reprint), vol. 6, pp. 226–227.

44. Lingard, *History*, vol. 6, p. 228 and note I, p. 282, Appendix, p. 685. Cf. H. Butterfield, *Man On His Past*, pp. 175, 185, 191.

45. Lingard, *History*, vol. 6, pp. 497–498; cf. G. Mattingley, *The Defeat of the Spanish Armada* (1959), pp. 82–84.

vious occasion, and his general, the Duke of Alva, had 'dictated the terms of peace in the Vatican'; but now 'revenge and ambition taught him a different lesson'. A document from Simancas gave Lingard the details of Philip's preparations for the Armada, including his demand for money from the Pope, 'the renewal of the censures promulgated against Elizabeth by former pontiffs', and his plans to have the investiture of the English throne conferred on him.[46]

After his 'ride westward', Sherburne was able to correct the information contained in Cameron's notes at certain points. Turning to the transcription of these notes which he had made earlier, Sherburne inserted certain corrections between the lines. Cameron had stated that Elizabeth engaged Don Carlos to assassinate his father, Philip II, but Sherburne added: 'This fact does not appear in the archives. T.S.'[47] Sherburne made similar corrections of Cameron's notes in the next letter of the same month, as, for example, when he writes alongside a statement of Cameron's: 'This fact is not clear, at least the corresp: does not bear it out. T.S.'[48]

Indeed Sherburne seems to have been a more able and critical researcher than Cameron. Both of them worked under Lingard's supervision; they searched for material under each 'head of enquiry' which was sent to them. This type of supervision, though restrictive, had its advantages. For neither of them was entirely dispassionate in his search for evidence, and Cameron in particular was so anxious 'to discover the practices of Elizabeth',[49] that there was a danger of his sending opinions instead of facts. But Lingard exercised a restraining influence, demanding facts and names to substantiate any opinion that they sent to him; and they were willing to admit when an opinion could not be verified by documents. Moreover, they both made it quite clear in their letters when they were merely expressing opinions and when they were actually stating facts derived from the documents; and it was in these facts alone that Lingard was interested. Sherburne was particularly good, as we have seen above, in basing his statements on the documents; he also copied out extracts for Lingard and was much more ready than Cameron to break free from the restrictions of his special commission and introduce 'unconnected gleanings' of his own from the documents.

Having made his transcription of Cameron's notes, Sherburne went on to add his own much more important contributions: 'Thus far Mr Cameron. The following unconnected gleanings valeant quantum valere possunt. Dn. Guerau d'Espes [or de Spes] was amb: at Eliz: court in 1568. In a letter of the 18 Dee: of that year he writes to his master... in a letter of 8th Jan: 1569...'. There follows an extract in Spanish from this dis-

---

46. Lingard, *History*, vol. 6, p. 498.
47. Sherburne to Lingard, Valladolid, Feb. 19th 1823, UCA, Lingard Transcript 1550.
48. Sherburne to Lingard, Feb. 28th 1823, UCA, Lingard Transcript 1551.
49. Cameron to Sherburne, Nov. 26th 1832, UCA, Lingard Transcript 1458 (re-addressed to Lingard).

patch of de Spes of about fifteen lines. So Sherburne was now definitely copying his information, not merely enjoying an 'ocular' inspection of it. He continued:

I have seen Philip's very earnest letters to the Pope begging his holiness would not proceed to extremities with Eliz: written at the time she accuses him of attempting her life. – I have also seen Philip's demand that Allen should be made Cardinal, and have the power to confer on him, Philip, the investiture of the kingdom of England, if the armada succeeded. The whole of Allen's & Parsons' correspondence with Philip is in the neighbourhood, but it has not been possible for me to read it over... I saw Philip's letter in his own hand to the emperor of Germany... I have found the following dispatches.[50]

Then there are descriptions of dispatches of Quadra[51] to his master of 1559 and 1561, and other dispatches of 1564 and 1566, the contents of which can be seen reflected in the first edition of Lingard's volume on Elizabeth.[52] Sherburne concluded with the remark that:

These as well as the other extracts are in the words of the dispatches from which they are copied; some I leave in the original for your own translation. Had my time been less taken up I could have liked to peruse Allen's & Parsons' letters: this has been impossible, & the time for your publication does not admit delays. I am therefore anxious not to lose a post.

One of the problems which Lingard hoped to solve with the help of the Simancas documents was the affair of Dr. Rodrigo López, Queen Elizabeth's Portuguese physician. English historians had always accepted the official statement first published in *A True Report of Sundry Horrible Conspiracies of late time detected to have... taken away the life of the Queenes most excellent Majestie* (1594), that López, in the pay of Philip II, had tried to poison Elizabeth in 1594 – a crime for which he had paid with his life. As late as 1894, A. Dimock, in an article on this subject, could speak of the 'almost inconceivable baseness of Philip and his ministers' who had been able to 'suborn a man who had been handsomely treated, and was not even "one of the faithful", to betray his trust and murder his mistress'.[53]

Lingard, in 1823, had not been convinced by the official account of this episode. He wrote to Cameron in Spain, but Cameron could find nothing about it at Simancas.[54] Similarly, Sherburne 'looked in vain for Philip's counter manifesto concerning López and the events of 1594'.[55] So Lingard, in his *History*, could only describe his suspicion of the old story

---

50. Sherburne to Lingard, Feb. 28th 1823, UCA, Lingard Transcript 1551.
51. Alvaro della Quadra, bishop of Aquila, Spanish ambassador to Elizabeth 1559–63.
52. Lingard, *History*, (1st ed., 1823), vol. 5, p. 628, note 81.
53. A. Dimock, 'The Conspiracy of Dr López', *English Historical Review*, 9 (1894), p. 470. Dimock referred to W.H. Prescott for the 'ethics' of Philip.
54. Sherburne to Lingard, Feb. 28th 1823, UCA, Lingard Transcript 1551.
55. *Ibid.*

and suggest that the value of the evidence against López was not great.[56] When the Simancas documents for this period were published at the end of the nineteenth century, the editor again questioned the type of evidence brought against López and referred to a letter from Simancas which 'goes very far to explain the facts upon which his guilt was mainly presumed' even though it did not actually prove his innocence.[57] Modern historians have been very critical of the old official version of this affair, and 'it has been demonstrated that López was never really proved guilty of the crime for which he was executed'.[58] The state of scholarship on this subject has not been advanced substantially since Lingard's statement of the case in 1823; we are still left with the assertion that there was 'no conclusive evidence' against López.[59]

In the next episode of this Simancas story, the activities of Lingard's agent became more pronounced. Sherburne was now taking extracts to a greater extent than hitherto, though he did not make it clear whether he was copying from originals or from extracts made by the friendly official at Simancas. Both Sherburne and Cameron were wisely obscure about how they obtained their information, and the best that we can do is to allow the agent to tell his own tale. In a letter of the spring of 1825, Sherburne wrote to Lingard:

Probably you have accused me of forgetfulness or neglect in not procuring, long ago, such information as the archives in this neighbourhood afford. The ill health and absence of the commissioner [at Simancas] has rendered it impossible till this day, & what I now offer concerning Eliz: is, perhaps, a repetition. –

Correspondencia de D. Gomez Suárez de Figueroa, Conde de Feria [Philip's ambassador in London, 1558–59] año 1559…

[There follows a long extract in Spanish]

Corresp: del Embas: Dn Álvaro de la Quadra, Obispo de Aquila [Spanish ambassador in London 1559–63] en 1559…

[Followed by an extract in Spanish]

Correspond: de Embajador Dn Guzmán de Silva, desde 17 de Abril 1564…

Año 1566…

Año 1568… [Extracts from the reports of de Silva and later dispatches]

Año 1569…

Año 1575…

…These different extracts were taken in the archives of Simancas after a careful reading of the original documents. Some dates are omitted

56. Lingard, *History* (1st ed., 1823), vol. 5, p. 535: 'How far these confessions [of two witnesses against López], made in the Tower, and probably on the rack, are deserving of credit, may be doubted'.

57. M.A.S. Hume (ed.), *Calendar of State Papers: Simancas IV. Elizabeth 1587–1603* (1899), Introduction, p. liii.

58. Merriman, *op. cit.*, vol. 4, pp. 558–559.

59. J.B. Black, *The Reign of Elizabeth 1558–1603* (Oxford, 1936), p. 355.

because not found in the originals. I see no difficulty in sending the extracts in Spanish, for you can thus have an opportunity of making the translation in your own way. The names are copied exactly, tho' it may require, in some cases, the skill of a Doctor to find out to whom they apply.[60]

The extracts in Spanish in this letter amount to about one thousand, six hundred and fifty words.

The next and final appearance of the Simancas archives in the Lingard correspondence occurred in 1832. In the autumn of that year Cameron wrote to Sherburne, who had returned by now to England, conveying certain information which the latter was to forward to Lingard. Cameron wrote:

> You will have seen by my last scrawl that I was desirous to serve Dr Lingard to the utmost of my power. ...but, as Dn. Tomas no longer presides over the department [at Simancas], I was obliged to request a friend to introduce me to his successor. After a long delay he disappointed me, and would only give me a line of recommendation. I gave the comission [sic] to Dn. John, who went to S. [Simancas] on the caballo of San Francisco... He met..., with a paper of which he took some notes, and which I shall subjoin.[61]

The extracts in Spanish taken from this particular document at Simancas comprise about one thousand, three hundred and eighty words; the document is that which Lingard described in an appendix to his later editions.[62]

Cameron added that 'should anything more come to light, you shall have a copy of it immediately', and the letter was forwarded by Sherburne to Lingard with the following interesting remark of his own on the cover:

> You have Mr Cameron's letter as it came to hand yesterday. He wrote in July, but nothing to the purpose. The work of the Librarian which has been published by the Academy of history, and contains the extracts, will be sent by the first opportunity. When I visited Simancas I recollect Dn. Tomás saying 'that bundel has furnished my materials, pointing to the papers on a particular shelf' [sic]. This was in 1823. When the extracts were made I know not, but about 1812 king Joseph ordered most of the papers to France, and altho' they were retaken at Vittoria, it is no ways improbable that some may be missing.

All through this Simancas correspondence we have been aware of a figure in the background who maintained a studied obscurity. It is that of the friendly official at the Archives, the one who supplied materials for 'oral', then 'ocular' inspection. This was Don Tomás González, canon of Plasencia, who, in 1815, had been chosen by the newly restored Ferdinand VII of Spain[63] to restore order in the Simancas Archives after the confu-

---

60. Sherburne to Lingard, April 16th 1825, UCA, Lingard Transcript 1552.
61. Sherburne to Lingard, Nov. 26th 1832, UCA, Lingard Transcript 1458.
62. Lingard, *History* (4th ed., 1823), vol. 8, p. 458, note X (Appendix).
63. M. Gachard (ed.), *Retraite Et Mort De Charles-Quint au Monastère de Yuste* (Bruxelles, 1854), vol. 1, Preface, p. xi.

sion caused by 'the depredations of the French invader, subsequent neglect, and the partial return of the papers which followed the peace'.[64] He
succeeded in his mission,[65] making, for example, a set of indexes which
were used later by Bergenroth,[66] and also found time to make extracts
from the sixteenth-century documents which he published in the
Memorias de la real academia de la historia (1832). Volume VII of this
work was devoted to Anglo-Spanish relations in the reign of Elizabeth:
Apuntamientos para la historia de Felipe II...y la reina d'Inglaterra.
Lingard made use of this publication in his later editions. Don Tomás left
the Archives in 1832 and this, as we saw above, was a blow to the chances
of research of Lingard's helpers in Spain; his absence through ill-health in
1825 had previously obstructed their research.[67] He died at Madrid in
1833.

When publishing his volume on Elizabeth in 1823, Lingard could claim
that he had 'joined much important information from the archives of
Simancas in Spain, where Philip II deposited all the dispatches which he
received from his ambassadors in the different courts of Christendom',
and that, from this and other sources, he had 'derived much information...
which in a great measure has hitherto been withheld from the knowledge
of the English reader of history'.[68] It is interesting, too, that Lingard
received information from certain materials which are no longer available.
Sherburne, in February 1823, sent an account – with quotations – of a dispatch to Philip II from his ambassador in England in 1561. Quadra,
according to Sherburne, said that 'so current is the rumour that Eliz: lives
with Robert Dudley that in one of the audiences which I had of the Queen
she took upon herself to treat on this matter with me, & showed me la dis-
posición de su camera y alcoba'.[69] An account of this dispatch was given
also by Gonzalez in the *Apuntamientos* (1832),[70] but it has never
appeared, to our knowledge, since, and we are reminded by Conyers Read
that this work 'contains notes and transcripts of dispatches now lost'.[71]

64. William Stirling, *The Cloister Life of the Emperor Charles The Fifth* (2nd ed., 1853),
Preface, p. xx.

65. *Ibid.*

66. G.A. Bergenroth (ed.), *Calendar of... State Papers...at Simancas* (1862), vol. 1,
Introduction, p. ix.

67. See above, p. 120.

68. Lingard to Mawman, May 10th 1823, UCA, Lingard Transcript 470.

69. Sherburne to Lingard, Valladolid, February 28th 1823, UCA, Lingard Transcript 1551.

70. González's account is as follows: 'The rumours that Elizabeth now indulged in the most
intimate intercourse with Leicester became so brim, that in one of the audiences with De
Cuadra she tried to exculpate herself, showing him the arrangement of her private apart-
ments...' (T. González, *Documents From Simancas Relating To The Reign of Elizabeth
(1558–1568)*, first published in Spanish, 1832, edited and translated by Spencer Hall, 1865, p.
70).

71. Conyers Read, *Bibliography of British History – Tudor Period* (2nd ed., Oxford, 1959),
no. 874, p. 73.

This brings us to a mystery which may never be solved. In a letter of 1823, Cameron said that there existed at Simancas the correspondence between Philip II and Elizabeth's 'Camerera Mayor' who 'communicated the secrets of the court to him, & among other things Eliz.s crim: intrigues with the Earl of Leicester (called in the corresp: Lord Robert)'.[72] If this correspondence was ever published 'it will show the virgin queen in her true colours'.[73] But Cameron had obviously not seen this correspondence himself because he was not able to give the name of the maid: 'The Camerera mayor I take to be the first Lady of honor, her name is in the correspondence, but they did not tell it me because they did not know how to pronounce it'.[74]

Sherburne then went to Simancas to try to establish the name of Philip's correspondent, but he, too, failed: 'I could not meet with the name of the Camerera mayor, but am promised it shall be found for next post'.[75] Yet Don Tomás Gonzáles seemed to know about these letters for when Sherburne returned to the task of locating them, he wrote that the commissioner was unfortunately absent from the Archives and was unable to direct Sherburne to the letters 'at the distance to which he is removed'; but 'what I learnt from him, in general, was, that the details placed Eliz: in the lowest place of dissoluteness & infamy'.[76] Lingard was still pursuing these letters, through the medium of his agents, in 1832, but no trace of them could be found and Sherburne concluded that they may have been lost when part of the Simancas Archives was taken to France in the days of Napoleon.[77] Was this correspondence an invention of the fertile imagination of an official at Simancas? Or were these letters lost, leaving only a memory of their contents in the minds of people who had seen them years before? They have not reappeared, as far as we know. Lingard went so far as to mention them in part of a footnote, and suggested that the elusive 'Camerera mayor' was 'probably the marchioness of Winchester'.[78] This might be considered a lapse in Lingard's usually high standard of source criticism and examination; but he mentions them only once, in a footnote, in the manner of an 'aside', and in conjunction with another document on which he is basing his main point.

We cannot leave the story of Lingard and the Simancas Archives without noticing a letter of 1840 in which Lingard replied to Tierney,[79] who

72. Sherburne to Lingard, Valladolid, February 28th 1823, UCA, Lingard Transcript 1551. Here Sherburne is transcribing Cameron's notes for Lingard.

73. Cameron to Sherburne, Valladolid, January 10th 1823, UCA, Lingard Transcript 1457 (forwarded to Lingard). Cf. 'it [the correspondence] exhibits a shocking picture of Elizabeth's lewdness, total want of principle, & readiness to comit [sic] every crime' (Ibid.).

74. Sherburne to Lingard, February 19th 1823, UCA, Lingard Transcript 1550. Here Sherburne is transcribing Cameron's notes for Lingard.

75. Ibid., but here Sherburne is writing on his own part.

76. Sherburne to Lingard, Valladolid, April 16th 1825, UCA, Lingard Transcript 1552.

77. Cameron to Sherburne, November 26th 1832, UCA, Lingard Transcript 1458, (forwarded to Lingard with this note by Sherburne added on the cover).

78. Lingard, History (6th ed., 1883 reprint), vol. 6, pp. 659–660, note 2.

79. M.A. Tierney, who produced an edition of Dodd's Church History of England from 1500 to the year 1688, chiefly with regard to Catholicks, in the years 1839–43.

had asked for a copy of one of the Simancas dispatches.   Lingard answered:

> I have no copy of the dispatch at Simancas or it should be at your serv-
> ice. When Mr Sherburne was president at Valladolid, he went at my
> request to Simancas. But the archivist would not allow him to read or
> write. With the rail between them, the former read the papers which Mr
> Sherburne wanted, and all he could do was to retain in his memory as
> much as he could, & write it down on his return. Hence I hardly made
> any use of his communication, unless, as in this instance, it was con-
> firmed aliunde.[80]

It may be of some significance here that in the same letter, Lingard, now approaching seventy years of age, goes on to make the comment: 'But my memory grows very treacherous with respect to papers... one of them [his eyes], the right is evidently growing more and more clouded every day, & the best I can do is to take care of the other.'[81] We have other instances in the letters of loss of memory,[82] and of Lingard – troubled with a painful illness – trying to remember where he had obtained certain information;[83] for he did not keep all the materials out of which he built his history.[84] At any rate, from a knowledge of the actual letters that he received from Spain, it seems that he did not do complete justice to his own source in this letter written at a much later period of his life. We know that Sherburne did in fact copy extracts from the Spanish materials,[85] though in the earli-er part of the story Cameron had been allowed only 'oral' and then 'ocu-lar' inspection of them and had to rely on memory.[86] We must remember that the historiographical significance of the episode was not so apparent to Lingard as it is to us, and that he did not write his letters for the benefit of future students of the history of historiography. Certainly Lingard would not have had the dispatch for which Tierney asked, since his mate-rials were in the form of paraphrases or extracts. It may be that, while informing Tierney that he did not have what the former required, Lingard repeated a statement of the case which he had made years before, during the early part of the Simancas story, when it had been correct,[87] and inad-vertently misrepresented the case for the later part of the story.

80. Lingard to Tierney, March 11th 1840, UCA, Farm Street Transcripts, Lingard Transcript 819. Lingard usually used his Simancas references with some other authority, but exceptions are seen in the *History* (1883 reprint), vol. 6, p. 189, note, p. 498, note 1, p. 660, note 2.

81. *Ibid.*

82. Lingard to Tate, May 30th 1844, UCA, Lingard Transcript 679: 'My memory is so treacherous that I may be mistaken...'

83. Lingard to Walker, October 29th 1848, UCA, Lingard Transcript 1293.

84. Lingard to Tierney, May 27th 1848, UCA, Farm Street Transcripts, Lingard Transcript 847.

85. See above, pp. 117, 119.

86. See above, pp. 110, 113, 114..

87. 'Perhaps I should observe to you that in quoting the records at Simancas, I do not men-tion the No. or the page &e. as in quoting other documents. This arises from the jealousy of

Throughout this description of Lingard's contact with the Simancas Archives we have been aware of the unsatisfactory nature of the medium by which he gained his information. The amateurish activities of Lingard's enthusiastic but unskilled helpers were hindered by the rigid rules and regulations which governed entry to these Archives. Cameron and Sherburne worked spasmodically and under great difficulties; the most that could be expected from them would be paraphrases of documents with some hasty and not infallible extracts in Spanish. Lingard was very conscious of all this and used the information from Spain very carefully.[88] Yet the two agents managed to convey the meaning of the documents correctly, as may be seen if we compare their work with the later published materials.

We would say now, of course, that the historian must see the documents for himself. But it would be unhistorical to use our modern standards of scholarship as criteria for work in Lingard's day, though he, indeed, pointed the way to future trends in many aspects of his craft. This was not the age of the professional historian and Lingard could not afford the time or the money for a journey to Spain. Moreover, the Archives had not been opened officially, so that he would probably not have been able to see the documents in any case.[89] Lingard was the first Englishman to have attempted to use material from the Simancas Archives in the interests of English history. This act of initiative, apart from the new information gained, is worth recording. He anticipated later historiographical developments by using a source which was able to throw new light at various points on the history of England; and his introduction of foreign source material, like that of the Simancas Archives, into his *History*, played an important part in the production of the 'first modern narrative of the two critical centuries of English history'.[90]

the Spaniards, or rather from the standing orders of the place. The officers will not allow my friend to take any notes. He can only read there [earlier, the papers had been read to him], and write down what he remembers when he leaves.' (Lingard to Mawman, spring 1823, UCA, Lingard Transcript 469).

88. Compare the information in a letter from Sherburne to Lingard, November 26th 1832, UCA, Lingard Transcript 1448, with Lingard's published account of the documents in *History* (4th ed., 1837–38, vol. 8, note x, p. 458, appendix), and with the Simancas documents published in M.A.S. Home (ed.), *Calendar of State Papers: Simancas IV. Elizabeth 1587–1603* (1899), pp. 101–104.

89. Lingard did manage to go to Rome where, with the support of certain English bishops and a cardinal, he gained entry to the Vatican Archives; but this is another story.

90. G.P. Gooch, *History and Historians in the Nineteenth Century* (2nd ed., 1952), p. 273.

7

EVERY PICTURE TELLS A CATHOLIC STORY: LINGARD'S *HISTORY OF ENGLAND* ILLUSTRATED AND THE TRANSITION IN CATHOLIC HISTORIOGRAPHY

ROSEMARY MITCHELL

John Lingard's *History of England*, first published between 1819 and 1830, was a highly significant and pioneering work in the field of British historiography. This point is ably made by Edwin Jones in his recently published work *The English Nation: The Great Myth* (1998), where he shows how Lingard's critical and source-based approach to history undermined the traditional Protestant interpretation of the English past. This chapter will take a rather different slant on the *History* by examining the illustrated edition[1] published in 1854–55 by the Catholic publisher Charles Dolman and largely illustrated by Catholic artists. It will not only explore Lingard's textual attack on the dominant Protestant narrative of English history, but will also examine how Dolman's edition of the *History*, through its images, highlighted this conflict between the accepted version of the English past and an erudite Catholic reinterpretation of it. Dolman's propagandistic repackaging of Lingard's text would clearly have disturbed its author. But the difference between the publisher and the historian was one of means rather than ends: Dolman was explicit where Lingard was discreet, but both reflected a mid-century transition in English Catholic historiography. This change was the result of evolutions within the English Catholic Church itself and within the framework of Victorian Catholic historiography: the illustrated 1854–55 edition can be seen to represent a transition from the conciliatory and rationalist approach of the late eighteenth-century Cisalpine historians – of whom Lingard was, in a sense, the last representative – and the more confident approach of late nineteenth-century and early twentieth-century Catholic historians.

The Religious and Historiographical Background

An initial examination of the early nineteenth-century background to the Dolman illustrated edition of the *History* will take in both the religious and historiographical contexts in which the author and his work appeared. In the context of this volume, there is no need to dwell on the difficulties confronting the Catholic writer of a national history in early nineteenth-century Britain. In the dominant narrative of the national past, Protestantism had been enshrined since at least the seventeenth century as an important element in the formation and expression of the English

---

1. The 1854–55 edition appeared in two formats: a ten-volume cloth-bound version and a five-volume leather-bound one. References here are all to the ten-volume version.

national identity.[2]   A traditional Protestant calendar had been developed
which celebrated events such as the defeat of the Spanish Armada and the
failure of the Gunpowder Plot.   It effectively distinguished the English
nation from most of its continental neighbours, with their Catholic calendar of feasts and festivals[3].   History textbooks informed the English people of the iniquities of the Church of Rome and its adherents, detailing (for
instance) the violent temper and bloody deeds of Queen Mary I.[4]   With
Protestant texts went Protestant iconography: for all their contempt for
religious imagery, English Protestants appreciated the impact of the visual.   Bishop Ullathorne recalled that schoolboys habitually stuck pins
through the eyes of Queen Mary in the illustrations of their history books.[5]

Nevertheless, there were some signs of change in nineteenth-century
Britain.   The Romantic movement led to a more sympathetic perception of
the medieval Catholic Church, and both ecclesiastical ruins and nostalgic
reconstructions of medieval society featured in Romantic imagery.   Such
perceptions – sentimental though they often were – could fuel historical
reinterpretation by encouraging the study of architectural remains and
documentary sources which eighteenth-century philosophical historians
had often considered too barbaric and recondite to repay attention.   These
changes in the intellectual climate were made possible at least partly by a
slackening of the political prejudices against Catholics.   With Catholic
Emancipation in 1829, much of the well-worn political debate surrounding the issue of the double allegiance of Catholics to the British
Government and the Pope was now rendered obsolete.   However, these
changes should not be exaggerated: Romantic sympathy for the medieval
Catholic Church did not always lead to a tolerant attitude to the modern
Catholic Church.[6]   The anti-Catholic demonstrations of the nineteenth
century were firmly rooted in an atmosphere of popular suspicion, reinforced by anti-papist pronouncements of such figures as Lord John Russell

---

2.   While David Loades identifies the reign of Mary I as the crucial moment when
Protestantism and the national identity became linked, Anthony Fletcher suggests that the origins of Protestant nationalism can be found in the opposition of the country gentry to Charles
I's Arminian policies.   D. Loades, 'The Origins of English Protestant Nationalism' and A.
Fletcher, 'The First Century of English Protestantism and the Growth of National Identity',
both in S. Mews (ed.), *Religion and National Identity* (Oxford, 1982), pp. 297–307 and
309–18.   Linda Colley in *Britons: Forging the Nation 1707–1837* (1992; this ed., London,
1994), pp. 11–54, identifies Protestantism as the fundamental force in the creation of the eighteenth-century British identity.

3.   D. Cressy, *Bonfires and Bells: National Memory and the Protestant Calendar in
Elizabethan and Stuart England* (London, 1989).

4.   For instance, see E. Penrose ('Mrs. Markham'), *A History of England* (1832; London,
1846 ed.), pp. 274, 277.

5.   L. Madigan (ed.), *The Devil is a Jackass* (Leominster and Stratton on the Fosse, Bath,
1995), p. 13.

6.   This was evidenced in Robert Southey's *The Book of the Church* (1824), a Romantic and
High Church polemic in defence of the Church of England apparently published as a response
to Lingard's *History of England*: while admiring the social structure of late medieval England
and advocating the establishment of Anglican sisterhoods, Southey supported the existing State

and Charles Kingsley.[7]   For most Protestants, national identity and Protestantism, Church and King, still remained firmly linked.

While Protestant reactions to the Catholic Church were now ambiguous, the Church itself was experiencing a period of revival and apparent expansion. Historians have traditionally identified this revival as a 'Second Spring', either boosted by the release of Catholics from civil and religious disabilities, or else imposed by a triumph of the Ultramontane party over Old Catholics. Reinterpretations of the eighteenth-century English Catholic community and of the impact of Ultramontanism and an admittedly small body of Oxford converts have been made by such historians as John Bossy and Mary Heimann.[8] As a result, the Second Spring has been seen as a matter of continuity as well as change, a gradual evolution from a largely robust and vital eighteenth-century Church: it has been identified less as a matter of actual conversion and growth, and more as a matter of bringing nominal Catholics into active observance and creating a distinctly Catholic life-style, based not on entirely new 'Roman' beliefs and devotions, but ones already accepted in the English Catholic tradition. This balance of continuity and change – which will be described here by the word transition – is reflected in the 1854–55 edition of *The History of England*, which can now be pictured within the context of a more complex and variegated pattern of gradual Catholic revival. Historian, publisher and illustrators must all be examined against this background, before an analysis of the text and images of the 1854–55 edition.

Lingard: A Historian in Transition

The first edition of Lingard's *History* appeared between 1819 and 1830; it was revised and republished several times before Lingard's death in 1851. Given this timeframe, it is natural to attribute many of the alterations of his text and shifts of emphasis in his arguments to the passage of events. Initially very restrained in his comments on religious issues in the 1820s – when successive Emancipation Bills seemed on the point of becoming law – Lingard later felt less anxious about the introduction of material 'respecting the penal laws which I had withheld in the former [editions]'.[9] It is, however, unlikely that his historical opinions really changed radically in the course of writing and revising the *History*. As he once commented, 'whatever I had said or purposely omitted has been through a motive of serving religion'.[10] Lingard could be persuasive or

and Church establishment, opposing Catholic emancipation. See S. Gilley, 'Nationality and Liberty, Protestant and Catholic: Robert Southey's Book of the Church' in S. Mews (ed.), *Religion and National Identity* (Oxford, 1982), pp. 409–432.

7. See K.L. Morris, 'John Bull and the Scarlet Woman: Charles Kingsley and Anti-Catholicism in Victorian Literature', *RH*, vol. 23, no. 2, pp. 190–218.

8. J. Bossy, *The English Catholic Community 1570–1850* (London, 1975), pp. 295–322; M. Heimann, *Catholic Devotion in Victorian England* (Oxford, 1995).

9. Haile and Bonney, p. 347.

10. *Ibid.*, p. 167.

polemical according to the demands of political necessity. It is the presence of both defensive and offensive approaches, which signals his status
as a transitional figure, both as a Catholic and a historian.

Of course, much of Lingard's intellectual and religious outlook identifies him as an Old Catholic. He was a late associate of the Cisalpine
group, which included such figures as Joseph Berington, Charles Butler,
and John Kirk. Rationalist theologians and philosophical historians, products of the Enlightenment, they advocated proto-democratic reforms in the
Church which would limit papal authority in non-essentials by local customs and wishes. They promoted ecumenical and conciliatory views,
believing that Catholics should integrate themselves into English society,
placing less emphasis on peculiarly Catholic customs and institutions. In
politics, they presented themselves as sincere supporters of the English
constitution, loyal subjects and advocates of liberty: they believed that
Catholics should co-operate with the State and should offer concessions in
order to gain the vote. In a Whiggish manner, they emphasised the sepa-
rateness of politics and religion, of the State and the Churches.[11]

Lingard's own views were clearly strongly influenced by these opinions. He, too, preferred to play down the expression of Catholic distinc-
tiveness, feeling that discretion was the better part of valour: he held, for
instance, that the 1850 restoration of English bishoprics should have been
made with less pomp and circumstance.[12] He had little sympathy for the
Ultramontanes; he was unimpressed by the new 'Romish' practices of
clergy such as Nicholas Wiseman; he was suspicious of the conversions of
J.H. Newman and W.G. Ward.[13] His personal relations with Protestants,
especially Nonconformists, were warm, and in an ecumenical spirit, in
1841 he published a catechism designed to be used by Protestants as well
as Catholics.[14] A supporter of religious emancipation and secular state
education, Lingard believed that the separation of religious from political
issues would free Catholics from the Protestant accusation of an unpatri-
otic double allegiance. He consistently argued that it was possible to be
Catholic and English, loyal to the Church and to the Crown.
Nevertheless, however loyal English Catholics pronounced themselves to
be, the early nineteenth-century Protestant interpretation of history always
appeared to subvert their claims. In response to this problem, Cisalpine
historians had developed an interpretation of English history, which portrayed loyal English Catholics resisting the Ultramontane demands of a
self-seeking papacy and the religious orders. This led them down antiquarian paths rarely frequented by the eighteenth-century historian, for
their endeavours rested on the Continental monastic tradition of source-
based research, pioneered by the Maurists and Bollandists.[15] But it gave

11. Chinnici, pp. 39–106.
12. Haile and Bonney, pp. 360–61.
13. *Ibid.*, pp. 304–10, 321–26.
14. *Ibid.*, pp. 283–85.
15. For the Maurists and Bollandists, see D. Knowles, *Great Historical Enterprises and Problems in Monastic History* (Edinburgh, London, etc., 1963), pp. 3–62. For Lingard's

them the means to revise the dominant national narrative of Protestant historians, which was rarely based on any original research. Berington and Butler – the pioneers of this historiography of Catholic nationalism – were friends to, and models for, the younger Lingard: many of their views resurface in his *History*, and he adopted their approach to archival research.

The Cisalpinist influence on Lingard can be seen in his decision, in the *History*, to adopt a style of argument which appeared to be more conciliatory than confrontational. He stressed his impartial examination of original sources, rather than indulging in polemical rhetoric, resting his case on the facts which he had gathered and avoiding drawing out the full implications. So restrained was the narrative of the *History* that it was initially published by a Protestant publisher, Joseph Mawman, and was probably aimed more at scholars than the general public.

But despite Lingard's restraint – indeed, almost because of it – his *History* did not escape criticism from reviewers. One of his critics, H.J. Todd, accused the historian of partial statements and evasions of the truth, 'artfully clothed with the captivating exterior of much excellent writing and great apparent candour'.[16] With much justification, Lingard defended his text from such criticism by assertions of his strict truth to his authorities. Nevertheless, Lingard's opponents were not entirely mistaken in their criticisms – Lingard's facts, however true and however impartially conveyed, were undoubtedly intended to overturn the traditional Protestant interpretation of the national past. While the Cisalpinist historians attempted to write Catholics into the national narrative on the grounds of their patriotism, Lingard seems to have been more aware that this narrative – in which Protestantism and national progress were portrayed as providentially linked – was not one to which he could merely attach addenda: it needed to be systematically dismantled. To identify Lingard too fully with the Cisalpines, as I think J.P. Chinnici has done, limits understanding of the more aggressive aspect of his Catholicism. Eamon Duffy rightly highlights the difference between Berington's dismissive attitude to the papacy, particularly in the middle ages, and Lingard's more enthusiastic one.[17] Influenced by Romantic historiography, there was a rampantly Catholic side to Lingard's character, which gave him no wish to avoid controversies with Protestants: indeed, his role

acquaintance with their work, see Chinnici, pp. 107–13 and P. Phillips, 'John Lingard and *The Anglo-Saxon Church*', *RH*, vol. 23 (1996), pp. 180–181. Phillips speculates convincingly on the possibility that Lingard became familiar with the works of Mabillon and the Bollandists as early as the 1790s during his education at Douai.

16. H.J. Todd, *A Reply to Dr Lingard's Vindication of his* History of England *as far as respects Archbishop Cranmer* (London, 1827), p. 134. Henry Todd was a fast-stream Anglican clergyman, chaplain in turn to several earls, sometime Keeper of Manuscripts at Lambeth Palace, and a royal chaplain in ordinary. From 1820, he was rector of the valuable Yorkshire parish of Settringham.

17. E. Duffy, 'Ecclesiastical Democracy Detected, III: 1796–1800', *RH*, vol. 13 (1975), p. 143.

in ushering in a new age of religious controversy in early nineteenth-century England has been emphasised by both Leo Gooch and Sheridan Gilley.[18]

In the first two decades of the nineteenth century, Lingard was a leading polemicist for his Church. Energetic debates with the Whig atheist and historian John Allen and H.J. Todd in the 1820s, over the *History*'s treatment of such issues as the character of Cranmer and the St. Bartholomew's Day's Massacre, showed that Lingard did not lose his controversial edge as he grew older. Revisions of later editions of the *History*, too, made its text openly more pro-Catholic. However, the full controversial potential of the apparently restrained text of the first edition of the *History* was revealed – not so much by Lingard's subsequent revisions – as by the publication of William Cobbett's *History of the Protestant Reformation in England and Ireland* (1824–26), which was based on facts derived from Lingard's *History*.[19] The anti-Protestant extremism of this work showed how controversial the artfully-presented content of Lingard's *History* could be.

Lingard, Dolman and the Illustrators

Lingard's careful balance between the confrontational and the conciliatory was destabilised in the 1854–55 edition of the *History* by the attitude of the Catholic publisher, Charles Dolman. More than twenty years Lingard's junior, Dolman had devoted his early career to the publication of Catholic periodicals. From 1838 to 1844 he was publisher of the *Catholic Magazine*, which was intended to promote harmonious relations between Catholics and Protestants and to explain Catholicism to a wider audience. Simultaneously, however, he was the publisher and proprietor of the less apologetic *Dublin Review*, the voice of a more militant Catholicism. In 1845, he founded his own periodical, *Dolman's Magazine*, a moderate publication, which – unlike the *Dublin Review* – avoided the controversial issues of Irish politics. A colourful figure in the Catholic Revival, with links to the Ultamontane party, Dolman also turned his popularising skills to use outside the sphere of the periodical: he was the publisher for several works by A.W.N. Pugin, whose passionate identification of Gothic architecture with an idealised vision of the medieval Catholic Church made no concessions to Protestant sensibilities. In 1850, Dolman embarked on the high-profile publication of *de luxe* editions of Catholic classics, such as Lingard's *History*.[20] For a small publisher in the precarious Victorian publishing world, this was an extravagant gesture.

18. L. Gooch, 'Lingard v. Barrington, *et al.*: Ecclesiastical Politics in Durham, 1805–1829', above, pp. 35–64; S. Gilley, 'John Lingard and the Catholic Revival', in D. Baker (ed.), *Renaissance and Renewal in Christian History* (Oxford, 1977), pp. 313–327.

19. W. Sambrook, *William Cobbett* (London, 1973), p. 136.

20. R.A. Mitchell, 'Charles Dolman', in H.C.G. Matthew and B. Harrison (eds.), *The New Dictionary of National Biography* (forthcoming, Oxford, 2004).

No great admirer of Catholic publishers, Lingard had a high opinion of Dolman as 'the only one among us that a gentleman can trade with'.[21] However, the relationship between author and publisher was subject to strain almost from its beginning. Dolman was the publisher for Lingard's 1841 *Catechetical Instructions*: as his correspondence with Mrs. Thomas Lomax shows, he was less than delighted when Dolman published a second edition of this work without offering him the chance to revise it, pricing it above the level Lingard considered suitable.[22] By the 1840s, Lingard was something of an anachronism in the Catholic world, and Dolman's more propagandist and entrepreneurial style alarmed him. In 1848, he wrote to Edward Price:

> I shall disappoint Mr Dolman. He is too fond of puffing... I think such things disadvantageous in the long run. People are too discerning now not to see the object − , and on that account think contemptuously of the work.[23]

The historian's attitude to his publisher − a mixture of respect and anxiety − suggest more subtle differences between the two than the labels of Old Catholic and Ultramontane can really explain: neither belonged wholly to either party. But it cannot be denied that Dolman was the representative of a more confident and propagandist phase of the Catholic Revival than Lingard ever inhabited. In the 'puffing' Advertisement for his edition of the *History*, Dolman also commented on Lingard's restrained style, which he interpreted very perceptively:

> Dr Lingard has done [his account of the Reformation] with exquisite tact. The superficial reader may think him cold when narrating the sufferings of Catholics during the long continuance of the penal laws; the acute thinker will rise from the perusal of Dr Lingard's pages with a much stronger abhorrence... of that wasting series of persecutions, than if the author had coloured his narrative with even the most indignant and burning eloquence. Dr Lingard states the fact precisely as it occurred: he leaves the inference to the reader's own reflections. Few would ever suspect him of being a Catholic.[24]

These comments suggest that Lingard's intention was far closer to Dolman's than the historian would like to admit: the difference was more of style than substance. This was aptly illustrated in the tussle over a new preface for the *History*: the ageing and weary Lingard was clearly unwilling to write one, no doubt believing that the book would speak for itself, but Dolman eventually persuaded him to produce one which the historian privately described as 'boastful and rather criminatory of others'.[25] It was clearly not challenging other historians' views, so much as publicising it,

21. Haile and Bonney, p. 327.
22. *Lingard-Lomax Letters*, p. 105.
23. Haile and Bonney, p. 348.
24. Advertisement in [Anon.], *A True Account... of the Gunpowder Plot* (London, 1851).
25. *Lingard-Lomax Letters*, p. 154.

which distressed Lingard here: less than a year previously, in 1849, he had been deliberately inserting material into his revision of the *History* to counter T.B. Macaulay's unflattering portrait of James II. But – characteristically – he had attempted to do it 'as if I knew nothing about Macaulay, when I wrote it'.[26]

While Lingard was alive, he could at least attempt to restrain his publisher. After the historian's death, when Dolman selected the illustrations for the edition of 1854–55 – reprinted from the earlier revised edition of 1851 referred to in the quotations above – he was free to express his own more militant brand of Catholicism. The illustrations used by Dolman are closely related to Lingard's themes and arguments, but they highlight the historian's defence of Catholicism and attacks on Protestant prejudices in a decidedly less subtle way than the text of the *History*.

In the task of exposing the polemical content of Lingard's text, Dolman was seemingly aided by like-minded Catholics, as determined as he to break the dominance of a Protestant historical iconography. He used the services of three artists – one a fellow Catholic, one a possible Catholic, and one not yet identified.[27] The first and more prolific illustrator was James Doyle, brother of the better-known Richard Doyle, with whom Lingard had had a tenuous link through his friend, Rev John Walker.[28] The eldest son in a devout Catholic family, James Doyle early showed an interest in history and genealogy. After painting and exhibiting a number of literary and historical genre paintings, in the 1840s he began work on a book entitled *A Chronicle of England, BC 55–AD 1485*, which he both wrote and illustrated.[29] Although it was not published until 1864, this work clearly influenced the pro-Catholic iconography of Dolman's edition of Lingard's *History of England*. The other main influence was the first illustrated edition of the *History* – the 1837–39 edition. It included a small number of pro-Catholic images which later appeared in the Dolman edition,[30] but did not present a systematic scheme of Catholic historical iconography. Doyle's *Chronicle* offered a range of new subjects to reme-

26. *Ibid.*, p. 148.

27. The information concerning the illustrators is taken from the advertisement in *A True Account... of the Gunpowder Plot*, but the Christian name of Doyle is not mentioned. However, the Doyle concerned is almost certainly James. The signature on the relevant illustrations in Lingard's *History* is closest to that of James; and the style of illustration is almost identical with that of illustrations known to be his in *The Lover's Stratagem* (1849) and his own *A Chronicle of England, BC 55–AD 1485* (1864).

28. *Lingard-Lomax Letters*, pp. 160–61. This connection links Lingard to a younger world of rather more rampant Catholics: the historian sent an early draft of his preface for Dolman's edition to Walker, commenting to Mrs. Lomax, 'He will flare up, I am sure. It is too meek for him: without vigour and pretension: he will criticize it unmercifully. So much the better: for he will suggest some new & perhaps useful idea' (p. 150).

29. For Doyle's life and career, see R.A. Mitchell, 'James Edmund Warren Doyle', *The New DNB*.

30. These included, for instance, 'The Marriage of Philip and Mary' (frontispiece to volume vii). The subject would naturally have appealed to Lingard, who was born in Winchester, where the marriage took place.

dy this deficiency: while the first illustrated edition of Lingard's *History* had illustrated the traditional scene from King John's reign of the King signing the Magna Carta, both the *Chronicle* and Dolman's edition (Fig. 1) carried very similar illustrations of the earlier Oath at Edmondsbury – a scene which put Catholic clergy into the equation of English constitutionalism.[31]

Doyle's style in both illustrations shows his attraction to the so-called 'German manner' of line-drawing. This style was extremely popular in the 1840s and 1850s, when the art of the German Catholic Revival school, the Nazarenes, and their successors, was enjoying some influence in English history painting circles, particularly in the monumental works prepared for the Westminster Hall competition.[32] For Doyle and other Catholics of his generation, the adoption of this distinctive 'German' style of illustration would have had a spiritual significance. Doyle's style thus linked him with Dolman, as one of a generation committed to a more Romantic and explicit expression of their Catholic faith.

One of the other two illustrators was Howard Dudley, born in London, the son of an Irishman from Tipperary. At an early age, he moved to Sussex: he determined at the age of fourteen to illustrate works of local history and antiquities, and setting up a printing press of his own, he published several antiquarian works.[33] Dudley's parents were Quakers, a denominational allegiance which he may well have shared:[34] as a member of another Nonconformist body, he would have understood the Catholic sense of exclusion from many aspects of national life. His style suggests that he was very much a hack draughtsman and engraver, with a tendency towards melodrama and the picturesque.

The History of England *Illustrated*

The text and illustrations of the 1854–55 edition of Lingard's *History of England* will now be explored. This examination will consider both the conciliatory and controversialist approaches adopted by the author, and reveal how the illustrations selected enhanced and emphasised the points made by the text. Like his Cisalpinist mentors, Lingard sought to write Catholics into the national narrative, portraying them as loyal subjects and active supporters of the English constitution, laws, liberties, and civilisation. This approach is seen in Lingard's exploitation of the universal applause for Alfred. He reminded his audience that this ideal king, popularly seen as one of the founders of English constitutional government,

31. J.E. Doyle, *A Chronicle of England, BC 55–AD 1485* (London, 1864), 222; J. Lingard, *The History of England* (London, 1854–55), vol. 2, frontispiece.

32. W. Vaughan, *German Romanticism and English Art* (New Haven, Conn., and London, 1979)

33. R. Engen, *A Dictionary of Victorian Wood-Engravers* (Cambridge and Teaneck, NJ, 1985), p. 77.

34. J. Glover, 'Juvenile Researches, or the Diligent Dudleys', in *Sussex County Magazine*, vol. 22 (1948), p. 50.

was also a devout Catholic 'deeply impressed with religious sentiments, which influenced him throughout life'.[35] His loyalty to the Church and selfless service of the English people were thus linked, a point stressed in Dolman's accompanying illustration of 'The Baptism of Gothrun' (Fig. 2). Most nineteenth-century history book and textbook illustrations of Alfred showed him burning the cakes, as a harpist in the camp of Guthram, as the patron of learning and law, or engaged in the defence of England against the Vikings.[36] Here he was portrayed as the sponsor of Guthram as the vanquished Viking is baptised into the Catholic Church.[37] The clerics are standing, while the most of the laity (probably Guthram's companions) kneel; Alfred and the officiating cleric stand facing each other on a raised dias, as the king gently bows, introducing his convert and godson. Alfred's conquest over the Danish invaders is seen as a spiritual as well as a military victory. The scene suggests sacred and secular powers acting in harmony, with a faint emphasis on the deep respect of the temporal powers for the Catholic Church.

If good kings are seen as loyal Catholics, good Catholics – especially the clergy – are seen as loyal supporters of the English constitution. When the king lacked the virtues of Alfred, Lingard argued, the clergy intervened to protect justice and law. Lingard described the burial of the ruthless William the Conqueror at Caen: the funeral was interrupted by an aggrieved subject, Asceline Fitz-Arthur, who had long sought justice from the king. It was the clergy, Lingard indicated, who promised him repayment for the land the king had stolen from him. The accompanying illustration (Fig. 3) reinforced the point: Asceline points dramatically at the ground, to indicate what has been taken from him, while a portly prelate prepares to respond to him. In the background, a monk holds a cross symbolically above the corpse of the king and the scene raging round it.[38]

Other Catholic clergy, too, were shown supporting the law: Thomas Becket, for instance, was portrayed by Lingard – not as so much as the defender of clerical privileges against the secular power – but as the advocate of ancient constitutional liberties against the novel encroachments of the Norman kings.[39] Even unpromising and unappealing Cardinals such as Henry Beaufort and Thomas Wolsey were seen as pillars of the state. Despite his ostentation and wealth, Wolsey was described as generous with money, interested in the reform of the Church and of the legal system for the benefit of the poor, as well as a patron of learning and the universities.[40] Moreover, Lingard argued, he was the only man capable of dealing with Henry VIII.[41] An illustration of Wolsey's arrival at the Abbey of

35. Lingard, *History* (1854–55), vol. 1, p. 102.
36. See R. Strong, *And When Did You Last See Your Father? The Victorian Painter and British History* (London, 1978), pp. 114–16, for examples.
37. Lingard, *History* (1854–54), vol. 1, facing p. 108.
38. *Ibid.*, vol. 1, p. 255 and facing.
39. *Ibid.*, vol. 2, pp. 68–69.
40. *Ibid.*, vol. 4, pp. 191–194.
41. *Ibid.*, vol. 4, p. 264.

Leicester (Fig. 4), on the point of death, reinforces this image of a public hero – Benjamin West's extremely popular painting, *The Death of Wolfe* – itself based on descents from the Cross – springs to mind momentarily, as the Cardinal sinks amid a crowd of monks and crucifixes, which remind the viewer that this hero belongs to the Catholic Church. The image is decidedly ambiguous: it draws on a tradition of similar illustrations of Wolsey's last moments, both in textbooks and history books, and therefore does not seem an unusual subject.[42]   But these presentations – often inspired by the penitent Wolsey of Shakespeare's *Henry VIII* – preached predominantly the message of humility through the mighty fallen. The image in Dolman's edition, however, depicting the dramatic arrival, rather than the deathbed itself, allowed the illustrator to make a less apologetic point about Wolsey as a national and a Catholic hero.[43]

After the mid-sixteenth century, Catholic appearances as the supporters and protectors of English liberties were rare, and the other central strand of Lingard's conciliatory argument was now introduced. This dealt with the problem of papal supremacy: Lingard argued that this authority, exercised by the Popes with wise moderation, was beneficial for the English, and did not create a conflict of loyalties with an Englishman's allegiance to his king and country. In his narrative of the Middle Ages, therefore, Lingard departed from the Cisalpine interpretation of history to attempt to establish a favourable picture of the papal supremacy as an external spiritual power upholding justice and liberty. For instance, in narrating the dispute between the Pope and King John over the appointment of Langton as Archbishop of Canterbury, Lingard emphasised Pope Innocent's moderation: before issuing an edict of excommunication, Innocent 'proceeded with deliberation and allowed his disobedient son time to repent'.[44] Lingard ably argued that John's submission to the Pope – usually viewed as derogatory to English national sovereignty – was not disgraceful, as vassalage was common in that age. Indeed, the barons consented to it because

> it offered a protector, to whom, as superior lord, they might appeal from the despotic government of [John][45]

So much for this famous affront to English independence: as Edwin Jones notes, Lingard managed to place medieval English history within a much-needed European framework, liberating it from the anachronistic national-

---

42. See, for instance, plate 93 in R. Bowyer, *A Series of One Hundred and Ninety-One Engravings (in the Line Manner) by the First Artists in the Country Illustrative of the 'History of England'* (London, 1812). These engravings were taken from a series of paintings which formed a gallery of images illustrating David Hume's *History of England* (1754–62).

43. Lingard, *History* (1854–55), vol. 4, facing p. 264. The composition is essentially the same as that of the illustration of this subject in volume 6 of the 1837–39 edition of Lingard's *History*: the illustrator of that edition, however, seems to have been more interested in the fan vaulting of the abbey porch than the scene unfolding beneath it.

44. *Ibid.*, vol. 2, p. 161.

45. *Ibid.*, vol. 2, p. 166.

ist isolation into which earlier Protestant historians had taken it.[46]   The absence of the traditional anti-Catholic illustration of John submitting to Pandolph is not, in this context, surprising.

Later constitutional crises offered more of a challenge to the historian: the Popes supported Henry III in his conflict with Simon de Montfort, which might have appeared, to the nineteenth-century reader, to put them on the opposite side from constitutional liberty.   But Lingard portrayed Clement IV and his envoy, Ottoboni, as the voices of moderation and clemency in the midst of political turmoil.[47]   Papal peace-making was, in fact, a subject on which Lingard was frequently eloquent.   He protested:

> Europe would have been plunged in perpetual wars had not pope after pope laboured incessantly for the preservation, or restoration of peace...[48]

The good effects (in the main) of papal intervention were but one side of Lingard's argument concerning the supremacy: the other was the proof of Catholic loyalty.   Lingard was determined to show that Catholic subjects in the past denied any temporal supremacy to the Pope, and were true English patriots, loyal to the crown and/or constitution.   When, during the reign of Edward III, the Pope laid claim to the first fruits of benefices and to temporal authority over England, Lingard showed the English people firmly replying that they would only accept the spiritual authority of the Pope – a principle which, he asserted, modern Catholics also maintained.[49] Under Protestant governments, Lingard argued, Catholics were always loyal.   He dwelt on the unshakeable allegiance of Edmund Campion, an English missionary priest arrested by the authorities.   When asked if he admitted Elizabeth I's title to the throne, Campion replied that he took her 'not only for queen, but his lawful queen'.   Campion and two others were later executed, 'praying with their last breath for the queen as their legitimate sovereign'.[50]   The loyalty of Catholics was again emphasised by the historian in the case of the Penderells, who helped the young Charles II to escape after the Battle of Worcester.   According to Lingard, one of their sisters commented to the suspicious king, 'I would die sooner than betray you', and their mother visited Charles and blessed 'God that he had chosen her sons to preserve... the life of their sovereign'.[51]   Dolman enthusiastically completed Lingard's apotheosis of this ideal loyalist Catholic family by adding an illustration (Fig. 5) of Charles in Spring Coppice, near White Ladies, on the day after the Battle (two days before he hid in the oak-tree at Boscobel, a mile away).   No less than three Penderells attend the rather sullen prince: one stands before him, clutching a musket and

46. E. Jones, (Stroud, 1998), especially pp. 184–94.
47. Lingard, *History* (1854–55), vol. 2, p. 234.
48. *Ibid.*, vol. 3, pp. 75–76.
49. *Ibid.*, vol. 3, p. 132.
50. *Ibid.*, vol. 6, pp. 167–68.
51. *Ibid.*, vol. 8, p. 157.

with his head respectfully uncovered, occupying the visual (and moral) centre of the picture; another keeps watch in the distance; and a third approaches with refreshments for their royal guest.[52]

But Lingard was not afraid to be controversial in the *History*, particularly in this last revision of his most important work. Even his claims to have carefully researched his narrative – true though they are – repay closer attention. Edwin Jones has shown that Lingard's brilliantly pioneering use of the practically inaccessible Simancas archives – years before G.A. Bergenroth made the supposed first British examination of them – was directed by specific, overtly Catholic objectives, such as clearing the character of Philip II of Spain from several charges, including that of plotting the assassination of Elizabeth I.[53] Much of this controversialist approach is immediately obvious in the text: he reinterpreted Catholic characters favourably, and Protestant ones unfavourably, in an attempt to break the traditional Protestant interpretation of English history.

Lingard's most radical reinterpretations, inevitably, concerned the characters and events of the Reformation. He redeemed the character of Mary I by portraying her as a merciful sovereign, who executed only three guilty parties after the crisis of her accession.[54] He excused the executions of heretics which took place in her reign, by pointing out that 'the extirpation of erroneous doctrine was inculcated as a duty by the leader of every religious party' and Mary 'only practised what *they* taught'.[55] However, one of the Catholic historian's most concentrated efforts at vindication involved Mary, Queen of Scots. Lingard prudently avoided making openly favourable statements, but his narrative of her career implied a sympathetic reappraisal. He denied that Mary was a member of a Catholic League to exterminate Protestants, claiming that it was intended merely to secure freedom of worship for Catholics.[56] In discussion of the murder of Darnley, he was clearly inclined to support Mary's cause, opining that there was 'no credible evidence' that she even knew of the plot to kill him.[57] He also exonerated her of any intent against the life of Elizabeth during the Babington Plot,[58] and highlighted the failure of the prosecutors at her trial to produce the originals of the letters on which they based their case against her.[59] He described how, when her death warrant was read aloud to Mary, she swore her innocence of any plotting against the life of Elizabeth, on a Catholic Testament, adding that she was being executed for her faith.[60] This presentation of Mary as not just a victim, but a Catholic martyr, was heightened by Dolman's choice of this scene for illustration

52. *Ibid.*, vol. 8, facing p. 156.
53. E. Jones, 'John Lingard and the Simancas Archives', above, pp. 105–124.
54. Lingard, *History* (1854–55), vol. 5, p. 211.
55. *Ibid.*, vol. 5, p. 259.
56. *Ibid.*, vol. 6, p. 61, footnote 1.
57. *Ibid.*, vol. 6, p. 70.
58. *Ibid.*, vol. 6, p. 199.
59. *Ibid.*, vol. 6, p. 211.
60. *Ibid.*, vol. 6, p. 225.

(Fig. 6).[61] Most images of Mary illustrated either events related to her marriages or her execution, tending to portray her as a romantic heroine.[62] This illustration – with its faint suggestion of Jesus before the High Priest or Pilate – presents her as a Catholic martyr: the inclusion of the Catholic Testament on her desk and a cross around her neck (not to mention an hour-glass signifying our common mortality) invite a religious rather than a sentimental response. Doyle or Dolman were deliberately breaking with the traditional iconography, which allowed both Protestant and Catholic to meet on the grounds of nostalgic sympathy for a beautiful victim.

Lingard also attempted to rehabilitate the infamous James II, although he was guarded in his account of this king's extremely controversial reign. He described the king's aims at the opening of his reign as reaching no further than religious and civil toleration for Catholics, and argued that, given his own beliefs, this was essential to his security as a monarch.[63] With this conciliatory argument, he neatly avoided making any unrealistic claims concerning James's progressive views, while presenting the Anglican opponents of toleration as both unreasonable and almost rebellious. He was restrained, too, in his narrative of Judge Jeffrey's 'Bloody Assizes' after the Monmouth Rebellion, but he commented, for instance, that the claim of Alice Lisle – a much lamented Protestant victim of the trials – to be unaware of the guilt of those rebels whom she sheltered in her house was 'a mere pretence'.[64]

As this criticism of Alice Lisle showed, Lingard did not limit his onslaught on the traditional Protestant narrative of national history to the rehabilitation of Catholic figures and their actions: he also directly attacked Protestant heroes and their actions. The Reformation, while exciting Lingard's contained rage, offered him the opportunity to sever the traditional link between national progress and the adoption of the Protestant faith by the English people. Lingard drew unappealing portraits of many English Reformation figures to whom he attributed the lowest of motives – rather than evangelical principles – for their actions. Anne Boleyn, whom the Protestant historians viewed as a proto-Evangelical, was dismissed by Lingard as 'no more a Protestant than Henry',[65] while he portrayed Henry VIII as both cruel and greedy. Farcical pretexts for the dissolution of the monasteries were welcomed by the king, Lingard argued, whose love of power was only exceeded by his thirst for money,[66] while the evidence against the monks was collected by 'clerical adventurers of very equivocal character'.[67] Even Protestant historians found few

---

61. *Ibid.*, vol. 6, frontispiece.
62. See Strong, *And When Did Your Last See Your Father?*, pp. 128–35, for a consideration of the Victorian iconography of Mary, Queen of Scots.
63. Lingard, *History*, vol. 10, p. 63.
64. *Ibid.*, vol. 10, p. 89.
65. *Ibid.*, vol. 5, pp. 1–2.
66. *Ibid.*, vol. 5, p. 27.
67. *Ibid,* vol. 5, pp. 28, 48.

redeeming features in Henry VIII, but Lingard cast his net more widely. Describing the reign of Edward VI, he commented that the Protestant zeal of the Duke of Somerset and the rest of the governing Council was really stimulated by 'the prospect of reward'.[68] Not only the Protestant figures of the Reformation were condemned, but the general results of the change were deplored. In a rare digression from the narration of political and ecclesiastical affairs, Lingard briefly delved into social history to shame Protestant historians:

Within the realm poverty and discontent generally prevailed ... the poor began to resort to the more populous towns in search of that relief which had formerly been distributed at the gates of the monasteries.

The Catholic historian was determined to shatter the link between true patriotism and Protestantism inherent in the dominant historical narrative of the English past. The early Protestants, Lingard argued, despite their claim to wish for nothing more than religious freedom, were disloyal and tyrannical: that hero of the Scottish Reformation, John Knox, for instance, preached doctrines which justified rebellion against legitimate (Catholic) authority.[69] Lingard was clearly alert to the logical inconsistency of Protestant monarchs, such as Elizabeth I, who branded their Catholic subjects as disloyal, while encouraging rebellion for religious motives by aiding Protestant rebels in France and the Netherlands: the Armadas were, for him, the deserved punishment for such 'perpetual interference'.[70] Lingard disputed the Protestant interpretation of Elizabeth's reign as a national Golden Age: he described Sir Francis Drake and his men, traditionally regarded as the imperialistic heroes of the period, as 'no better than public robbers and assassins'[71], and he deplored the lack of real civil and religious liberties.[72]

The theme of Protestants as no champions of true religious freedom – and thereby, of civil and national progress – was continued in Lingard's narrative of the events of the seventeenth century. The Puritans were, he argued, poor protectors of religious freedom: he commented that the trial and execution of Archbishop Laud was the result of 'religious, and not political rancour', adding with an impartial disdain that Laud and his Puritan persecutors were 'equally obstinate, equally infallible, equally intolerant'.[73]

But it was the Popish Plot, of all seventeenth-century events, which aroused Lingard's animus against Protestant extremism most fully. On the fact of a routine triennial meeting of the Jesuit order in London, Lingard argued, Titus Oates and his associate Tonge raised 'a huge superstructure of malice and fiction,'[74] supported by forged letters. When Oates told his

68. *Ibid.*, vol. 5, p. 123.
69. *Ibid.*, vol. 6, p. 16.
70. *Ibid.*, vol. 6, p. 116.
71. *Ibid.*, vol. 6, p. 235.
72. *Ibid.*, vol. 6, p. 324.
73. *Ibid.*, vol. 8, p. 42.
74. *Ibid.*, vol. 9, p. 173.

tale before the Council, Lingard continued, his narrative seemed so improbable and his character exhibited 'such baseness and dishonesty' that his hearers were both bewildered and amazed.[75] The king, questioning Oates, easily proved the factual inaccuracies of his story.[76] This scene – which stressed the fraudulence of Oates and, therefore, the gullibility and/or bigotry of anyone who seriously believed his tales – was appropriately selected for illustration.[77] The King and his councillors – among whom are a couple of Anglican prelates – look on with apparent scepticism and disapproval, as the sharp-chinned and unappealing Oates delivers his testimony. Lingard described the subsequent trials for conspiracy and treason and executions of innocent Catholics as nothing less than 'judicial murders'.[78]

To create a real sense of the Protestant injustice and cruelty exhibited during the Popish Plot, Lingard chose to highlight the trial and execution of the Catholic Lord Stafford. This elderly man, he wrote, was accused by Oates and other informers, whose characters were 'a sufficient condemnation of the cause which they appeared to support'.[79] Lingard commented that Stafford's spirited defence during his trial and his 'Christian piety and fearless deportment on the scaffold' broadcast his innocence to the general public.[80] This unusual subject is chosen for illustration (Fig. 7).[81] An apparently subdued crowd (and a picturesque old house) occupy the foreground, while Lord Stafford is led off towards the Tower of London, a gloomy reminder of the ruthless executions of numerous other unfortunate (and often innocent) individuals. In addition, Lingard contrasted the fraudulent Popish Plot and its innocent Catholic victims with the rampantly pro-Protestant Rye House Plot and its undoubtedly guilty perpetrators. He was unsparing in his treatment of the Protestant heroes of the Rye House Plot, William, Lord Russell and Algernon Sydney, exposing Sydney as a double-dealer in the pay of France[82] and Russell as traitor to his king by intent if not action.[83]

Although Lingard was reserved in his defence of the Catholic James II, he was less restrained in his criticism of the Protestant heroes of the period: James, Duke of Monmouth and William of Orange, later William III. While William of Orange was denounced as an ambitious schemer rather than a defender of English liberties,[84] Monmouth was subject to an even more devastating character assassination. Lingard portrayed the captured

75. *Ibid.*, vol. 9, p. 176.
76. *Ibid.*, vol. 9, pp. 176–77.
77. *Ibid.*, vol. 9, frontispiece.
78. *Ibid.*, vol. 9, p. 189.
79. *Ibid.*, vol. 9, p. 241.
80. *Ibid.*, vol. 9, p. 248.
81. *Ibid.*, vol. 9, facing p. 248.
82. *Ibid.*, vol. 10, p. 39–44.
83. *Ibid.*, vol. 10, p. 34–35.
84. *Ibid.*, vol. 10, p. 187.

Monmouth as a coward willing to accept life on any terms,[85] and a cruel husband, who was openly unfaithful to his wife. In prison, the reader was informed, he received her first visit coldly; at her last visit, he was civil but unconcerned when her distress resulted in a fainting fit. This scene was chosen for illustration (Fig 8):[86] the indifferent Monmouth stands aside with his arms folded, while his wife collapses artistically, supported by two gentlemen, a guard, two maids and a couple of watching children. The attention and the pity of the viewer is focused thus on the wronged but loving woman, and little sympathy is evoked for the soon-to-be-dead Duke. The text reminded the reader that, to his death, Monmouth remained unrepentant of both his long extra-marital affair and his treasons:[87] his lack of loyalty to his country and King is thus linked to his marital infidelity. This illustration is particularly interesting in view of the nineteenth-century condemnation – often reflected in popular historical paintings[88] – of the similarly loose morals of Monmouth's father, who (in Protestant eyes) multiplied his sins by a rumoured deathbed conversion to Catholicism. Dolman and Dudley have clearly shown that the Protestant son was no better than the Catholic father.

The Future of Catholic Historiography

Lingard's aim, in writing the *History*, was to produce a history of England which could and would be read by Protestants, to write English Catholics into the dominant narrative of the history of the nation. To some extent, he achieved this: his impartial tone and meticulous research won him the qualified approval of even his most strident critics. But his critique of the traditional Protestant interpretation of English history, supported by pioneering analysis of his sources, led him also towards the creation of a rival Catholic history of England. Lingard was not simply a Cisalpine historian, although he used some of their conciliatory arguments; he was also a Catholic who shared with other younger and more militant Catholics – men such as Dolman and Doyle – a desire for the defence and revival of the Catholic Church. In the 1854–55 edition of Lingard's *History*, the controversial content of the text, often disguised by the historian's impartial tone, was pointed up and highlighted by the choice of illustrations. Here this transitional work foreshadowed the developments of later-nineteenth-century Catholic historiography.

Later Victorian Catholic historians – such as the Redemptorist Bridgett, the Jesuit John Morris, and Anne Hope – were to work in the shadow of Lingard, and they exhibited his critical concern to examine and cite sources and authorities. They used the results of their researches pointed-

85. *Ibid.*, vol. 10, p. 84.
86. *Ibid.*, vol. 10, facing p. 85.
87. *Ibid.*, vol. 10, pp. 85–87.
88. A classic example is W.P. Frith's *King Charles the Second's Last Sunday*, exhibited in 1867.

ly to expose errors in the Protestant national narrative and to chronicle uniquely Catholic aspects of English history, to an extent which Lingard would have considered as far too aggressive, separatist, and propagandist. Gone indeed was the deceptively impartial tone of Lingard's narrative, with its aim to be equally palatable to both Catholic and Protestant: these historians examined and celebrated the English Catholic Church, its adherents, and its heritage, for themselves rather than in the context of a national history, and they combated, openly and robustly, as Catholics, the errors of Protestant historiography.[89]

The direction and approaches of the research of such as Bridgett, Morris, and Hope prepared the way for the confrontational style of Aidan Cardinal Gasquet, the most important turn of the century Catholic historian.   In such a work as his *Henry VIII and the Dissolution of the Monasteries* (1888), Gasquet fore-grounded a controversial issue and directly attacked the traditional Protestant interpretation of events, bluntly declaring in his introduction that 'the national character of honesty and fairness has been permanently warped' with respect to the reality of medieval monasticism.[90] Equally, Catholic historians followed the lead of Bridgett, Morris, and Hope in their continuing exploration and celebration of the English Catholic past: the foundation of the Catholic Record Society by such individuals as John Hungerford Pollen the younger, and its steady publication of documents relating to recusant history is an example of this pursuit.   Lingard would surely have found such developments imprudent and would undoubtedly have described Cardinal Gasquet as a 'puffer'; yet the transitional 1854–55 Dolman edition of his *History* was itself one indicator of the future of Catholic historiography.

89. R.A. Mitchell, 'Thomas Bridgett', 'John Morris', and 'Anne Hope', in *The New DNB*.
90. A. Gasquet, *Henry VIII and the Dissolution of the Monasteries* (2nd ed., London, 1888), vol. 1, p. xiii.

8

JOHN LINGARD AND THE LITURGY

Emma Riley

During the past one hundred and fifty years very little has been written about John Lingard's liturgical theories and opinions, probably because his liturgical writings have not been easily to hand, and because his best known work is as an historian. Nevertheless, a careful study of Lingard's liturgical views is worthwhile and enlightening both for historians, whose chief interest is in Lingard himself, and for those with an interest in the English Roman Catholic liturgy of the nineteenth century.

The focus of this chapter on Lingard's liturgy will be his *Manual of Prayers on Sundays and During Mass,* which was published in Lancaster in 1833. In this work his liturgical ideas are encountered most fully, since it was the only specifically liturgical book that he produced. Nevertheless, this study will also draw information from other sources, most notably his letters and writings, especially those penned under the pseudonym of Proselytos, in the *Catholic Magazine.* Finally, in order to appreciate and understand Lingard's *Manual* more fully, it will be compared with other prayer books of similar date and intent, for it is in comparison with these works that we can appreciate the strengths of Lingard's book.

Lingard compiled his prayer book with his congregation in Hornby specifically in mind and it is unlikely that he envisaged its reaching a wider audience.[1] In fact Lingard's friend Robert Tate, a well-known preacher and subsequently president of Ushaw College, adapted Lingard's work for the use of his own congregation in 1840. Otherwise we know that Lingard gave copies to friends, as evidenced by his gift to his correspondent Mary Frances Sanders (later Mrs. Thomas Lomax) in 1835.[2] Essentially, however, Lingard's prayer book is a local one and so it will be interesting to study the book's relationship with other local manuals. It is important to remember, however, that Lingard's *Manual* arose out of his belief that other works, especially the exceptionally popular *Garden of the Soul* first published by Richard Challoner in 1740, were in some ways deficient and therefore not the best material to put into the hands of the Hornby community. It is appropriate, for a full understanding of Lingard's *Manual*, that we briefly examine the popular works, which he found defective, as well as other local prayer books, in order to appreciate fully just how apt Lingard's work was and to explore the rationale behind his liturgical ideas.

---

1. This congregation was comparatively small in number, seldom producing more than one hundred Easter communicants: J. Bossy, *The English Catholic Community, 1570–1850,* Darton, Longman and Todd, (London, 1975), pp. 302–303.
2. John Lingard to Mary Sanders, January 31st 1835, *Lingard-Lomax Letters*, p. 25.

John Lingard's *Manual* is in no sense an innovation; it comes in a long line of similar works which started to appear from the end of the seventeenth century.   The first such was John Gother's *Instructions and Devotions for hearing Mass*, first published in 1699.   Gother, a Catholic priest and convert from Presbyterianism, was one of the first post-Reformation Catholics to recognise that it would be beneficial for a congregation to be able to follow the Mass itself, rather than be engrossed in their own devotions during its celebration.   Most typically, many in the congregation would have been saying the Rosary or some form of morning prayers as the priest was saying Mass; these devotions, whilst pious and spiritual activities in their own right, were essentially unrelated to the liturgy of the Mass.   Gother clearly stated in *Instructions and Devotions for Hearing Mass* that the best way to hear Mass was 'to accompany the priest, in offering with him, to Almighty God, the sacrifice of the body and blood of Christ under the forms of bread and wine.'[3]   Gother's work sought to aid congregational understanding since it included a full translation of the Ordinary of the Mass, the first translation to be published in England.   Earlier, in 1698, Gother had also produced a series of volumes, collectively entitled *Instructions for the Whole Year*.   These books contained Gother's reflections on the Epistles and Gospels chosen to be read at Sunday Masses throughout the liturgical year; they reveal Gother's concern that the people should understand and benefit spiritually from the whole of the Mass.   This concern was to be echoed by Lingard, yet by few others.   We also see that Gother's liturgical ideas were similar to those later held on the continent by moderately progressive Catholics of the Enlightenment who saw the liturgy as a vital tool for instructing the laity. Aidan Nichols has emphasised this aspect of the Enlightenment in recalling that the:

> movement was distinguished by rampant didacticism. Franz Oberthur, for instance, who defined divine worship as 'a solemn means of teaching, nourishing, and promoting religion in the Christian Church', regarded teaching as the liturgy's main goal.[4]

Lingard has often been regarded as a late Enlightenment thinker[5] and later in this chapter we shall see that his prayer book, although relatively brief, was also didactic.

After Gother, the next significant devotional manual to be published was Richard Challoner's *Garden of the Soul*, which first appeared in 1740; it was one of the most important Roman Catholic works to appear in this country after the Reformation.   There would be no exaggeration in claim-

---

3. J. Gother, *Instructions and Devotions for Hearing Mass*, (?London, 1744 ed.), p. 1.

4. A. Nichols, O.P., *Looking at the Liturgy: A Critical View of its Contemporary Form*, Ignatius Press (San Francisco, California, 1996), p. 25. Oberthur was an ecclesiastical commentator who published *Idea biblica Ecclesiae*, from which the quotation in this extract is taken.

5. See Chinnici; J. A. Hilton (ed.), *A Catholic of the Enlightenment: Essays on Lingard's Work and Times*, North West Catholic History Society, (Wigan, 1999).

ing that his work was the single most influential devotional work for English Roman Catholics up to the end of the nineteenth century, both in its effect upon congregations and in the inspiration it provided to authors of other devotional manuals. Most significantly for this study, Challoner's work contains a substantial chapter entitled 'Instructions and Devotions for Hearing Mass'. This chapter, as its title suggests, falls into two distinct sections: very full instructions for hearing Mass, including technical information regarding the significance of the Mass, and a more devotional section, which provided commentary and prayers to accompany the succeeding stages of the Mass. Challoner's work was, however, essentially different in style from that of Gother, for it was far less strictly liturgical. Whilst Challoner's devotions adhered closely to the structure of the Mass, he did not provide a translation of the complete rite. For example, whilst Challoner translated the *Gloria*, *Credo*, *Sanctus*, *Agnus Dei* and *Pater Noster*, he provided only paraphrases of much of the Canon of the Mass, and a devotional prayer with a strong emphasis on personal sinfulness in place of the *Confiteor*. This format was less liturgically accurate and less didactic than Gother's work; it was consequently unlikely to meet with Lingard's wholehearted approval. Lingard's comments on Challoner's work should provide little surprise:

in many respects, a beautiful garden, containing some of the choicest flowers of devotion, but it is badly *laid out*, and wants *weeding* very ill.[6]

He was even less flattering about Challoner's treatment of the Mass, for he found fault with the intelligibility and accuracy of the late Vicar Apostolic's translations. Lingard reflected:

[Challoner's Latinisms] have the effect of rendering the prayers obscure, and sometimes unintelligible to an ordinary reader. Prayers for the use of the people, should be as easy to understand as possible, and scrupulously correct in their language and expression.[7]

Lingard gives several examples to emphasise his point. He objected particularly to the reference to Jesus as 'the Angel of the Great Council' included in Challoner's prayer after the elevation of the Eucharist during the Canon: Lingard believed that there was no justification in the Latin text of the Mass for the use of this title and furthermore he held it to be meaningless.[8] So whilst Challoner's *Garden of the Soul* was to provide inspiration for other manual writers, Lingard's *Manual* should be viewed more as a reaction against the perceived inadequacies of Challoner's work, and as an attempt to put an accurate and instructive manual into the hands of his congregation at Hornby.

Other manuals for nationwide use were to appear, most significant amongst them being *The Key of Heaven*, first published in 1755 by John Sadler of Liverpool. This work did contain the text of the Ordinary of the

---

6. *The Catholic Magazine*, vol. 5, (1834), p. 85 (Lingard's own emphasis).
7. *Ibid.*, p. 80.
8. *Ibid.*, p. 86.

Mass in two parallel columns, Latin and English, along with a separate chapter of devotions for Mass. This division meant that *The Key of Heaven*, like the *Garden of the Soul,* contained both liturgical and devotional material but in a rigidly separate format, which was perhaps less able to capture the imagination of the reader.

Clearly, however, despite the relative proliferation of the well-known manuals, some priests, with Lingard amongst them, felt the need to provide smaller and more readily accessible books better tailored to their local congregations. One of the first of these to appear was *Prayers to be said Before and After Mass and in the Afternoon, on all Sundays and Festivals in the Catholic Chapels of Preston and Blackburn. To which is Added the Ordinary of the Mass*. This work was prepared and compiled by two brothers, Joseph[9] and William Dunn, and Nicholas Morgan, all three of whom were priests in the Preston and Blackburn area. The prayer book was first published in Manchester in 1805 and was intended for use in the urban Lancashire chapels staffed by these three priests. A similar work, though one which seems to have been destined for wider use, is *Instructions and Prayers Before, At and After Mass for Sundays and Holydays. As used in the Northern District*; a work published, again in Manchester, in 1830. Both of these texts, like Lingard's later manual, are much more narrowly focused than those prayer books intended for a national audience. The local manuals were compiled to meet a specific need: that of preparing for and following the Mass. Works such as the *Garden of the Soul* and *The Key of Heaven* were intended to provide a prayer companion for almost every eventuality.

In the same way, the prayers intended for Preston and Blackburn congregations and those compiled for the Northern District were quite similar in both construction and content and it seems highly likely that the compiler of the later *Instructions and Prayers* had some knowledge of the earlier work of the Dunns and Morgan, which was, after all, used in a related, though smaller, geographical area.

The prayer book written for the congregations of Preston and Blackburn is divided into four sections, three of which centred on the Mass: prayers before Mass, the Ordinary of the Mass, thanksgiving prayers after Mass, and prayers to be said on Sunday afternoons. The prayers before and after Mass are heavily dominated by psalms, some of which originated in Sunday's Office of Lauds, or Morning Prayer. Consequently, the reader of this work finds that the opening of the prayers before Mass begin in the same manner as the Divine Office:

Priest: O God! Thou wilt open my lips;
Clerk: And my mouth shall declare thy praise.
Priest: O God! Incline unto mine aid.
Clerk: O Lord! Make haste to help me.[10]

---

9. See T.G. Holt, S.J., 'Joseph Dunn of Preston from his Correspondence', in J.A. Hilton (ed.), *Catholic Englishmen*, (Wigan, 1984).

10. *Preston and Blackburn*, p. 3.

It is interesting to note that this opening prayer, like much of the Tridentine Mass, is in the form of a dialogue between priest and clerk during which the congregation must have felt somewhat marginalised. Following this brief dialogue passage comes a series of psalms and canticles; it is unclear whether the intention was that these be recited – either as a whole or antiphonally – by the congregation, or whether they too were to be restricted to priest and server. The psalms chosen include Psalm 1, which is also to be found in the Office of Lauds, and Psalm 116. Two canticles also occur in the opening section of the prayers before Mass: the *Benedictus es Domine* from 1 Chron. 29, appointed for Lauds on a Sunday, along with the Canticle of Zechariah, the *Benedictus*, always said at Morning Prayer. The psalms of praise (Pss. 148, 149 and 150), which give Lauds its name, are not, however, included in this introductory service. This collection of psalms, canticles, and a brief reading from Deuteronomy, is rounded off with a prayer expressing the sanctity of Sunday, the congregation's need of divine forgiveness and a desire to reach the eternal happiness of heaven. The service then continues with long prayers of intercession for the sick and for the dead – including the *De profundis* – and acts of faith, hope, love, and contrition. Finally there is a prayer before Mass, linking instruction with devotion, since it outlined some of the reasons for saying Mass:

> And now, O God, behold we thy people presume to appear before thee this day, to offer up to thee by the hands of thy minister, and by the hands of our great high-priest, Jesus Christ, thy Son, the unbloody sacrifice of his body and blood, as a perpetual commemoration of his passion and death, his resurrection and ascension.[11]

This prayer is followed by prayers of intercession on behalf of non-Christians, the lapsed, the king and royal family, those in government, all Christendom, the sick, the local church community; and the series ends with a prayer for the dead.

There then follows the centrally important translation of the Ordinary of the Mass, provided so that the congregation could better follow the prayers of the Mass and to encourage a more full participation in the liturgy, rather than abandoning the people to their own individual prayer. This translation was provided pretty much in full although, as is common in many manuals of prayer, the *Confiteor* and the prayer of absolution which followed it are omitted from the text. This is almost certainly because the priest authors of these devotional works were afraid that their readers might think that they received sacramental absolution from this prayer just as they did at Confession. Of course this was not the case; and, given that in the nineteenth century sacramental absolution was seen as a prerequisite for reception of Holy Communion, it is unsurprising that priests did not want to sow confusion in the minds of their flocks. Indeed, the

---

11. *Ibid.*, p. 12.

assumption that the reader would make only a spiritual communion is clearly made in this work, since a description of the priest's communion is accompanied by a reflective prayer which encourages the lay person to make a spiritual communion at this time.

Generally, this translation of the Ordinary of the Mass is closely liturgical since it offers accurate translations of the Mass texts coupled with brief descriptions of the priest's actions. Nevertheless, it has one significant drawback: in place of the Proper of the Mass devotional prayers are provided. For example, in place of the Gradual and the Tract the reader is exhorted to say a prayer extracted from Challoner's *Garden of the Soul*:

How wonderful, O Lord! is thy name thro' the whole earth. I will bless our Lord at all times, his praise shall ever be in my mouth. Be thou my God and my protector; in thee alone I will put my trust, let me not be confounded for ever.[12]

Whilst these prayers are appropriate to the point in the Mass which has been reached, they in no way compensate for the lack of seasonal variety resulting from the total omission of the Proper. The lack of the Proper can be explained in terms of economy of cost and size, but when we come to study Lingard's *Manual* it will become clear that some variety could be included even in a brief and conveniently small format.

As I have already mentioned, the prayers for the Northern District are essentially similar to those for the congregations of Preston and Blackburn. The structure of the two manuals is almost identical: both included prayers before Mass, much of the translated text of the Ordinary of the Mass, and prayers to be said after Mass; the only difference being that the prayers for the Northern District do not make any provision for afternoon prayers. The chief difference between these two manuals, however, is in their prayers before Mass. The prayers for the Northern District are far less dependent on the use of psalms and do not derive their material from the Office of Lauds, in the way that the Dunn and Morgan service seems to have done. The later Northern work includes long acts of faith, hope, charity and contrition, clearly intended to be said as a dialogue between priest and clerk. Then comes a prayer for the sick identical to that found in the prayers for Preston and Blackburn, and this is followed by the *De profundis*, included both as a reflection on personal sinfulness and as prayer for the dead. After this is to be found a lengthy litany which again reflected on personal sinfulness in pretty much all its manifestations, and asks that God should protect the supplicants from temptation, have mercy on them in their sins, and also have mercy on their deceased friends and benefactors.[13] Finally comes the last prayer to be said before Mass, which

---

12. *Ibid.*, p. 20.

13. Interestingly this litany was very typical of the era in its view of society: *viz.* 'Teach us to be submissive to our superiors, condescending to our inferiors, faithful to our friends, and charitable to our enemies', *Northern District,* p. 7, and cf. the slightly later outpourings of Victorian hymnody, for example Mrs. Alexander's 'All things bright and beautiful' which contained the lines, now expunged, 'The rich man in his castle,/ The poor man at his gate.'

in fact contains the first specific reference to the Mass itself. This prayer is almost identical to that contained in the prayers for Preston and Blackburn and enumerates in the same way the reasons for offering the sacrifice of the Mass. The similarity regarding this prayer in these two works strongly suggests that the writer of the prayers for the Northern District knew, and derived material from, the earlier work.

Overall these prayers do not seem to provide a particularly well-considered preparation for the Mass, especially since it is only in the last prayer that preparation itself is actually mentioned; rather these prayers are heavily dominated by a consideration of sinfulness. Furthermore, congregational participation in these devotions does not appear to have been encouraged since the text is constructed in the form of a dialogue between the priest and the clerk, leaving the congregation somewhat marginalised, even if the latter understood these vernacular texts rather better than the Latin texts of the Mass.

The section of this work devoted to the Ordinary of the Mass is entitled 'Instructions and Devotions for Hearing Mass'. Such a title might lead the reader to expect this section to be more devotional than liturgical in contrast to its counterpart in the prayers for Preston and Blackburn. This is, to some extent, the case, for whilst the devotions provided in the Northern District's manual follow the structure of the Mass closely, often alternative devotional prayers are offered here in place of, or at least in addition to, the prayers of the Ordinary. For example, at the beginning of Mass, the following suggestion is made for devotion after the priest has made the Sign of the Cross:

> He [the priest] then recites with the clerk the 42nd psalm, *Judica me Deus, etc.* – that is – Judge me, O God, *etc.* which you may recite with them, or pray as follows:...[14]

The alternative is one of self-offering to God, asking God to help the supplicant to be contrite and then to respond mercifully. This prayer actually puts more emphasis on sin and contrition than the psalm in the Ordinary of the Mass. At other points in the Mass, however, the prayers suggested are more liturgical, and in fact on many occasions direct translations of the prayers in the Ordinary are provided: for example the *Gloria* and the Creed are fully translated. Interestingly, unlike the prayer book for Preston and Blackburn, the *Confiteor* is also fully translated in this text, although the prayer of absolution at the end is significantly altered to read:

> May the Almighty God be merciful to me, and forgiving my sins, bring me to life everlasting. May the Almighty and merciful Lord give me pardon and remission of all my sins. Amen.[15]

This revision of the prayer subtly alters the meaning of the Latin original so it becomes a hopeful dialogue between the sinner and God without any hint of guaranteed forgiveness, priestly intervention, or sacramental abso-

---

14. *Northern District*, p. 11.
15. *Ibid.*, p. 12.

lution. The revised prayer replaces the supplication: *Misereatur vestri omnipotens Deus, et dimissis peccatis vestris, perducat vos ad vitam aeternam;*[16] this original prayer implied a greater certainty of God's forgiveness, sounding much more like words of absolution than the Northern District alternative.

In a similar vein to the Dunn and Morgan manual, this work omits the Proper of the Mass, offering instead devotional prayers; so, for example, in place of the Epistle we find a devotion which also appeared in *The Key of Heaven* and, in a modified form, in the prayers for Preston and Blackburn:

> Be thou, O Lord, for ever praised, for having given thy holy spirit to the blessed prophets and apostles, and taught them these sacred truths which redound to thy greater glory and our great good. We firmly believe THEIR WORD, because we know it to be THINE. Give us, we beseech thee, the happiness to understand from thy *Church*, by their instructions, what is profitable for us, and grace also to practise the same, to the end of our lives.[17]

This prayer seems to allow the people to lay aside any responsibility for reading the Scriptures themselves, an idea which would accord with the oft-cited opinion that the Catholic hierarchy feared personal Bible reading in case of incorrect interpretation. Certainly, however, this is not the general tenor of the work for the Northern District; for when the Gospel is reached the author suggests that the people should either read their own edition of the Gospels, or, failing that, read his selection of 'Gospel truths', a list of aphorisms taken from the works of the Evangelists. Whilst these pithy statements, which include extracts such as 'What doth it profit a man if he gain the whole world, and lose his own soul?',[18] could not replace the richness of the Proper, they do go a step further than the simply devotional prayers suggested for Mass-goers in Preston and Blackburn.

Another difference between these two local works is the more detailed descriptions and explanations of the priest's actions provided in the prayers for the Northern District. These explain the ceremonial actions and also signal the point in the Mass that has been reached, since short extracts from the Latin of the Ordinary are quoted.

The concluding sections of the two works are similar. The Last Gospel, the beginning of the Gospel of St. John, is translated in full and then prayers to be said after Mass are added. In keeping with the prayers recommended to be said before Mass, the Dunn and Morgan manual includes more material from the Divine Office in the concluding prayers than the Northern District manual. Thus the congregation in Preston and Blackburn said the *Te Deum* and the *Benedicite*. After these had been

---

16. May almighty God have mercy upon you, and, forgiving you your sins, bring you to life everlasting.

17. *Ibid.*, p. 14 (the manual writer's emphasis).

18. *Ibid.*, p. 15; Mt. 16:26.

recited, however, the material in the manuals is remarkably similar: Psalm 19, which concludes with the words, 'O Lord save the King; and hear us in the day when we call upon thee', was said for the monarch, evidently to demonstrate that Catholics were loyal subjects. The final prayers are also similar.

Generally then the prayers intended for the Northern District are fuller and more devotional than the more liturgical prayers found in the Preston and Blackburn manual. Nevertheless the large quantity of material shared between the two works clearly indicates that the author of the later prayers for the Northern District had knowledge of the earlier book.

Returning now to Lingard's *Manual*, we find perhaps a more carefully considered and more complete work than the other local manuals of prayer. Professor John Bossy, who looked at all three manuals of prayer, comments that Lingard's version:

> gives an impression of considerable formal beauty and appropriateness, and it strikes me personally both as a genuine creative achievement in its own right and as the successful culmination of a phase of liturgical experiment.[19]

This is an interesting and accurate reflection, since Lingard's work can be seen as a more complete and better crafted example of the genre. Lingard's manual was almost certainly written in reaction to the inadequacies he perceived in existing prayer books. I discussed earlier Lingard's difficulties with Challoner's *Garden of the Soul*, a work that, while acknowledging its merits, he believed to be poorly organised, and whose text of the Ordinary of the Mass he thought to be inaccurately translated.[20] In general, Lingard seems to have found the existing manuals to be less than ideal, and he was acutely aware of the importance of the vernacular prayers said before Mass, both for Catholics and for visiting Protestants. In response to a letter from his friend and regular correspondent Robert Tate he wrote:

> You wish to have my notions respecting a reform of our service in great towns. My notions are that the English Prayers should be such as would at least instruct and edify Protestants; that they should be read slowly, distinctly and devoutly and that the sermon should be well composed and well delivered. For of the Mass Protestants understand nothing; it is only by the prayers and sermon that you can induce them to repeat their visits and think of the doctrines of our religion.[21]

In this letter Lingard eloquently expresses much of his liturgical *raison d'être*; he was determined that the liturgy in general, and the prayers before Mass in particular, should be simple to comprehend, edifying, prayerful, and dignified. These sentiments are also expressed in Lingard's writings as Proselytos in the *Catholic Magazine* in 1833. Lingard had

---

19. Bossy, *English Catholic Community*, p. 376.
20. See above, p. 145.
21. John Lingard to Robert Tate, December 7th 1831, UCA, Lingard Transcript 623.

intended Proselytos' liturgical reflections to form a series in the periodical, but his remarks met with such vehement criticism that his contributions ceased after just one article. Nevertheless, we can learn a great deal about Lingard's rationale even from this short piece. Assuming the character of a recent convert to Catholicism, Proselytos, Lingard wrote:

> It chanced one morning while I was staying in a provincial town, that I saw several persons enter what seemed a public building. I had the curiosity to follow and found myself in a Catholic chapel. I was pleased with the simplicity and neatness of its ornaments, and edified by the silence and apparent devotion of the congregation.
>
> After a few minutes the door of the vestry opened, and the minister came forth, preceded by the clerk... There was indeed something very strange and apparently fantastical in his sacerdotal garments: but my antiquarian habits taught me to look upon them as antique, and therefore venerable... I was all attention; my expectation had been wound up to the highest pitch, but never alas! was man more miserably disappointed. The voice of the clergyman proved harsh and unmusical; his enunciation was quick and indistinct.[22]

Proselytos was, however, not only to be disappointed by the person of the priest; he also found the vernacular prayers unsatisfactory:

> instead of the solemn address to the Almighty, which I anticipated, he began with a prayer to the Virgin Mary, and a prayer too, which in my protestant [sic] judgement, bordered on impiety: for he begged her 'to deliver him and his flock from all dangers'... But from these reflections my attention was called away by a succession of short invocations to the virgin, uttered with the most surprising rapidity, to which the congregation responded 'pray for us' with equal rapidity. It seemed a race between priest and people. I had heard of protestant dancers, jumpers and ranters; I now thought myself amidst a set of Catholic gallopers.[23]

In this description we find mentioned much of what Lingard found most disagreeable in nineteenth-century liturgical practices: gabbled prayers, unnecessary archaism of language, improper and excessive use of Marian prayers, incomprehensibility. It was to counteract these tendencies, if only in his own village of Hornby, that Lingard compiled his prayer book.

Lingard's *Manual of Prayers on Sundays and During the Mass* bears eloquent testimony to his liturgical sensitivity. As we would expect, it is not a copy nor yet derived from other local manuals, some of which I have described above. It is broadly similar to them in construction, since it is divided into four main parts: prayers for Sundays, clearly intended to be said in the morning before Mass; a brief chapter entitled 'Prayers Before Mass'; a treatment of the Ordinary of the Mass; and finally, a very brief concluding section entitled 'Prayers after Mass', which in fact includes only the *Te Deum*.

The two opening chapters of Lingard's work are broadly similar in intent to the prayers before Mass included in the other two works that I have studied in detail. Both chapters are, clearly, intended to be used as a public devotion because many of the psalms which are included in the prayers have been rearranged to include responses. Whilst Lingard's prayers, like those for the Dunn and Morgan congregations in Preston and Blackburn, are heavily dominated by psalms, Lingard's approach to the use of the psalms is markedly different from that of the three other priests. Firstly, Lingard's choice of psalms is much freer since he did not seem to have been limited by the choice of psalms used in Sunday's Office of Lauds. Hence he selects psalms whose content was particularly apt for use on a Sunday: the first psalm he included was Psalm 94 which expressed a desire to praise God and come gratefully into his presence, indeed a psalm which was especially appropriate for a day devoted to the Lord. This psalm was to be recited with a congregational refrain 'Come, let us sing to the Lord, let our voices praise the rock of our salvation'[24] in a manner similar to the modern responsorial psalm. This meant that these prayers were not limited to dialogue between priest and altar server, but were opened up to wider and more appropriate congregational participation. Following this psalm, Lingard includes prayers which express a desire to keep Sunday holy and include the Lord's Prayer followed by extracts from two further psalms, Psalm 117 and Psalm 103, a further expression of thankfulness and praise. After this paean of praise, the general tenor of Lingard's prayers become more reflective, focusing on penitence and including Psalm 50, the *Miserere*. In one of Lingard's letters to Robert Tate we find the explanation for the inclusion of these prayers:

> I am much in Protestant company... and I have repeatedly heard well-educated Protestants remark that it seems strange to them that Catholics in their public service never pray for the forgiveness of sin: at least that they never heard any such prayers when they have been in Catholic chapels. That such remarks may not be made in the service here, I always say the *Miserere* with its appendages.[25]

This letter, like Lingard's writings as Proselytos, show his clear concern for Protestant opinions and sensibilities; it also demonstrates that the prayers he set were intended for public recitation. Nevertheless, the Protestant criticism to which Lingard was responding does not appear to be entirely just for, as I have already noted, the other local prayer manuals certainly do include reflections on personal sinfulness, with the prayers written for the Northern District including a lengthy litany focusing on this very subject. These other two works do not, however, include the *Miserere* in their prayers before Mass and so omit the most recognisable of the psalms asking for mercy and forgiveness. Certainly, Lingard expands the theme of penitence although his prayers cannot be seen as a

---

24. Lingard, *Prayers*, pp. 3–4.
25. John Lingard to Robert Tate, probably written in 1836, UCA, Lingard Transcript 632.

morbid dwelling on sin, which was to be a characteristic of some later works such as the Jesuit John Morris' *Manual of Prayers for Youth*, first published in 1893, and which treats the Mass rather like the Stations of the Cross as a Passion devotion.

Following on from Lingard's penitential prayers, his *Manual* reverts to the use of extracts from psalms of praise, including Psalm 26 which, rather aptly, express a great love for God's house, and Psalm 106. This section of the prayers is concluded with a range of intercessory prayers for the Church, the nation, the sovereign, and for friends, family and the wider world. The inclusion of a prayer for the reigning monarch is typical of these local prayer books: the prayers express a genuine concern for, and good will towards, the sovereign and government, although one might surmise that they have also been included at least partly to mollify Protestant and state fears regarding resurgent Roman Catholicism. Certainly, however, a desire to make his service agreeable to Protestants was, as we have already seen, a major motivation for Lingard who was consistently irenical in his approach to non-Catholics.

Having completed the chapter of 'Prayers on Sundays', Lingard's manual then moves on to a section devoted to prayers to be said immediately before Mass. In effect, this section is a continuation of the earlier chapter, but this chapter contains Lingard's first specific reference to the Mass. Here Lingard echoes the other manual writers whose works we have already studied, although he was the only one to acknowledge the fact that only the last few prefatory prayers are specifically oriented towards the Mass. Lingard's prayers before Mass are very brief, consisting of the brief invocation: 'Let us pray that God would pour his holy spirit into our hearts, and prepare us to offer to him with proper dispositions the sacrifice of the Mass.'[26] This is followed by another psalm extract, this time from Psalm 83, which again expresses a love for God's house. Here the prayers before Mass conclude.

It can be seen that Lingard's prayers are in some way similar to those intended for use in Preston and Blackburn and in the Northern District. Nevertheless, when the three works are read together, it is difficult to argue that Lingard's introductory meditations are not superior. As I have demonstrated, Lingard's choice of psalms is particularly apt; his treatment of the psalms is also especially effective, for he does not simply reproduce them in full, as did the other manual writers, but rather he rearranges them, providing either extracts or psalms with congregational responses. This method suited Lingard's desire to provide fully comprehensible material for the reader as well as allowing congregational participation. It also makes Lingard's prayers more appropriate and better tailored to the specific needs of Sunday worship than those of the other manual writers; they can be said to have fulfilled Lingard's intention to be instructive to out-

---

26. Lingard, *Prayers*, p. 14.

siders, for few who heard them could fail to be impressed by Lingard's view of the need to praise God and the centrality of Sunday worship.

Lingard's treatment of the Mass itself is also effective. True to its time, it combines liturgical and devotional elements, although liturgical qualities dominate. Lingard translated many of the Mass texts directly, including the *Gloria*, Creed, Lord's Prayer and *Agnus Dei*, although, like the other writers of local manuals that we have encountered, he did not translate the *Kyrie* and succeeding prayer of absolution in full. At this point he provided a devotional alternative which, whilst it implored God the Father, Son and Holy Spirit to look upon his people with mercy and to send them consolation and joy, did not give any hint that their sins might have been forgiven.[27]

Lingard's approach to the Canon of the Mass perhaps reveals the most about his rationale as a liturgist. He translated this central part of the Mass completely and also added passages of Scripture to aid reflection at the elevation of the Eucharist. His attitude to the Canon reveals much about Lingard's approach to the vernacular treatment of the Mass in general: he believed clear translations were important; he sensed the need for some devotional additions to the translation, and he valued Scripture very highly. Thus in Lingard's work we do not find the scant treatment of the Proper of the Mass encountered in the two earlier manuals. Instead, Lingard provided one translated text for the Epistle (1 Peter 2:11), for the Gospel (Matthew 6:24), and for the Collect in the main body of the manual; then he offered variant texts in an appendix at the back of the book. That Lingard did the latter should come as no surprise to the reader, since his belief in the accessibility of Scripture is ably evidenced by his work on the Gospels, *A New Version of the Four Gospels: with notes critical and explanatory*, published in 1836. In his setting of the liturgy for Palm Sunday he further stressed the importance of the Word of God, describing the scene in a letter to his friend John Walker:

> For the Passion I have a man seated at the bottom of the chapel, and facing the altar, who when I begin the Passion, reads it in English in a loud voice, so that everyone may hear it, a great advantage to the people... and is much liked... as several who have come from Lancaster for the day have assured me.[28]

This inclusion of translated texts, both written and spoken, certainly made Lingard's liturgy a more effective rendering of the true sense of the Mass and also made the Mass a more effective didactic tool: the impact of the read Passion in particular, was evidently considerable. In all things Lingard's watchwords were clarity and comprehensibility, no more so than in this manual which concluded simply with the *Te Deum*.

To conclude, therefore: this brief comparison of Lingard's *Manual of Prayers on Sundays and During Mass* with other manuals of the period

---

27. *Ibid.*, pp. 17–19.
28. John Lingard to John Walker, March 26th 1850, UCA, Lingard Transcript 1415.

highlights a number of points. Firstly, I think it is fair to say that Lingard produced a more polished prayer book than his contemporaries, although one that was similar in intention to their work, and drawn up along similar lines. Certainly it is clear that Lingard was concerned with clarity of translation, easy comprehensibility and as full an inclusion of Scripture as the constraints of space would allow; in this I believe him to have been more the child of John Gother than of Richard Challoner. Lingard was also a late son of the Enlightenment for he, like Oberthur, was convinced of the central role of the liturgy in teaching Protestants and Catholics alike. Overall, Lingard had much to say about the power of the liturgy: he stressed the ability of God's Word to reach people's hearts; he recognised the importance of good liturgy as a means of drawing more people to the Church and to teach them about its beliefs; and he firmly believed that in order for the liturgy to speak to the congregation they had to understand what it was saying; in fact, we may say from our post-Vatican II standpoint that indeed he was prescient.

ABBREVIATIONS

Lingard, *Prayers*	John Lingard, *A Manual of Prayers on Sundays and During the Mass* (Lancaster, 1833).
Northern District	*Instructions and Prayers Before, At and After Mass, for Sundays and Holydays. As used in the Northern District. Embellished with Engravings* (Manchester, 1830).
Preston and Blackburn	*Prayers to be said Before and After Mass and in the Afternoon, on all Sundays and Festivals in the Catholic Chapels of Preston and Blackburn. To which is added the Ordinary of the Mass* (Manchester, 1805).

9

THE *NEW VERSION OF THE FOUR GOSPELS*

PETER PHILLIPS

In the summer of 1836 Lingard published anonymously *A New Version of the Four Gospels*. In many ways it is, as Wiseman appreciated, a rather startling work. In the first place, this is a translation of the Gospels from the Greek text, rather than the familiar and authorised Latin Vulgate. The layout and translation is also striking. Lingard has a predilection for inverted commas, no doubt to emphasise the metaphorical overtones of a phrase: 'kingdom of heaven' is frequently highlighted in this way, as is 'the word' in the prologue of John's Gospel. Christ is throughout rendered by its Hebrew equivalent, Messiah, gospel becoming 'good tidings': thus the opening of Mark's Gospel reads: 'The beginning of the good tidings of Jesus Messiah, son of God' (Mark 1:1). For the most part good plain English terms are preferred to the Latinisms and technical theological language of the accepted translations. Lingard uses 'worship' rather than 'adore' 'because *worship* is an English, *adore*, a Latin word';[1] generally he prefers 'trust' to 'faith', but, challenged by his publisher, Lingard asked John Walker about this as he had translated '*fides tua te salvam fecit*' as 'thy faith has saved thee' (Luke 7:50): 'Turn it in your mind. Ought not the word in both passages be the same?'.[2] Perhaps rather more contentiously, 'favoured (of God)' replaces 'full of grace' in the angel's greeting to Mary (Luke 1:28). As one might expect from the historian, the notes and introduction are marked by a strongly historical and critical cast, but they lack the rigorous textual analysis that later scholars have come to expect. Lingard inverts Mark 9:12 and 13, arguing their present order to be 'the mistake of some copyist'. His solution to the oft-noted problem of Luke's reference to a census at the time of Quirinius' governorship in Syria ten years too late to relate to Jesus' birth (Luke 2:2) is to reject the reference as a late interpolation resulting from the similar 'carelessness of a copyist'.

This was all rather too much for Wiseman. John Henry Newman and the Tractarians, on the other hand, had rather fewer problems with his approach and Lingard was able to write to Walker of hearing favourable reports from Oxford.[3] The work was reviewed by Wiseman in the *Dublin*

---

1. *Lingard-Lomax Letters*, August 23rd 1836, p. 66.
2. Lingard to John Walker, January 26th [1837], UCA, Lingard Transcript 902.
3. John Lingard to John Walker, January 7th 1839, UCA, Lingard Transcript 908. Newman in his Tract 85, published in 1838, had a similarly radical view of the human fashioning of divine inspiration: 'As God rules the will, yet the will is free... so He has inspired the Bible, yet men have written it. Whatever else is true about it, this is true, – that we may speak of the history, or mode of its composition, as truly as that of other books; we may speak of its writers of having an object in view, being influenced by circumstances, being anxious, taking

Review.[4] This itself is a strange piece: in seventeen closely printed pages only twenty-five lines deal directly with the *New Version of the Four Gospels* and it is only in his concluding paragraph that Wiseman offers a positive reflection on the work before him:

> Throughout the notes and preface there is a drift which cannot be overlooked, and which has our cordial approbation; it is to place the gospels in their proper light, as narratives not intended to form a complete digest of our Saviour's life, but as 'occasional pieces,' so to speak, suggested by particular circumstances, and primarily directed to readers possessing different qualifications from ours, who could understand much that to us must be obscure. The impression on the reader's mind, after having perused this edition, must be, that Christianity never depended, for its code or evidences, upon the compilation of these documents, and that they never could have been intended for a rule of faith. Considering the work in this light, we have an additional pleasure in bearing witness to the learning, diligence, and acuteness of its author.[5]

With hardly any direct reference to Lingard's text, Wiseman takes the opportunity of calling for an authorised revision of the Douai-Rheims version. To continue to call it so, he claims, 'is an abuse of terms' for it 'has been altered and modified till scarce any verse remains as it was originally published.[6] While agreeing with Challoner's excision of Latinisms, Wiseman considers that Challoner 'weakened the language considerably'[7] and further inaccuracies have been introduced in editions since Challoner.[8] Using a detailed analysis of specimen texts, for the most part taken from the Old Testament, Wiseman carefully argues the point that a translator of the Vulgate must read it against 'a minute and often complicated study of the original texts';[9] Wiseman argues that it is only by doing this that nuance and ambiguity in the text can be appropriately clarified.[10]

---

pains, purposely omitting or introducing things, leaving things incomplete, or supplying what others had so left. Though the Bible be inspired, it has all such characteristics as might attach to a book uninspired, – the characteristics of dialect and style, the distinct effects of times and places, youth and age, of moral and intellectual character. I observe, then, that Scripture is not one book; it is a great number of writings, of various persons, living at different times, put together into one, and assuming its existing form as if casually and by accident.' ('Lectures on the Scripture Proof of the Doctrines of the Church', *Tracts for the Times*, vol. 5, 1838, No. 85, p. 30).

    4. *Dublin Review*, April 1837, pp. 475–492.

    5. *Ibid.,* p. 492.

    6. *Ibid.,* p. 476.

    7. *Ibid.,* p. 478.

    8. Lingard himself commented on Challoner's version in a letter to George Silvertop: 'it appears to me that Dr Challoner's version is the Protestant authorized version, adapted to the Vulgate. At least he seems to have had the Protestant version before him and to have adopted it generally' (John Lingard to George Silvertop, June 24th 1839, UCA, Walker Transcripts, Lingard Transcript 376).

    9. *Ibid.,* p. 478–479.

    10. For example Wiseman shows that in the Vulgate version of Wisdom 8:21 *continens* (ἐγκρατής) is translated 'continent'; elswhere in the sapiential literature it is translated as

Wiseman's article is an erudite and important piece, but hardly a review of a translation of the Gospels. In the last two paragraphs of the article Wiseman turns to the *New Version* itself and, while accepting that some of the revisions in vocabulary are pleasing, he finds others, Messiah for Christ, for example, and good tidings for gospel, 'unnecessary, and likely to startle ordinary readers'.[11]

In the first months after publication, Lingard was anxious to preserve his anonymity, revealing his authorship only to his closest friends. In late June, or early July, he reported to Mary Sanders that the work had just come out: 'it is pretty well got up, and with no great multitude of blunders considering that I could not correct the press. I must ask your acceptance of a copy: but I know not how to get it to you. For, if it be known to come to you from me, it will be known that I am the author, which for certain reasons I must keep secret'.[12] In an undated letter from this period to Robert Tate, Lingard admits that he is under a promise to his publishers not to be found in 'evangelical company'. The play of anonymity appealed to Lingard and he joked about the identity of the translator with Tate:

> If I were to *guess* I should say he is a Jesuit: for I understand that his object in his preface was to awaken in the minds of his Protestant readers doubt of the propriety of putting even the earliest part of Scriptures into the hands of uneducated people, whilst Jesuitically enough, he pretended to be doing nothing more than warning Scripturists of the manner in which they ought to read it. He has however been disappointed; for such is the horror of popery excited in the minds of the orthodox by the Conservative press, that not a copy has been ordered by Protestant booksellers.[13]

Lingard used the occasion of the same letter to seek Tate's advice on the translation of the word 'scandal', a word which 'not one catholic in twenty, not one protestant in a hundred takes... in its scriptural signification'. Lingard is tempted by 'cause of sin', (or perhaps even better 'fall' rather than 'sin'), but acknowledges that this is weak as it substitutes an interpretation for a translation of the straight metaphor. Lingard's letters to John Walker of Scarborough raise similar queries about the translation.[14]

These were all members of Lingard's intimate circle of friends. The secret was soon out, however. By August Lingard's authorship was rumoured in Liverpool,[15] and at the beginning of the following year the cat was out of the bag: Lingard wrote to Mary Sanders releasing her from her

---

'contain', or 'possess': *continens* thus does not signify *qui se continet* (one who restrains himself), but one who contains or holds something else (pp. 479–480).

11. *Ibid.,* p. 492.

12. *Lingard-Lomax Letters,* ?June/July 1836, p. 64.

13. Lingard to Tate, [September 1836], UCA, Lingard Transcript 632.

14. Lingard to Walker, April 1st 1836, UCA, Lingard Transcript 898; no date [1836], Lingard Transcript 900; 26th January [1837], Lingard Transcript 902.

15. *Lingard-Lomax Letters,* August 23rd 1836, p. 66.

obligation of silence but asks her, for the sake of his publishers, to refrain from admitting that she *knows* it to be his.[16]

One might hazard the suggestion that here lies the explanation for Wiseman's rather odd contribution to the *Dublin Review*. Amongst the uncatalogued Wiseman manuscripts at Ushaw are two undated drafts; one entitled 'On a Revision of the Douay version of the Scriptures and the original texts', the other 'Remarks on the New Version of the Gospels by a Catholic'. The *Dublin Review* piece follows the former in some detail. The latter, a detailed and strong critique of Lingard's translation, is not referred to. It is hard to know how these two drafts are related. Could Wiseman have withdrawn the detailed criticism of *A New Version of the Four Gospels* on hearing rumour of Lingard's authorship and replaced it at the last minute with a scholarly but relatively innocuous discussion of some principles of translation? It seems likely. Wiseman might have balked at public criticism of his former teacher which might have resulted in unseemly divisions within the Catholic community.

Wiseman's unpublished, twenty-four page manuscript offers a detailed critique of Lingard's translation and concludes with a forthright condemnation:

> I have noticed only some of its most glaring defects. I have been silent respecting a great number of other passages in which the translation appears vicious. No Biblical scholar, I should suppose, will peruse this version and its notes without pronouncing that the author has completely failed in attempting to improve on other versions, and in giving an originally true view of the meaning of the Sacred Text.

Wiseman takes issue with Lingard verse by verse, sometimes on minor points, sometimes on major questions of translation. Wiseman rejected 'repent' as an adequate translation of μετανοείτε (Matthew 3:2) because Catholic authors understand the word as including 'not only repentance, or change of heart, but a disposition to atone for our sins by penitential works'. This is, of course, a major crux of anti-Protestant apologetic, Protestant versions following the Greek, Catholic versions the Vulgate. In his early preface to a new edition of Ward's *Errata of the Protestant Bible* (1810) Lingard had made precisely this point, supporting the Vulgate reading by comparing it with Matthew 11:21/Luke 10:13 ('they had done penance in sackcloth and ashes') and by reference to the Fathers who always style the performance of penitential works μετανοείν, and 'who', he adds rather ungraciously, 'probably understood the real import of their own language as well as Protestant translators'.[17] In his *New Version* Lingard is simply attempting to provide an accurate rendering of the Greek text, justifying his choice in a carefully nuanced footnote which concludes 'though there can be no true repentance which produces not reformation, there is often a reformation which is not produced by repen-

---

16. *Lingard-Lomax Letters*, 8th/9th January 1837, p. 73.
17. John Lingard, *Ward's Errata of the Protestant Bible*, (Dublin, 1810), p. 8.

tance'. Ronald Knox, here, as in many places, is on Lingard's side of the debate, finding Lingard's footnote 'admirable', and adding that the translation *poenitentiam agere* ('to do penance') was the only option available for Jerome in translating μετανοεῖτε into Latin as *poenitet* has to be impersonal, except in the participle.[18]

Wiseman was particularly concerned to challenge Lingard's rendering of κεχαριτωμένη as 'favoured (of God)' (Luke 1:28) and we might agree at this point that Lingard's version is inadequate. In a long note on the passage Wiseman cites

Beza who rejects the *gratiosa* (favoured) of Erasmus, [and who] says that it was a new word adopted by St Luke to express an idea quite different from *gratiosa*. Indeed when we consider that in the New Testament the word χάρις, *gratia*, generally signifies not favour of a natural order, but a *supernatural* favour which we call divine grace, we can safely conclude that in the intention of the sacred Penman the word χαριτόω signifies an infusion of divine grace, and that in a copious degree... Now it is the opinion of many Biblical scholars that the vulgate in all its important parts was translated for the use of the Latin Christians under the eye and with the sanction of St Peter himself or some other apostle. Can we then doubt that the translator understood the genuine meaning of κεχαριτωμένη much better than moderns and that in rendering it *gratia plena* he conformed to the understanding of the primitive Fathers and Christians?

Knox, like Wiseman, was to accept the traditional reading of the angelic address, 'Hail, thou who art full of grace', but he follows Lingard in preferring 'favour' to 'grace' in Luke 2:52: Lingard's version runs, 'And Jesus improved in wisdom, and stature, and favour, both with God and man'. Knox comments pertinently, 'Is there really any sense in saying that our Lord grew in grace with men?'[19] Lingard is at least trying to be consistent as he wrestled with the import of Luke 1:28, and he has the Revised Version and the New English Bible, as well as the Jerusalem Bible on his side. He does, however, opt for 'grace' earlier at Luke 2:40, suggesting this translation preserves the ambiguity inherent in the Greek original which can be understood as either heavenly beauty or divine favour.

Lingard was a historian, not a Biblical scholar, but many of his insights are sound. Much to Wiseman's consternation, he questions whether Jesus publicly proclaimed himself to be Messiah. He was unusually sensitive to the influence of particular context on the shaping of Jesus' message and its significance for our own understanding of the Gospels, being prepared to

18. Ronald Knox, *On Englishing the Bible*, (London, 1949), p. 22.
19. Knox, *op. cit.*, p. 21. Lingard was quite prepared to use the word 'grace' when he thought it necessary. Ward in his *Errata of the Protestant Bible* (see below) accused the Protestant translators of translating χάρισμα as gift (1 Tim. 4:14; 2 Tim. 1:6). Lingard asserts that in scriptural language χάρισμα is never properly rendered 'gift', there is always included a supernatural element better described as *grace* (p. 5).

go as far as suggesting that many 'passages, though strictly applicable to the Jewish converts, had no reference to the form of discipline to be established in the Churches of Gentile origin' (p. xv).[20] He is equally prepared to acknowledge that the knowledge of the earthly Jesus 'was limited, like his power, to the object of his mission' (see note on Matthew 24:36). Above all, Lingard recognises with later scholars the vital function eschatology plays in interpreting the Gospels: the times in which Jesus lived were utterly determined by the expectation of the coming of the kingdom of God. Lingard is quite clear that the metaphors here are of activity, not place: expressions like 'the coming of the son of man', 'the coming of his kingdom', 'his coming in his kingdom' point to the same 'manifestation of that kingly authority'. He points out 'perhaps it would be an improvement, if, in some passages βασιλεία were translated *sovereignty*, instead of *kingdom*' (see notes on Matthew 10:23 and Luke 17:20). As he was to remark a few years later to George Silvertop, his school-mate at Douai and one who had played a leading part in the stereotype controversy of 1813:

> You mention Lingard's version – that version I understand was made not for the sake of the version but of the preface and of a few of the notes, and the object of the translator was to induce some readers at least to consider the question seriously and without prejudice when he thought that they would come to the same conclusion with him; that the books are only occasional tracts written for the use of certain contemporaries without any view to the instruction of future ages. He has been urged frequently to continue with the Epistles, but has often desisted after beginning for this important reason, that he cannot understand them. He is convinced that the Christians before the destruction of Jerusalem and in daily expectation of that event, had among them a conventional language on certain subjects which none but the initiated could understand...[21]

This is a useful summary of an introduction to the *New Version of the Four Gospels* which is itself a model of brevity.

It could be that Wiseman misunderstands the intention behind Lingard's work. In later years Wiseman seemed keen to marginalise Lingard's significance; he sought to undermine the suggestion that it was Lingard whom Leo XII had created Cardinal *in petto* in 1826.[22] Lingard's obituary in *The Tablet,* declaring 'its sympathies and whole soul to be with Rome and Ultramontanism', professes a similar reserve, criticising his

---

20. *New Version*, p. xv.

21. John Lingard to George Silvertop, June 24th 1839, UCA, Walker Transcripts, Lingard Transcript 376. For the Stereotype controversy see note 26.

22. Nicholas Wiseman, *Recollections of the Last Four Popes and of Rome in their Times*, (London, 1858), pp. 207–215; Wiseman suggests that the Pope had Félicité de Lamennais in mind. The priest and historian Mark Tierney, Lingard's first memorialist and 'one of Wiseman's most vocal opponents in the ranks of the English clergy' (Richard J. Schiefen, *Nicholas Wiseman and the Transformation of English Catholicism* (Shepherdstown, 1984), p. 71) defended Lingard's reputation against the Cardinal's claims (see Schiefen, pp. 270–272).

old-fashioned and now outmoded Gallicanism.[23] For *The Tablet* Lingard
belonged to 'a school now diminishing, and of which the influence is failing' and as such his work 'will sink somewhat in public estimation...
not... owing to inaccuracies, or misrepresentations, or to obsolete style,
but to another feeling, to the growing dislike of his school, to the abandon-
ment of local peculiarities, and a more healthy sense of the strength and
beauty of Rome'. For Wiseman and the author of *The Tablet* obituary the
question had become a matter of defining English Catholic identity firmly in Ultramontanist terms: *A New Version of the Four Gospels* is for *The
Tablet* yet another indication of Lingard's Gallican inclinations. The fact
that Bishop Kenrick of Philadelphia speaks highly of Lingard and
acknowledges that he follows him freely in his own edition of *The Four
Gospels* which was published in the United States in 1849 might at first
seem to offer further indication that Lingard should be placed firmly in
this camp: Kenrick, as Archbishop of St. Louis, was to be one of the leading figures of the opposition at Vatican I.[24]

Joseph Chinnici, though taking a more positive view of Lingard in his
study of the historian than does the Cardinal, develops the point at some
length in suggesting that Lingard's translation of the Gospels 'represented
a concrete example of the Cisalpine approach to preaching the message in
the environment of the Second Spring'.[25] Chinnici sets Lingard's work in
a context shaped by the Scottish priest and biblical scholar Alexander
Geddes and the subsequent attempts of Charles Butler and the Catholic
Board to disseminate a cheap stereotyped edition of the New Testament in
1813.[26] I do not find this particularly helpful; moreover I suspect it fails
to appreciate the internal development within Lingard's thought. Though
agreeing with Charles Butler on many questions, Lingard seems to have
differed from him on the question of the use of Bibles in schools, as the
letter to George Silvertop testifies:

> You mention the great controversy respecting the Scriptures. For my
> part, I cannot think that the point in question is worth a straw. No
> Protestant child will ever become Catholic by reading the Catholic
> translation, nor Catholic become Protestant by reading the Protestant
> version. In fact the Scriptures appear to me the most unfit book in the
> world to be used in Schools. The Bible abounds in passages unfit to
> meet the eye of children and nine-tenths of the book are above their
> comprehension – one half, I suspect, beyond the comprehension of
> those who pretend to teach it. But it is now the fashion or rage, and we
> must submit to it.[27]

23. *The Tablet*, vol. 12, no. 589, July 26th 1851, pp. 473–474.
24. Lord Acton considered Kenrick to be, with Strossmayer, Darboy, and Hefele the best
men of the Council: see Christopher Hill, *Lord Acton* (New Haven & London, 2000), p. 222.
25. Chinnici, p. 149.
26. See R.C. Fuller, *Alexander Geddes 1737–1802* (Sheffield, 1984); Hugh Pope, *English
Versions of the Bible* (London, 1952); P. Phillips, 'Catholic Biblemongers: Silvertop or
Copperbottom?', *Northern Catholic History*, 43, (2002), pp. 39–46.
27. John Lingard to George Silvertop, June 24th 1839, UCA, Walker Transcripts, Lingard
Transcript 376. For the controversy over Butler's attempt to support an interdenominational

Lingard certainly had his roots in the Cisalpine tradition and is most clearly representative of the tradition in his first book, *The Antiquities of the Anglo-Saxon Church* (1806), a position which continued to influence his liturgical thought. In his controversial writings, on the other hand, and in *The History of England* (1819–1830), we see a different position emerging. As Lingard grows in confidence we find him preparing to take on the English establishment and to challenge its self-definition in a way rather different from his Cisalpine forebears. In this he is more of an ally to his former pupil and future Cardinal than Wiseman himself realised, though Lingard's approach was to remain far more subtle and more under-stated than Wiseman's was to be.

A New Version of the Four Gospels belongs within the tradition of Lingard's controversial writings, both public and private. The primary purpose of the book is to show that Scripture cannot be read independently of tradition. In a forthright note on John 13:15, for example, he muses over whether the washing of the feet should be regarded as a sacrament:

> Did [the Lord] not command his disciples to wash one another's feet, and attach the promise of grace to the ceremony? There does not appear to me any stronger proof *from scripture* that baptism and the eucharist are sacraments, than that this washing of the feet is also one. It is, indeed, true that it was never considered such; and that shows that the first Christians interpreted these writings by the doctrine which they had already imbibed from their instructors.

Lingard's intention is to assert the authority of the Church and a passing remark on Matthew 10:2, backed up with a series of patristic references, betrays his underlying loyalties: 'Peter is here called the first, not in number only, but in rank.' Like the majority of his Catholic contemporaries, Lingard considered the Vulgate to be a translation of an earlier and more accurate Greek manuscript than any currently available Greek text. Lingard's notes to the *New Version* underline the point: for example at Matthew 8:30, Lingard adds 'the learned reader will observe that I frequently prefer the Latin to the Greek text' and for the most part he is correct in so doing.

The insights of modern scholarship might correct Lingard on matters of detail, but his comments to Silvertop remain not far from the truth:

> You ask what I think the best version extant. I answer the Vulgate without a doubt, and, if we take the Christian Scriptures only (and with these as Christians we are chiefly concerned) a version better than the present Greek original. Nor is this my opinion alone. You remember at the dinner at poor Mr Mawman's, with respect to which we have sometimes laughed at the expense of the late Mr Blundell. Mr Freund was of the party. He sat next to me and told me after a long study of the subject he had come to that conclusion. The reason is this, that it appears to have

school for the poor in London at which Bible reading would form the staple of religious education, see Bernard Ward, *The Eve of Catholic Emancipation* (London, 1911), vol. 2, pp. 161–165.

been an interlineary version, rendering the Greek Text word for word, and therefore representing to us a Greek Ms much more ancient than any which exists at the present day. You will see that as a version it must be more fair and honest than any made in these later ages because it was made above a thousand years before the controversies, which now divide Christians, had any existence; and therefore the translator could have had no bias towards any particular system regarding such controversies: a bias which must influence the mind when passages are susceptible of several meanings. This happens much oftener than you would imagine, particularly in the construction of participles, and when the form of assertion or command is the same. Thus for example the much quoted text 'Search the Scriptures'; in the original or in the Latin may mean either that, or 'You search the Scriptures'; for both forms are alike in these languages, but the ambiguity cannot be preserved in English. Another cause is that the translator lived when Greek was a spoken language and was probably master of the colloquial Greek in which the books are written. But modern translators are acquainted only with classical language and seek to illustrate the New Testament from passages in the Greek poets, who lived many centuries before, which appears to me as strange as if some learned man, a thousand years hence, be supposed to get hold of one of our present newspapers and undertake to point out its meaning by passages from Chaucer and Shakespeare. Excuse this dissertation. I ran into it unwittingly. I am unable to answer your question respecting St Jerome and have not books by me to consult. He made, I believe, some alterations in the Old Testament books in the Vulgate: or rather some alterations in them have been adopted from him. The Vulgate Version was originally made by a native of Africa. In St Jerome's time it was but one of a great number of versions. How it happened at last to exclude the others, even that called Vetus Itala, I know not.[28]

The currently available printed Greek version, and the text which Lingard translated, was that first published by Robert Estienne in the sixteenth century and known universally as the Textus Receptus. This was the version on which the English Authorized Version of 1611 depended. Although introducing a critical apparatus which recorded variant readings collated from the different manuscripts available, this text was based on a late and significantly corrupt manuscript tradition. Jerome's Vulgate Gospels, though merely a thoroughgoing fourth century revision of the existing Old Latin text, was based on a much earlier and more secure manuscript tradition. It might well be that Lingard's decision to translate the more unsatisfactory Greek text, but that on which the Authorized Version is founded, is an example of a subtle polemical intent. The notes are not generally openly controversial in tone, but the careful reader might discern the occasional pull of a polemical undertow. Lingard gently takes issue

28. John Lingard to George Silvertop, June 24th 1839, UCA, Walker Transcripts, Lingard Transcript 376.

with Herbert Marsh in his interpretation of Mark 7:19, and, more importantly, cites Wiseman's *Horae Syriacae* in refutation of an understanding of the words of institution as merely representational on the grounds that Aramaic had no other way of expressing representation other than by the expression 'This is my body' (Mark 14:22): Wiseman offered more than thirty words by which Aramaic is able to express representation rather than identity, which Jesus could have used had he so wished.

Lingard approached the text with an open mind and with the vigorous independence which was his wont. For example, while he preferred the Vulgate reading of *justitiam* (δικαιοσύνη, religious duties) to the ἐλεημοσύνη (kind deed, alms) of the Textus Receptus version of Matthew 6:1, and here he is followed by modern scholars, he follows the Textus Receptus, which generally opts for a smoother reading, for John 12:47, preferring μὴ πιστεύσῃ (believe not) to the Vulgate's *non custodierit* (keep not), the latter being the preferred modern reading (μὴ φυλάξῃ). Lingard notes that his Greek text of Matthew 6:33, and in three other places in Matthew's Gospel, has 'kingdom of God' rather than Matthew's preferred 'kingdom of heaven' and asks 'was the alteration here accidental on the part of the Evangelist, or of his Greek translator, who might be betrayed, without noticing it, into the use of his native idiom?' Here the Vulgate and Textus Receptus collude in what might be thought to be a misreading significantly absent from the great fourth century Codex Sinaiticus which was finally to be published by Tischendorf in 1862.

Two early works are of particular significance in the evolution of *A New Version of the Four Gospels*: Lingard's Preface to a reprinting of the long-standing work of anti-Protestant polemic, Ward's *Errata of the Protestant Bible,* and his pamphlet *Strictures on Dr. Marsh's 'Comparative View of the Churches of England and Rome'*. In 1810 Lingard prefaced the new edition of Ward's *Errata of the Protestant Bible* by taking up the gauntlet thrown down by the Dublin prebendary Edward Ryan's *Analysis of Ward's Errata of the Protestant Bible* and he does so with some panache, providing a detailed and closely argued review of Ryan's pamphlet, sharply polemical in tone.[29] The Douai-Rheims Bible made its contribution, often unsung, to correcting the readings of the Authorised Version,[30] but the work remained incomplete. Lingard depicts the irony of a 'scriptural Church... originally founded on a false translation of the scriptures...

29. First published 1688. For Thomas Ward, see Geoffrey Scott, OSB, 'Thomas Ward and Hexhamshire: Catholic Apologetics in the Tyne Valley', *Northern Catholic History*, 41, (2000), pp. 32–37. The fourth edition was published by Richard Coyne, (Dublin, 1810) with a preface by Lingard. Lingard's preface seems also to have been published separately as a pamphlet in its own right: 'Defence of Ward's Errata to the Protestant Bible' (Dublin, 1810). A fifth edition was published by James Duffy (Dublin, 1841) to which was appended 'Letter VII' (in answer to Richard Grier's reply to Ward) from John Milner's *A Vindication of the End of Relgious Controversy* (London, 1822). This must be the only time Lingard and his esrtwhile antagonist Bishop Milner were published together as apparent allies between the same covers.

30. See, for example, J.G. Carleton, *The Part of Rheims in the Making of the English Bible* (Oxford, 1902).

every old *woman*, both male and female [becoming] an adept, if not in knowledge of the Bible, at least in the prejudices and errors of its translators'.[31] Whether such errors were by ignorance or design remained a matter for dispute, but Lingard is prepared to follow Ward in arguing that corroborative evidence suggests the latter. Rather ungenerously, Lingard claims that Pope Adrian II's grant of Ireland to Henry II, depriving the twelfth century Ryans of their Irish estates, sowed a seed of resentment against Rome that came to fruition in Ryan's attack. It is all the stuff of the cut and thrust familiar to the readers of much nineteenth century religious controversy: rather artificial, stylised, and not particularly edifying.

Within the rhetoric of debate, however, Lingard is beginning to plot for himself the basic principles appropriate to Biblical translation. Lingard's Preface reveals a historian's sensitivity to textual criticism, a study still relatively in its infancy, and some ability to evaluate variant readings of the Hebrew, Syriac, Arabic, Ethiopic versions, that of the Chaldaic paraphrast, as well as the more familiar Greek and Vulgate versions, at least by way of contemporary hand-books and dictionaries.[32] At one point he is able to correct a mistranslation in the Latin translation of the Samaritan Pentateuch by reference to the original Genesis 37:35.[33] Perhaps the Douai-Rheims Bible had opted for an over-literal rendering of the Vulgate, introducing into its English text a multitude of Latinisms, but an inner consistency of translation was one of its strengths. It is with inconsistency that Ward, and Lingard following him, charge the Protestant translators, a 'verbal legerdemain'[34] which at many points imposes a translation which supports Protestant doctrine. They discuss examples touching on the main heads of Reformation controversy: justification, merit, the doctrine of the Sacraments.

A further principle of good translation is an attempt to render a word in a manner akin to the good usage of the present day. Ryan accuses the Catholic Version of mistranslating πρεσβύτερος as 'priest' rather than 'elder'. Lingard responds that function and common usage suggests 'priest' as a more appropriate translation of the word and he poses a challenge: surely it would be incorrect to translate the Latin sentence, '*Episcopus Londoniensis cum majore civitatis et duobus ecclesiae presbyteris visitavit universitatem Oxfordiensem*' as 'the overseer of London,

---

31. *Errata*, p. 1.
32. The Library at Ushaw possess copies of the four great early Polyglot editions of the Bible: the Complutensian (Alcala, 1514–1517), the Plantin (Antwerp, 1569–1572), the Paris (Paris, 1629–1645) and Walton's (London, 1657), texts all at least noted by Lingard in his controversy with Bishop Barrington in 1807 (see *A Collection of Tracts on Several Subjects*, Keating (London, 1826), p. 29). There are also copies of Houbigant's *Biblia Hebraica* (Paris, 1753), Kennicott's *Vetus Testamentum Hebraicum* (Oxford, 1776), and Tremellius' *New Testament* (Geneva, 1569). Apart from the Walton Polyglot, which came to Crook Hall as part of the library of Edward Dicconson (see Alistair MacGregor, *The Library of Edward Dicconson*, Ushaw College Library, 2002), it is not known whether the other volumes were at the College in Lingard's time.
33. *Errata*, p. 10.
34. *Errata*, p. 11.

with the greater of the city, and two elders of the church, visited the generality of Oxford'. Literal consistency would suggest that if 'bishop' and 'priest' are rendered 'overseer' and 'elder', 'disciple' and 'angel' should be rendered 'scholar' and 'messenger', but this thoroughgoing consistency is not demanded by Protestant versions.[35] Perhaps the Douai-Rheims Version might also be susceptible to such criticism, but to demonstrate this was not the object of Lingard's study.

Lingard returns to the theme a few years later in the pamphlet, *Strictures on Dr. Marsh's 'Comparative View of the Churches of England and Rome'* which came out during the first half of 1815. Charles Butler had sent him Herbert Marsh's book on the Synoptics and had recomended Marsh, who was known to him, as a worthy opponent. Butler thought highly of Marsh who had studied under Michaelis in Göttingen and was one of the first to popularise German critical methods in Britain; he was by this time Lady Margaret Professor of Divinity in Cambridge. Butler suggested to Lingard how Marsh's work might be tackled: 'I think a most powerful attack on him might be made by shewing how the whole of the Protestant Creed is founded on Tradition... according to [his system of the origination of the Gospels] many of the texts in the scripture must have been delivered through 8 or 10 hands before they attained the place which they now hold in the Gospel.'[36] This was indeed the line Lingard followed in his pamphlet by inquiring whether the reformers 'by rejecting the authority of tradition, have not in effect destroyed the authority of scripture, taken away the security of religious belief, and undermined the very foundations of Christianity.'[37] Lingard's point is that Scripture and tradition, far from being independent sources of doctrine, belong together and that outside the tradition of authentic interpretation 'the written word is of itself a dead letter' and a variety of contending interpretations lead only to the breakdown of unity and the numerous creeds of the reformed churches. Here we find already set out the theme Lingard takes up again in *A New Version of the Four Gospels*: 'the manner in which the New Testament is composed, of occasional and unconnected tracts, shews that it was not designed by the apostles – nor by the Spirit of God – to be the only rule of faith'.[38] Lingard recognised the contradiction that John Henry Newman, not yet a Catholic, was to tease out in his *Lectures on the Prophetical Office of the Church*: 'the Bible does not carry with it its own interpretation'.[39] This was first published in 1837, the year after Lingard's *New Version* appeared. Lingard in his earlier debate with Marsh illustrated his argument with four examples not unfamiliar to Newman: a rigor-

35. *Errata*, p. 6.

36. Charles Butler to John Lingard, November 4th 1814, CUL Add. Ms. 9418.

37. 'Strictures on Dr. Marsh's "Comparative View of the Churches of England and Rome"' in *A Collection of Tracts on Several Subjects connected with the Civil and Religious Principles of Catholics* (London, 1826), p. 392.

38. *Collection of Tracts*, p. 406.

39. John Henry Newman, *The Via Media of the Anglican Church* (London, 1901), vol. 1, p. 245. See Ian Ker, *John Henry Newman* (Oxford, 1988), pp. 139–144.

ously asserted doctrine of *sola Scriptura* can provide grounds neither for Scriptural inspiration itself, nor for the canon of Scripture; similarly, neither the doctrine of infant baptism, nor the observation of Sunday can be deemed certain from Scripture alone.

Even while Lingard was in the process of translating *A New Version of the Four Gospels* he was drawn into a more private controversy regarding the Scriptures. His new-found friend, Mary Frances Sanders, had been exiled from home and family after her conversion to Catholicism and her father invited his friend, John Dalby, vicar of Castle Donnington, to enter into controversy with her. Lingard's letters to her during this period are peppered with ammunition for the dispute. As we might expect, questions of Scripture and tradition play a central place: 'may you not say', writes Lingard, 'how you cannot conceive that without tradition he can prove the books of the new testament to be the word of God?'[40] Dalby was to publish his own discussion of Scripture in the very year of the publication of *A New Version of the Four Gospels* and Lingard himself draws the parallel.[41]

It seems, then, that it is religious controversy which provides the context in which we can best understand Lingard's intention in publishing his translation of the Gospels. Its origins lie in the anti-Protestant polemic of the early pamphlets. But Wiseman was not altogther wrong in his assessment: Lingard's work transcends the boundaries of mere polemic. It is perhaps the freedom and the independence of mind which Lingard brought to the task of translating the Gospels that particularly unsettled Wiseman, but it is these very qualities which make *A New Version of the Four Gospels* so modern. An edition, acknowledging Lingard's authorship, was published in 1851, but many in the Catholic community remained ill at ease with Lingard's version; it was disliked at Ushaw from the start, and Edmund Winstanley, the Rector of the English College, Lisbon, felt constrained to write a damning letter about it to Wiseman suggesting that the translation was 'calculated to do mischief to the British Catholics, by leading them to a false view of some important parts in the Gospels and to a depreciation of the Vulgate as the only authentic version of the Originals'.[42] For the most part, however, it is Lingard's views that have stood the test of time. In bringing the rigours of a historical method to the Gospel texts, Lingard, in his introduction and notes in particular, raises issues which show him to be an astute and thoughtful Biblical comentator not unmindful of questions which would tax the minds of a future generation of fine New Testament scholars.

---

40. *Lingard-Lomax Letters*, p. 30. For Dalby see *Lingard-Lomax Letters*, p. 174, note 59.
41. *Lingard-Lomax Letters*, p. 61. Dalby's work has not been identified.
42. Lingard to John Walker, January 26th [1837], UCA, Lingard Transcript 902; Edmund Winstanley to Nicholas Wiseman, June 16th 1852, Winstanley's Letter Books, vol. 5, Lisbon College Archives, Ushaw.

10

OFF DUTY: LINGARD'S LETTERS TO WOMEN

JOHN TRAPPES-LOMAX

John Lingard was an excellent and prolific letter-writer,[1] and well over two thousand of his letters survive. For the most part, as one would expect, they are concerned with historical questions and with the affairs of the English Catholic Church; for the most part too his correspondents are men and very often Catholic priests. All this lends a special interest to his letters to his two regular female correspondents, one of whom was a Unitarian. Lingard's ninety-nine surviving letters to Mary Frances Sanders (1814–1875; married Thomas Lomax on June 15th 1837) run from 1835 to 1851; they have now been published,[2] but were not available to Martin Haile and Edwin Bonney for their *Life and Letters of John Lingard*. His 111 letters to Hannah Joyce (c. 1809–1892; married William Ridyard on December 30th 1847) run from 1841 to 1850; they are in the library of Harris Manchester College, Oxford, and I am greatly obliged for permission to read and excerpt them; they were used by Haile and Bonney, but have not been published. The majority of the letters to Mrs. Lomax were lost before her death; many of those that do survive concern private family matters, so there does not appear to have been any deliberate censorship. On the other hand Mrs. Ridyard wrote to Mrs. Newmann asking that if she inherited the letters she should 'destroy any of a private nature that she find among them' (Oct. 17th 1878); it should therefore be borne in mind that this collection may be neither complete nor representative; for example, if it were complete, we would expect to find a letter of consolation on the death of Dr. Shepherd.

Both of his female correspondents were highly intelligent and well read; Miss Sanders certainly and Miss Joyce presumably received their education at home in clerical households. Rev. Charles Sanders was an Anglican clergyman in Lincolnshire, and his only daughter distressed him deeply by becoming a Catholic in 1834. Miss Joyce's father, Jeremiah Joyce,[3] was for many years Secretary of the Unitarian Society and had the distinction of being imprisoned on an unsustainable charge of treasonable practices in 1794, but was released without trial; his daughter Hannah was a life-long Unitarian. After his death she was brought up by William

---

1. See Appendix 2.

2. John Trappes-Lomax (ed.), *The Lingard-Lomax Letters*, CRS 77 (2000). Letters in this collection are cited both by date and by page number.

3. For the career of Jeremiah Joyce (1763–1816), cf. *DNB* and J. Seed, 'Jeremiah Joyce, Unitarianism and the Radical Intelligentsia in the 1790s', *Transactions of the Unitarian Historical Society*, 17, (1981), pp. 97–108. That Hannah was his youngest daughter appears from *The Gentleman's Magazine*, 1 (1848), p. 304, but I have been unable to find the exact date of her birth.

Shepherd,[4] Unitarian minister at Gateacre near Liverpool, and author of the celebrated *Life of Poggio Bracciolini* (London, 1802), for which he was awarded a Doctorate by Edinburgh University; he was a staunch ally in the fight for Catholic political and educational rights,[5] and had been in correspondence with Lingard since at least 1824. The immediate cause of Miss Joyce's writing to Lingard may have been the stay which Shepherd invited Lingard to make when he came to Liverpool to give evidence in the disputed will case of Blundell v. Camoys, which he did on September 2nd 1840. In her memoir of Lingard she writes, 'by degrees my fear of trespassing on the kindness of Dr. Lingard wore away under the influence of his benignant temper, & I used to write to him freely & often, to ask his opinion on any book I was reading, or for information on any subject'; she would also pass on political and literary news. She was of course greatly impressed by Lingard:

> polished and charming as were his manners to all, I always considered that towards our sex they were peculiarly winning, combining the high bred courtesy of the finished gentleman, with the chivalrous attentions which I have been accustomed to attribute to the foreign priest of the old school.

Lingard possibly feared jealousy among his female correspondents; Miss Joyce seems to have learned nothing of Mrs. Lomax until after Lingard's death, but they must have then got in touch, for the biography of Lingard among the Joyce papers is in fact in Mrs. Lomax' hand and is a version of her accounts of Lingard quoted in CRS 77 pp. 4–9. Mrs. Lomax knew (so far as one can tell from the surviving correspondence) little of Miss Joyce; all that she hears of her is a reference to the first letter that Lingard received from the latter:

> What convert has Mr. Morris[6] made at Wakefield? I have a correspondent, a Miss Joyce, a very amiable unitarian girl near Liverpool, who told me that she had met Mr. Morris, but was "disposed to feel some unkindness towards him for having stolen a lamb from their flock at Wakefield, in a Mrs. Kendall, an act of petty larceny" (Oct. 16th 1841; p. 118).

To Miss Joyce herself he had turned the accusation aside with gentle humour: 'in former times he was in the habit of stealing young ladies' hearts: so that he is an old hand at petty larceny, and you must not be surprised at his carrying off the Kendall lamb' (Sept. 8th 1841). On the other

---

4. For the career of William Shepherd, cf. *DNB* and F. Nicholson and E. Axon, 'The Manuscripts of William Shepherd at Manchester College, Oxford', *Transactions of the Unitarian Historical Society*, 2 (1922), pp. 119–130.

5. For the relations between Catholicism and Unitarianism, cf. G.M. Ditchfield, '"Incompatible with the Very Name of Christian": English Catholics and Unitarians in the Age of Milner', *RH*, 25, (2000), pp. 52–73.

6. Rev John Morris (?–1855) was the priest at Wakefield and had received Miss Sanders into the Catholic Church.

hand, when Miss Joyce was looking for a situation for a Mrs. Thellwall, he writes:

> I am the most unlikely man in the world to meet with a suitable situation for her, living as I do out of catholic society, and having scarcely a catholic female correspondent. However nil desperandum. The manner in which you interest yourself in her favour is deserving of the highest praise and the warmth of your charity is a reproach to the coldness of mine (May 18th 1843).

Much though Lingard teases Mrs. Lomax for her 'Jesuitism', he was quite capable of employing equivocation himself; his letter would scarcely have led Miss Joyce to suspect that there was one Catholic lady with whom he had such an intimate correspondence.

It is impossible to study the surviving correspondence without admiring the skill with which Lingard adapts the content of his letters to the interests and predispositions of the recipients; as a result there is surprisingly little overlap. This is very noticeable in the field of politics: Mrs. Lomax was, unlike Lingard, a Tory. In one of his earliest letters to her he assures her that

> in politics I see not the difficulty of joining your faith as a catholic with your opinions as a Tory. Many catholic gentlemen do not, who are as violent at present as any tories – I mean in the conservative interest. The tories at present abuse us, because they find that religious abuse is a powerful engine with the ignorant and the bigotted. But that is all – and that will soon pass away (June 6th 1835; p. 139).

Miss Joyce had been brought up in the tradition of radical dissent, and with her Lingard takes an active political rôle. Thus when the Unitarians were alarmed by the possible defeat of the Dissenters' Chapels Bill, which was to secure them in the legal possession of Dissenting chapels that had come into their hands,[7] Lingard lobbied hard on their behalf: 'I wrote also to Mr. Howard of Corby[8] to solicit his vote, telling him that he was bound to give it in your favour for all the services which the Unitarians had rendered us in the long struggle for emancipation – and requesting him to suggest the same to his kinsman, the earl of Arundel and Surrey' (May 15th 1844). He had also written 'to Mr. Silvertop...[9] to solicit the vote of Mr. Standish and of other members of his acquaintance, putting it on the ground of rendering one good office for another'. After the Bill went to

---

7. Cf. Ditchfield, *op. cit.*, p. 62.

8. Philip Henry Howard of Corby (1801–1883) was M.P. for Carlisle; Henry Granville Fitzalan-Howard, Earl of Arundel and Surrey (1815–60), eldest son of the Duke of Norfolk, was M.P. for Arundel; cf. J.A. Stack, 'Catholic Members of Parliament who Represented British Constituencies, 1829–1882: a Prosopographical Analysis', *RH*, 24 (1999), pp. 335–353.

9. George Silvertop (1775–1849) of Minsteracres, co. Northumberland, was a wealthy Catholic landowner and a life-long friend of Lingard's; they had been at Douai together. Charles Strickland Standish (1790–1863) was also of Catholic landed gentry stock and was M.P. for Wigan; cf. Stack, *op. cit.*

the Lords, Lingard continued his efforts: 'I cannot find that I am personally known to any protestant members of the house. Of the votes of the
catholic members you are, I think, secure. Still I will not fail to urge your
claim with them to the best of my power, and write to them or some of
them immediately' (July 8th 1844).

Their political sympathies made Dr. Shepherd and Miss Joyce regular
visitors to Lord Brougham[10] at Brougham Hall just outside Penrith; it was
during their journeys to or from that place that they were in the habit of
calling on Lingard. But Lingard did not feel obliged on that account to
conceal his opinion of Brougham; he hoped that Shepherd will 'enjoy
himself at Brougham Castle; yet I do not envy him for I cannot help thinking that my Lord has a spice of insanity about him. I shall be delighted to
see the Dr. again at Hornby' (Sept. 26th 1843). It might be added that
Lingard was not inclined to encourage overnight visits; he expresses his
regret that a proposed visit must be given up; his house has only one spare
bed, and the inn 'is so miserable a place that you could not possibly be
comfortable there a single day' (Sept. 16th 1845). The privilege of staying overnight at Hornby was confined to very close friends like George
Silvertop and Mrs. Lomax herself. Other visitors were not greeted with
enthusiasm; thus a Mr. and Mrs. Holden will be welcome on Miss Joyce's
recommendation, 'though I am not very fond of exhibiting my infirmities
and oddities to strangers' (Dec. 25th 1846). Whereas to Mrs. Lomax he
writes (for example):

I shall be happy to see your Ladyship and family on Tuesday... Tell the
Peri and the Comte [her two eldest children], that I have been growing
stronger every day since I heard of the distinguished honour, which they
think of doing me: and if they beat me in a race up and down my walk,
I will do them the honour to dine with them, an honour wh[ich] I have
not done to any other individual for several years (Oct. 12th 1849; p.
153).

Lingard felt free to express his disapproval of Daniel O'Connell[11] to
Miss Sanders: 'Like you I am prejudiced against O'Connell. He is an
Irishman, therefore hasty, imprudent, offensive' (Spring 1836; p. 158). To
Miss Joyce he expresses a more benevolent interest on hearing that she

---

10. Henry Peter Brougham (1778–1868), Baron Brougham and Vaux, Lord Chancellor
1830–1834; Whig politician; legal and social reformer. Lingard was not alone in attributing to
him 'a spice of insanity', cf. R.K. Huch, *Henry, Lord Brougham, the Later Years 1830–1868*,
(Lewiston NY, 1993), p. 216: 'There is still a persistent view that Brougham, if not insane, at
least was "disturbed"... if "disturbed" is taken to mean someone in a state of agitation, it is
quite an appropriate description. His pacing, his talking to himself, compulsive need for information, and his frequent tomfoolery are evidence of an active mind not an unbalanced one.' In
spite of Lingard's comments about Brougham to Miss Jocye, it might be noted that Brougham
is to be numbered among the guests who visited the Mission House in Hornby. He also contributed towards the subscription towards the portrait by Lonsdale which was presented to
Lingard in 1834.

11. Daniel O'Connell (1775–1847), Irish politician, was elected M.P. for co. Clare in 1828
and thus brought about Catholic Emancipation in 1829; devoted himself to securing the repeal

will be present at a banquet for him: 'Tell me how he looks. I have never seen him since he was a boy at Douai, when he was too young... to be worth my notice... and I dare say that I never thought proper, never deigned to speak to him. How little I knew then of the great man that he was destined to be!' (March 2nd 1844). Later he expresses pleasure at O'Connell's release: 'Had L[or]d Abinger been alive, I fear O'Connell would still have been in prison' (Sept. 13th 1844). Apart from O'Connell there is little mention of Ireland; the potato blight is mentioned on September 12th 1846, but only with reference to England, and he recommends to Miss Joyce harricots [*sic*] as an alternative, giving a recipe from his youth in France, and signing himself as 'De Lingard, cuisinier en chef'. There was one occasion when the problems came closer to home, and he writes to Miss Joyce: 'I have attended two women, Irish, dying of fever at Kirby Lonsdale [about 8 miles away], but came off safe. I shall go no more there, for I find Kirby is nearer another chapel than to mine' (July 4th 1847).

On the other hand the controversies of Lancashire Catholicism are of interest to Mrs. Lomax, and Lingard's letters to her at the relevant times are full of references to such matters as the Brindle Will Case.[12] Miss Joyce, like everybody else, took a strong interest in this, but gets no insider's gossip, merely an expression of regret that she has missed the ensuing libel trials:

> It was certainly great presumption in the parties, Sherburne and Eastwood, to have the cause tried here [Lancaster] instead of Liverpool, and so prevent you from being present: as however there were two actions for libel against the Orange editor of the Lancaster Gazette, Quarme, and as he pleaded justification, and Eastwood and his wife had both promised Quarme to come forward at the Liverpool assizes, and prove the truth of the libels as witnesses I flattered myself that you would still be able to gratify your curiosity. But alas! all his courage, and that of Eastwood has evaporated: and Sherburne was informed on Sunday that both causes would be undefended (April 4th 1843).

Lingard no doubt would have been able to tell her much to 'gratify her curiosity' but refrained from doing so.

---

of the Act of Union; convicted in Feb. 1844 on a charge of creating disaffection and discontent, and in May 1844 fined £2,000 and sentenced to a year's imprisonment, but the conviction was quashed on appeal to the House of Lords in September. Between conviction and sentence he visited England and was honourably received by the reformers at Liverpool and elsewhere. James Scarlett, Lord Abinger (1769–1844) was a lawyer and Tory politician; he was appointed Chief Baron of the Exchequer in 1834.

12. This arose from the will of William Heatley of Brindle Lodge co. Lancs., who died in 1840 leaving very large sums for ecclesiastical purposes to the secular clergy (notably Rev. Thomas Sherburne); the husbands (in particular Thomas Eastwood) of Heatley's two nieces contested the will and denounced the seculars; apart from the newspaper controversies and the law suits, the affair also led to the establishment of the Select Committee on Mortmain; cf. Trappes-Lomax, *op. cit.*, pp. 14–16 and, for the libel cases, pp. 202–4.

Lingard was less reluctant to pass on adverse comment directed against the Jesuits and in his first letter to Miss Joyce he tells her of the hostility to the Jesuit plan for a day school in Liverpool, which was looked upon by the monks and seculars 'as a scheme to monopolise the education of the better classes among the catholics in Liverpool, and then carry them off to Stonyhurst, whereas they are mostly sent to the colleges of the other two parties. But this may be all false for I know no more of Liverpool matters than of the transactions in Pekin' (Sept. 8th 1841).[13] This is anyhow not so harsh as what he wrote to Miss Lomax, a professed admirer of the Jesuits: 'You think the Jes[uits] of old could not be like those of the present day. They had piety, zeal, learning, and were after all in my opinion old women... In my historical researches I have seen enough to persuade me of the truth of that assertion' (Spring 1836; p. 57). Female Religious, unlike their male counterparts, earned Lingard's commendation, and he wrote to Miss Joyce: 'Of the Irish sisters of charity I know nothing: but on the continent one of the order is worth half a dozen clergymen. The services which they render to the poor are most valuable' (Oct. 14th 1841). Similarly he expressed to Miss Sanders his admiration for the Prioress of the community at Princethorpe: 'She is a very good looking woman, and apparently young – but nuns always look ten years younger than they are. I admire her much for her goodness and her talents' (Aug. 7th 1835; p. 43).

Lingard's references to Miss Sanders' fondness for the Jesuits are a regular feature of the early stages of the correspondence: 'I must be indebted to your company for my proficiency in Jesuitism' (March 13th 1836; p. 55); 'having learned to act the jesuit from you' (Jan. 28th 1837; p. 74). Likewise he directs some of his humour at the female sex: 'every woman is by nature a jesuit' (Feb. 15th 1837; p. 76); 'Now my piety dislikes to be encumbered with letters on a sunday morning: however my curiosity – surely I must have been intended for a woman... peeped at them... but I had the resolution not to peep into yours, that my mind might not be thinking on womanish trash, when it ought to be fixed on other objects' (Dec. 5th 1837; p. 86). Jokes of this sort almost disappear after the first few years of the correspondence, perhaps because Lingard was too good a letter-writer to be willing to repeat himself. But even in old age he could revert to such irreverence as this, addressed to her son: 'If you dare so to do, Tell that mischievous shrew, Your Mammy, Today is the feast of St Jammy' (July 25th 1850; p. 160). In the first letter that he wrote to her he

---

13. Lingard was more direct in writing to Bishop Brown: 'the salus animarum cannot be the real object of the Fathers [i.e. Jesuits]; otherwise having made the proposal they would have been satisfied, when they were told by the bishop that the salus animarum did not require a church there – who ought to be the best judge, the bishop or they? no: there is another object, to sweep away to Stonyhurst all the boys of Catholic parents in easy circumstances, a consequence which will be, as I mentioned in my last, very injurious to *your district*, by depriving you of many who at the same time would be missionaries and have property of their own' (Feb. 14th 1842; Liverpool Diocesan Archives).

shows himself anxious to avoid misconceived gossip, and declines an invitation to Pleasington Hall (where she was a guest) for fear of being considered 'a pilgrim, always directing my steps towards a certain shrine, wherever that shrine may be' (Jan. 31st 1835; p. 23); yet in that same year he invited her to Hornby, which caused some comment: 'It must be flattering to you to be the subject of so much conversation. Be that as it may, I am proud that my name should be coupled with yours' (Summer 1835; p. 42). He had already addressed her as 'Literatissima Puella, Hurrah! from your Valentine' (Feb. 14th 1835; p. 29), and the same innocent flirtatiousness continues till the end of his life, when she is still addressed as 'Valentina' (Feb. 14th 1850; p. 153).

There is no attempt to convert Miss Joyce, though there is a little gentle teasing of her as a 'heretic': 'My Dear Madam, The box – the Christmas box – is arrived. Let me thank the fair artiste, heretic though she be – In fact, I almost think I value it the more on that account. The pattern is beautiful – the work is beautiful – I hardly know what to find fault with, unless it be the cost – it is far too costly for the poor vicar of Hornby' (Dec. 6th 1842). Likewise:

You know Mr. Pusey[14] is building a protestant or Puseyite convent in the isle of Wight. He sent the intended abbess Miss Young to Birmingham that she might visit the nuns there, and get some insight into the internal management of the convent. She did so to some purpose for she took up her abode within the convent, and purposes to make her profession there in place of the isle of Wight. He called on her some time ago, and spent the day with her, without eating or drinking, but weeping and entreating her to return to his convent in the island. There, you heretic, see what it is to get among nuns! (Jan. 13th 1843).

He also sent her a copy of his translation of the Ave Maris Stella, in which he had quietly substituted 'thine handmaid' for 'thy children' in the last couplet, so that Miss Joyce's version runs:

Do thou, bright Queen, Star of the Sea,
Pray for thine handmaid, pray for me.

Lingard no doubt hoped that this would be more efficacious than any arguments.

Miss Sanders on the other hand received much theological instruction, which would have had the effect of bolstering her new-found Catholicism as well as providing her with arguments to use against Rev. John Dalby, a friend of her father, who was seeking to persuade her to return to Anglicanism. Thus he covers transubstantiation, the inadequacy of seek-

---

14. Rev. Edward Bouverie Pusey (1800–82), a leading figure in the Oxford Movement. In 1839 he was already interested in founding Anglican Sisterhoods on the model of the Catholic Sisters of Charity, and in 1841 he himself visited Catholic convents in Ireland. However it was not until 1845 that the first such Sisterhood was established near Regent's Park; cf. H.B. Liddon, *Life of Edward Bouverie Pusey*, 4 vols. (London, 1893), 3, pp. 1–32.

ing the truth from scripture alone, the position of St. Peter in the apostolic church, and the intercession of the saints:

> If Mr. Dalby teaze you still about the supposed ubiquity of the saints (otherwise they cannot hear the prayers of those who invoke them) refer him to the text where our saviour, to deter men from scandalizing his little ones, tells them that their angels always see the face of his father who is in his heaven... By whatever means this knowledge is communicated to them, by the same God may communicate to the Saints the prayers of those who invoke them (Jan. 31st 1835; p. 24).

In the same letter he seeks information from Miss Sanders about how Protestants are likely to view his Prayer Book: 'If you ever honour me with another letter, tell me – for you can judge better than any of us – whether there be anything in the book to hurt the feelings of a protestant, or to strengthen his religious prepossessions against our worship'.

One topic of Catholic interest occurs fairly often in both sets of letters, and it illustrates well the distinction between the gossipy and irreverent nature of the correspondence with Mrs. Lomax and the more formal and restrained manner in which he wrote to Miss Joyce. Bishop Brown[15] is not treated entirely seriously in the letters to Mrs. Lomax. Before his consecration he had acquired a number of nicknames: 'Mr. Alderman Brown! Alderman George. I am delighted with the soubriquet. Never shall he be the pilgrim or the wanderer henceforth, but the alderman, and who knows but under the new constitution of boroughs he may be made Alderman of Lancaster? How great he would be!' (Summer 1835; p. 40). Nor were his opinions taken very seriously: 'if they wish to see me, let them come here, as did the Alderman and Mr. Walker yesterday. The first looked very glum till a glass of champagne gave a lustre to his eye, and a smile to his lips. Yet Walker at parting whispered to me that I was in disgrace. Why, I know not, and what is worse, I care not' (Autumn 1835; p. 45). The first comment on Brown after his consecration is not one of unqualified approbation: 'I have no doubt that he has a becoming confidence in his own judgment: and I have also, so that I expect he will always act judiciously, unless it be in a moment of excitement, when he is accustomed to express himself perhaps too warmly, or unless he allow himself to be warped by the notion of popularity' (Sept. 15th 1840; p. 101). Nor did he conceal his disapproval of Brown's intention to absent himself from Sherburne v. Quarme: 'I was vexed with Dr. Brown; I wrote him word that he was doing Eastwood a great service by staying away, and advised him to go to Liverpool, pending the trial, and show himself in court... He replied that on the last trial he was present, and the effect on his shattered nerves was

---

15.   Rev. George Hilary Brown (1786–1856); Vicar Apostolic of the Northern District 1840–50; Bishop of Liverpool 1850–56; cf. Gillow, 1, pp. 320–1, and P. Doyle, '"A Tangled Skein of Confusion": The Administration of George Hilary Brown, Bishop of Liverpool 1850–1856', *RH,* 25 (2000), pp. 294–303. Before his consecration he had been priest at Lancaster.

such that he resolved never more to expose himself to it again' (Aug. 23rd 1842; p. 124). Brown is initially treated with more forbearance in the letters to Miss Joyce, and excuses are made for his failure to return the calls of Dr. Shepherd:

> but the bishop is a man of sense and learning, though several years of ailment, and dangerous ailment too, has made him rather brusque and fidgetty. Three years residence during the winter in Italy has entirely restored his health to my very great surprise: and I shall be happy if his residence at Eaton enable him to get rid of the habits which he acquired during his long illness (Aug. 8th 1844).

However Lingard eventually gave up making excuses: 'I am sorry so many disappointments occur in your calls at Bishop Eaton' (Nov. 13th 1845); 'I am vexed at the bishop. If I were you, I would never invite him again' (Jan. 15th 1846). To Mrs. Lomax he is far from complimentary about the Bishops in general: 'Dr. Tate... has been... several times designed for bishop. But there is a remora somewhere. He is always thrown overboard, though infinitely more fit than most of those who by some chance or other are chosen' (July 15th 1849; p. 151).

The two ladies' experience of marriage was very different. Miss Joyce selflessly looked after Dr. Shepherd until his death on July 21st 1847, but did not long postpone marriage thereafter; Lingard soon had cause to congratulate her: 'You have reason from the character you give Mr. Ridyard to rejoice in the prospect before you' (Dec. 19th 1847). After the ceremony he gives thanks for his portion of the wedding cake and adds, 'I'll never more believe a woman. Here I have been mourning Miss Joyce's hard fate for a long time, as if she were never more to enjoy good health, and lo! she has been marrying, and is jaunting all over the country in pursuit of pleasure' (Feb. 16th 1848). It may be that Lingard's prognostications of marital harmony were fulfilled; Miss Joyce was old enough to know her own mind, and we hear nothing of troublesome in-laws or of misbehaviour on the part of the husband. In any event there was little time for problems to arise before the cessation of the correspondence. By way of contrast Mrs. Lomax married at 23, and we hear much intimate gossip about her relationship with her husband, about her children and about her in-laws. There was no occasion for this where Mrs. Ridyard was concerned, but in any event the relationship was perhaps not personal enough to allow of it, though Dr. Shepherd is the object of humour and gratitude and concern: 'Most assuredly Dr. Shepherd is grown an old woman to suppose it possible that I could object to a letter from you. No: I do not believe it. The truth is that he is jealous; and therefore tell him to his teeth from me, that, say what he will, I shall always be proud and happy to be honoured with an epistle from Miss Joyce' (Sept. 8th 1841); 'Thank Dr. Shepherd for his exertions in favour of the poor Catholic children' (Dec. 30th 1841); 'let me wish you joy of your generalship with respect to the obstinacy of the Doctor. Never mind his scolding if you preserve his health' (Jan. 13th 1844).

Mrs. Lomax was faced with many family problems and disputes. Lingard's loyalty to her is absolute, and there is never a hint that there might be anything to say on the other side. This was easy enough before her marriage, when her problems arose from her expulsion from her parental home in consequence of her conversion to Catholicism; Lingard's advice is considered and tactful: 'Listen not to the advice of zealous but imprudent friends. You have come to a wise determination. A controversy with Mr. Sanders could be productive of no benefit; it might lead to an everlasting separation' (May 17th 1835; p. 35); 'I thank you for your hymn so excellent and beautiful, expressive of real not fancied feeling... I am confident it will awaken in Mr. Sanders feelings which he will find it difficult to resist' (Summer 1836; p. 60). Other difficulties began to occur within a year of the marriage; first with Mrs. Lomax' mother-in-law: 'I am vexed that you should allow yourself to be annoyed by the remarks or even censures of any old lady' (April 26th 1838; p. 90). By the following year Mrs. Lomax was on bad terms with at least two of her brothers-in-law: 'You appear to have formed a very high notion of both the Kentish Jesuit and the Lancashire Otter hunter: otherwise you would not allow their words or deeds to affect you so much. Dismiss them from your thoughts...' (May 25th 1839; p. 98). The death of Mrs. Lomax' second son called forth a brief mention:

> Allow me to condole with you... He is gone to heaven: yet you grieve on his account, I have no doubt: for I never yet met with a mother who was willing that her child should go to heaven before herself. How wonderfully our lots are cast here below! I was celebrating the seventieth anniversary of my birthday, and at the same time the little innocent was taken away before he had seen the first anniversary of his. However, vouloir ce que Dieu veut, c'est la seule science, qui nous met en repos (Mar. 1st 1841; p. 106).

Infant death was so ordinary an event that Lingard, having thus expressed his sympathy, goes on to ordinary gossip about the weather and the Brindle Will Case, not failing to mention, 'that a few days ago my only, and my favourite cat died of old age... She was occasionally a plague at breakfast and dinner: but even then she broke the dull monotony of a solitary meal. This I mention that you may understand that however you may interfere with my habits, when you come to visit me, yet even that will be a pleasure to me. If I lose one cat, I shall be grateful for another'.

Thomas Lomax himself seems to have become increasingly erratic, although marriage to a Catholic younger son with a comfortable income must have seemed an answer to prayer when her conversion to Catholicism had made Mrs. Lomax an exile from her own home and a dependant on the charity of Miss Butler of Pleasington Hall near Blackburn. In the summer of 1844 he was sent to prison in Lancaster to await trial on a charge of assaulting a young woman on the streets of Preston; his brothers paid her off and the prosecution was never brought; Thomas went to stay with his brother James so as to keep him away from the temptations of Preston. Lingard alludes to this with commendable tact in a letter of congratulation on the birth of Mrs. Lomax' second daughter: '[Dr. Lingard] is also inclined to draw a favourable augury from the visit which her papa paid to her on her arrival, and the intelligence that he is staying with his brother, Mr. James Lomax' (Sept. 21st 1844; p. 131). There was no improvement, and Lingard remained staunch in his support:

I infer... that you were dissuaded from insisting on the deed of separation, and consented to live with Sir Thomas again... So it appears that after the reconciliation there has been another outbreak, and another attempt of the opposite party to divert hostilities. That you have out-witted them, is not surprising: that they will not soften and subdue your resolution, is more than I will pretend to foretell. You have them, how-ever, in your power, and will, I trust, keep the ascendancy which you possess, even if in other things you relent (July 5th 1845; p. 133).

The contest continued: 'I know not which to admire the most, the perse-verance and acharnment [*sic*] of your enemies in annoying you, or your tact and judgment in defeating them. I most heartily wish you success' (Oct. 29th 1850; p. 161). In the last surviving letter Lingard concludes by offering congratulations on 'the continued improvement in the moral con-duct of Sir Thomas' (Mar. 14th 1851; p. 164).

Lingard's health is a frequent topic in his letters, and Miss Joyce in par-ticular received regular bulletins on the subject. She was well aware of Lingard's sufferings, and in her memoir of him she writes:

I have occasionally seen him in his little book room at Hornby, in extreme torture, but still conversing with those around him with unal-tered serenity, his countenance calm and placid, the large drops of per-spiration on his brow, wrung from him by his agony, alone testifying to the intensity of his pain. By and bye, with a still equable expression of countenance he would rise, and gently and quietly leave the apartment.

He knew her well enough to give her a detailed account: 'Do forgive this long description. I would not have gone into the particulars, were it not to convince you that I am not shamming' (Sept. 5th 1845); however the description must have seemed too detailed for a maiden lady, and it has been removed. Mrs. Lomax on the other hand was less squeamish, and she preserved the following:

For a long while the spasm which prevents the egress of the water from the bladder has been exceedingly tight: and I, in forcing the barrier with the catheter have wounded the passage... [the medical man] took off the water twice yesterday: but the quantity of clotted or coagulated blood which came away with it was truly awful. I was obliged to rise thrice last night through the pain (July 23rd or 24th 1848; p. 139).

In general there is much less about his health in the letters to Mrs. Lomax, no doubt because he had so many other topics about which he could gos-sip with her.

This element of mere gossip is of much greater importance in his letters to Mrs. Lomax, not merely because the relationship was much closer, but because they had so many acquaintances in common; it is no exaggeration when Lingard begins a letter with 'Madame la Gossipe', and concludes it with 'I am, O Gossippissarum Gossippississima, Tibi devotissimus, Joannes Gossippus' (May 16th 1849; p. 147). It was Lingard's claim that he lived a retired life and knew nothing of the wider world: 'For 30 years I have made it an invariable rule never to originate any question with the Eccles[iastical] authorities, never to intrude, never to interfere... I live an unconcerned spectator of the movements in our little world: or rather, instead of being spectator, I live in a happy ignorance of most that is going on. I do not hear as much in twelve months, as you hear in a week' (May 13th 1841; p. 110). That being so, he was always happy to receive information: 'how are the sisters at Plessington and Grimsargh. Of both I have heard accounts, which I hope are not true. Do tell me' (Sept. 30th 1838; p. 93). Mrs. Lomax' Jesuit connections enabled her to provide Lingard with information from that quarter: 'Have you heard any remarks on my ninth volume? I wish to learn, how I have pleased the Jesuits' (Jan. 11th 1839; p. 95). She could also defend him when he was attacked by the opponents of the seculars: 'it was very kind of you to involve yourself with certain persons by becoming my advocate. But why did I want an advocate? I cannot conceive. I always thought myself something of a favourite with F. Trappes.[16] Certainly he cannot be offended that I have resisted the impudent and unjust demand made by Mr. Riddell on the executors of Mr. Rutter' (March 1st 1841; p. 107). Lingard closes one letter with: 'There is gossip for you. Beat it, if you can' (April 27th 1849; p. 147), and the remarkably heterogeneous contents of that letter give a flavour of the correspondence as a whole: he mentions the ceremonies ensuing on the death of a Pope; the activities of Padre Ventura[17] and others during the short-lived Roman Republic; the collection of bones at Borwick co. Lancs.; a double entendre for the amusement of Mrs. Lomax' nine-year old son (an entry in an account book of 1713: 'This day William Skirrow drove his cart through my bakside [sic]'); the relationships of Revv. Daniel Hearne and Francis Trappes with Bishop Brown; Samuel Lover's unwillingness to visit Lingard on account of Lingard's repeatedly expressed dislike of Lover's portrait of him; Rev. John Walker's tutoring of some of the sons

16. Rev. Francis Trappes (1791–1871) was a secular but had been trained at Stonyhurst; he was a strong opponent of the Vicars Apostolic, particularly in support of the rights of the lay patrons of Catholic chapels. Rev. Henry Rutter (1755–1838) had been appointed to the mission of Dodding Green, co. Westmorland, by the Riddells of Cheeseburn Grange, co. Northumberland, who claimed the right of patronage; Lingard as his executor was in dispute concerning the salary received by Rutter; cf. *Lingard-Lomax Letters*, pp. 16–19.

17. Gioacchino Ventura (1792–1861), a Theatine, characterised by Lingard as an '*ultamontanist enragé*' (Lingard to Bulter, Feb. 19th 1829, CUL, Add. Ms. 9418), published a violent attack on Lingard's *History* in the *Journal Catholique*, which was re-published as an unlicensed Italian pamphlet (1828) (See Haile & Bonney, pp. 234–235). Ventura spent his later years as an exile in France after his support of Mazzini's proclamation of the Roman Republic on the Piazza Navona (1848) made him *persona non grata* in the Papal States.

of the Catholic aristocracy; songs for her son to sing with Lingard's neighbour's daughters on his next visit.

The letters to Miss Joyce are less varied. Apart from Lingard's health, there are a number of discussions of historical matters, notably the vagaries of Miss Strickland,[18] who 'has written an introduction from which nothing of importance can be learned, unless it be that Q Mary was a bird-fancier' (Nov. 7th 1842), and 'Miss Strickland has corrected one blunder only out of a dozen' (Jan. 27th 1843). There is comment on matters of contemporary interest; to those already mentioned we might add Lingard's opinion of Fr. Matthew[19] after he had visited Dr. Shepherd: 'I believe him to be a good and humble man, who has not suffered his head to be turned by the applause which he has received and has merited' (Aug. 25th 1843), together with some banter about Dr. Shepherd's failure to be converted to total abstinence: 'How I have laughed at the figure which Dr. Shepherd must have made when he heard that he was to take the pledge' (Sept. 1st 1843). Lingard's open-mindedness on 'scientific' topics is also in evidence, and on observing that his correspondent will 'have been initiated... in the mysteries of Mesmerism' (Sept. 12th 1846), he remarks that there may well be truth in it, for there is much that is not seen or understood, as formerly electricity, and even now the causes of cholera and the potato blight.

The greater intimacy of the relationship with Mrs. Lomax is reflected above all in the way in which he entrusts her with information that he would entrust to nobody else. Thus very early in their relationship he confided to her alone ('arcana sunt tibi soli commissa') the information that he had read a letter of the bishops before it was sent to Rome, though he does not tell her that he had in fact written it; his motive was to put her in a position to authoritatively deny certain rumours about its contents (Summer 1835; p. 42). He makes arrangements for her to receive a copy of his translation of the Gospels, although others must not know that he is the author: 'I must ask your acceptance of a copy: but know not how to get it to you. For, if it be known to come to you from me, it will be known that I am the author, which for certain reasons I must keep secret' (Summer 1836; p. 64). He told her of his anxiety not to meet Bishop Briggs:[20] 'I want much to see Thompson of Weldbank, and propose going there as soon as I know (remember not to blab this out,) that Dr. Briggs has left Lancashire. My reason for not going before is, that he may perhaps fall in with me; and perhaps ask my opinion respecting matters with

18. Agnes Strickland (1796–1874); enthusiastic but inaccurate historian; author of *Lives of the Queens of England,* 12 vols. (London, 1840–8).

19. Rev. Theobald Mathew (1790–1856); Irish priest and temperance advocate; visited England in 1843.

20. Rev. John Briggs (1789–1861); Vicar Apostolic of the Northern District (which then included Lancashire) 1836–40; of Yorkshire District 1840–50; Bishop of Beverley 1850–61; cf. Gillow, 1, pp. 295–6, and G. Bradley, 'Bishop Briggs and his Visitations of the North', *RH,* 25 (2000), pp. 174–91.

which I have no concern' (Oct. 1836; p. 71). She was the first to be let into the secret of Lingard's authorship of a satirical poem about Robert Peel[21] in the *Lancaster Guardian* a month previously: 'Twas saucy, but no one knew the author' (March 20th 1837; p. 78). She was also the first to hear of Lingard's grant from the Privy Purse: 'as you know so much, you may as well know all... This morning I received from London an answer to one of mine merely acknowledging the receipt by me of the £300. The writer expresses his satisfaction that I had accepted it: for it was a present from the Queen! But must be kept secret. Do you do so. For no one else shall know of it' (23 March 1839; p. 98). Mrs. Lomax also received a fuller account of Lingard's involvement in the Brindle Will Case: 'Now that you have been involved in the business, I mean to tell you what I believe to be the entire fact. But remember that you are una de multis: that is that you are, though a woman, able to keep a secret, for if it were revealed to anyone it might involve me in quarrels, which I could wish to avoid' (July 8th 1842; p. 122).

Mrs. Ridyard did not write regularly towards the end of Lingard's life – there is only one letter dated later than 1849 – knowing (as she says in her memoir of him) how much the effort of replying exhausted him; by way of contrast there are eleven letters to Mrs. Lomax from 1850 and 1851. The last letter to Mrs. Ridyard, an expression of thanks for the Ridyards' customary Christmas present of cod and oysters, is a long one. It contains the opinion that Pio Nono might have acted differently on the Restoration of the Hierarchy if he had consulted Lingard, but the ensuing troubles 'will all end in smoke'; in any event, 'we all live in peace and harmony here. The new curate, a Mr. Shields from Durham, a mere boy in appearance, and a most simple well-meaning man in reality, and I are on good, on the best terms; only Mr. Dawson,[22] his Lord and lay rector, compels him to go about for petitioners against us. At the same time D[awson] and I are great friends. His anticatholic propensities and intrigues are ignored by me' (Dec. 27th 1850). The last words of the correspondence are moving and valedictory: 'whatever providence may mete out for me... I shall always retain a grateful sense of your unvarying kindness to me, and feel a lively interest in your health and happiness. Believe me, Dear Madam, Very sincerely yours, John Lingard'.

Lingard's significance to the modern world lies of course in his achievements as a historian and in his influence on the development of English Catholicism. His letters to women provide a useful reminder that he was also a singularly estimable and engaging human being.

---

21. Sir Robert Peel (1788–1850); Tory politician; despite his earlier opposition he introduced the measure granting Catholic Emancipation in 1829; in 1837 he was leader of the Conservative opposition and had committed himself to the maintenance of the established constitution in Church and State.

22. Pudsey Dawson succeeded to the Hornby Castle Estate in 1840 on the death of Lingard's friend, Admiral Sandford Tatham.

APPENDIX 1

LINGARD'S PUBLISHED WORKS

1. Books and Pamphlets

1. *The Antiquities of the Anglo-Saxon Church*, Edward Walker, Newcastle, 1806, 2 vols., 8vo.; 2nd. edition, Walker, Newcastle, 1810, 8vo.; Philadelphia, 1841, 12mo. [for 3rd. edition, see 34 below].

2. *Letters on Catholic Loyalty*, [Henry Cotes, John Lingard & others], originally published in the *Newcastle Courant*, Walker, Newcastle, 1807, 8vo., pp. 36.

3. *Remarks on a Charge Delivered to the Clergy of the Diocese of Durham by Shute, Bishop of Durham, at the Ordinary Visitation of that Diocese in the year 1806*, Walker, Newcastle, 1807, 8vo.; 2nd edition, Keating, London, 1807, 8vo., pp. 52; 3rd edition, enlarged, Walker, Newcastle, 1807, 8vo., pp. 47.

4. *A Review of a Pamphlet entitled "A Protestant's Reply"*, Mitchell, Newcastle, 1807, 8vo., pp. 38.

5. *A Vindication of the "Remarks on the Charge of the Bishop of Durham"*, Hodgson, Newcastle, 1807, 8vo., pp. 57.

6. *A General Vindication of the "Remarks on the Charge of the Bishop of Durham", containing a Reply to a Letter from a Clergyman of the Diocese of Durham (second edition); a Reply to the Observations of the Rev. Thomas Le Mesurier, Rector of Newton Longville; a Reply to the Strictures of the Rev. G.S. Faber, Vicar of Stockton-on-Tees; and some Observations on the More Fashionable Methods of Interpreting the Apocalypse*, Hodgson, Newcastle, 1808, 8vo., pp. 102. Reprinted several times.

7. *A Letter to a Clergyman of the Diocese of Durham in Answer to His Second Letter to the Author of the Remarks on the Bishop of Durham's Charge*, Preston & Heaton, Newcastle, 1808, 8vo., pp. 62.

8. *Remarks on a late Pamphlet entitled "The Grounds on which the Church of England Separated from the Church of Rome, Reconsidered by Shute, Bishop of Durham"*, Booker, London, 1809, 8vo., pp. 64.

9. *Errata to the Protestant Bible*, by Thomas Ward. With a Preface by the Rev. J.L., Coyne, Dublin, 1810, 8vo.; Coyne, 1841, 8vo.

10. *Defence of Ward's Errata to the Protestant Bible.* By the Rev. J.L., Coyne, Dublin, 1810, 12mo.

11. *The Controversy between the Rev. John Lingard and Shute Barrington, and the Rev. T. Mesurier*, Coyne, Dublin, 1811, 8vo., [includes 3, 4, 6, 7, 8].

12. *Documents to Ascertain the Sentiments of British Catholics in former ages respecting the Power of the Popes*, Booker, London, 1812, 8vo., pp. iv+38 and Appendix, pp. 15.

13. *Tracts Occasioned by the Publication of a Charge delivered to the Clergy of the Diocese of Durham by Shute, Bishop of Durham*, Walker, Newcastle, 1813, 8vo., pp. xii+376, [includes 3, 4, 6, 7, 8]. Translated from 3rd edition into French, Paris, 1829, 8vo.

14. *The Faith and Doctrine of the Roman Catholic Church proved by the testimony of the most Learned Protestants, by the author of a Protestant Apology*, [Preface by John Lingard], Coyne, Dublin, 1813, pp vxiii.[1]

15. *A Review of Certain Anti-Catholic Publications, viz, a Charge delivered to the Clergy of the Diocese of Gloucester in 1810, by George Isaac Huntingford, D.D., F.R.S.; A Charge delivered to the Clergy of the Diocese of Lincoln by George Tomline, D.D., F.R.S.; and Observations on the Catholic Question, by the Right Hon. Lord Kenyon*, Booker, London, 1813, 8vo., pp. 88: 2nd and 3rd editions.

16. *Examinations of Certain Opinions advanced by Dr. Burgess, Bishop of St. David's, in two recent Publications, entitled "Christ, and not Peter, the Rock of the Christian Church" and "Johannis Sulgeni versus hexametri in laudem Sulgeni patris, Menevensis Archiepiscopi"*, Wardle & Bentham, Manchester, 1813, 8vo., pp. 51.

17. *Strictures on Dr. Marsh's "Comparative View of the Churches of England and Rome"*, Booker, London, 1815, 8vo., pp. 88.

18. *Observations on the Laws and Ordinances which Exist in Foreign States Relative to the Religious Concerns of their Roman Catholic Subjects*, Keating & Brown, London, 1817, 8vo., pp. 39; 2nd edition, Dolman, London, 1851, 8vo., pp. iv+28.

---

1. Lingard provided this brief preface for Coyne's publication of the work by Christianus [William Talbot] who had earlier written *The Protestant Apology for the Roman Catholic Church*, Fitzpatrick, Dublin, 1809, which included a long introductory essay, signed Irenaeus. This essay has been attributed to Lingard by Gillow (*Bibliographical Dictionary*), followed by Haile & Bonney, Chinnici and others, but Philip Cattermole is correct in pointing out (*John Lingard: The Historian as Apologist*, Ph.D. Thesis, University of Kent at Canterbury, 1984, p. 328) that Irenaeus is to be identified with the Irish theologian and Church historian, John Lanigan (see *DNB*).

Keating and Brown brought out an extract of this pamphlet, printed by the desire of the author, with an abbreviation of Lingard's preface:

The Confessed Intimacy of Luther with Satan, at whose suggestion he abolished the Mass as recorded by himself. To which is prefaced, an introduction by The Rev. John Lingard, Keating and Brown, London, 1821, pp. vi, 18.

19. *Plowden's "Case is Altered", Corrected in a Restatement of Thompson's "Case Stated"*, Harris, Liverpool, 1818, 8vo.[2]

20. *History of England, from the First Invasion by the Romans to the Accession of William and Mary in 1688*, London, 1819–30, 8 vols., 4to., preface, vols. 1–3, dated Hornby, May 1, 1819; vol. 4, October 15, 1820; vol. 5, May, 1823; vol. 6, July 4, 1825; vol. 7, 1829; vol. 8, 1830; the first six published by J. Mawman, the two last by his successors, Baldwin and Cradock; 2nd edition, Mawman, 1823–30, 14 vols., 8vo.; 3rd edition, Mawman, 1825–30, 14 vols., 8vo.; 4th edition, Booker, 1837–9, 13 vols., 12mo., corrected and enlarged; 5th edition, Dolman, 1849–51, 10 vols., 8vo.; 6th edition, Dolman, 1854–5, 8vo., 10 vols.; 7th edition, London, Nimmo, 1883, 10 vols., 8vo.; *Histoire d'Angleterre, depuis la premiere invasion des Romains,* translated from 2nd edition by M. le Chevalier de Roujoux, Paris, 14 vols., 1825–1831; the 2nd French edition (Paris, 1833–8, 21 vols., 8vo.) was continued to 1837 by M. de Martes and personally revised by Lingard; *Istoria d'Inghilterra*, translated from 2nd edition by Domenico Gregori, 8 vols., Roma, 1828–1833. There are also German and American editions.

21. *The Charters granted by different Sovereigns to the Burgesses of Preston, in the County Palatine of Lancaster*, Preston, 1821, 8vo., pp. iv+95.

22. *Supplementum ad Breviarium et Missale Romanum, Adjectis officiis Sanctorum Angliae,* Londini, Keating and Brown, 1823, 8vo., pp. 105; Index and Approbation, pp. 3.

23. *A Vindication of certain passages in the Fourth and Fifth Volumes of the History of England,* Mawman, London, 1826, 8vo., pp. 112; 2nd edition, London, 1827; 3rd, 4th and 5th edition (with postscript in answer to Dr. Allen's Reply, etc.), Mawman, London, 1827, 8vo., pp. 120.

24. *A Collection of Tracts on several subjects connected with the Civil and Religious Principles of Catholics,* by the Rev. J. Lingard, D.D., Keating and Brown, London, 1826, 8vo., pp. xi+479, [includes Nos. 3, 4, 6–8, 12, 15–18].

25. *Remarks on Mr Henhofer's Secession from the Romish Church with a brief statement of Conversions of Protestants to the Catholic Faith*, Preston Society for the Defence of Catholic Principles, Thomson, Preston, 1827, pp. 12.

26. *Sermons for tile Different Sundays of the Year and some of the Festivals and on other Important Subjects,* By the Rev. Thomas White, arranged from his MSS by the Rev. John Lingard, D.D.,

---

2. Although Lingard had a large hand in preparing this pamphlet, it was revised by Richard Thompson, and Lingard never owned it as his.

London, 1828, 2 vols., 8vo., pp. xi+407, vii+472; Dolman, London, 1841, 2 vols., 8vo.

27. *Remarks on the "Saint Cuthbert" of the Rev. James Raine, M.A., etc.*, Preston and Heaton, Newcastle, 1828, 8vo., pp. 68.

28. *A Manual of Prayers for Sundays and Holidays*, Clark, Lancaster, 1833, 18mo., pp. 48; second and further editions (enlarged by the Rev. Robert Tate), Croshaw, York, 1837, 18mo., pp. 178; further editions, 1840, 1844.

29. *A New Version of the Four Gospels*, with Notes, critical and explanatory. By a Catholic, London, Booker, 1836, 8vo., pp. xx+421; Dolman, London, 1846, 8vo.; 1851, 8vo.

30. *Letter to the Lord Chancellor on the Declaration made and subscribed by her Majesty*, James Ridgway, London, 1837.

31. *The Widow Woolfrey versus The Vicar of Carisbrooke: or Prayer for the Dead. A Catholic Tract for the Times*, Catholic Institute Tracts, London, 1839, 8vo.

32. *Is the Bible, the only Rule? or, Doubts and Queries, respectfully addressed to the Rev. J.H. Green Armytage, one of the Lecturers against Popery at St. Anne's. By a Lancaster Idolator*, Milner, Lancaster, 1839, 8vo., in two parts, pp. 11, 18; 2nd edition, Lancaster, 1887, 12mo.

33. *Catechistical[3] Instructions on the Doctrines and Worship of the Catholic Church*, Dolman, London, 1840, 12mo.; 2nd edition, pp. 139; new edition, London, 1844, 18mo.

34. *The History and Antiquities of the Anglo-Saxon Church, containing an account of its Origin, Government, Doctrines, Worship, Revenues, and Clerical and Monastic Institutions*, 3rd edition, London, Dolman, 1845, 2 vols., 8vo.; 4th edition, London, 1858, 2 vols., 8vo.; 5th edition, Baker, London, (reprinted from plates of 4th edition).

2. Articles, Letters and Reviews

Note: This list includes letters to Journals, but not letters to Newspapers. Following nineteenth century custom, such items are generally unattributed, and are at times hard to identify. With a few additions, the list follows Haile & Bonney's identification of the pseudonymous personae assumed by Lingard in his letters to *The Catholic Magazine & Review*. It is a topic which needs further exploration and more material may indeed come to light.

---

3. 'a printer's blunder' – Lingard intended *Catechetical* (see *Lingard-Lomax Letters*, p. 104).

1. 'A reply to the observations of the Edinburgh Review on the Anglo-Saxon Antiquities', *The Pamphleteer*, vol. 7, (1816), pp. 532–544 [signed J. Lingard].

2. *'Flavii Cresconii Corippi Johannidos seu de bellis Libycis libri vii, editi ex codice Mediolanensi musei Trivultii, opera et studio Petri Mazzucchelli, Collegii Ambrosiani Doctoris, Mediolani, anno MDC-CCXX'*, *The British Critic, New Series*, vol. 1, (Jan. 1826), pp. 309–322 [review article, unsigned].

3. *'Eusebii Pamphili, Caesariensis Episcopi, Chronicum bipartitum, nunc primum ex Armeniaco Textu in Latinum conversum, adnotationibus auctum, Graecis Fragmentis exornatum, opera P. Jo. Baptistae Aucher, Ancyrani, Monachi Armeni, et Doctoris Mechitaristae, Venetis, 1818, 2 vols. 4to.'*, *The British Critic, New Series*, vol. 2, (April 1826), pp. 78–93 [review article, unsigned].

4. 'A Letter of Dr Lingard to Mr Butler, in reply to the Charge [brought against him by Dr Phillpotts]' & 'Doctor Lingard's Reply to Doctor Phillpotts further charge' in Charles Butler, *Vindication of the Book of the Roman Catholic Church*, John Murray, London, 1826, pp. 214–223, 228–236.

5. 'Lingard's History and the Edinburgh Review', *Catholic Miscellany*, vol. 6 (Dec. 1826), pp. 408–410 [signed Investigator; this letter was first published in the *British Press*, October 15th 1825].

6. 'On the Litanies', *The Catholic Magazine & Review*, vol. 1 (Oct. 1831), pp. 546–547 [signed H.Y.].

7. 'Miracle of St. Januarius', *The Catholic Magazine & Review*, vol. 1 (Sept. 1831), pp. 484–487; vol. 2 (Feb. 1832), pp. 35–44 [signed H.Y.].

8. 'A translation of those Psalms which usually occur in Catholic Books of Devotion', *The Catholic Magazine & Review*, vol. 1 (Dec. 1831), pp. 670–677; vol. 1 (Jan. 1832), pp. 730–739; vol. 2 (April 1832), pp. 161–169; vol. 2 (June 1832), pp. 327–333; vol. 2 (Nov. 1832), p. 701 [unsigned].

9. 'Catholic Martyrs', *The Catholic Magazine & Review*, vol. 2 (March 1832), p. 110–112 [signed H.Y.].

10. 'The Benedictional of St. Aethelwold, Bishop of Winchester, ed. John Gage, Nichols & Son, 1832', *The Catholic Magazine & Review*, vol. 2 (Sept. 1832), pp. 419–424 [review article, signed H.Y.].

12. 'Roman College and Benedictionals', *The Catholic Magazine & Review*, vol. 2 (Sept. 1832), pp. 557–558 [signed H.Y.].

13. 'Proselytos on his conversion', *The Catholic Magazine & Review*, vol. 3 (Jan. 1833), pp. 17–22; vol. 3 (Feb. 1833), pp. 126–133; vol. 3 (April 1833), pp. 302–309 [signed Proselytos].

13. 'On the Doxology', *The Catholic Magazine & Review*, vol. 3 (Feb. 1833), pp. 133–134 [signed H.Y.].

14. 'On the Douay Catechism', *The Catholic Magazine & Review*, vol. 3 (June 1833), pp. 457–460; vol. 4 (Aug. 1833), pp. 33–35 [signed Proselytos].

15. 'Proselytos on the Litany of Loretto', *The Catholic Magazine & Review,* vol. 4 (Sept. 1833), pp. 111–113 [signed Proselytos].

16. 'Sacerdos on the Garden of the Soul', *The Catholic Magazine & Review,* vol. 5 (Feb. 1834), pp. 85–87 [signed Sacerdos].

17. 'Angla's reply to Hibernus', *The Catholic Magazine & Review*, vol. 5 (Feb. 1834), pp. 88–89 [signed Angla].

18. 'Sacerdos in reply to Missionarius' letter', *The Catholic Magazine & Review*, vol. 5 (April 1834), pp. 232–234 [signed Sacerdos].

19. 'Sacerdos in reply to Paulinus', *The Catholic Magazine & Review*, vol. 5 (Sept. 1834), pp. 591–595 [signed Sacerdos].

20. 'Angla on the Prayer-books', *The Catholic Magazine & Review*, vol. 5 (April 1834), pp. 220–223 [signed Angla].

21. 'Anglus in defence of Angla', *The Catholic Magazine & Review*, vol. 5 (July 1834), pp. 448–449 [signed Anglus].

22. 'Catechistes on the Catechism', *The Catholic Magazine & Review,* vol. 5 (Feb. 1834), pp. 89–93; vol. 5 (March 1834), pp. 142–146; vol. 5 (April 1834), pp. 203–206 [signed Catechistes].

23. 'Catechistes Junior on the Catechism', *The Catholic Magazine & Review*, vol. 5 (July 1834), pp. 457–461; (Aug. 1834), pp. 508–513; (Nov. 1834), pp. 715–719 [signed Catechistes Junior].

24. 'On Protestant Ordinations', *The Catholic Magazine & Review,* vol. 5 (Aug. 1834), pp. 499–503; vol. 5 (Nov. 1834), pp. 704–715; vol. 5 (Dec. 1834), pp. 774–782; vol. 6 (May 1835), p. 221 [signed J. Lingard].

25. 'H.Y. on Cranmer's Letter to Henry VIII', *The Catholic Magazine & Review,* vol. 5 (March 1834), pp. 162–168; vol. 5 (April 1834), pp. 223–231 [signed H.Y.].

26. 'John Wycliffe, the Reformer', *The Catholic Magazine & Review,* vol. 5 (June 1834), pp. 366–371 [signed H.Y.].

27. 'Protestantism the Greatest Enemy of the Church in England', *The Catholic Magazine & Review,* vol. 5 (Dec. 1834), pp. 762–766 [signed J.L.].

28. '"Ave Maris Stella" ("Hail, Queen of Heaven")', *The Catholic Magazine & Review,* vol. 5 (Sept. 1834), p. 607 [translation, signed Pros.].

29. 'Letter to the Lord Chancellor', *Dublin Review*, No. 4 (Jan. 1838), pp. 265–267 [a version differing only slightly from the pamphlet, 30 above].

30. 'Dodd's *Church History of England*, M.A. Tierney, vol. 1, London 1839', *Dublin Review*, No. 6 (May 1839), pp. 395–415 [review article, unsigned].

31. '*Origines Liturgicae, or Antiquities of the English Ritual*, William Palmer, 2 vols., Oxford, 1832; *A Treatise on the Church of Christ; designed chiefly for the use of students of theology*, William Palmer, 2 vols., London, 1838; *A Sermon preached at the Chapel Royal in St James' Palace, on the First Sunday after Trinity*, Walter Farquhar Hook, London, 1838; *Tracts for the Times by Members of the University of Oxford*, 4 vols., London, 1840', *Dublin Review*, No. 8 (May 1840), pp. 334–373 [review article, unsigned].

32. 'Fr. John Hudleston', in Samuel Jefferson, *The History and Antiquities of Leath Ward in the County of Cumberland with Biographical Notices and Memoirs* (Carlisle, 1840), pp. 476–479.

33. '*En Quelle Année Anne Boleyn, depuis mariée a Henri VIII, et mise a mort par son ordre, quitta-t-elle la France et retourna-t-elle en Angleterre?*', *Mémoires de l'Académie des Sciences morales et politiques: Savants Étrangers* (Paris, 1841), tom. 1, pp. 609–631 [signed J. Lingard].

34. '*The Apostolical Jurisdiction and Succession of the Episcopacy in the British Churches*, William Palmer, London, 1840; *Origines Liturgicae, or Antiquities of the English Ritual*, William Palmer, Oxford, 1839', *The Dublin Review*, No. 11 (Aug. 1841), pp. 167–196 [review article, unsigned].

35. 'Inscription at Autun', *The Catholic Magazine*, New Series, vol. 5 (Jan. 1841), pp. 25–29 [unsigned].

36. 'A letter on the alleged suppression by Catholics of the Second Commandment from the Rev. John Lingard to Philip H. Howard, Esq., M.P.', *The Catholic Magazine*, New Series, vol. 6 (July 1842), pp. 429–431 [signed J. Lingard].

37. 'Alma Redemptoris', 'Ave Regina', and 'Salve', *The Catholic Magazine*, Third Series, vol. 1 (May 1843), pp. 270–271 [translations, unsigned].

38. 'Perran-zabuloe', *Dolman's Magazine*, 3 (1846), pp. 133–145 [unsigned].

APPENDIX 2

LINGARD'S LETTERS AND PAPERS

In a will dated May 20th 1840, Lingard appointed as his executors George Brown, Bishop of the Lancashire District, but known to Lingard as the former missioner in Lancaster (and often the butt of Lingard's humour), and James Crook of St. Alban's, Blackburn, appointed Vicar General of the District in 1848. Five years later in an additional note Lingard instructed them to send to Ushaw 'any of my papers to be thought worth keeping' (UCA, Lingard Transcripts 190, 191). Lingard was an assiduous letter writer and wrote a remarkable number of letters; at some periods, for example, he was writing more than one letter a week to his friend John Walker, missioner in Scarborough. Inevitably some letters have been lost and it is noticeable that most of the extant letters belong to the last twenty years of his life. Lingard is known to have destroyed parts of his correspondence; he wrote to Tate, for example, in 1846, admitting that 'about four or five years ago I burnt all such papers as I did not wish to fall into the hands of my executors' (Lingard to Tate, August 21st 1846, UCA, Lingard Transcript 719). His letters record other such episodes. Much has been preserved, however, and in recent years, with the more systematic cataloguing of archives, further material has turned up.

Many of Lingard's financial papers were collected up by James Crook, his executor, and are now lodged in the Liverpool archdiocesan deposit at the Lancashire Record Office in Preston (RC Lv: Boxes 75 & 76). Lingard's executors sent to Ushaw a considerable collection of notebooks, unsorted jottings, transcripts and manuscript material, as well as many of his letters; this material forms the foundation of Ushaw's holdings of Lingard Papers. In September 1851 Robert Tate sent his letters from Lingard to Ushaw (130 letters, 1831–1850, Lingard Transcripts 623–754a) and Newsham, Ushaw's President, promised to put them with his (100 letters, 1837–1850, Lingard Transcripts 521–622) (see Newsham's letter of thanks to Tate, September 20th 1851, UCA, UCH 80a); soon, too, must have been added the vast correspondence represented by the letters from Lingard to John Walker of Scarborough (530 letters, 1836–1851, Lingard Transcripts 899–1450). A further addition to the collection came in November 1896 when Frederick Antrobus of the London Oratory sent to Ushaw the letters from Lingard to his publisher Joseph Mawman, procured by Dolman from Mawman's executor and sent to Tierney (65 letters, 1818–1827, Lingard Transcripts 454–520, & one not transcribed). Other letters remain in private hands, and in the archives of parishes and other institutions. The interests of autograph collectors have resulted in a few individual letters being scattered far and wide; Lingard's hand is represented in such collections in the British Library, the Bodleian Library, the National Library of Scotland, and as far afield as the Houghton Library, Harvard.

Some of the material was dispersed from the outset. John Walker had gone over to Hornby to be with Lingard on his deathbed. He too was gathering material. Mark Aloysius Tierney, similarly anxious to get his hands on Lingard's papers, was full of complaints that Brown was unsuitable as an executor and had let Walker rifle Lingard's drawers for papers. Walker appeared to have acquired Lingard's Scrapbook and Tierney could not be sure that he had returned all the letters he had at first appropriated (Tierney to ?, Nov. 30th 1851, UCA, LMisc 6). Walker, it seems, was attempting to persuade Blackwoods to publish a complete edition of Lingard's works and corresponded with George Rigg to ask him to approach the Edinburgh publishers (George Rigg to John Walker, Edinburgh, no date, UCA, LMisc 1).

The historian Mark Aloysius Tierney was also making a collection of Lingard manuscripts on his own account. Tierney, prodded into action by a posthumous attack on Lingard in *Brownson's Quarterly Review*, wrote a brief and, it must be admitted, rather disappointing, memoir of Lingard in the *Metropolitan and Provincial Catholic Almanac*, (London, 1854, pp. 3–25); this was also published in a enlarged and revised version as an introduction to the sixth edition of Lingard's *History of England* (1854). Tierney himself had been a correspondent of Lingard's and was able to gather a considerable quantity of material from various sources. Some material he borrowed from Ushaw, including the Lingard-Butler correspondence and the correspondence A–Y arranged by Michael Gibson, (list in Tierney's hand, July 25th 1852, UCA, UCH 9) and he managed to obtain the Scrapbook from Walker. At some stage, it seems, the Scrapbook was returned to Ushaw; Tierney retained the remainder. After Tierney's death (February 19th 1862) a long search for the whereabouts of this material proved fruitless although it was thought to be at St. George's, Southwark: Lingard's 'Journal of a Tour to Rome and Naples in the summer of 1817' did turn up and was returned to Ushaw by John Butt (Arundel, March 11th 1883, UCA, UCH 205, 32). Butt also explained that some personal letters had been returned to Mrs. Lomax and some to Canon Husenbeth. John Bamber made a further search (1883) in Southwark, again without success. He did however find another group of Lingard letters which he proposed to send to Lancaster for Walker to transcribe (see below; John Bamber to Mgr. Wrennall, May 4th 1883, UCA, UCH 205, 39).

Part of Tierney's collection (consisting mainly of correspondence of Lingard, Robert Gradwell, Charles Butler, John Jones, Edward Price and Tierney himself) was passed on by Tierney to Canon Estcourt, who gave it to Joseph Stevenson, working at the time as librarian at Oscott; he, in turn, had the collection with him when he entered the Society of Jesus in 1877. The letters were bound at the British Museum in 1887 and deposited in the Jesuit Archives in Farm Street (Joseph Gillow to Edwin Bonney, March 4th 1910, March 12th 1910; John Hungerford Pollen, introduction to Farm Street Transcripts, March 16th 1910, UCA). A further major portion of this collection was lost altogether: it seems that this material was left at Arundel Castle, where Tierney had been chaplain from 1824 until his death in 1862, and on the death of the fifteenth Duke of Norfolk in 1917 passed into the hands of a London bookseller, remaining unnoticed in the cellars until only recently; it was purchased by the Cambridge University Library (CUL, Add. Ms. 9418) in 1996. This deposit of over 600 items includes the Lingard-Butler Correspondence, a considerable collection of other letters, as well as some important personal papers, notably the grant of the triple doctorate to Lingard by Pius VII and signed by his Secretary of State, Cardinal Consalvi.

John Walker's nephew, William Walker,[1] on the staff at Ushaw until 1856 and eventually moving to St. Peter's, Lancaster from 1869 until his death in 1893, began systematically to make transcriptions of Lingard's letters during his years at Lancaster. He borrowed some from Ushaw (letters to Kirk [very few], Newsham, Tate, and Walker), and wrote to borrow holdings from others who he knew possessed letters from Lingard. These he copied into a series of soft-backed notebooks, sometimes in full, sometimes merely as extracts. The notebooks and a number of original letters were passed on to Joseph Gillow in January 1890 and were given by him to Ushaw in March 1910.

Walker's transcripts and notebooks make up 26 volumes: 2 volumes cover Lingard's letters to Tate; 13 volumes cover the correspondence with John Walker (with an additional early letter to John Rigby of Lancaster, 1817); 4 volumes cover the letters Walker borrowed from Southwark comprising the correspondence between Lingard and Rock and Lingard and Oliver. These volumes provided the source for the Lingard Transcripts 363–372 (Lingard-Rock) and 386–450 (Lingard-Oliver). Photostat copies of the former were kindly sent to Ushaw by the Southwark diocesan archivist, who also most generously deposited the original copies of Lingard's letters to Oliver in the Ushaw Archives in 1984. A further volume of the series is made up of transcripts of Lingard's letters to George Silvertop of Minsteracres, Lingard Transcripts 373–387, which is particularly important because the whereabouts of the originals are currently unknown. Walker also wrote to Mrs. Ridyard and he was able to transcribe a small part of her collection of Lingard letters (Lingard Transcripts 755–785): as Miss Joyce, she, together with her guardian, the Unitarian, Mr. Shepherd of Liverpool, had been frequent correspondents of Lingard's and the correspondence is now lodged in the archives of Harris Manchester College, Oxford (111 letters from Lingard to Miss Joyce, letters to Mr. Shepherd and some additional items). There are five other volumes containing miscellaneous notes and transcripts (Kirk, Butler and a few other items, some of which were omitted from the later typed transcripts and include 3 letters to Charles Blundell, 1826–1828).

1. See Joseph Gillow, 'Provost Walker and "Lingard" ', *Ushaw Magazine*, vol. 20 (1910), pp. 149–153.

Preparations for the writing of Lingard's biography, *The Life and Letters of John Lingard* (Herbert & Daniels, London, 1911), by Edwin Bonney and Martin Haile (*vere* Marie Hallé) marked the next stage in the gathering of Lingard papers at Ushaw. Bonney now had Walker's transcripts and Joseph Gillow offered further help by contacting John Hungerford Pollen at Farm Street who arranged for the transcriptions of the Farm Street material to be sent to Ushaw. Bernard Ward provided transcripts of the letters at St. Edmund's, Ware; he went through the material in the Westminster Archives, and arranged for the letters at the English College, Rome, to be copied. They discovered a few sources but searched in vain for other material, particularly Lingard's letters to Mrs. Thomas Lomax which were rumoured to have been deposited in the Westminster Archives; these letters in fact remained with her family and were eventually edited by John Trappes-Lomax and published by the Catholic Record Society in 2001.

This material collected for Lingard's biography was gathered into 11 large ring binders: Lingard to Newsham; Lingard to Mawman; Lingard to Tate; Lingard to Walker (3 vols.); Lingard to Various Others; Letters to Lingard A–M; Letters to Lingard N–Y; Farm Street Transcripts (Tierney); Various Transcripts.

Other deposits were made to the collection at Ushaw. Mention has been made above of the Oliver letters. To these must be added Lingard's letters to John Coulston of the Lancaster Bank (85 letters, 1831–1848, including 50 undated; a group of these remain untranscribed, suggesting they were given to Ushaw after c. 1951, see below) and a group of early letters to John Orrell (14 letters, 1803–1810).

At the request of the historian Philip Hughes, a series of typed transcripts were made of the Ushaw collection of Lingard letters and transcripts (c. 1951). These include copies of autograph letters, the letters transcribed by Walker, and the transcripts collected by Bonney from Farm Street, St. Edmund's College, Ware, the archives of the Archdiocese of Westminster, the Northampton diocese, the English College, Rome, Oscott (Birmingham Archdiocesan Archives), Stonyhurst, Downside, and elsewhere. Each transcript has been numbered and this numeration is customarily used as a supplementary reference to the letters. The typed transcripts have been collected into 24 volumes: one set is held at Ushaw; another set is lodged at the University of Notre Dame, Indiana.

The following catalogue lists first Lingard's papers, for the most part collected at Ushaw, as was his wish. It goes on to give the location of original Lingard letters: those included in the Hughes transcripts, as well as letters which were not recorded in the series. It also notes other letters, for which there is evidence, but whose present whereabouts are unknown.

1 Lingard's Papers

Ushaw College Library	*Antiquities of the Anglo-Saxon Church* (proof sheets with autograph corrections: 2 files, incomplete)
	History of England, vols. 1–5 (bound proofs with autograph corrections)
	History & Antiquities of the Anglo-Saxon Church (proof sheets with autograph corrections; incomplete)
	Commonplace Book (beginning Feb. 6th 1824)
Notebook	Journal, 1800 (notes on history reading: Carracioli, Gibbon, and other jottings; note on Bishop Alexander Cameron)
Notebook	Sales of 1st and 2nd edition of *Antiquities of the Anglo-Saxon Church*
Notebook	Hornby Obligation Masses (John Lingard & George Gibson) 1815–1863
Notebook	Journal of a Tour to Rome and Naples, 1817 (notebook and 3 fascicles)[2]
Notebooks (3)	Fair copies of Occasional Verses, etc.
Notebook	Psalms & Canticles on Translation
Notebook	List of 18th century Jesuits (recording date of birth, entry & profession)
Notebook	Practice of Living in Union with Christ
Notebook	A First or Shorter Catechism & A Second Catechism
Notebook	Translation of Psalms; Prayers for Sunday; First or Shorter Catechism (Part); historical notes
	Note (publisher's advertisement?) on Wiseman's *Horae Syriacae*
Personal Papers	Copy (dated November 8th 1792) of Baptismal Certificate
	Fides ordinum (December 20th 1794): tonsure & four minor orders

2. Although the Notebook was never published, the three fascicles appeared in a lightly edited version made by Edwin Bonney, *Ushaw Magazine*, vol.17, July 1907, pp. 160–178; December 1907, pp. 248–271.

		Fides ordinum (December 22nd 1794): diaconate
		Fides ordinum (April 18th 1795): priesthood
		Brief of DD (August 24th 1821)
		Diploma of the Accademia di Religione Cattolica (August 10th 1822)
		Certificate of Royal Society of Literature (June 24th 1824)
		Diploma of the Société d'Archéologie d'Avranches (April 5th 1839)
		Faculties for Yorkshire District (April 20th 1842)
		Dispensation from Eucharistic Fast (August 7th 1850)
	Pocketbook	Household inventory (Crook Hall?)
		Sick list (Ushaw, 1809?)
		Old Chapter consults 1667–1681
		Extracts from Smelt's letters to Eyre (1790)
		Scrapbook
		Unsorted papers (4 files)
Cambridge University Library	Personal Papers	Oath of Allegiance to George III (Winchester, 1791)
		Fides ordinum (December 20th 1794): subdiaconate
		Celebret (Rome, 1817)
		Passports (1821 & 1825–8)
		Brief of DD (August 24th 1821)
	Verses & manuscript notes	

2 Miscellaneous Manuscript Criticism

British Library	Gladstone Papers	William Gladstone, Digest of *History of England* (1837)
		Digest of 'Did the Church of England Reform Herself?', *Dublin Review*, 1840, no date
Ushaw College Library	Wiseman Papers	Nicholas Wiseman, 'Remarks on the New Version of the Gospels By a Catholic' [1836]
National Library of Wales	William Floyd	Remarks on historians

3 Lingard's Letters

Note: in the following catalogue 'correspondence' includes letters from other correspondents to Lingard; 'other items' refers to occasional manuscript and printed material, and letters between other parties which Lingard sent on to correspondents, or letters which, for various reasons, have been included in the collections. Personal papers and memorabilia have also been noted where appropriate. 'Transcribed/untranscribed' indicates whether the letters have been included in the series of transcriptions at Ushaw or not, although it must be recognised that a letter still to be found amongst the originals has occasionally been missed in this series, and from time to time a transcript has been made of an original letter now apparently missing.

i) Britain

Birkenhead

Shrewsbury Diocesan Archives	letter to Eugene Egan (1843?)	untranscribed	Shrewsbury Box

Birmingham

Archdiocesan Archives	letters to: John Kirk (6 letters; 1815–1832); Samuel Jones (1 letter; 1805); other items and correspondence	transcribed	

Bury St. Edmunds

private collection	letters to Mary Frances Lomax (99 letters; 1835–1851)	untranscribed	see John Trappes-Lomax, *The Letters of Dr John Lingard to Mrs Thomas Lomax*, CRS, 2000

Cambridge

University Library	letters to Charles Butler (40 letters; 1810–1829) and others; other items and correspondence (over 600 items)	untranscribed	CUL Add. Ms. 9418
	letters to John Gage Rokewode (1815–1842)	untranscribed	CUL Hengrave Deposit

Downside Abbey

	letters to Thomas Joseph Brown (3 letters; 1839–40)	transcribed	
	letters to: Joseph Booker (1 letter; [1836]); Charles Dolman (6 letters; 1851); miscellaneous letters (3 letters; 1840s) and papers	untranscribed	

Durham			
Dean & Chapter Library	letters to Cuthbert Sharp (2 letters; late 1830s)	untranscribed	
Edinburgh			
National Library of Scotland	letters to various correspondents (3 letters; 1840–1847)	untranscribed	see published catalogue
Scottish Catholic Archives	letter to Bishop Alexander Cameron (1811)	untranscribed	
University Library	letter cover (1824)	untranscribed	see published catalogue
Hornby			
Hornby Castle	letters to: Sandford Tatham, Pudsey Dawson, and others (1826–1837)	untranscribed	see Emmeline Garnett, *John Marsden's Will*, Hambledon Press, London, 1998
St. Mary's Church	miscellaneous items and memorabilia	untranscribed	
Leeds			
Diocesan Archives	letters to: William Gibson (3 letters; 1800–1817); Thomas Smith (18 letters; 1813–1828); John Bell (1 letter; 1824); Thomas Penswick (8 letters; 1823–1834); Richard Thompson (1 letter; 1840); John Briggs (22 letters; 1834–1842); other items and correspondence	untranscribed	
Leicester			
private collection	letter to Benjamin Dockray (1848)	untranscribed	

Liverpool

Archdiocesan Archives	letters to: John Orrell (11 letters; 1802–1809); Richard Thompson (4 letters; 1819–1830) and others	untranscribed	Orrell Papers
	letters to: George Brown (6 letters; 1841–1842); Henry Greenhalgh (4 letters; 1842); other items	untranscribed	

London

Archives of the British Province of the Society of Jesus	letters to: Mark Aloysius Tierney (44 letters; 1826–1850); John Jones (5 letters; 1833–1834); Edward Price (44 letters; 1846–1849); other items and correspondence	transcribed	Lingard Correspondence
	letters to: Joseph Dunn (4 letters; 1813–1825); Nicholas Sewell (5 letters; 1821–1822); C.P. Cooper (1 letter, 1839 [copy]); George Oliver (1 letter; 1839)	untranscribed	Letters of Non-Jesuits
British Library	letters to: Lord Stourton; Hugh Clifford; George Oliver; and a reply from Clifford (4 letters; undated, mid-1820s)	untranscribed	BL, Clifford Papers
	letters to various correspondents (7 letters; 1823–1845)	untranscribed	see published catalogue

Location	Description	Status	Repository
Southwark Diocesan Archives	letters to Daniel Rock (12 letters: mostly undated, 1830s)	transcribed	
	letters, correspondence and other items included with Tierney's notes for his memoir of Lingard; Howard's Historical Notebooks; and in a copy of Dodd's *Church History* once in the possession of John Gage Rokewode	untranscribed	
Westminster Diocesan Archives	letters to: William Poynter (29 letters; 1809–1827); John Kirk (13 letters; 1819–1826); Robert Gradwell (6 letters; 1829–1831); James Yorke Bramston (2 letters; 1834–1836); other items and correspondence	Poynter, Kirk & some others transcribed; Gradwell & Bramston untranscribed	Archives of the Archdiocese of Westminster
	letters to: Henry Bagshawe (15 letters; 1840–1845); and Philip Henry Howard (1 letter; 1838)	untranscribed	*Dublin Review* Papers
	letters to: George Dunn (11 letters; 1838–1851); and Mr. Heaton (3 letters; 1828–1847)	untranscribed	St. Edmund's College Archives
Northampton Diocesan Archives	letters to Frederick Husenbeth (40 letters; 1828–1850)	transcribed	
	letters to Thomas Quinlivan (2 letters; undated, mid-1840s); and other items	untranscribed	

Oxford Bodleian Library	letters to various correspondents (2 letters; 1835)	untranscribed	see published catalogue
Harris Manchester College	letters to Hannah Joyce (111 letters; 1841–1850); and other items	largely untranscribed	Shepherd & Ridyard Papers
Penrith Skirsgill Park	letters to James Whiteside (100 letters; 1840–1849); and other items	untranscribed	
Preston Lancashire Record Office	letters to: John Higgin (c. 78 letters; most-ly undated, 1830–1836); Pudsey Dawson (1 letter); Sandford Tatham (c. 17 letters; mostly undated, 1830–1836); and others; household, financial and executors' papers including letters to James Crook (4 letters; 1842); other items and corre-spondence[3]	untranscribed	
Skipton Broughton Hall	letters to Stephen Tempest (2 letters; 1811)	untranscribed	Broughton Hall Mss. Box 14
Stonyhurst College	letters to various correspondents (4 letters; 1830s)	transcribed	

3. *Papers of British Churchmen 1780–1940* (London, 1987) identifies a group of Lingard's sermons in the Lancashire Record Office. It would appear that these sermons contained in an uncatalogued box of miscellaneous material, which includes papers relating to Lingard's estate, should be attributed to James Crook, one of Lingard's executors.

Ushaw College	letters to: John Coulston (85 letters; 1831–1848); Joseph Mawman (65 letters; 1818–1827); Charles Newsham (100 letters; 1837–1850); George Oliver (64 letters; 1827–1850); Robert Tate (130 letters; 1829–1850); John Walker (530 letters; 1836–1851); John Orrell (13 letters; 1807–1810); and others; other items and correspondence	largely transcribed	
ii) Abroad			
Harvard, Mass. Houghton Library	letters to various correspondents (2 letters; 1840–1843)	untranscribed	see published catalogue
Lisbon English College	letters to: Edmund Winstanley (1 letter; 1824); Ignatius Collingridge (1 letter; 1849)	untranscribed	(Archives now located at Ushaw College)
Rome English College	letters to: Robert Gradwell (29 letters; 1817–1821); Richard Thompson (1 letter; no date) and others; other items	transcribed	
Scots College	letters to Paul Macpherson (5 letters; 1817)	untranscribed	
Propaganda Fide	letter to Charles Acton (1839)	untranscribed	

Valladolid

English College	letter to Thomas Sherburne (no date; 1822–3)	untranscribed	
(iii) Unknown Location			
	letters to Charles Blundell (3 letters; 1826–1828);	untranscribed	UCA, Walker transcripts
	letter to John Rigby (1 letter; 1817);	untranscribed	UCA, Walker transcripts
	letters to George Silvertop (15 letters; 1837–1848)	transcribed	UCA, Walker transcripts
	letters to: Henry Howard (33 letters; 1835–1841); Philip Henry Howard (2 letters; no date) with other items[4]	untranscribed	Historical Mss. Commission, UK National Register of Archives
	letters to James Johnson (12 letters; mostly undated, 1846–1850)	untranscribed	T. Cann Hughes and others, *John Lingard: A Learned Lancashire Priest*, Lancaster, 1907

4. A transcript of these letters made by Dr. Philip Cattermole has recently been lodged at Ushaw College.

PORTRAITS OF LINGARD

1 James Ramsay, c. 1819–1822, Ushaw College, Oil on canvas, 56" x 43": half length, aged about fifty: seated and wearing a close-fitting white wig; dressed in a black coat and white neck tie; curtains behind, revealing books [Fig. 9].

Engraved several times, including: Hopwood; Fox (Line, $5^{1}/_{4}$" x $4^{3}/_{8}$", published Colnaghi & Co. and printed by Tomkins, London, June 5th 1823). Hopwood's engraving was also published in France by Baudry, Paris. A photograph of the portrait provides the frontispiece for J.P. Chinnici, *The English Catholic Enlightenment*, Patmos Press, Shepherdstown, 1980.

Gillow (vol. 4, p. 278) claims that this portrait was painted in 1819. The books to the left of the picture can be identified as Lingard's *History* volumes three and four, suggesting that it was painted to mark the publication of volume four of the *History* in October 1820, or afterwards. An engraving of the portrait was made to sell with the second (octavo) edition of the *History* (1823). The portrait came to Ushaw College in the late nineteenth century, seemingly after 1892, for it is not mentioned in W. Dallow's Inventory of the Ushaw paintings of that date; an undated notebook (possibly 1900–1910?) refers to the portrait as 'from Newcastle by Ramsay presented by Miss Dunne' (is she to be identified as the sitter of the portrait of Miss M.E. Dunn, exhibited by Ramsay at the Royal Academy in 1851?). Lingard had a small circle of friends in Newcastle who singly or severally might well have been responsible for commissioning the work. In the absence of firm evidence it is impossible to trace the portrait's earlier provenance, but a tempting suggestion might be that it was commissioned, or at least purchased from the artist, by the Catholic businessman George Thomas Dunn (see P. McGuiness, 'Some Notes on the Dunn Family of Newcastle upon Tyne', *Northern Catholic History*, 14, Autumn 1981, pp. 15–24), who had some involvement in Lingard's financial affairs. Haile & Bonney record that 'it pleased neither the painter nor himself' (Haile & Bonney, p. 337).

Note on the Artist

James Ramsay (1786–1854) was born in Sheffield and entered his father's business as a portrait and miniature painter in 1801. He left Sheffield in 1803, making London his base for the next forty years, although he made frequent visits to the north and especially Northumberland. In 1816 he painted his first portrait of Thomas Bewick, the engraver and naturalist, who had prepared two engravings for Lingard's first book, *The Antiquities of the Anglo-Saxon Church* (1807). This portrait was exhibited at the Royal Academy that same year and was engraved many times. In 1819 Ramsay was in the North East again and painted *The Ruins of Tynemouth Castle and Lighthouse* and *View of the Harbour of North and South Shields* as well as several portraits. He worked in Newcastle in 1820 and 1822, exhibiting one of his most famous paintings, *The Lost Child*, a view of Newcastle. He exhibited in the North, in both Newcastle and Carlisle as well as in London, at the Royal Academy, the British Institution, and the Society of British Artists, before settling permanently in Newcastle in 1847. Ramsay died in Newcastle in June 1854, aged 68.

Ramsay's paintings, *Peter's Repentance* and *Peter's Denial of Christ* were exhibited both in Liverpool and at the Royal Academy in 1814, and *Christ giving sight to the Blind* was exhibited at the Academy in 1822; this painting now hangs at Ushaw. Amongst his portraits were paintings of Lingard's acquaintance, Henry Brougham, and members of several Catholic families, including John Townley; the Clifford and Weld families, including a portrait of the future Cardinal Weld (1829); Henry Howard of Corby Castle (1843); the Riddells, including a posthumous portrait of Bishop Riddell (1848, now at Ushaw), the newly appointed Vicar Apostolic of the Northern District, who had died of typhus while ministering to his flock in the slums of Newcastle.

DNB; Marshall Hall, *The Artists of Northumbria*, 1982; Algernon Graves, *The Royal Academy: a Complete Dictionary of Contributors*, Graves & Bell, 1905–1906; Algernon Graves, *The British Institution 1806–1867*, George Bell & Son, 1908; Edward Morris & Emma Roberts, *The Liverpool Academy & Other Exhibitions of Contemporary Art in Liverpool*, Liverpool University Press & National Museums & Galleries on Merseyside, 1998.

2 James Lonsdale, 1834, Ushaw College, oil on canvas, 56" x 43": three-quarter length, aged sixty-three: seated in palatial room at a desk, wearing black coat and breeches and holding a quill [frontispiece].

Engraved by H. Cousins (Mezzotint 16$^{1}/_{2}$" x 13", published by Agnew & Zanetti, 1836). An engraving of this portrait provides the frontispiece to Haile & Bonney, *Life and Letters of John Lingard*, Herbert & Daniel (1911), but is misattributed to Ramsay.

This portrait, for which Lonsdale eventually received £83 (Lonsdale to Coulston, March 4th 1835, UCA, LMisc 15), was paid for by subscription and presented to Lingard by a group of friends, including the Lord Chancellor, Lord Brougham. The idea for the scheme seemed to have originated with Gillison Bell of Melling Hall (Coulston to Sir G.A. Lewin, Sept. 3rd 1833, UCA, LMisc 10) but John Coulston of Lancaster, Lingard's friend and banker, did the organising, writing a series of letters inviting a subscription of two guineas from members of Lingard's immediate acquaintance (There is a printed list of the seventy-one subscribers amongst the Lingard papers at Skirsgill Park). Lonsdale painted the head from life on a visit to Hornby and finished the painting at his London studio. It was exhibited at the galleries of the Society of British Artists, Suffolk Street, in 1834 (No. 195) and arrived in Hornby the following year. Coulston saw it in London and reported to Lingard that he considered it '*a Hero* of the collection... the cuff of the coat being somewhat turned back, displays a very delicate white hand, such as never belonged to your frame... In the right hand which hangs in a manner quite *dégagé*... is a pen, not such as you use at present, but such a one as was to be found in your inkstand when in Low Figures [a junior class at Douai]... The likeness is strikingly perfect and reflects great credit on the skill of the artist. I met Ramsay the other day and spoke to him of the Portrait. He promised to see it' (Coulston to Lingard, July? 1834, UCA, LMisc 11; Mrs. Lomax who first came to know Lingard at about this time records that, though 5' 9" or 5' 10" in height, Lingard had remarkably small feet and hands, *Lingard-Lomax Letters*, p. 5). Lingard was pleased with the portrait and considered it the best likeness of himself acknowledging to Coulston that is was 'a noble painting, and a splendid present' (Lingard to Coulston, no date, UCA, LC 308).

Note on the Artist

James Lonsdale (1777–1839) was born in Lancaster and travelled to London to become a pupil in the studio of George Romney. He was based in the city for the rest of his life. Lonsdale was appointed portrait-painter in ordinary to both the Duke of Sussex and to Queen Caroline and exhibited frequently at the Royal Academy, hanging 138 pictures, but was never elected a member. Lonsdale played a significant role in the founding of the Society of British Artists, at which he was also a regular exhibitor. Amongst his portraits were those of Henry Bathurst, Bishop of Norwich, and of William Manning (1814), father of the future Cardinal. He painted Henry Brougham (1822) and Charles Howard, 11th Duke of Norfolk (1815), both exhibited at the Royal Academy. In about 1816 he also painted the portraits of John Marsden, Giles Bleasdale and George Wright, Lingard's near neighbours, and central characters in the Hornby Castle Dispute (see Emmeline Garnett, *John Marsden's Will: The Hornby Castle Dispute 1780–1840*, The Hambledon Press, 1998). There is a Crucifixion by Lonsdale, after a painting of van Dyck in St. Michael's Church, Ghent, in the Catholic Church of St. Mary and St. Michael, Garstang.

DNB; Algernon Graves, *The Royal Academy: a Complete Dictionary of Contributors*, Graves & Bell, 1905–1906; Algernon Graves, *The British Institution 1806–1867*, George Bell & Son, 1908; Jane Johnson, *Works Exhibited at the Royal Society of British Artists 1824–1893*, Antique Collectors Club, 1975.

3 Samuel Lover, 1837, location unknown, miniature, aged sixty-five: seated in a Victorian high-backed chair and holding a book.

Engraved by L. Stocks. The engraving provides the frontispiece to the fourth edition of Lingard's *History of England*, 1837 [Fig. 10].

Lingard describes sitting for this portrait in letters to Mrs. Thomas Lomax: 'I was ill of the influenza, and on thursday morning last about 8 in popped a miniature painter from London, sent post haste by my publishers to take and transplant my phiz into the first volume of my new edition. Never was there such a bore. I have each day been sitting to him from breakfast till dinner, and by him from dinner till bed-time. I hoped he would have done on saturday. Alas! He is dissatisfied with his performance – and so in truth was I though, having learned to act the Jesuit from you, I praised it with the hope that he would make no further attempt. He sought to catch my likeness he said, when I turned suddenly, and smiled: he wished to make me cheerful, and he made me merry, aye a boon companion over a good glass of wine. I have insisted that he shall finish tomorrow. But will he!' (Lingard to Mrs. Thomas Lomax, Jan. 28th 1837, *Lingard-Lomax Letters*, pp. 74f.). 'Lover thought, as *you* say, that I am difficult to draw. He complained that I was continually changing countenance, In his ambition to excel Lonsdale, he would paint me looking at him full in the face. He failed. I was like a boon companion carousing and asking my companions to drink with me. He tried me again in another position, and succeeded as he thought and Mr. and Mrs. Proctor thought [Proctor was the Anglican incumbent at St. Margaret's, Hornby], but not as I did, I see myself every morning when I shave, and if I have formed any notion of my own features, I say it is not like me. His reply is, that I never see myself, when I look around sharply and fix my eyes on another – He is not only a songster: I met the other day with an advertisement of 'Tales Etc. of Ireland', second series, by Sam Lover' (Lingard to Mrs. Thomas Lomax, March 21st or 20th 1837, *Lingard-Lomax Letters*, p. 78). Lover entertained Lingard with some of his compositions (Lingard to Mrs. Thomas Lomax, Feb. 15th 1837, *Lingard-Lomax Letters*, p. 77) but the latter was not to be mollified: he repeatedly expressed his 'very strong dislike' of this likeness (Lingard to Mrs. Thomas Lomax, April 27th 1849, *Lingard-Lomax Letters*, p. 147).

Note on the Artist

Samuel Lover, RHA, (1797–1868), born in Dublin, was the eldest son of a Dublin lottery-office keeper and money-changer, who disapproved of his youthful aptitude for literature and the arts. Lover grew to be well known in Dublin society, combining an interest in the writing of ballads and Irish tales with book illustration and miniature painting; he was elected an Associate of the Royal Hibernian Academy in 1828, a full Member the following year. In 1832 his miniature of Paganini won acclaim in Dublin. By 1835 he had moved to London, making amongst others a miniature of Brougham in his Chancellor's robes. He published his first novel, *Rory O'More, a National Romance*, in 1837, the year of the Lingard miniature. This novel, he turned into the first of his stage works and, after failing eyesight led him to abandon the painting of miniatures in 1844, he began a series of one-man stage shows, 'Irish Evenings' which he performed with some considerable success in Britain, Canada and the United States. Song writing, and some painting and landscape drawings, continued to keep him occupied and he completed two libretti for works by Balfe. After his health failed in 1864, he retired to the Channel Islands where he died in 1868. A man of varied talents and an attractive and winsome personality, he had no great talent for miniatures. Basil Long notes, 'Lover is not considered to have been a very good miniaturist' (Long, p. 280) and Lingard concurred with this judgement.

DNB; B. Bernard, *The Life of Samuel Lover RHA*, 1874; Basil Long, *British Miniaturists*, Geoffrey Bless, London, 1929; Walter George Strickland, *A Dictionary of Irish Artists*, Shannon, Ireland, 1962.

4a Thomas Skaife, 1848, National Portrait Gallery, miniature on ivory on card, $2^{13}/_{16}$" x $2^{3}/_{16}$": aged seventy-seven: head and shoulders, seated and looking to right, left hand raised to cheek, wearing close-fitting black wig.

This miniature remained in the artist's family until about 1900 when it was raffled and won by a maidservant. Haile & Bonney (p. 336) record it as having been lost, but it turned up in Carlisle and, having gone through a number of hands, was eventually purchased by the National Portrait Gallery in 1963. With the miniature is a note in the hand of the artist: 'This Original Miniature of Dr Lingard was painted by me at the learned Historian's residence Hornby in 1848 and from which the engraving was taken which illustrates the Library Edition of the history of England Published by Dolman / Thos Skaife / The Last Portrait for which Dr Lingard sat to any artist.'

4b Thomas Skaife, 1849, lithograph [Fig. 11].

Published in large format by Maclure, Macdonald and Macgregor and engraved by E.F. McCabe as the frontispiece to Dolman's fifth edition of Lingard's *History* (1849).

The lithograph was taken directly from one of the sketches Skaife made of Lingard while preparing the miniature of 1848 (Skaife to Lingard, Feb. 10th 1849, CUL, Add. Ms. 9418). Skaife later thanking Lingard for a copy of the *History* and, confessing that he had 'committed matrimony', proffered the suggestion that the lithograph 'though a tolerably good likeness is in my opinion inferior to the miniature' and proposed next time to get the miniature itself engraved (Skaife to Lingard, Jan. 7th 1851, CUL, Add. Ms. 9418).

Note on the Artist

Thomas Skaife, *floruit* 1840–1852, remains something of an unknown figure. He worked in Liverpool and in London, exhibiting a number of miniatures at the Royal Academy between 1846 and 1852. Skaife painted a portrait of Lady Bulwer Lytton in Geneva which was exhibited at the Academy in 1848. We know from his correspondence with Lingard that he married the proprietor of a school in 1850.

Richard Walker, *Regency Portraits*, National Portrait Gallery, 1985; Algernon Graves, *The Royal Academy: a Complete Dictionary of Contributors*, Graves & Bell, 1905–1906; Daphne Foskett, *Miniatures Dictionary and Guide*, Antique Collectors Club, 1987.

Additional Note

The correspondence (UCA, Bonney Correspondence) between Marie Hallé (*alias* Martin Haile) and Edwin Bonney in preparation for their *Life and Letters of John Lingard* refers to a picture of John Lingard as an old man in the garden which was in Marie Hallé's possession. If this is a copy of the late nineteenth century photograph of a priest in cassock and biretta saying his office in the garden at Hornby which is preserved in the Shepherd-Ridyard Papers, Harris Manchester College, Oxford, it is sadly not a picture of Lingard.

NOTES ON CONTRIBUTORS

Leo Gooch is currently Secretary to the Catholic Record Society. He has written widely on various aspects of eighteenth-century northern Catholic history. In 1995 he edited the correspondence between Robert Banister and his nephew Henry Rutter for publication by the North West Catholic History Society: *The Revival of English Catholicism: The Banister-Rutter Correspondence 1777–1807* (Wigan, 1995).

J.A. Hilton is editor of *North-West Catholic History* and has written extensively on the Catholic history of the North-West, publishing *Catholic Lancashire* (Chichester,1994) and *A Reasonable Service: Two Essays on Lingard* (Wigan, 1998), as well as editing *A Catholic of the Enlightenment: Essays on Lingard's Work and Times* (Wigan, 1999).

Edwin Jones retired in 1994 after thirty years as headteacher of a Catholic comprehensive school in South Wales, receiving an O.B.E. for services to education some years earlier. In 1998 he published *The English Nation: The Great Myth* (Sutton, 1998), which was followed by a study of Lingard's historical method, *John Lingard and the Pursuit of Historical Truth* (Sussex Academic Press, 2002).

Rosemary O'Day is Professor and Head of the History Department at the Open University. She is a specialist in the social history of the English Reformation and the author of, amongst other books, *The English Clergy, The Emergence and Consolidation of a Profession 1558–1642* (1979), *The Debate on the English Reformation* (1986) and *The Professions in Early Modern England: Servants of the Commonweal* (2000).

Rosemary Mitchell is Lecturer in History at Trinity and All Saints College, University of Leeds. As well as working on *The New Dictionary of National Biography,* she has published a monograph on the relationship between text and illustration in Victorian history books: *Picturing the Past English History in Text and Image 1830–1870* (Oxford, 2000).

Peter Phillips, a priest of the Shrewsbury diocese, taught Systematic Theology at Ushaw College before returning to his diocese as a parish priest in Shrewsbury. He has written a number of articles on nineteenth-century Catholic history and is currently working on a biography of John Lingard.

Paul Richardson is a post-graduate research student in the Theology Department at Durham University where he is researching into the history of the development of the Catholic Press in Britain.

Emma Riley is a research student in the History Department at Lancaster University and is currently completing a thesis on approaches to liturgy and architecture in the English Roman Catholic Church during the nineteenth century.

Michael Sharratt, a priest of the Hexham and Newcastle diocese, is Vice-President of Ushaw College, where he also teaches Philosophy. He has a particular interest in the scientific tradition of the recusant period and has published articles on Natural Philosophy at Douai College as well as a biography of Galileo, *Galileo: Decisive Innovator*, (Blackwell, 1994).

John Trappes-Lomax taught Classics at Christ's Hospital and Stonyhurst. He has recently edited *The Letters of Dr. John Lingard to Mrs. Thomas Lomax (1835–51)*, volume 77 of the Records Series of Catholic Record Society Publications (London, 1999).

Fig. 1: J. E. Doyle, 'The Barons at Edmondsbury swearing to obtain the Great Charter',
J. Lingard, *The History of England* (1854–55), vol. 2, frontispiece.

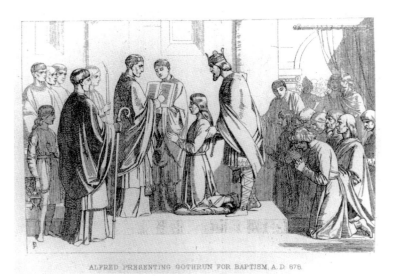

Fig. 2: J.E. Doyle, 'Alfred presenting Gothrun for Baptism A.D. 878',
Lingard, *History* (1854–55), vol. 1, facing p. 108.

Fig. 3: H. Dudley, 'The Burial of William I',
Lingard, *History* (1854–55), vol. 1, facing p. 255.

ARRIVAL OF CARDINAL WOLSEY AT THE ABBEY OF LEICESTER.

Fig. 4: H. Dudley, 'The Arrival of Cardinal Wolsey at the Abbey of Leicester',
Lingard, *History* (1854–55), vol. 4, facing p. 264.

ESCAPE OF CHARLES II AFTER THE BATTLE OF WORCESTER

Fig. 5: J.E. Doyle, 'Escape of Charles II after the Battle of Worcester',
Lingard, *History* (1854–55), vol. 8, facing p. 156.

DEATH WARRANT READ TO MARY, QUEEN OF SCOTS.

Fig. 6: J.E. Doyle, 'Death Warrant read to Mary, Queen of Scots',
Lingard, *History* (1854–55), vol. 6, frontispiece.

LORD STAFFORD LED TO EXECUTION.

Fig. 7: H. Dudley, 'Lord Stafford led to Execution',
Lingard, *History* (1854–55), vol. 9, facing p. 248.

LAST INTERVIEW BETWEEN THE DUKE OF MONMOUTH AND HIS WIFE.

Fig. 8: H. Dudley, 'Last Interview between the Duke of Monmouth and his wife',
Lingard, *History* (1854–55), vol. 10, facing p. 85.

Fig. 9: John Lingard by James Ramsay, c. 1819–1822.

Fig. 10: John Lingard, engraving by L. Stocks, after the miniature by Samuel Lover, 1837.

Fig. 11: John Lingard, lithograph by Thomas Skaife, 1849.

Fig. 12: St. Mary's Church, Hornby.

Fig. 13: The presbytery at Hornby.

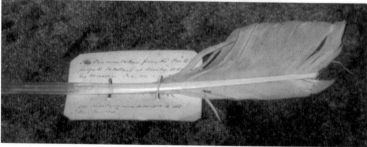

Fig. 14: Inkstand, black inlaid with silver, formerly belonging to the poet Cowper, a gift to Lingard from Lady Throckmorton, and quill used by him.

INDEX

Compiled by Meg Davies

References in italics refer to Figures,
located between pages 212 and 213.

Abbot, John, 71–72, 77.
Abinger, James Scarlett, Baron, 7, 174.
Acton, John, 1st Baron, 163 n. 24.
Adrian II, Pope, 167.
Albot, Richard, 18.
Alfred the Great, in Lingard's *History*, *2*, 133–134.
Allen, John, 130.
Allen, William, 82, 87, 114, 118.
'Amicus Justitiae', Lingard as, 67–68.
Andrews, William Eusebius, 4, 66, 67–69, 74.
Anglo-Saxonism, 23–34; and Christianity, 29, 30–31, 33; manifest/latent, 24; and Normans, 32–33, 134; and the Other, 24–27, 31–33; and racism, 26–27; and religion, 27–28; and settlement of Britain, 28–30, 32; and slave trade, 29–30; and Vikings, 31–32, 134.
Anti-Catholicism, 36–38, 53–54, 126–127; in Durham, 35, 41, 49–58.
Appellant priests, 83, 87.
Aristotle, in seminary curriculum, 12–13, 19.
Arundel and Surrey, Henry Granville Fitzalan-Howard, Earl, 172.
Auckland, George Eden, 1st Earl, 61.
Ave Maris Stella, 4, 176.

Bagshawe, Henry Richard, 77–80.

Bamber, John, 192.
Banister, Robert, 12, 15–17, 21.
Barrington, Shute, Bishop of Durham, 35–64; and Anglican supremacy, 43–44; and anti-Catholicism, 3, 35, 36–37, 40–56, 58, 62; *Charge* of 1810, 52; *A Charge Delivered to the Clergy*, 3, 41, 43–44, 46, 48, 50, 54; and charity, 36–37, 46; *The Grounds ... Reconsidered*, 52; *The Grounds on which the Church of England Separated from the Church of Rome*, 41, 48, 50; and Lingard, 40–55; *Vigilance, A Counterblast*, 53.
Bayle, Pierre, 19.
Beaufort, Cardinal Henry, 134.
Beaumont, Col., 48, 49.
Becket, Thomas, 79; in Lingard's *History*, 66, 134.
Bell, Gillison, 206.
Bell, Matthew, 63.
Bentham, Jeremy, 19.
Bergenroth, G.A., 106 n. 5, 107–108, 121, 137.
Berington, Joseph, 16; as Cisalpinist, 43, 84, 128–129; and history of the Reformation, 85–87, 88, 94, 102.
Bernard, Sir Thomas, 45.
Bewick, Thomas, 205.
Bible: Authorized Version, 165, 166–167; Douai-Rheims, 158, 166–168; Greek text, 5, 157, 160–162, 164–166; and inspiration, 157, 168–169; Latin text, 157, 158, 160, 164–167, 169; personal reading, 150; and tex-

Bible—*continued*
 tual criticism, 167, 168; and tra-
 dition, 164, 168–169; transla-
 tion, 157–169.
'Black Legend', 115.
Blackwell, George, 87.
Boleyn, Anne, 82, 97, 98, 99–102,
 138.
Boleyn, Mary, 99, 100–101.
Bonner, Edmund, 90, 91.
Bonomi, Charlotte (*née* Fielding),
 46.
Bonomi, Ignatius, 46.
Bossy, John, 127, 151.
Boucher, Joan, 91.
Brahe, Tycho, 14, 15, 16.
Brennan, Charles, 69.
Bridgett, Thomas, 141–142.
Briggs, John, Bishop of Beverley,
 182–183.
Brindle Will Case, 174, 177–178,
 179, 183.
British Empire, in Lingard's writ-
 ings, 29, 34.
Brougham, Peter Henry, 1st
 Baron Brougham and Vaux, 7,
 173, 206, 207, 208.
Brown, George Hilary, Bishop of
 Liverpool, 175 n. 13, 177–178,
 181, 191–192.
Burgess, Thomas, Bishop of St.
 David's and Salisbury, 53,
 56–57, 63.
Burnet, Gilbert, *History of the
 Reformation,* 83, 90, 91, 92–93,
 97–99, 105, 108.
Butler, Alban, 14–15, 21.
Butler, Charles, 15, 46, 58, 192;
 and Bible translation, 163, 168;
 and emancipation, 2; and history of the Reformation, 88–90,
 91–93, 97, 102; and liberalism,
 84, 128–129; and periodical
 press, 65, 66.
Butt, John, 192.

Camden, William, 83.
Cameron, Alexander, 109–111,
 113–114, 117–120, 122–124.
Campion, Edmund, 88, 136.
'Candidus', and Lingard's
 History, 67–68.
Catherine of Aragon, 96, 99,
 100–101, 110–113.
*Catholic Advocate of Civil and
 Religious Liberty,* 69.
Catholic Board, 65, 66, 163.
Catholic Committee, 84, 86.
Catholic Emancipation, 1–2, 3,
 23, 33, 126; and English laity,
 38–39, 40; and Irish Catholics,
 39–40; and Lingard, 46–47,
 127; and loyalty of Catholics,
 82–83, 84, 87–88, 126, 128; and
 nineteenth-century history, 83,
 84, 92, 102, 104; opposition to,
 35–59; and periodical press, 65;
 support for, 60–64.
Catholic Magazine and Review,
 65–66, 69–73, 130; and catechism, 76; and Lingard, 69,
 71–73, 75–76, 143, 151–152;
 and liturgical reform, 73–75,
 143, 151–152; and loss of readers, 76–77; and miracles,
 71–72; and Wiseman, 70,
 75–76.
Catholic Record Society, 142.
**Catholic Relief Acts (1778,
 1791),** 23, 40, 63, 82, 87.
Catholic Relief Bills: of 1813, 66,
 88; of 1825, 62.
Catholicon, 65, 77.
Catholic's Prayer Book, The, 73.
Challoner, Richard: and Douai-
 Rheims Bible, 158; *Garden of
 the Soul,* 75–76, 143, 144–145,
 146, 148, 151, 156.
Charles II, 5, 7, 136–137.
Chinnici, Joseph P., 67, 70, 129,
 163.
Church of England, and

Church of England—*continued*
Anglican supremacy, 43–44, 58, 60.

Church and state, 2, 4–5, 31, 36, 38–40, 128; and Barrington, 42–43, 52; and Berington, 85–86; and Lingard, 47–48; and Paley, 55.

Cisalpinism, 2, 4, 23, 31; and emancipation, 84; and historiography, 93, 125, 128–129, 133–135, 141; and Lingard, 129, 163–164; and periodical press, 65–67, 70–71, 76.

Clarke, Samuel, 19.

Cleveland, William Henry Vane, Marquess, 61.

Cobbett, William, *The Protestant Reformation*, 6, 82, 95–96, 103–104, 130.

Collier, Jeremy, *Ecclesiastical History*, 83, 90, 91, 94, 108.

Collins, Anthony, 19.

Congregation of the Index of Prohibited Books, 13–14, 15.

Conscience, individual, 2, 31, 49, 89.

Copernicus, Nicolas, 13–16.

Coronation Oath, and Catholic Emancipation, 59–60.

Cotes, Henry, 47–48, 49, 50, 52, 56.

Coulston, John, 194, 206–207.

Cranmer, Thomas, 96, 103, 130; in Lingard's *History*, 82, 91–92, 97–98; in Protestant history, 91–92, 97–98, 99.

Criticism, postcolonial, 23–34.

Crook Hall seminary: establishment, 2, 23; library, 18; Lingard as Professor of Philosophy, 2, 9, 17–21, 36; Lingard as Vice President, 2, 41; teaching methods, 9–12.

Crook, James, 191.

Curr, Joseph, 74.

Dalby, John, 169, 176–177.

Darnell, William, 64 n. 60.

Davies, R. Trevor, 115.

Dawson, Pudsey, 183.

Descartes, René, 12, 17, 19.

Dimock, A., 118.

Dissenters, and Catholic Emancipation, 37, 43.

Dixon, R.W., 98.

Dodd, Charles, *Church History of England*, 78–80, 90.

Dolman, Charles: and *Catholic Magazine*, 130; and *Dublin Review*, 78, 80, 130; and Lingard's *History*, 125, 130–133, 135, 136, 137–138, 141–142; and Lingard's papers, 191.

Dolman's Magazine, 130.

'Douai Dictates', 9–12, 17.

Douai, English College: continuation of traditions, 9–18; curriculum, 9–12; disputations, 10–11, 15–16, 17; founding, 87; and Lingard, 2, 9, 11, 23; and Newtonianism, 2, 14–16; and philosophy course, 12–13, 19, 21.

Douai-Rheims Bible, 158, 166–168.

Douglas, Bishop, 53 n. 35.

Dover, Secret Treaty (1670), 6–7.

Doyle, James E., 132; 'Alfred presenting Gothrun for Baptism A.D. 878', *2*, 134; 'The Barons at Edmondsbury swearing to obtain the Great Charter', *1*, 133; *A Chronicle of England*, 132–133; 'Death Warrant read to Mary, Queen of Scots', *6*, 137–138; 'Escape of Charles II after the Battle of Worcester', *5*, 135–137.

Doyle, Richard, 132.

Drake, Francis, in Lingard's *History*, 139.

Dublin Review, 77–80, 130, 157–158, 160.

Dudley, Howard, 133; 'Last Interview between the Duke of Monmouth and his wife', *8*, 141; 'Lord Stafford led to Execution', *7*; 'The Burial of William I', *3*, 134; 'The Arrival of Cardinal Wolsey at the Abbey of Leicester', *4*, 134–135.

Duffy, Eamon, 129.

Dunn, George Thomas, 205.

Dunn, Joseph and William, 146–150, 153–154.

Durham: anti-Catholic clergy, 35, 49–58, 64; Barrington-Lingard controversy, 3, 35–64; pro-Catholicism, 35–36.

Eastwood, Thomas, 174, 177.

Edinburgh Review, 58.

Edward III, 136.

Elijah Index (Rev. Henry Cotes), 49, 50, 52.

Elizabeth I: Bull of Deposition, 87–89; excommunication, 114–116; and Philip II of Spain, 114–119, 121–122, 137; and Reformation, 85–87, 88–90, 96, 101, 136, 139.

Ellison, Cuthbert, 49.

Emancipation Act (1829), 3, 23, 35, 62–64, 82, 126.

English College in Rome, 2, 55, 70, 194.

Estienne, Robert, 165.

Eucharist: and devotional manuals, 143–156; and Real Presence, 43, 45, 47, 50, 52.

Exequatur, 38, 66.

Eyre, Thomas, President of Ushaw, 3, 9, 53.

Faber, Frederick, 56.

Faber, George Stanley, 50, 51–52, 56, 58.

Felton, John, 88.

Fenwick, J.R., 48.

Ferdinand II of Aragon, 6, 110–112.

Ferdinand VII of Spain, 120–121.

Fletcher, Anthony, 126 n. 2.

Fletcher, John, 67, 73.

Fontana, Cardinal, 69.

Foxe, John, *Book of Martyrs*, 83, 89, 96, 103, 108.

French Revolution, 23; and Catholic Emancipation, 40, 42–43, 50; and Douai College, 2, 9, 19; and influence of Rome, 42, 45.

Frith, John, 91.

Froude, J.A., 115.

Fuller, Thomas, 83.

Gachard, M., 106.

Galileo Galilei, 13–14, 15.

Gallicanism, 2, 4, 31, 163.

Garden of the Soul; see Challoner, Richard.

Gardiner, Steven, 90, 91.

Gascoyne, John, 70, 72.

Gasquet, Cardinal Aidan, 142.

Geddes, Alexander, 163.

General election 1807, 2–3, 40–41, 47–49, 62.

George III, and Catholic Emancipation, 2, 40–41, 59–61, 82.

Gibbon, Edward, 24–30, 32.

Gibson, George, 48 n. 26.

Gibson, William, Vicar Apostolic of Northern District, 3, 37 n. 3, 39, 53.

Gilley, Sheridan, 130.

Gillow, John, 3, 53.

Gillow, Joseph, 193–194.

Gillow, T., 48 n. 26.
Gilly, William, 46.
González, Don Tómas, 120–122.
Gooch, Leo, 130.
Gother, John: *Instructions and Devotions for Hearing Mass*, 144, 145, 156; *Instructions for the Whole Year*, 144.
Gothic Revival, 4, 130–131.
Gradwell, Robert, 6, 70, 192.
Gregory I the Great, Pope, 30.
Gregory XVI, Pope, 70.
Grey, Charles (later Lord Howick and 2nd Earl Grey), 35, 36, 39, 48, 49, 57, 61–62.

Hail Queen of Heaven, 4, 176.
Haile, Martin and Bonney, Edwin, 170, 194, 205, 206, 209.
Hall, Edward, 83, 101.
Hardinge, Gen. Sir Henry, 61.
Harpsfield, Nicholas, 83.
Hay, Bishop, 39.
Haydock, George Leo, 16–17.
Hearne, Daniel, 181.
Heatley, William, 174 n. 12.
Heimann, Mary, 127.
Heliocentrism, and Catholic teaching of science, 14–15, 16.
Henry II, 79.
Henry III, 136.
Henry VII, 110–112.
Henry VIII, 96–101, 103; and Anne Boleyn, 97, 98, 99–101; and Catherine of Aragon, 96, 99, 100–101, 110–113; and Cranmer, 91, 98; and dissolution of the monasteries, 92–97, 138–139; motivation, 82, 92–94, 138–139.
Herschel, William, 20.
Heylyn, Peter, 83, 85, 90.
Hierarchy, restoration of, 1, 23, 38, 128, 183.
Hill, Christopher, 33.

Hippisley, Sir John Cox, *Report on the Law and Ordinances*, 4.
History: and Cisalpinism, 93, 125, 128–129, 133–135, 141; and context, 82, 90–91, 102–103; and politics, 84–85, 88–104, 128; Protestant, 1, 91–92, 101–102, 125, 128–129, 137–139, 141–142; and revisionism, 1, 5–6, 8, 92; source-based, 128–129, 141–142; Whig intepretation, 7, 83, 112.
History of England (Lingard), 3, 4–6, 54; and Anglo-Saxons, 25; and British Empire, 29, 34; and Catholic Revival, 127, 131; criticisms, 66–68, 128, 181 n. 17; editions, 127, 130, 131–132, 141, 192; illustrations, 6, 125, 132–142, 207; and international perspective, 6, 105, 109, 135–136; and Milner, 66–68; and Philip II, 115–121; preface, 131–132; and Reformation, 5–6, 34, 82, 89, 91–92, 95, 97–103, 104, 130, 137–139; and revisionism, 1, 5–6, 8, 164; and Secret Treaty of Dover, 6–7; and Simancas Archives, 105–124; sources, 6, 23, 98, 105–124, 125, 129.
Hodgson, Joseph, 2, 12, 16–17, 19–21.
Hollingsworth, N.J., 52, 54, 56.
Hook, W.F., 91, 98.
Hooper, John, 97.
Hope, Anne, 141–142.
Hornby: Lingard as incumbent, 3, 23, 53, 55, 105, 143, 152; Lingard's visitors at, 7, 173, 176; the presbytery, *13*; St. Margaret's (CE) Church, 7, 208; St. Mary's Chapel, 3, *12*, 23.
Hornby Castle Dispute, 207.
Howard, Philip Henry, 78, 172, 206.

Howick, Lord; see Grey, Charles.
Hughes, Philip, 194.
Hull, William, 53 n. 35.
Hume, David, *History of England*,
   24–29, 32, 83–84, 99, 105.
Husenbeth, Frederick Charles,
   71–72, 74–75, 192.

Identity, national: and
   Catholicism, 34; and
   Protestantism, 1, 38, 83,
   125–127, 139, 141–142.
Illustration: German Catholic
   Revival style, 133; in Lingard's
   History, 6, 125, 132–142.
Index of Prohibited Books,
   13–14, 15, 75.
Infallibility, papal, 47, 84.
Instructions and Prayers Before,
At and After Mass, 146,
   148–151, 153–154.
Ireland, and Catholic
   Emancipation, 39–40, 59–61,
   63, 95.

James II, in Lingard's *History*,
   132, 138, 140.
Janson, Baldwin, 65.
Jenkinson, John Banks, Dean of
   Durham, 46.
Jesuits: in Lingard's correspon-
   dence, 175, 181; in nineteenth-
   century history, 87, 88,
   139–140.
John, King of England, 135–136.
Jones, Edwin, 125, 135–136, 137.
Jones, John, 192.
Joyce, Hannah (later Mrs.
   Ridyard), 7, 170–178, 182–183,
   193; and Brindle Will Case,
   174; and Jesuits, 175; and
   Lingard's health, 180, 182; mar-
   riage, 178; and O'Connell,
   173–174; and politics, 172–173.

Joyce, Jeremiah, 170.

Keating, Broen and Keating (pub-
   lishers), 65.
Kellison, Matthew, 13.
Kemble, John Mitchell, 24.
Kenrick, Thomas, Archbishop of
   St. Louis, 163.
Kenyon, Lord, 54, 59.
King, William, 19.
Kingsley, Charles, 127.
Kirk, John, 5, 128; and Catholic
   periodical press, 67, 69–70, 73,
   75–77.
Knox, John, 139.
Knox, Ronald, 161.

Laity: and Emancipation, 38–39,
   40; and liturgy, 43, 143–150,
   153–156.
Lambert, John, 91.
Lambton, George ('Radical Jack';
   later Earl of Durham), 35.
Lambton, R.J., 49.
Lancashire, and Catholicism, 174,
   177.
Latimer, 47–48.
Latimer, Hugh, 97.
Latin: and Lingard's Gospel
   translation, 157, 158; in liturgy,
   43, 44–45, 145; in seminary
   education, 9–11, 17–18.
Laud, William, Archbishop of
   Canterbury, 139.
Le Mesurier, Thomas, 50, 51, 56.
Lee, John, 67.
Leo XII, Pope, 3, 55, 162.
Liberalism, Catholic, 65–66, 84,
   128–129.
Liddell, Sir H.T., 49.
'Liege Subject' (Rev. Henry
   Cotes), 47–48.
Lingard, John: education at
   Douai, 2, 9, 11, 23.

Lingard, John—*continued*
  As historian. In general, 183; Anglo-Saxonism, 23–34; and Barrington, 3, 40–55; formation, 2; method, 41–42; in period of transition, 1–2, 23, 125, 127–130; and politics, 89–92, 97–104, 128; and Reformation, 89–91, 95, 112; revisionism, 1, 5–6; and Simancas Archives, 105–124, 137.
  Honours. And Académie Française, 3, 23; papal doctorate, 3, 23, 193; Privy Purse grant, 183; and Royal Society of Literature, 3.
  Personal life. Final illness and death, 1, 192; friendships, 3, 6–7, 55, 105, 159, 173; health, 80, 180; as letter writer, 6–7, 170–183, 191; letters and papers, 191–204.
  Portraits, frontispiece, 9, 10, 11, 205–210.
  Religious life. As Cardinal *in petto,* 3, 55, 162; and liturgy, 4, 73–76, 143–156; as Old Catholic, 128, 131; ordination, 2; as parish priest, 3, 23, 53, 55, 105, 143.
  As teacher. At Crook and Ushaw, 2, 3, 9–11, 13, 17–21, 23, 36, 41–42, 65; at Douai, 2.
  Writings. In general, 184–190; *The Antiquities of the Anglo-Saxon Church,* 2, 4, 23, 41–42, 164, 205; *Catechical Instructions,* 128, 131; *Documents to ascertain the Sentiments of British Catholics,* 53; *A General Vindication,* 51; *Manual of Prayers on Sundays and During the Mass,* 4, 143–145, 151–156, 177; *New Version of the Four Gospels,* 5, 155, 157–169, 182;

Observations on the Laws and Ordinances, 54; and periodical press, 67–68, 69, 71–73, 75–76, 77–80, 151–152; *Remarks on a Charge...,* 41, 44–46, 49–50, 53; *A Review of Certain Anti-Catholic Publications,* 54; *Strictures on Dr. Marsh's 'Comparative View',* 168; *Theses Philosophicae,* 20; *Vindication of Certain Passages,* 100; *A Vindication of The 'Remarks',* 50, 51; see also *History of England.*
Lisle, Alice, 138.
Litany of Loreto, 73–74, 75.
Liturgy: and Lingard, 143–156; and Litany of Loreto, 73–75; and simplicity, 4, 75–76.
Loades, David, 126 n. 2.
Locke, John, 12, 16, 17, 19, 20, 36.
Lomax, James, 179–180.
Lomax, Mrs. Thomas; see Sanders, Mary.
Lomax, Thomas, 170, 179–180.
Londonderry, Charles Stewart, 3rd Marquess, 61.
Long, Basil, 209.
Lonsdale, James, portrait of Lingard, *frontispiece,* 173 n. 10, 206–207.
López, Rodrigo, 118–119.
Losh, James, 64.
Lover, Samuel, 181, 208–209; 'John Lingard', *10,* 207–208.
Loyalty, Catholic, 36, 82–83, 84, 87–89, 92, 126, 128, 151; in Ireland, 39–40; in Lingard's *History,* 133–134, 135, 136.

Macaulay, T.B., 132.
Mariana, Juan de, 109, 111, 113.
Marsh, Herbert, 54, 166, 168.
Martyn, Francis, 70, 72.

Mary I, and persecution of Protestants, 89–91, 115, 126, 137.

Mary, Queen of Scots, *6*, 116, 137–138.

Mass: and communion in one kind, 43, 45; and devotional manuals, 143–156; translations, 144–145, 147–148, 151, 155.

Mathew, Theobald, 182.

Mawman, Joseph, 5, 129, 191.

Maynooth College, Lingard declines professorship, 55.

McDonnell, Thomas Michael, 67–68, 70, 71, 73–77.

Methodists, and Catholic Emancipation, 37.

Milbanke, Ralphe, 48–49.

Milner, John, Vicar General of Midland District, 5, 42 n. 15, 50, 91; and Catholic periodical press, 4, 65–69, 71; and emancipation, 88; *The History ... of Winchester*, 84–85, 88, 89–90; *Letters to a Prebendary*, 88, 89; and Lingard's *History*, 66–68; and Reformation history, 88, 89–90, 91–95, 97–98, 103; as Ultramontanist, 65, 84, 87; *A Vindication of the End of Religious Controversy*, 166 n. 29.

Ministry of All the Talents, 2, 40–41, 42, 48.

Miracles, in periodical press, 71–72.

Monasteries, dissolution, 92–97, 138–139.

Monmouth, James, Duke, *8*, 140–141.

Monmouth rebellion, 138.

Monthly Review, 84–85.

Morgan, Nicholas, 146–150, 153–154.

Morris, John, 141–142, 154, 171.

Motley, J.L., 115.

Natural philosophy: Catholic teaching, 13–14; at Crook Hall and Ushaw, 9, 18, 19–20; at Douai, 9, 13–16.

Newcastle Courant, 3, 47–48.

Newman, J.H., 55, 128, 157, 168.

Newsham, Charles, 10, 17, 191.

Newton, Isaac, *Principia Mathematica*, 13, 15.

Newtonianism, at Douai College, 2, 14–16.

Nichols, Aidan, 144.

Norman Conquest, 32–33, 134.

Northumberland, Hugh Percy, 2nd Duke, 36, 49.

Northumberland, Hugh Percy, 3rd Duke, 48, 49, 62–63.

Oates, Titus, 139–140.

Oath of allegiance, 1, 60, 62, 87.

Oath of Supremacy, 86.

Oberthur, Franz, 144, 156.

O'Connell, Daniel, 51, 77, 173–174.

Old Catholics, 128, 131.

Orrell, John, 194.

Orthodox Journal, 4, 66–69.

Oscott College, Lingard declines presidency, 55.

Oscott Conference, 74–75.

Other: Anglo-Saxons as, 24–27, 31–33; Vikings as, 31–32.

Oxford Movement, 79–80, 157.

Palgrave, Francis, 24–26, 28, 32, 108.

Papacy: and Philip II of Spain, 114, 116–118; and Reformation, 85–86; and spiritual authority, 36, 88, 135–136; and temporal authority, 60, 85–86, 88–89, 128, 135–136.

Parsons, Robert, 83, 86, 87, 114, 118.

Paul IV, Pope, 85, 116–117.
Peach, Edward, 70, 73, 75.
Peel, Robert, 61, 183.
Penal Laws, 87; repeal, 1–2, 31, 82, 127.
Perceval, Spencer, 41.
Percy, Sir Hugh (later 3rd Duke of Northumberland), 48, 49, 62–63.
Periodicals, Catholic, 3–4, 65–80, 130; and Cisalpinism, 65–67, 70–71, 76; and Lingard's *History*, 66–68; and miracles, 71–72; see also *Catholic Magazine and Review; Dublin Review.*
Persecution: of Catholics, 86–87, 89–92, 102–103, 140; of Protestants, 89–92, 97, 102–103, 115, 137.
Persons, Robert; see Parsons, Robert.
Petre, Bishop Francis, 38.
Petre, Edward, 73.
Philip II of Spain: and Elizabeth I, 114–119, 121–122, 137; and papacy, 114–118; and Simancas Archives, 6, 105–106, 113–115.
Phillips, Thomas, 90.
Phillips, Peter, 128–129 n. 15.
Phillpotts, Henry: and anti-Catholicism, 35, 49–50, 51–52, 57–59; and Barrington, 49–50, 57–58; and Emancipation, 3, 58–60, 63–64.
Philosophy: Aristotelian, 12–13, 19; at Crook Hall and Ushaw, 18–19.
Pius V, Pope, 88, 114.
Pius VII, Pope, 3, 69, 193.
Plowden, Charles, 84, 87.
Plowden, Francis, 86.
Pole, Reginald, 83, 91, 99–101.
Politics: and history, 84–85, 88–104, 128; and Lingard's correspondence, 172–173.

Pollen, John Hungerford, 142, 194.
Popery, and Protestantism, 36–38, 42, 50–53, 55.
Popish Plot, in Lingard's *History*, 139–140.
Postcolonial criticism, 23–34.
Powlett, William, 61.
Poynter, William, Bishop, 4–5, 38, 54 n. 37.
Prayer books: and Lingard's *Manual*, 143–145, 151–156, 177; for local use, 143, 146–151, 153–154; for nation-wide use, 143–146.
Prayers to be said Before and After Mass, 146–151, 153–154.
Pre-millennialism, 51–52, 56.
Prescott, W.H., 115.
Press; see periodicals.
Price, Edward, 131, 192.
Primitive Methodists, and Catholic Emancipation, 37.
Propaganda, anti-Catholic, 2.
Propaganda, Sacred Congregation of, 17, 38, 69.
Protestantism: and national identity, 1, 38, 83, 125–127, 139, 141–142; and persecution of Catholics, 86–87, 89–92, 102–103; and Popery, 36–38, 42, 50–53, 55.
Pugin, A.W.N., 4, 130.
Puritans, in Lingard's *History*, 139.
Pusey, Edward Bouverie, 176.

Quadra, Alvaro della, 118, 119, 121.
Quarterly Review, 85, 99–100.
Quin, Michael Joseph, 77–78.

Racism, and Anglo-Saxonism, 26–27.

Radicalism, and Catholic Emancipation, 37–38.
Ramsay, James, 205–206, 207; 'John Lingard', *9*, 204.
Ranke, Leopold von, 6, 115.
Ravensworth, Henry Thomas Liddell, 1st Earl, 61, 63.
Read, Conyers, 121.
Real Presence, 43, 45, 47, 50, 52.
Reformatio Legum Ecclesiasticarum, 91–92.
Reformation: and Authorized Version, 167; historical sources, 83–84, 98, 105–124; in Lingard's *History*, 5–6, 34, 82, 130, 137–139; in nineteenth-century history, 84–104, 105, 112, 115–116; as political act, 88–104; social effects, 93–97, 103, 139; as spiritual movement, 92–93, 101–103.
Ridley, Nicholas, 97.
Rigby, John, 193.
Rigg, George, 192.
Rippon, Cuthbert, 64 n. 60.
Robertson, William, 106–107, 109.
Romanticism, and Catholicism, 126, 129, 133.
Rome, English College, 2, 55, 70, 194.
Russell, Lord John, 126.
Russell, Matthew, 48.
Russell, W., 63 n. 58.
Russell, William Lord Russell, 140.
Rutter, Henry, 10, 181.
Ryan, Edward, *Analysis of Ward's Errata*, 166–167.
Rye House Plot, in Lingard's *History*, 140.

Sadler, John, *The Key of Heaven*, 145–146, 150.
St. Bartholomew's Day Massacre, 116, 130.
St. Edmund's College, Ware, 2, 9, 194.
Sanders, Charles, 170, 179.
Sanders, Mary Frances (later Mrs. Thomas Lomax), 170–174, 192, 194, 208; and confidences, 182–183; conversion to Catholicism, 7, 169–170, 179; and Dolman, 131, 132 n. 28; and gossip, 174, 177–183; and Jesuits, 175; and Lingard's health, 180; and Lingard's *Manual*, 143, 177; and Lingard's *New Version*, 159–160, 169, 182; marital problems, 178–180; and theological instruction, 176–177; and visits to Lingard, 173, 176.
Sanders, Nicholas, 83.
Scarlett, James (later Lord Abinger), 7, 174.
Science: and 'Copernican Revolution', 13–15; at Douai, 14–16; and Lingard, 2, 9, 12, 18–21, 182.
Scott, Sir Walter, 24, 32–33.
Second Spring, 127, 163.
Selby, Thomas, 48 n. 26, 49.
Sharp, Sir Cuthbert, 109 n. 18.
Shepherd, William, 170–171, 172, 178, 182, 193.
Sherburne, Thomas: and Brindle Will Case, 174, 177; and Simancas Archives, 109, 113–114, 123–124.
Silvertop, George, 162, 163, 164–165, 172, 173, 193.
Simancas, Spanish State Archives, 6, 105–124, 137.
Skaife, Thomas, 209–210; 'John Lingard', *11*, 209.
Slave trade, 23, 29–30, 35.
Smith, Bishop Thomas, 38, 53, 54 n. 37.
Smith, Sydney, 42, 55.

Smithson, Sir Hugh (later 1st Duke of Northumberland), 62 n. 56.

Southey, Robert, 58, 126 n. 6.

Spanish Armada, 116–118, 126, 139.

Spes, Guerau de, 114, 117–118.

Spinoza, Benedict, 19.

Stafford, William Howard, 1st Viscount, 7, 140.

Stephenson, George, 50–51, 56.

Stocks, L., 'John Lingard', *10*, 207.

Stourton, Lord, 6–7.

Strathmore, 10th Earl, 48.

Strickland, Agnes, 182.

Strype, John, 83, 92, 97, 104.

Sumner, John Bird, Bishop of Chester, 63.

Surtees, Robert, 56.

Sydney, Algernon, 140.

The Tablet, obituary of Lingard, 4, 162–163.

Tacitus, Publius Cornelius, *Germania*, 26, 28.

Tate, Robert, 178; and *Catholic Magazine and Review*, 71–72, 74, 76; correspondence with Lingard, 74, 76, 191; and Lingard's *Manual*, 143, 151, 153; and Lingard's *New Version*, 159.

Tejada, Mariano Gil de, 76.

Tempest, Sir H.V., 49, 63.

Test Acts, 37, 82.

Throckmorton, Sir John, 86.

Tierney, Mark Aloysius: and *Dublin Review*, 78–80; and Lingard's papers and letters, 192–193; and Simancas Archives, 122–123; and Wiseman, 162 n. 22.

Tiran, M., 106.

Todd, Henry John, 91–92, 98, 129–130.

Tolkien, J.R.R., 26.

Tories: and Catholic Emancipation, 35–36, 41, 42, 48–49, 57–59, 61, 63, 172; and Church and State, 42; and radical critique, 95.

Townley, John, 206.

Townsend, George, 58.

Tractarians, 79–80, 157.

Tradition, and scripture, 164, 168–169.

Transalpinism; see Ultramontanism.

Trappes, Francis, 181.

Trotter, Thomas, 52.

Turner, Sharon: and Anglo-Saxonism, 24–28, 32; and Philip II, 115; and Reformation, 101–102, 103.

Ultramontanism, 4, 128, 162–163; and history of the Reformation, 84, 86–87, 93; and Milner, 65, 84, 87; and periodical press, 71, 130–131; and Second Spring, 127.

Uranos, discovery, 20.

Ushaw College: and Barrington, 45–46, 49; curriculum, 11–12; and Douai disputations, 10; establishment, 3, 23, 53; library, 9, 18; and Lingard Papers, 191–194; Lingard as Professor of Philosophy, 2, 9–11, 13, 17–21, 36; Lingard as Vice President, 2, 52, 53, 65; teaching methods, 9–11.

Valladolid: English College, 6, 109, 113, 114, 123; Scots College, 6, 109.

Van Mildert, William, Bishop of Durham, 35, 62–63, 64.

Ventura, Gioacchino, 181.
Vergil, Polydore, 101.
Vikings, as Other, 31–32.
Vulgate Bible, 157, 158, 160, 164–167, 169.

Walker, Edward, 54.
Walker, John, 181–182; and Bishop Brown, 177; and *Catholic Magazine and Review*, 74–75; correspondence with Lingard, 7, 17, 78, 155, 191, 193; and death of Lingard, 192; and Doyle, 132; and Lingard's *New Version*, 157, 159.
Walker, William, 193–194.
Ward, Bemard, 194.
Ward, Thomas, *Errata of the Protestant Bible*, 160, 161 n. 19, 166–167.
Ward, W.G., 128.
Watson, Robert, 115.
Watson, William, 83, 87.
Weedall, Henry, President of Oscott, 70–71, 72.
Wellington, Arthur Wellesley, 1st Duke, 3, 59–63.
Wesley, John, 37.
Wesleyan Methodists, and Catholic Emancipation, 37.
Wharton, Richard, 48, 63.
Wheeler, James, 67 n. 12.
Whigs: and Catholic Emancipation, 35–36, 48–49, 63–64; and Church and State, 128; and history, 7, 83, 112, 130; and Norman Yoke, 33.
White, Thomas, 67.
Wilberforce, William, 45.
Wilkinson, William, 15, 21.
William I the Conqueror: burial, *3*, 134; and Norman Conquest, 32.
William III (William of Orange), 140.

William the Silent, 115.
Williams, John, 47.
Winstanley, Edmund, 169.
Wiseman, Card. Nicholas, 1, 5, 128, 164, 166; and *Catholic Magazine and Review*, 70, 75–76; and *Dublin Review*, 77–79; and Lingard's *New Version*, 157–163, 169; and Ultramontanism, 4, 162–163.
Wolsey, Cardinal Thomas, *4*, 5, 99, 100–101, 103, 134–135.
Women, Lingard's correspondence with, 7, 170–183; see also Joyce, Hannah; Sanders, Mary Frances.
Wyatt's Rebellion, 89–90.

Zurita, Gerónimo de, 109, 111, 113.